Katherine

With Love + Blessings, Diane Pomerance

Katherine

A WOMAN OF VISION

‿

Diane Pomerance

POLAIRE PUBLISHING

Dallas, Texas

Published in the United States by Polaire Publishing

Printed in the United States of America
ISBN 13: 9781936315000
ISBN: 1936315009

Dedication

I wish to thank the wise, visionary, charming, and charismatic Katherine Hayward for the powerful bond and deep friendship we shared as well as the extraordinary joy we experienced in learning together and from each other. I deeply admired her determination and perseverance in attempting to discover the Truths of Life, and her deep desire to share her discoveries with those equally passionate about finding life's meaning and purpose. Her work was inspired and inspiring. She was the catalyst responsible for what she jokingly referred to as "lighting my pilot light"—igniting my innate longing and desire to find the meaning and purpose of life and achieve self-realization—and encouraging me to explore, study, examine, and investigate the meaning and purpose of my life.

She was both my guide and travel companion throughout so many spiritual journeys and discoveries. She awakened me to the potential all human beings have to be so much greater, wiser, kinder, more compassionate, and more creative and expansive in ways we would never have thought possible. She spoke of the Godseed within us and the development, maturation, and fruition of this seed as we learn to identify and utilize our innate abilities and manifest our true potential. She saw God in everyone and everything and viewed every experience as an opportunity to evolve spiritually. To her, it was one's attitude toward all events and circumstances that mattered above all else. Grace and gratitude are cornerstones of her teachings.

I give thanks also to the many other great teachers I have known: Maharaj Charan Singh Ji, Swami Muktananda, Sri Daya Mata, Krishnamurti, Rev.

Kanjitsu Iijima, Swami Chidvilasananda, and to such life coaches and teachers as M. Scott Peck, Dr. Leo Buscaglia, Elizabeth Kubler-Ross, Jean Houston, and Jack Canfield. All have influenced both my heart and mind, and I live each and every day acknowledging and utilizing the profound wisdom they have imparted to me. Thankfully, their work has inspired and continues to inspire millions of people all over the world.

Table of Contents

Acknowledgments

⌒

THERE ARE SO MANY PEOPLE and organizations I would like to thank for their contributions to this book—Randy Simmans and the Denton Public Library, in particular, for their guidance, generosity, and support.

I am grateful for such long-time friends and colleagues Laurie Ackerman Rausch, Linda Schleider Davis, Beverly DeMenna, and Linda Nelson who knew Katherine and supported our work together.

I am grateful to Steve and Bill Harrison and the staff of Bradley Communications for their wise counsel and advice. They have been very, very helpful to me in so many ways throughout the last fifteen years— Steve, Martha Bullen, and Geoffrey Berwind, in particular. It is through Bradley Communications that I was introduced to my wonderful, creative, patient, and highly intuitive editor, Heidi Grauel.

I would be remiss if I did not express my deepest gratitude to Linda Nelson who typed the original manuscript of the book on her IBM Selectric typewriter in 1982 and to my dear friend and colleague Laura Rodgers who fell in love with the manuscript in 2014 and volunteered to help edit and reformat it into a Word document (no easy undertaking!). Laura and I spent many an afternoon reading passages of the book aloud to one another to "hear" it told as a story.

There are many other friends and colleagues who deserve my praise and gratitude. You know who you are, and I cannot thank you enough—Karen Lee Cohen, Jeannie Nadel, Kathy Tracy, Nikki Darling (who appeared in my life in the nick of time!), the wonderful staff and members of Unity

Spiritual Center of Denton County, and Crystal Wood, publisher and creative force of Tattersall Publishing.

Blessings upon you and all who read and benefit from Katherine's extraordinary story.

Introduction

KATHERINE SEDONIA DAVIES HAYWARD, BORN in Wales in 1899, was a remarkable woman. Teacher, psychic, medium, healer, philosopher, and visionary, she became my spiritual teacher in 1979, shortly after I moved from New York to West Hollywood, California, to pursue a career in the entertainment industry.

After running into an old college friend of mine, Michele, who had moved to Los Angeles several years before me, our friendship was rapidly rekindled and we discovered that we only lived within a few miles of each other. It was Michele who told me about her spiritual teacher, Katherine Hayward. She invited me to attend a free Sunday morning meeting at Katherine's home in West Hollywood. After describing Katherine's unique abilities and philosophy to me, I happily agreed to join her.

From Michele I learned that at age sixty, Katherine, after countless years of utilizing her psychic abilities and communication with the so-called "dead" and "Spirit Beings," had proven in the United Kingdom and all over the world that there is no death. After many decades of researching and studying and implementing many of the world's great religions, she synthesized what she viewed as the highlights or best of various religions and philosophies and, drawing upon her own amazing experiences, she ultimately formulated her own philosophy of life. After advising and counseling world leaders and notable public figures, Katherine "retired" to Los Angeles.

As planned, I met Michele at Katherine's Spanish style duplex bungalow. It was very cozy and quaint, and its art and furnishings were very

English with antiques, chintz, pastel landscapes, and fresh flowers in vases everywhere. There were approximately thirty or so chairs of all sorts gathered around a large circle extending throughout Katherine's lounge and living room.

I arrived at about 10:45 a.m. Many people were already seated; others straggled in one or two at a time. By 10:50, the room was full, and yet, people continued to come into the room—many sitting on the floor. At precisely 10:59 a.m., Katherine gracefully and elegantly made her way through a doorway and took her seat upon a comfortable and elegant armchair.

Katherine was seventy-nine years old. She was a small, attractive woman with bright red hair (obviously not her natural color!) who was wearing a rather exotic, vibrantly colored and richly embroidered kaftan. Her jewelry was tasteful and becoming. She spoke with an aristocratic British accent and in a deep contralto voice. She reminded me of—in appearance as well as her wit, charm, and charisma—the popular and highly regarded British actress Dame Judi Dench.

Katherine warmly, but with reserve, greeted her audience and began sharing information that I imagine was startling to some of the attendees. "There is no death," she stated calmly and matter-of-factly. "The real you is neither the mind nor the physical body but rather the Power that motivates them," "All life is energy operating at different rates of vibration," "Life on Earth is a school in which we learn to attain spiritual evolution and self-realization in the manner of the great sages, teachers, and masters of all time."

Katherine believed in reincarnation and that we visit the Earth many, many times in various circumstances and in many different physical bodies until we ultimately achieve mastery over our minds, bodies, and emotions— until we learn to love, respect, and appreciate one another, our planet and the whole of life. She taught that all of us are connected and interrelated and are as one living, breathing organism.

I was twenty-eight years old when I was introduced to Katherine, and I had studied and researched many of the world's religions and philosophies. I thoroughly enjoyed Katherine's talk and found her to be most knowledgeable, engaging, and intriguing. She also had a delightful sense of humor and was quite theatrical. I definitely wanted to study with this woman. After the meeting, I made an appointment to see her. From the moment we met, we shared a deep bond and powerful connection. I happily and gratefully became Katherine's student and, eventually, her protégé.

I was blessed and privileged to study and work with Katherine and to have her as my beloved teacher and dearest friend. At one point, about six or seven months after I met her, I awoke one morning with the very strong conviction that I would be writing Katherine's biography. I approached her one Sunday morning after her meeting and told her my plan. She was going away for a brief holiday and said that she would think about my suggestion. When she returned from her trip, as we prepared for one of our lessons, she hugged me warmly and said, "Yes, my dear, you will write my life's story, and from hereon, you are no longer my student but, rather my colleague, my coworker." Needless to say, I was elated by her response, and from that point on we were virtually inseparable.

I spent countless hours recording our interviews. I have kept these recordings and hope to share them with those who are interested in Katherine's work and vision of the future. Katherine firmly believed that human beings are far greater than they presently believe themselves to be; that they have unlimited potential for discovering their own divinity and for helping themselves, one another, and our planet to evolve and transform into something far greater and more powerful than we can imagine.

I have spent much time and energy in spiritual reflection, exploration, and research. I am most grateful for the joyful and extraordinary experiences, wisdom, and information that Katherine shared with me. That we would come to know one another during this lifetime does not appear to me as coincidence. Rather, it seems the inevitable outcome of sharing many lives together and wishing to be of service to our fellow human beings at this most critical juncture of our Earth's history. I have been blessed and privileged to serve our planet, our people, and creatures alongside Katherine Hayward.

Diane Pomerance
Aubrey, Texas
July 2015

CHAPTER 1

A Decision

ELIZABETH DAVIES WAS A SMALL woman of indefatigable strength and courage. Rarely one to concede to failure or defeat, she exercised her great strength of will to achieve whatever she might desire. Once she made up her mind to pursue a particular course of action, there was generally no human being, no external event which could circumvent or cause her to deviate from her chosen path. She was unyielding.

Only on rare occasions had Elizabeth been known to hesitate before or remain dubious after she had arrived at a decision. At these times, she would state firmly, matter-of-factly, "All right, Lord, I've done my share of the work. Now it's your turn. Show me the way." And, somehow, her questions and difficulties would be resolved to her satisfaction.

Now, then, despite much seeming evidence to the contrary, she knew in her heart that all was well. Once or twice during the past several months she had anxiously wondered if the decision had been too hastily made, if, indeed, it had been the wisest decision. But on these occasions, as now, she would simply shrug her shoulders and casually dismiss all doubts and fears. *What's the use of bothering about it anyhow? The decision's been made. For better or worse, I am going back to England—back home.*

"Home"—what comfort, what relief, what inexpressible joy the word brought to her heart. How long, how difficult had been the separation from those she loved. *Has it really been seven years since I've seen dear Mum and Dad?* she marveled. It seemed impossible. Tears suddenly stung her eyes as she recalled the enormous sacrifice and will it had required to wrench herself free from all she loved—friends, family and home—seven years ago. Then, briefly, the painful series of events which transpired over the years and had culminated in her recent decision to return home flashed before her. She was soon lost in reverie.

A jabbing pain which pierced through her lower abdomen served as a brusque reminder that she was not yet back home amongst loving relatives and her doting husband. *Dear God, please let this journey be over soon,* Elizabeth prayed silently, her pale lips clenched, as the pain continued to penetrate the whole of her abdomen now. Taking a deep breath, she slowly, deliberately made her way back to the cabin.

The boat continued to sway back and forth uneasily. *Thank goodness the children are still asleep,* Elizabeth thought, as she gazed lovingly upon the three tiny forms lying peacefully in bed in the late afternoon stillness. "I do so need quietude and rest," she sighed aloud, to no one in particular, vaguely parroting the orders she had received from her physician prior to the journey.

Wearily, she crawled into bed. Lying upon her back, she gently massaged her swollen abdomen, and she immediately began to feel better. The color gradually returned to her cheeks. As the pain began to subside, she continued to ruminate. *We're almost home, we're almost home, we're almost home.* Over and over again the happy phrase passed through her mind, like the jingles she used to chant as a little girl. She knew that the journey was nearly over, and was fully aware that with every moment which elapsed she was drawing closer to the joyous occasion during which she would find herself in the arms of her husband, Gwilym, among her family, at home in peace at last. With the pleasant thought of home in her mind, she closed her eyes and drifted off into a light slumber, the suggestion of a smile playing about her lips.

It had not been an easy voyage by any means. Elizabeth and her three small children had set sail from New York in June of 1899, nearly a week ago. Unaccustomed as they were to ocean travel, they were unprepared for the ceaseless motion of the ship. The large liner rocked back and forth prompting even the stalwart Elizabeth to spend much of her time aboard the vessel in her cabin. She could not remember when she felt so helpless, isolated, and queasy. And yet, although there were many difficulties inherent in such a journey, Elizabeth firmly and capably handled each situation which arose, consciously minimizing her own physical discomfort and limitations. Despite her small stature—she was only an inch and a half above five feet and petite—Elizabeth possessed great physical stamina. Seldom had she experienced illness of any variety. Her physical solidity seemed to be reinforced by her pragmatism, her firm grasp of reality, and by the efficiency with which she confronted the details of life.

The less romantic soul may have been inclined to overlook Elizabeth's physical beauty—her large brown eyes, the abundant, soft, chestnut hair, the clear complexion, the small, even features—and perceive only a dedicated, uncomplicated young mother whose plans and dreams were firmly rooted in reality. Physical beauty was of little interest or concern to her, however, and she patiently sought to secure her own particular brand of happiness which consisted simply in the safety, health and comfort of her loved ones. Assuredly, she would never have agreed to undertake so arduous a journey in her condition, had she not been convinced that she was so doing for the ultimate happiness and well-being of her family

"Thank the Lord for Mr. Allen's kind offer," Elizabeth had remarked early in the voyage to little Della, breathing a deep sigh of relief. For this thoughtful gentleman had provided assistance in the single area she had required it, eradicating what had been a source of considerable fear and anxiety. Gwilym had been able to afford only second-class accommodations for his wife and children which, under normal circumstances would have proven sufficiently comfortable. Unfortunately, however, Elizabeth had observed on her first night at sea, several large rats scamper from one side of her tiny cabin to the other. She had nearly fainted from shock and fear. Had she merely heard them, she might have been more tolerant. But when she noticed several of the creatures—their eyes glaring and whiskers twitching menacingly—at the foot of her bed and then on the chest of drawers near the children, she did not know what to do. The sight of them was simply too much to deal with in her condition, at eight months pregnant.

Overhearing Elizabeth describe her dilemma to one of the stewards, Mr. Allen had graciously come to her rescue, volunteering to exchange his own luxurious first-class quarters for hers. Having seriously doubted her ability to continue the journey under such circumstances and fearing for the life of the child she carried, Elizabeth gratefully accepted the offer. How Mr. Allen's heart had gone out to the brave little woman as she extended her dainty hand, smiled demurely and in a tremulous voice, expressed her appreciation for his kindness and generosity! Henceforth, he became her dear friend and companion, looking after her and the children with paternal solicitude and allowing no one to disturb them in any way.

Amidst even the most frightening and disagreeable circumstances, Elizabeth had been both proud and pleased to observe that the children had never behaved more beautifully. It was with genuine admiration, pride, and no little amusement that she received their earnest attention. "You mustn't disturb Mummy," she would overhear Della admonish the others in her most grown-up and maternal voice. "She's been through an awful strain and needs her rest. Let's all go for a walk together on deck and allow her to relax."

"But we only just took a walk," little Cora would wail. "I don't want to go out again." "C'mon let's do as Della says," young Gwilym would mutter grudgingly. "After all, she's usually right." And Elizabeth would keep her eyes closed and bite her lip to keep from laughing, as she pretended to be asleep until the children had put on their coats and mittens and silently tip-toed out of the room.

What a blessing they truly are, Elizabeth would think to herself. *And what a comfort.* For Gwilym, Della, and Cora (ages seven, five, and three, respectively), sensing their Mum's need for solitude and serenity, tenderly looked after one another, dispelling each other's fears and worries by openly discussing the future.

"When we settle down in Cardiff," Della was fond of saying in an authoritative manner, "life shall be very pleasant for all of us. Mum and Dad, Grandfather and Grandmother, Uncle Thomas and Aunt Elvira—all of us shall be together forever and ever. We shall have a perfectly lovely house—with a beautiful rose garden and a swing—and lots and lots of playmates who live nearby."

Little Cora's eyes would sparkle with excitement as she listened to the description of life to be. And even her more sophisticated brother seemed to be mesmerized by Della's words. "Life in England is not at all like life in America," Elizabeth had assured them, and now they were looking forward with great anticipation to their new home.

Even at this very early age, Della and the others—who adored both their Mum and Dad—possessed a keen intuitive awareness of the vast differences which existed between them in nature, temperament and personality. Although Mum was basically jovial, magnanimous and kind-hearted, she was also rather nervous, highly strung and irritatingly unpredictable. For example, one could never determine the best time to confess one's failings or misdeeds to her, for sometimes she would react tenderly and sympathetically, at other times, she was as likely to explode in anger. On still other occasions, she would look terribly hurt and disappointed and shake her head sadly as though she had been betrayed by one whom she had trusted implicitly.

Dad, on the other hand, was in every way as kind and generous, as warm-hearted as Mum, but he always appeared calm and collected and was refreshingly consistent. One was seldom surprised or disappointed by Dad's reactions. Gentle, courteous, and dignified, rarely did he exhibit the engaging and intriguing volatility displayed by his wife. No one could deny that Mum was spontaneous—even impulsive—exploding into gales of hearty laughter one moment, maintaining a stony silence the next, arguing heatedly after that. Dad, on the other hand, was cautious, deliberate, and methodical—generally even-tempered and poised. Rarely could they recall seeing Dad overtly angry or ruffled or in any way unsteady. Neither could they imagine him without the delightful twinkle in his eye which seemed to imply that life was not to be taken as seriously as one might expect.

In reality, it was Gwilym who ruled the family. But he did so with such subtlety and grace and with such utter lack of concern for maintaining appearances, that most outsiders regarded Elizabeth as the more dominant of the two and the ruler of the household. Only the children and those intimate with the Davies knew that it was really Gwilym—with his finely developed sense of justice, integrity and sensitivity—who actually governed their home and who was not only the head of the family, but also its conscience, guardian, and anchor.

Whereas Elizabeth was earthy and resourceful—a pragmatist—who was largely ignorant of and unconcerned with the lofty aims and ideals espoused by those of a poetic or philosophical bent—Gwilym was contemplative and analytical—rich in wisdom and in character—a practical philosopher who taught his children to confront all of life's challenges with faith, quiet courage, and gentle dignity.

The entire family had been severely tested when they were forced to contend with the tragic death in 1898 of the little girl who had been the first-born of the Davies' children. Suddenly, inexplicably, little Catherine Sedonia, only seven years old, had contracted a severe case of spinal meningitis. Despite the desperate measures which had been taken to save her life, she was dead within a matter of a few days. Elizabeth was inconsolable. If not overtly her "favorite" child, Catherine Sedonia was nonetheless very special to her. There had been something very strange, oddly compelling about this child with the honey-colored hair and large, deep brown eyes that seemed to see right into the heart of a person. Catherine Sedonia had rarely smiled; even at her early age, she had sensed that life was to be taken seriously. Seldom had she laughed or giggled, cried aloud, whined, thrown tantrums, or displayed any of the emotions or interests normally associated with a child her age. Nor did she engage in any of the typical childhood games and activities. She was simply not interested. Gentle and good-natured, and universally adored and petted, this little girl preferred her own private world to any other. For many hours every day she would sit silently alone or lie on the veranda humming softly, her eyes closed, totally absorbed in her thoughts and dreams.

"What an extraordinary child," various friends or neighbors would remark. "She is not of this world."

"No, I don't believe she is," Elizabeth would smilingly concur, as she studied her daughter's slender form, luminous eyes, ivory skin, and delicate features. She had not been offended by such remarks, for she felt them to be true. *She's far too kind and good to be of this earth*, she would think to herself. Then, feeling a great surge of love well up in her for the gentle little girl, she would rush over and embrace her.

Then, suddenly, the beautiful little girl was gone—forever. And Elizabeth was heartbroken. It was not as though Catherine Sedonia had been the first child they had lost to illness; they had survived the deaths of two other children as well in 1894 and 1895. But these had been mere infants, and had not touched their lives as deeply as had Catherine. Yet the fact remained—Elizabeth had borne the loss of three children within five years. For a while, life was hardly worth living—the burdens of life seemed too heavy to bear, and Elizabeth fell into a self-pitying, despondent state of mind, as she was forced to yield to the inevitable. Then, to her intense joy and astonishment, within a relatively short period of time after Catherine Sedonia's death, she discovered that she was pregnant, and life was full of hope and promise once again.

The children believed that it was Catherine's death that had been largely responsible for their mum's sudden, urgent desire to leave Pennsylvania and to return home to her native England. But, in fact, there were many factors involved in the decision to return home. For, if truth be known, Elizabeth had grown weary of the rigorous way of life, the unfamiliar routines and hardships and prejudicial attitudes of many of the people toward immigrants in America and was homesick for her family and loved ones. Also, for no logical reason, she felt fiercely compelled to give birth to the child she was now carrying on English soil.

On how many different occasions had the children overheard fragments of conversation to this effect between Mum and Dad? "Catherine Sedonia's death has broken my heart," Elizabeth would say quietly, her brown eyes filling with tears, her lips quivering with emotion. "She is the third baby I have lost in this country."

"I know, love," Gwilym would state sympathetically. He, too, had deeply loved the sensitive little girl, and her death had come as a great blow to him.

"I want to go home, Gwilym. To Mum and Dad and the family. I want our next child to be born and to grow up in perfect health in England." She stated all this firmly, as though she had given the subject careful consideration.

"Now, be reasonable, Elizabeth," their dad would respond patiently, scrutinizing his wife's countenance. "It is not America that is in any way responsible for the deaths of our children. You know full well that such tragedies occur not only here but in England and in every country in the world."

"Perhaps I am not making much sense," Elizabeth admitted grudgingly, rather embarrassed. "I can't explain it logically. It's just a feeling I have—the powerful conviction that we no longer belong here—that we should return to England and raise our children there—where they will be amongst family, friends, and loved ones—and no longer among total strangers of unknown origin and breeding who have come here from all parts of the globe . . . Besides all that, I miss England—her tranquility and beauty. I miss Mum and Dad, my brothers and sisters," her voice broke. She had not been financially able to afford to visit England and the years away from them took their toll upon her. She gulped and the tears spilled forth. "Oh Gwilym, I guess I just miss home—my true home." And she would collapse into her husband's arms weeping, while he would gently wipe away her tears, stroke her tumbled hair, and soothe her in the same manner in which he had so often comforted the children following a nasty fall, or after they had experienced a deep hurt, disappointment, or sorrow.

"There, there, love. It's all right. I understand," Gwilym comforted her softly, gently tilting her face until her eyes looked directly into his. "It's quite natural that you're homesick. After all, we've been away from England for so long. Although Catherine's death was difficult for all of us to bear, I fear it has affected you most deeply. You were closer to her than the rest of us. Such an extraordinary child—so wise for her age. And she took you into her confidence. Yet God, in His infinite wisdom and mercy, saw fit to take her from us. And we are expected to carry on."

His voice would drop off as if he, too, were not quite certain as to how one might carry on. Then regaining his composure, he would say quietly with restored confidence, "It will be all right, my love. All will be well, I promise . . . Feel any better now?"

Elizabeth would nod. How thankful she was for Gwilym's presence. He was so tender, so infinitely soothing that she longed to remain in his arms forever. With him nearby she felt that nothing could harm her and that everything would soon be all right.

Gwilym seemed to be thinking aloud now, "You know, business has been poor in recent months. Perhaps," he said slowly, "if you are sincere about returning to England, I shall write to my brother, Thomas, in Cardiff, South Wales, on our behalf to determine the possibility of entering into a business partnership with him there. Does the idea appeal to you?"

"It's a wonderful idea," breathed Elizabeth, heartened by the mere prospect of returning home. "Well, then, I shall write to Thomas immediately. In the meantime, we shall have to give the issue serious consideration. We must avoid drawing any hasty or careless conclusions. Let us patiently await Thomas' reply and then decide. All right?" And Elizabeth would nod happily, her tear-stained face now radiant and youthful, the effect resembling the sun's welcomed appearance following a thunderstorm.

Temporarily assuaged, Elizabeth returned to her household tasks and responsibilities with renewed vigor and optimism until impatience or despondence once again overcame her and the necessity to approach her husband arose once more. It was not until Gwilym's business began to falter, however, that he began to seriously consider permanently returning to England. Nearly all of the small inheritance he had received from his parents had been invested in the modest hotel he had purchased upon coming to America seven years ago and then operated along with his cousin, with whom he had always felt a deep bond. The business had been moderately successful until the past year or so when it was adversely affected by a severe statewide depression and the constant strikes and fierce wage battles which erupted among the coal miners. Now, cognizant of both his wife's desire to return home and of the enormous effort which would be required of him to rebuild a viable business structure in Pennsylvania during these difficult times, Gwilym became increasingly receptive to the idea of resettling in the United Kingdom. Yet, because he still had some hope of succeeding in America and had developed genuine admiration and fondness for its people, he was reluctant to make the final decision. Instead, he advised his wife that it must be she who made the final decision whether or not the family returned.

Elizabeth was only too pleased to comply, even though Gwilym assured her that the responsibility of making such a decision was great and that she must exercise caution, wisdom, and prudence. Despite this sound advice, Elizabeth arrived at her decision instantaneously and emotionally. "We shall return to England," she announced to her family one evening after supper, her eyes shining with joy, her face radiant. None were surprised by the announcement. There had been an air of suppressed excitement and gaiety about her ever since Dad had decided to write to Uncle Thomas.

Not long afterward, Gwilym received word from Thomas indicating that he would, indeed, be a welcome addition to the coal-exporting business he now owned and operated almost single-handedly. "How fortuitously timed is your inquiry regarding a partnership," Thomas had written. "Only three weeks ago did I come to realize that far too great a responsibility had fallen upon my shoulders and that I was in dire need of assistance. Do, then, come as soon as possible. It is with great relief and anticipation that I look forward to your return to Cardiff." Elizabeth had positively glowed with satisfaction upon hearing the words as Gwilym read them aloud. The letter seemed a hearty endorsement of the decision she had already made.

CHAPTER 2

Home at Last

⸺❧⸺

ONLY A FEW WEEKS FOLLOWING the arrival of Thomas' letter, Gwilym set sail ready to start a new career and to establish a new home for his family in South Wales. It had been decided that Elizabeth and the children would remain in Pennsylvania until Gwilym was comfortably situated and could well afford their passage to England.

Oddly enough, no one experienced remorse or apprehension. They were convinced that the decision would prove advantageous. All were delighted with the prospect of establishing a new life in Britain.

It had been April when Gwilym set sail for Cardiff—nearly three months ago. Now, finally, his family was en route across the Atlantic to rejoin him in the northern port city of Chester where the boat was scheduled to dock and where they had decided to spend several days recuperating from the arduous journey. While in Chester, they would stay with Elizabeth's elder sister, Elvira and her family. Elvira had written to Elizabeth, explaining that she, too, was pregnant and was expected to deliver at approximately the same time as Elizabeth. "How lovely to be with you at such a blessed and joyous time!" Elvira had written. "I simply cannot wait to see you, my dearest little sister." Following their brief respite in Chester, they would complete the final phase of the journey and travel southward by train to Cardiff where Elizabeth could most comfortably and conveniently give birth to the child she was carrying. This was the plan they had devised. However, the plan that emerged was somewhat different.

First, the ocean journey was taking longer than the anticipated eight days due to the strong winds and rough seas. Second, Elizabeth was far more ill and uncomfortable than had been anticipated. Third, Elizabeth, partly due to her physical illness and the challenges of the journey itself, who had for so many months vehemently expressed her eagerness to return to Britain—along with the confidence that she had made the right decision—was now entertaining doubts regarding the efficacy of her decision.

As she and her babies drew ever closer to the United Kingdom, she grew increasingly apprehensive that the decision had been too hastily determined, too selfishly applied. Furthermore, she wondered if it had been prudent to forfeit the freedom, bounty, and beauty of life in the United States, and she wondered, as well, if it had been in the best interest of the children to uproot them and replant them in English soil. Deep in her soul, she felt a great love for America. Had it been fair to remove the children from this land of hope and freedom? During these moments of uncertainty, Elizabeth derived considerable strength and solace from the knowledge that she had followed her heart, obeyed her God, and had acted in accordance with what she regarded was in Gwilym's best interest and happiness. Upon Gwilym's suggestion, she had opened her heart to life—and then trusted it to direct her along the appropriate pathway. Having asked for guidance, she could only view her own notions and desires as superfluous and regard the outcome as divine will.

In fact, she had not really required Gwilym's advice along these lines. For she had been carefully taught by her father, James Coleman, a minister in the Wesleyan church, to consciously place her soul in God's keeping. And although she had never fully understood precisely what this entailed, she had always entrusted everything that was difficult or problematic unto the benevolent guidance of that unidentifiable power and source of life that her parents had referred to as "God." Far too sensible to trouble herself by questioning the existence or nature of such a power, she had accepted it as a matter of common sense and expediency. She found it most comforting and convenient to believe then, that she and her family were returning to England in accordance with God's will.

Nearly ten days after they had departed from New York City's harbor, Elizabeth and her three small children set foot on English soil. Weary and disheveled after the tedious days of preparing for the trip and then taking the difficult journey, they were, nonetheless, overjoyed to behold the castle, cathedral, great clock tower, and the medieval black and white timbered houses that Gwilym had described to them and that they knew signified the city of Chester. How tender was the reunion with Gwilym who simply could not stop smiling as he was encircled by four pairs of loving arms! Elizabeth was gratified to observe that he looked more handsome—and more at ease and content—than ever. It was obvious that life in Britain agreed with him.

Only for an instant did Elizabeth experience anything like regret or remorse. "Oh dear," she had murmured in an anxious tone loud enough for all to hear upon first setting foot on shore, "I believe I have made the wrong decision after all. We should never have left America." Fortunately, she was allowed no further opportunity for such reflection, for Gwilym teasingly placed his hand over her lips, hastily gathered her and the children into his arms, and gently lifted them into the hired carriage that would transport them to the home of Elizabeth's sister. Never again did she either express or experience any further uncertainty.

Approximately six weeks after their arrival in England, in Chester, on August 14, 1899, Elizabeth gave birth to a baby girl whom she subsequently named Katherine Sedonia in honor and memory of the little girl she lost in 1898. The child was dainty and rather delicate, but healthy and normal in every way, as Elizabeth had prayed it would be. Although it had been Elizabeth's intention to give birth to the child in Cardiff, she had been obliged to remain in Chester to assist Elvira in the delivery of her baby who had come only one week after Elizabeth and Gwilym had arrived at her home. Equally solicitous and eager to repay the kindness, Elvira insisted that Elizabeth remain with her until the birth of her child. And so it came to be that Katherine Sedonia Davies was born in Chester rather than Cardiff. Only one month after Katherine's birth—as soon as it was deemed advisable by the attending physician—the family boarded a train bound for their new home in Cardiff, Wales. Wales was a small country, comparable in size to the state of New Jersey, in the United States. The trip to Cardiff required a three and one-half hour train ride through the rural, unspoiled verdant countryside, mountains, and valleys.

From the moment she set foot back in Cardiff, in her new home, virtually everything about it appealed to Elizabeth. In truth, she had never been happier. What a fuss everyone made of her and the children, to be sure! Well-intentioned and doting friends and relatives welcomed their return to Cardiff warmly, making certain that they lacked nothing in the way of companionship or provisions. As might be expected, Elizabeth was in her element in the midst of such kindness, affection, and attention.

How easily, then, did they learn to appreciate their new surroundings! It did not take them long to discover the many advantages of life in a large cosmopolitan city. The capital of Wales, Cardiff was not merely a bustling commercial seaport, but an attractively arranged center of trade, communications, and culture offering diverse forms of entertainment and diversion and boasting a grand collection of governmental buildings, a castle, cathedral, several universities, theaters, shops, and first-rate museums. To the Davies, it afforded a refreshing change from the monotony and dreariness of life in rural Pennsylvania. It was not only Elizabeth who derived great pleasure and joy from city life, for the children loved being a part of the constant parade of human beings who lined the busy thoroughfares. They delighted in the colorful local markets wherein every imaginable variety of produce, handicrafts, and merchandise were displayed. They were overwhelmed by the elegant shopping arcades wherein one might purchase the finest and latest European fashions. And they were deeply impressed with the medieval ruins and great monuments. As Mum had promised, life in Britain was vastly different from that which they had experienced in America—and to their minds, ever so much more fun! Even Gwilym seemed to derive considerable benefit from the changes that had taken place—appearing far less solemn and preoccupied than he had during those final months in America.

A source of great pride and joy to all—but to Elizabeth in particular—was the tiny infant who had rapidly and successfully filled the void in their lives left by Catherine Sedonia. This new baby was every bit as beautiful, good-natured, and well-behaved as the original. She seldom cried, was rarely cranky or irritable, and had an odd, knowing smile that she exhibited at the most opportune moments as well as deep, penetrating eyes that seemed to perceive far more than one might expect. Everyone enjoyed indulging this child, and she would have become terribly spoiled had not Gwilym intervened in his firm but gentle manner. Even he, however, had difficulty resisting the slightest wish or whim of this tender, precocious little girl.

Within a few months of their arrival, the Davies were comfortably settled in a spacious three-story brick home on City Road in a pleasant residential middle-class neighborhood within walking distance of the commercial heart of the city. It was everything they might wish, and Elizabeth was especially delighted with the large backyard and the lovely rose garden in the front. In time, the entire family became so comfortable that it seemed they had never lived anywhere else.

CHAPTER 3

Cardiff

LIFE IN CARDIFF PROCEEDED SMOOTHLY for some time. The role of a middle-class Welsh housewife suited Elizabeth perfectly and, by 1904, five years after the birth of Katherine Sedonia, she had given birth to two more children—a little boy named Leonard and a little girl named Olwen. Preoccupied with the rearing of her children and with the numberless details which comprised the efficient maintenance of her household, she had little time for anything else. In the meantime, Gwilym continued to devote the vast majority of his time and energies to the coal-exporting business he now co-owned and operated with Thomas and from which he derived a moderate income.

The three eldest Davies children were now regularly attending school and assisting their Mum and Dad with the care of the three younger children. Now, five years old, little Katherine Sedonia had grown into a rosy, slender, fair-haired little girl with a sunny disposition and an inquiring turn of mind whereby she wished to know, as Elizabeth put it, "everything about everything and everybody." Insatiably curious, she was forever asking questions, often becoming frustrated as a result of the inadequate, careless responses she received in answer to her perpetual, "But why, Daddy?" or "On what basis, Mummy?" It did not take the perceptive child long to discover that adults did not always possess greater wisdom than she herself. It was with a keen sense of disappointment that she realized that with age did not necessarily come the answers to the endless stream of questions that had already arisen in her mind. She had sincerely hoped that this would be the case.

Katherine bore an uncanny resemblance to the sister for whom she had been named. She was of a similar nature and disposition as well. Gwilym could not help but marvel at the similarities, and he felt a special warmth and fondness for his little girl. She was an uncommonly sensitive child—eager to please, quick to forgive, and anxious to avoid friction or disturbance of any kind. In fact, she was unable to tolerate even the slightest disagreement without becoming physically ill, and when arguments erupted among family members, she would beg her dad to intervene.

"But, my Love, you mustn't take these things so seriously. They don't mean anything by it," Gwilym would assure his daughter after a nasty row had developed between Della and Cora.

"Oh yes they do, Daddy. They do mean it, and they say such awful things to each other. And I can tell they don't love each other when they fight. Otherwise they wouldn't. And I can tell they both feel badly afterward. But then I don't understand why they do it. Why do they try to hurt each other so, Daddy?"

"Because they don't know any better, my love," Gwilym would reply thoughtfully. "After all, they are just children. Perhaps when they get older, they will no longer fight."

"Yes, but Daddy," Katherine would persist, "you and Mummy fight, and you are older. You say dreadful things to one another. You hurt each other just like Della and Cora. Why do you try to hurt each other?"

"Because," Gwilym would admit after an uncomfortable pause, "we don't know any better either. Sometimes even grown-ups act like children. It makes no difference how old they get."

"Really, Daddy?"

"Really, my love."

"Well, I hope I shan't act like a child all my life."

"My dear, you do not behave like a child now." And studying the intense, serious little face, he could not help but kiss her tenderly on the cheek and hug his precocious daughter close to him. And while Katherine loved her mum, she worshipped her dad, regarding him as her mentor, trusted confidant, and as a limitless source of wisdom. To her, it seemed that he lacked nothing in the way of grace, charm, and knowledge, and she loved him unconditionally.

It was shortly after Katherine's fifth birthday that her eldest sister, Della (now eleven), was discovered to be a suspect tuberculosis victim. Although she remained under close medical scrutiny and supervision for some time, there was no noticeable improvement in her condition. Later, when her health actually began to deteriorate, local physicians could do nothing for her but recommend that she be sent to the country to recuperate. "The high altitudes—where the air is fresh and clean—are particularly beneficial to one in her condition," advised one of the many doctors the Davies had consulted.

They would not hear of sending little Della off alone to the country. Therefore, they had little alternative but to relinquish their lovely home on City Road and find a suitable residence in the countryside surrounding Cardiff. "I will go anywhere—do anything in my power to save my little girl's life," Elizabeth had stated unequivocally before her family. "No sacrifice is too great." All agreed.

Due to the urgency of the situation—for Della was growing worse daily—they had little time or opportunity to locate appropriate accommodations in the country. Thankfully, one of Gwilym's business associates came to their rescue in the nick of time, graciously volunteering to rent them his lovely summer retreat, The Cottage, which was ideally situated high in the mountains near Cardiff, a mere six miles away in a tiny village called Gwaelod-y-garth.

Accepting the kind offer immediately, the Davies hastily packed up their possessions and managed to relocate to Gwaelod-y-garth within several weeks' time. So suddenly had these circumstances arisen, however, that no one had given much thought to anything but the immediate future. There had been virtually no consideration of each individual's feelings or the long-range ramifications inherent in such a dramatic change in lifestyle. It was required of each one to adjust to the new environment to the best of his or her abilities.

It was not the village of Gwaelod-y-garth itself that in any way posed problems of adjustment; rather, it was the nature of rural life that was simply too dramatic a departure from the bustling life that they had known in Cardiff. Gwaelod-y-garth was a pleasant, tranquil village picturesquely situated high in the hills overlooking the scenic River Taff and a pretty town called Taff's Well which lay directly in the valley below. Consisting of approximately one hundred cottages clustered together, several shops and family owned and operated businesses, a general store, and a post office—daily life starkly contrasted with that of Cardiff. Most of the village's inhabitants had bought property here for precisely this reason, using the village as a weekend and holiday vacation spot. The Davies were thus numbered among the community's few permanent, year-round residents.

And yet, despite the obvious difficulties inherent in the transition, no one could deny the distinct benefits to be derived from country life. For Gwaelod-y-garth was truly a lovely spot offering magnificent wooded areas, sparkling rivers and streams which flowed gently through the slopes and valleys, emerald green meadows, snow-covered mountain peaks, and an abundance of vividly colored wild flowers and fruit trees. Never had they lived in an atmosphere of such persistent peace and awe-inspiring natural beauty. The children were able now, as never before, to romp freely in the woods and meadows; wade and swim in the sparkling rivers; to pick the ubiquitous wild flowers; to wander through the hills to their hearts' content; and from the luscious fruit trees they plucked apples, pears, and plums. They were able to indulge in limitless beauty whenever they wished.

Despite their initial misgivings the Davies came to love country life, for it afforded them a delightful change of pace from the old neighborhood and the normal run of activities. But they were able to enjoy themselves primarily as a result of the conviction that their stay in Gwaelod-y-garth was only temporary—rather like an extended holiday.

It was with mounting anxiety and disappointment, then, that they began to realize that they might never return to Cardiff—that it might be necessary to remain for quite some time—perhaps forever—in Gwaelod-y-garth. For by the time that several months had elapsed, it had become evident that Della's health had improved considerably and would continue to do so here.

For Katherine, in particular, this transitional period was difficult. Never having known anything but city life, she deeply missed its continuous excitement, activity, entertainment, diversion, and companionship. She had not before in her brief life experienced anything like the great silence, vastness, and loneliness of the country. Wistfully, she would recall the happy experiences she had shared with her brothers and sisters in the city. Her memories of all facets of city life were vivid: the comforting smells and sounds of the crowds on High Street, Queen Street, and City Road; the soothing hum of the electric trams, hansom cabs, and carriages on every road at all hours of the day and night; the savory fragrance of freshly baked breads, cakes, and pastries wafting from the interior of Howell's Bakery Shop; the ornate display windows of the elegant shops in the St. Mary's Street Arcade; the impressive and enticing array of fruits, vegetables, and flowers sold at the Open Air Market on Charles Street; the city streets at night still filled with people and a joyous vitality and camaraderie—gas lamps burning brightly on every corner and in many of the shops.

Katherine was frightened by the ceaseless stillness of the country both by day and by night, but particularly so by night. For then, everything seemed strangely silent, ominous, and foreboding. The darkness, with its accompanying quietude, made her terribly uneasy, as did the mysterious sounds that pierced the darkness—the wailing of unidentifiable animals; the whistling of the wind; the creaking of the house itself, the sense of isolation.

With all her heart she longed to return to Cardiff. And yet, little by little, she came to realize that this would not be. For her sister seemed to grow rosier, healthier every day, and in her heart, Katherine understood that it was essential to remain in the country for Della's sake. In time, she outgrew her childish fears and inhibitions and, like the others, came to appreciate the pretty cottage on the side of a mountain with its great rich land and beautiful gardens; the air that was always pure and fragrant, the pleasant climate, and the uninterrupted peacefulness. Yet she would never forget the busy, happy days she had known in Cardiff, and she vowed secretly to return to the city as soon as she was old enough to be able to do so on her own.

CHAPTER 4

The Tin Church

ALTHOUGH VASTLY DIFFERENT FROM THOSE of Cardiff, the country boasted all manner of interesting attractions and diversions. There were the frequent "jumbles," or rummage sales, held in the center of town; the various pageants and festivities sponsored by the Bethlehem Church; the frequent concerts and plays presented by the Independent Congregational Church; the magic lantern shows; the elaborate weekly dinners held for friends and family at home; the lengthy political, religious, and philosophical discussions following these dinners which extended late into the night; lovely walks in the country; the circus that visited nearby Hopkins Town several times a year—all held a charm and fascination of their own.

For little Katherine, the pattern that was to emerge as her life for the next several years was firmly established. Her weekdays were spent at the Gwaelod-y-garth County Primary School; late afternoons were shared with her best friend, six-year old Maravanuie Edmunds and other children who lived nearby. Saturdays were devoted to the exploration of the glorious countryside or, if need be, to whatever family activity had been planned by Mum and Dad. On Sunday, the family enjoyed a great mid-day dinner after which they walked half a mile to the Independent Congregational Church for the afternoon service. Katherine and her brothers and sisters attended Sunday school weekly. On Sunday evening, her Dad would read aloud from his favorite books which included everything from those of Alfred Tennyson to Frederic Harrison to T. H. Huxley. Often friends and neighbors would drop by to exchange local gossip as well as church, political, and domestic news. In short, it was a pleasant, peaceful, satisfying time period in no way remarkable except, perhaps, for its simplicity and subtle grace and charm.

Yet there were other elements that must be included among those that influenced little Katherine. The inspired rhetoricians who loudly proclaimed the virtues of temperance at church and who issued forth somber warnings of the eternal hell fire and damnation which assuredly awaited those who indulged in alcohol frightened Katherine terribly. For she knew that her beloved Dad drank on occasion, and she could not bear the thought of this dear, gentle man enduring the agony of eternal hell. Furthermore, her mum's fear compounded her own. For Elizabeth had been raised in a strict Christian household in which the consumption of alcohol was regarded as a sin and was absolutely forbidden. She was, therefore, convinced that Gwilym would burn in hell forever as a result of his indulgence. Nor could Katherine endure the vicious confrontations that took place following each of Gwilym's visits to the local pub.

"You've been at the pub again, haven't you?" Elizabeth would ask him in a nasty, accusatory tone. Her husband would merely nod, knowing perfectly well what was to ensue.

"You've been drinking that awful stuff and carrying on with those pals of yours? After I have begged you not to! After I have made it perfectly clear that I would no longer remain here with you if you continued to drink!"

Taking a deep breath, Gwilym would pause a moment or two and then reply calmly and with admirable patience, "Now, Liz, do be sensible. What harm could possibly result from a game or two of draughts with the boys and a glass of wine after a hard day at the office? Can you seriously imagine that after all the good I've done that God would see fit to send me to eternal hell? If it is a transgression to take a drink every now and then—and I personally do not believe it to be one—I am certain that God in His infinite mercy and wisdom shall forgive me. I assure you, my dear, there is nothing to fear."

"And I am equally certain that everyone who drinks defends the filthy habit that way," Elizabeth would snap, her eyes blazing with disgust and contempt. And on and on the argument would proceed in this manner until finally, Elizabeth would storm out of the room in a silent rage, indignant and frustrated that he would not heed her warnings or concede to what seemed to her a simple demand.

Fortunately, her explosions were always short-lived, and seldom did she remain bitter or upset for longer than a few minutes. Then, both the transgressor and his transgression would be forgiven and forgotten and the subject dismissed until similar circumstances arose once again.

It was not until Katherine intervened that Gwilym felt compelled to give up drinking altogether. The little girl, who could not tolerate the slightest disturbance, the least misunderstanding, lived in perpetual dread and fear of the nasty arguments that took place between her parents following each of her dad's visits to the pub.

Unbeknownst to anyone else, she was unable to fall asleep until she knew that her Dad had safely returned home. Silently slipping out of bed, she would sit on the stairway landing attired in nothing but her flimsy nightdress until she heard the comforting turn of her dad's key in the door. She would then trace his actions and whereabouts in the house by means of his footsteps on the hard wooden floors. First, the foyer, then the dining room, finally the lounge where she knew he would find her mother crocheting. Shivering from the combination of fear and cold, she would remain on the landing and eavesdrop until she knew that the inevitable confrontation had reached its conclusion. Finally, wearily, she would crawl back into bed and then as she had been taught in Sunday school, would pray to God to "make the awful fighting stop and to help Mummy and Daddy to be kind and to love one another."

One morning, several days after Katherine had heard several overly zealous members of the Band of Hope—a community group with a focus on teaching children in particular the importance of living a life free of alcohol—spreading their message about the evils of alcohol. Gwilym succinctly announced at the breakfast table his intention to return home late that evening. Katherine knew immediately that he was planning to meet his friends at the Inn, and her heart sank in anticipation of the inevitable consequences. Elizabeth was too absorbed in the feeding of little Olwen and

Leonard to take much notice of her husband's words, but Katherine was painfully aware of all that they implied. The too familiar scenario flashed before her eyes. Tremblingly, she recalled the ultimatum which Elizabeth had issued to Gwilym during their most recent argument, "If you ever again set foot in the pub, I will leave you. Do you understand me? I will pack up my belongings and go where you shall never find me." Katherine had known that these were no idle words, no empty threat. Her mum had meant every word she had spoken.

What will happen to all us all if mum leaves us? Katherine wondered miserably. She would have gladly shared her fears and worries with the others, but she was reluctant to upset anyone else. Following breakfast and throughout the seemingly endless day, Katherine prayed that the argument would somehow be averted, that the situation be resolved and that peace be permanently restored to the household. She was able to think of little else.

Finally, at half past nine in the evening, Katherine, vigilantly seated at her post on the landing, started, as she heard her dad's key turn in the front door. Grateful that he had safely arrived home at last, she next braced herself for the inevitable. There were several moments of heavy silence during which she felt that her parents were assessing of the situation. Although she hoped with all her heart that there would be no quarrel, she knew that it was too late. After several more minutes—which seemed like an eternity to the little girl, her mother spoke. Elizabeth's voice was tremulous, and Katherine noticed that it was also higher in pitch than usual.

"How could you, Gwilym? How could you so blatantly ignore my wishes and visit the pub again?"

The row had begun. This time, however, Katherine felt that she could not allow it to continue. *I have to do something*, she thought to herself in desperation, wondering how she might possibly intervene.

"I am sorry," Elizabeth was saying quietly, despair evident in her voice, "but I have made up my mind. Early tomorrow morning, I shall catch the first train for Cardiff." Never had Katherine felt more helpless. As the tears came to her eyes, she prayed from the bottom of her heart, *Dear God, please don't let my mum leave us. I love her. Please help us.*

As though in answer to her request and before she had a chance to really comprehend what was taking place, she found herself almost flying down the stairs as though she had been propelled by an unknown Power. She knelt on the floor before her parents. Tears streaming down her face now, she heard herself utter words that she had neither planned nor intended to speak. "Please, God, help us all. Please make the fighting end. Tell my Dad not to go to the Inn anymore, for he is making all of us so sad and frightened by drinking that nasty stuff which Mum says will send him to hell. And please don't let Mummy leave us—ever, God, as she says she will. For all of us need her so. I love Mummy and Daddy so much, God. But if Daddy doesn't stop upsetting all of us, then I don't want to go on living anymore 'cause I get so scared of what will happen. And I get so cold, God, waiting on the stairs for Daddy to get home at night. I don't know what else to do—so I'm asking You, God, to please help us, and to make all the fighting stop forever."

The room was completely still for several moments, as the impact of her words was felt. Gwilym and Elizabeth hardly dared look at one another. As Katherine wondered whatever had prompted her to address her parents in such a manner, she noticed that her mother's large brown eyes were filled with tears and that the expression on her dad's face was unlike any she had seen before.

With profound tenderness and remorse he spoke, "I am so sorry, my darling little girl. So very sorry." He held his arms out to her, and she tumbled happily into them. As he gently wiped the tears from her cheeks, he continued softly, caressing each syllable with his silken voice. "Daddy promises you that from hereon he shall never, ever go to the Inn again. He shall never again upset you or your Mum like this. Do you understand?"

Katherine nodded, feeling that nothing could equal the wonderful warmth of her dad's embrace. He continued slowly, thoughtfully, "But I would like you to remember, love, that Daddy has never been drunk. He is perfectly sober now, and despite what your mum thinks, there is no harm in having a little to drink every so often. The drink itself is not bad—only if he drinks too much can it be bad for anyone. And then, it's like when one eats too many sweets or too much food. Nevertheless, I promise that Daddy will never, ever go to the Inn again—and that there will be no further disagreement between your Mum and me on the subject. You have my word, love."

"Oh, Daddy, thank you so much," Katherine murmured contentedly, her face nuzzling his, as she nestled comfortably in her dad's arms. And observing the relieved expression in her mother's eyes, she could not help but feel gratified with the results of her intervention. *Mummy is so pretty when she isn't all worried*, she thought to herself. All of a sudden, she became aware of how exhausted she was—for it had required a great effort to keep her eyes open and to keep from continuously yawning. As her dad tenderly carried her up the stairs to her bedroom, she silently thanked God with all her heart for coming to her aid. How deeply and peacefully she slept that night! A man of his word, Gwilym never again set foot in the pub, and a glorious peacefulness and harmony pervaded the household for quite some time.

It was not too long after this episode that Katherine was introduced to a wonderful friend and cherished companion, who was of great comfort and assistance to her throughout her childhood. One unusually wet and bitterly cold February Sunday, Elizabeth felt ill-advised to send the children off to school, for it was a long journey in such weather. Yet she did not wish them to ignore the Sabbath day. It suddenly occurred to her that under such circumstances, it might not be a bad idea to send the children to the Tin Church—an odd, funny building made of tin and stone which served as the mountain annex to the local Catholic Church. Now the Tin Church—deriving its name from its bizarre appearance—had been a topic of considerable curiosity and speculation on the part of the children. If one had to attend Sunday school at all—and nearly everybody did—it seemed far more adventurous to go to the Tin Church than the sedate, ordinary looking Independent Congregational Church.

On this particular Sunday afternoon, then, it took the children only a few minutes to make the brief journey on foot to the Tin Church. On their way, they were relieved to observe the sun making its first appearance of the day. Upon their arrival, they were delighted to note that the interior of the building was just as peculiar as the exterior. How they would have appreciated the opportunity to explore the structure! Unfortunately, they were immediately put together with a lot of other children and then divided into individual classes on the basis of their age.

From here on, to Katherine's great disappointment, despite the novelty of the building itself, everything else was virtually the same as her regular Sunday school. The teacher was as stern, dull, and uninteresting as her own, and the lesson was equally uninspiring. She was bored. It was, in fact, a struggle to keep her eyes open.

Perhaps twenty minutes had elapsed when, suddenly, Katherine was startled out of her lethargy by an enormous clap of thunder and an awesome flash of lightning. Within seconds, the classroom had become very dark, and a heavy rain outside spattered and hissed fiercely. No one could concentrate upon anything but the drama unfolding outside the window. Great sheets of gray rain began to fall; and while it had been mid-afternoon only a few moments before, the sky was now an inky black, and it seemed as though it were the middle of the night. As the thunder and lightning increased in frequency and intensity, Katherine was unable to think of anything else. She had always been frightened of the dark, and now she was terrified. In no way was she comforted by the presence of her teacher and classmates. "I want to go home," was all she felt like saying. Silently, she prayed that the awful commotion outside would cease.

As if in response to her prayers, the superintendent of the school, Mr. James, appeared at the door of the classroom announcing his intention to hold a brief assembly for everyone in the main hall. Relieved just to get up from the hard, wooden chairs, Katherine and the others arose obediently and marched single file from their room.

There was much whispering and giggling as they settled into the hall. But then, a hush came over the youthful audience as the superintendent ascended the small platform and approached the lectern. Katherine liked him immediately, for he seemed kind and unaffected, and his eyes twinkled with irresistible warmth and good humor.

"Good afternoon to all of you, dear children," he said in a deep, soothing voice. "And it really is a good afternoon despite our rather unpredictable weather. Now, I understand that there are many of you who are frightened. Is this so?" Nearly everyone in the audience breathed a sigh of relief, then nodded in response. Mr. James continued, smiling sympathetically. "Now, I would like all of those of you who are frightened—just for a moment or two—to glance outside the window and observe what is taking place. Study the sky, and the trees. Look at the rain, and then try to appreciate it—remembering how helpful—indeed, necessary—it is to the growth of the fruits and flowers and vegetables and all living things. We cannot live without the rain, any more than we can live without the sun. The sun and the moon—night and day—warmth and cold—all are a part of the wonderful world which God has created for us. What each of you must learn to do is to look for the beauty which lies within everything and everyone. Notice the wisdom and love with which everything has been created. And although you are only little children, you must realize that all human beings experience great storms at one time or another, and that these storms serve to strengthen us—making us wiser and greater. Therefore, you have no cause for fear. It would be helpful for you to understand that exactly like the rain, these storms are a part of God's plan for us, and. that they seldom last very long.

"Today, on this rainy afternoon, there is something very special—rather—someone very special whom I would like to share with all of you dear children. And this someone is a man called Jesus. You see, God—the Creator of our world and of all life—as a result of His great love for all of us—has sent His beloved son, Jesus of Nazareth, to look after us—to guide and assist us whenever we are in need. The son of God is a gentle, loving man who truly loves all little children, and is a friend to each one who turns to Him in friendship. Jesus helps cast away all doubts and fears, and He brings peace to our troubled hearts and souls. Jesus has worked countless miracles in the past, and it is my belief that He continues to do so at the present time. If you love Him, if you turn to Him and have faith in Him, He will never let you down. He will never, ever fail you.

"Jesus is blessed with the ability to hear the word of God. And God is telling Him right this very minute to tell all of you that there is nothing at all to fear here this afternoon. Each of you is safe and will not be harmed in any way. So, do not feel frightened any longer, my little friends. Remember, that when you love Jesus, you are always under His protection. So love Him, pray to Him. He is always nearby. God bless you all.

"And now," concluded Mr. James in his warm voice and sincere manner, "let us all sing together a lovely hymn. We are no longer frightened of the darkness outside, are we? For we know that it will soon be light once again." And he began to sing with great enthusiasm, "Jesus Loves Me, This I Know."

Katherine was never fully able to explain what it was about Mr. James' simple talk that had affected her so deeply. Certainly, even in her brief life, she had attended numerous lectures, sermons and prayer meetings of a similar nature. Yet none had touched her as this one had.

While others had spoken of Jesus as a distant, forbidding historical figure "who died for man's sins," Mr. James had painted a vastly different portrait of the son of God—depicting him as tender and loving, gentle and forgiving, friendly, and accessible. Even as Mr. James had spoken, she believed that she had felt the loving influence of Jesus, and from that time forth she welcomed Him into her life as a friend, confidant, teacher, and guide.

She never spoke of her new friend to anyone else. He was far too special to describe in mere words. But truly believing all which Mr. James had said about Him, she approached Him frequently, turning to Him for help whenever she was in need, certain that He would never fail her. And, somehow, He was as real to her as any living person. But perhaps, most importantly, she felt that He loved her as much as she loved Him.

CHAPTER 5

The Transformation

⸻

TIME SEEMED TO FLY IN the country. By the time she was six, Katherine had adjusted perfectly to life in Gwaelod-y-garth, and she was now enjoying the games, relationships, and activities commonly associated with one her age. She had grown to love her new home. Her dad continued to be engrossed in business affairs, commuting daily—often six or seven days a week to Cardiff. Her mum's time was fully devoted to her home and family. Only her beloved rose garden offered Elizabeth any relief from the monotony of daily routine. While Gwilym, Della, Cora, and Katherine attended school, little Leonard and Olwen remained at home under Mum's careful supervision. Surrounded by loving friends and family, firmly established by now in the community, they all had adjusted to the concept that they would never return to the city, and they were content and at peace.

Then, suddenly, inexplicably, life altered dramatically for the Davies. Several weeks before Katherine's seventh birthday, she was stricken with double pneumonia compounded by pleurisy—illnesses, which, at the turn of the century in rural Wales, very often resulted in death. Having been advised as to the hopelessness of their daughter's condition, Elizabeth and Gwilym were disconsolate. They did everything in their power to circumvent her death, providing her with every available type of assistance as little Katherine valiantly struggled for her life.

No one had been prepared for this extensive battle of survival, for the illness had come about quickly—seemingly overnight—and without any warning at all. Many years later, Katherine recalled in detail the extraordinary events that led up to her illness:

I had been quite a strong, healthy child—playful, full of fun and vitality. One of my favorite games, and the last one I ever played, in fact, was that of piggyback whereby my friends and I would take turns carrying one another upon our shoulders.

I had been given one such ride on the shoulders of my best friend, Maravanuie Edmunds, one warm evening in late July. In order to be able to mount her shoulders, it was necessary for me to climb up on the split-rail fence first, for I was a small little girl. At any rate, it was getting rather late—past dusk, I think—and I thought, perhaps it was due to the lateness of the hour that I felt so weary, so exhausted. And although it was now my turn to carry Maravanuie on my shoulders, I realized that I was simply far too tired to do so. I told her this. And I remember thinking, I only want to go to bed. Unfortunately, Maravanuie was not terribly sympathetic and accused me of being unfair. Far too exhausted to argue, I simply advised her that I would be sure to carry her first the next time we played. But I could see that she was hurt and disappointed, and this upset me very much.

I had little choice but to turn back toward the house. It seemed to take a very long time to walk back, even though I had been perhaps only several hundred feet away from our front door. Once I finally got inside, I had to literally drag myself up the staircase leading to my bedroom, feeling all the while that something very strange indeed was taking place. On the way up, I called out to mum in a feeble voice, "Good night. I am going to bed." She was in the midst of entertaining some of our neighbors, and interrupted her conversation only briefly enough to remind me to "Make sure you wash your hands and feet." I remember thinking it rather peculiar that she had not, advised me to wash my face, as well, and to tuck myself into bed, as was her custom. I remember entering the water closet, changing into my nightdress, and then, finally, literally collapsing into bed. I was conscious of virtually nothing else for some time after this. Apparently, I was terribly ill.

The family physician, whom my parents had notified at once, advised them that there was no hope of my survival. Pneumonia, compounded by pleurisy was almost always fatal. In addition, he indicated that I had been carrying the illness for at least three or four days prior to my collapse. He said that I had the highest temperature he had ever seen, and that, frankly, he was surprised that I was still breathing. He could do nothing further.

Determined to do everything in his power to save my life, dad prayed and prayed. Suddenly, he remembered the name of a wonderful physician who lived on the other side of the River Taff. It had been claimed by many villagers that Dr. Risely, as he was called, had performed "miraculous" healings, and had saved the lives of many whom other physicians had regarded as incurable. Unfortunately, Dr. Risely's infant daughter had died recently in a tragic accident, and it was rumored locally that both he and his wife had become alcoholic. Prior to the death of his daughter, however, Dr. Risely had achieved great success in employing what would later become known as natural and holistic methods of healing. Dad felt it worth his while to contact Dr. Risely. In fact, this man was Dad's last hope. And so, he made the journey to the physician's home. With an eloquence borne of his desperate desire to save the life of his child, Dad managed to persuade Dr. Risley to see me.

Sobering up the physician first, he then escorted him to our home and to my bedside. Sadly, Dr. Risely could do little more than to confirm the prognoses made by the other physicians who had been called in to see me. They had regarded my death as imminent and inevitable. Like them, he could not comprehend how it was that I had managed to survive this long with such a high fever.

After taking my temperature once more, an idea suddenly occurred to the physician. "Quickly," he cried hoarsely to Mum and Dad. "Find me a blanket." Puzzled, Dad nonetheless obeyed.

In his worry and his haste, he could find only the rug which was used on our horse and trap. But Dr. Risely did not seem to take notice. Patiently, ever-so-gently, he mopped my feverish forehead, and simultaneously dipped the rug in boiling hot water. "We'll wrap her in the rug, and pray that she perspires. If she does, her body temperature will lower automatically." Dad and Mum watched in horror as the Doctor lifted me out of bed, placed the rug underneath me, and then wrapped me, my entire body, into it. He burnt his hands in the scalding water as he did so, but continued as though he were oblivious to the pain.

He kept me wrapped in the blanket for quite a while. Nothing happened for some time. Several hours later, however, it became apparent that Dr. Risely's experiment was successful. For I did perspire, and my body temperature dropped significantly. It was not too much later that I regained consciousness for a brief period of time.

Before regaining consciousness, however, something quite extraordinary, and unlike anything I had ever experienced before, took place. While everyone believed me to be in an unconscious state, I was, in fact, completely conscious but in another place altogether—a place of exquisite peace and beauty and light. While everyone believed that I was lying in bed, in reality, I was, in fact, floating above the bed some distance away. The atmosphere in which I was floating was unlike anything I had previously known in normal life, yet somehow extremely familiar. It was full of love and light. I noticed that there were on either side of me, lovely, radiant forms of light whom I somehow knew to be angels. They emanated a wonderful peacefulness and joy. I remember feeling quite astonished to perceive that these angels did not possess the wings I had always been taught to believe they had.

Intuitively, I loved them, and felt, in turn, their love for me. Therefore, I was quite perplexed when they advised me, for no apparent reason, to leave this wonderful place and return to

my physical body. "You must go back into the body, dear Child,"
they were saying. "You must, there is much for you to accomplish
in this lifetime. It is not yet time for you to leave the earth." They
became increasingly emphatic. But I was far from willing to heed
their advice, for I was perfectly content where I was. Observing
my physical body with total detachment, I had no desire to return
to it ever again. I felt so light and free—it was exhilarating!
And although I had no idea where I was, I liked being there. It
was indescribably beautiful—as were those radiant forms beside
me. Yet I began to feel rather uneasy, as the angels continued to
encourage me to return. "My dear, you will deeply regret it if you
do not go back," they were saying. "Go on now, go back. Go back."

And then, all of a sudden, I heard Mum cry out to me.
Her love for me, her worry and concern—were all evident in
her voice. And I remember feeling terribly sad and sorry for her,
and I wished that I could make her feel better. The next thing I
knew, I was no longer in the beautiful place. I felt myself re-enter
the physical body, and the sensation was dreadful. The contrast
between the world I had just left and the one which I re-entered
was great; and I felt deeply hurt and disappointed to be back in
the painful body after my excursion into a sphere of light and joy.
I did not wish to be back at all!

What was most startling of all, however, was the sudden re-
alization that I was not the same person who had inhabited my
body before. Major changes had been effected while I was out
of the body. Somehow, in some way, I was older, wiser, more
aware—as though I had left the body a child and re-entered it an
adult. Inexplicably, from the moment that I regained conscious-
ness, I was aware that I was different.

Shortly after I returned to the body, I regained consciousness
for a brief interval. Although I had consumed no food or liquid
for several days, I awoke with a terrible thirst and an intense
craving for some juice.

It had been believed that my death was imminent. Mum and Dad were weary and heartbroken by this time and had been advised to leave the room for a while. My brother Gwilym had received explicit instructions to remain by my bedside in case I should awaken unexpectedly or worsen or require any attention at all. Mum had been very disappointed with Dr. Risely's initial efforts, and she could hardly bear to watch me moan and writhe in agony under the scalding rug. Much of my hair had fallen out in conjunction with my illness; my skin was raw and red and rough—in short, I was a pitiful sight. Neither could stand to watch me suffer.

And so, my brother was alone with me in the bedroom. There was a glass of orange juice that had been placed on the mantle on the opposite side of the room from which I lay. And I can hear it now as distinctly as I did then—the strangely mature, adult voice—emanating from me, saying firmly, "Please pass me a drink. Do not be afraid to do so. Do not worry about disobeying the instructions which you have been given [he had been advised against providing me with any food or beverage lest I choke]. If I do not drink," I continued in my strange new voice, "I will not remain in the body. If, therefore, you wish me to survive, you will give me the drink."

I was certain that I would not choke, and Gwilym must have sensed this as well. For he immediately got up to retrieve the juice. Sitting by my side, he then gently held the glass to my parched lips. As I slowly sipped the cool liquid, I could actually feel my body respond. It was as though I were already beginning to grow stronger. And I realized, at this time, that I was here to stay. I cannot describe the horror of this realization.

Katherine was desperately ill for many weeks despite the brief foray into consciousness she had experienced in her brother's presence, and it was still widely feared that she might die. Even if she somehow managed to survive the illness, it was expected that she would be severely afflicted, possibly invalided for the remainder of her life. She was unconscious for the vast majority of each day which elapsed, and only at infrequent intervals did she awaken briefly in order to request a few sips of water or to go to the bathroom. When she did awaken, she suffered excruciating pain, for the boiling rug into which she had been strapped for so many hours, had severely burned her, and she felt as though her body were on fire. Every bone, every nerve, and muscle ached—even her face throbbed in pain. And the little girl longed only to escape from this intense, persistent pain, wishing never again to awaken to the agony which now characterized her daily life.

Ever so slowly, almost imperceptibly at first, the mental anguish became less acute, the physical pain began to diminish, and Katherine was on her way to recovery. Each day, she grew stronger, more alert. The periods of consciousness became lengthier and more frequent, and the idea of continuing to live became increasingly tolerable.

But Katherine was neither pleased nor displeased, satisfied nor dissatisfied with the so-called "progress" she was making—for she had little interest or desire or impetus to go on living. Her body seemed too difficult to support, her mind was tired and her spirit weary and she could not fathom upon what basis it was that her family and friends had been so elated by her recovery. Wistfully, she recalled the lovely place she had visited before re-entering the body; the exhilaration, the freedom and love she had experienced here, and the wonderful angelic beings who had served as her gentle companions during that brief but unforgettable period. She could not help but wonder in a dull, listless manner why she had been required to go on living, why the angels, whom she had intuitively loved and trusted, had so emphatically encouraged her to return to the physical body. In addition, she could not help but wonder why it was that she now felt so different than before.

For, indeed, she felt different in every way. There were no words or concepts with which she was familiar that could adequately convey how or why she felt this difference, but she was profoundly aware of it. And perhaps it is the word *awareness* that most aptly describes the nature of the changes that had taken place. It had been not as a result of, but somehow in conjunction with the experience she shared with the angels that she now seemed to possess greater perspective, deeper insight, an acute sensitivity toward—and heightened awareness of all that transpired around her. There was an increased subtlety and significance to each event; an expanded understanding of the natures of her friends and family members; the feeling of never being truly alone, even when no other human being was nearby; and the conscious realization that she, though a child, knew more about nearly everyone and everything than any of the adults who came to visit. It took her awhile to identify the nature of the transformation which had taken place and an even longer time to adjust to it. In the meantime, she wondered if others had perceived it. Was it as obvious to them as it was to her? It was difficult to determine.

One late Tuesday afternoon, several days after she had regained consciousness for the first time, Katherine was startled out of a deep sleep by loud knocking at the front door. Surprisingly alert and articulate after having been so abruptly awakened, Katherine boldly announced to her mum and those members of the family who were gathered in attendance around her bed, "You will find that it is Mrs. Williams who is at the door. You must not allow her into our home, now or at any other time. She and her husband are bad. Please see to it that the children are no longer permitted to visit them, for what happens at their house is unhealthy for them. The Williams are very bad people." As one might imagine, all were astonished by the strange outburst. Elizabeth gasped at the words, and then carefully scrutinized her daughter's countenance as if trying to determine both the motivation and interpretation of such a message. Sadly, she concluded that her daughter was still delirious.

Collecting herself, Elizabeth hastily tidied the scattered wisps of hair around her face, smoothed her apron, and made her way to the door. Meanwhile, Katherine's brothers and sisters simply stared at one another in disbelief—it seemed to them that the entire household had turned topsy-turvy since their sister's illness. Never had they heard her address Mum in such a manner before—with such evident conviction and authority. They were even more astounded, however, to overhear their mum exclaim in a peculiar voice, "Why good day, Mrs. Williams. How kind of you to call upon us."

"I was rather hoping to visit with Katherine this morning," Mrs. Williams stated politely. "How is the dear child?"

"Oh, better, thank goodness," stammered Elizabeth, feeling very awkward. "Unfortunately, she is still unconscious much of the time, and she has been delirious this morning. So, I am very sorry, but I do not think it advisable for her to have any visitors at the present time. Perhaps another day . . ."

Elizabeth was clearly unnerved and could hardly concentrate upon her conversation with Mrs. Williams as she attempted to recall the words Katherine had recently uttered. "The Williams are bad people. What happens at their home is unhealthy for children," Katherine had stated. *Whatever could have prompted her to say such dreadful things?* Elizabeth now wondered to herself.

"I quite understand," Mrs. Williams was replying sympathetically. "Whatever you feel is best. We hope to see her health greatly improved in the near future. Please convey to her our love and best wishes."

"Oh, I will, to be sure. Thank you for your concern," said Elizabeth.

"Good day, then."

"And a good day to you and to Mr. Williams." And soon, Mrs. Williams had disappeared.

For some moments after her departure, Elizabeth stood with her back to the door, trying to make sense of the puzzling situation. Although they were neighbors—the Williams lived in the home directly below theirs on the mountain side—they had never shared a close relationship. Elizabeth had always felt uncomfortable around them. *Why?* she wondered now. Then, she was reminded of their glibness, their subtle affectation in speech and dress, their false gaiety and the insincerity of Mrs. Williams smile. Elizabeth could always discern a genuine smile from one which was not. The more she thought about the matter, the more she realized that she had never liked the Williams. It had been of necessity that the couples were friendly.

Then Elizabeth caught herself, "Oh, pooh, silly nonsense!" she muttered. "Imagine a grown-up woman like myself paying attention to such childish prattle!" And, shrugging her shoulders, she dismissed the subject and returned to the tasks at hand. Nonetheless, a vague anxiety haunted her for some time following this incident. No matter how frequently she attempted to dispel all doubts and fears, she could not help but feel that there had been truth to her daughter's unusual pronouncement.

In a way, then, Elizabeth was not surprised to learn, within several weeks' time, that Mr. and Mrs. Williams had been caught in the act of child-molesting in their home and, as a result of this offense as well as substantial evidence accumulated indicating that they had committed various other criminal offenses, they had been compelled to leave the community permanently. Upon receiving this news from Hannah Jones, Elizabeth had to steady herself, and she frantically wondered how, where, and why her seven-year old daughter had acquired such information.

Undoubtedly, Katherine's powers of perception were uncanny. No one knew how or why she was able to "know," but all suspected that her abilities were in some way related to her recent bout with double pneumonia and pleurisy. Not only could the little girl predict what would take place in the future, but she also seemed to know just what people were thinking and feeling deep down inside.

"It's downright spooky," Katherine overheard her mum say to Gwilym on several occasions.

But Dad would only smile. "Nothing to worry about, love," he would say gently.

But no one felt completely comfortable around her any more. For she could tell when her brothers were lying or her sisters exaggerating. She could predict who would win a fight or an argument, or who would win an election or contest. And, she had a particularly irritating habit of penetrating a facade and uncovering the truth.

"Why don't you like Mr. Fitzwilliams, Daddy?"

And caught off-guard, Gwilym would stammer, "Oh, but I do like him, dear."

But both he and his daughter were acutely aware of the truth—that he was merely pretending to like Mr. Fitzwilliams. And whenever Gwilym would innocently evade her complex philosophical questions or attempt to simplify the answers, Katherine would know. And if the poor man dared to pretend to know when he did not, Katherine would always confront him with the truth.

"Why don't you simply say, Daddy, that you don't know?" At the age of seven, then, she was a powerful personality and a force to be reckoned with. She knew, and no one knew how she knew.

It was evident, then, to nearly everyone who had known Katherine prior to the illness, that drastic changes had taken place. Both her personality and her behavior were vastly different, yet no one could determine the primary cause of such changes. Certainly, no one could deny that externally her life had altered profoundly. Terribly frail and feeble now, Katherine was an invalid—one who was confined to bed and restricted to inactivity. Not only was she wracked with mortifying physical pain and forced to lead a bedridden existence, but she was required to contend, as well, with the inherent bitterness, confusion, and frustration that are aspects of any major and transforming illness. No longer able to share in the happy, active carefree days of her brothers and sisters, she felt singularly alone and lonely. And sensing the fear, sadness, and suspicion with which her friends and family now regarded her, she wished to avoid them. Worst of all was the pity evidenced in their eyes and through their voices. And it was more than she could bear, for she was a proud little girl.

There was one additional factor which contributed to her feelings of loneliness and alienation. During the latter, more critical phases of the illness, her beautiful, dark blonde, shoulder-length hair had begun to fall out in large clumps; and Dr. Risely had advised Gwilym to crop the remaining hair close to the scalp in order to salvage what was left and to facilitate the growth of the new hair. And so, in compliance with the doctor's orders, Gwilym had sheared Katherine's fine, fair hair, leaving only perhaps an inch's growth around the entire head. As a result, her appearance was most unusual. Catching a glimpse of herself in the mirror, the little girl was heartbroken. For many days afterward, she wept bitterly. So different, so bizarre and foreign looking was the image she beheld that she was hardly able to recognize herself. Under the curious scrutiny of her brothers and sisters who she knew felt sorry for her, Katherine was terribly shy and embarrassed. In time, she adopted the measure of sporting a crocheted hat to cover the shorn head. But the new awkwardness and self-consciousness prevailed throughout much of her youth and adolescence.

None of the children—except for Della—had been ill for any length of time, and now Katherine was aware of the special treatment, the great conscious effort involved in the kindness and attention directed toward her by her brothers and sisters. Sometimes she felt that she could not endure for a moment longer the fuss, the insincere compliments, the false bravado of those who came to visit. She felt she would scream if she heard the phrase, "How is little Katherine this morning?" one more time.

Having been such an active child, it was dull and tedious work to remain inert in bed while everyone else raced about the house in a flutter of activity. She wished more than anything to bounce freely about as she had before. Never had she given a moment's thought or consideration to the wonderful freedom she had known prior to the illness—how delightful it had been to stretch her limbs by walking and running; how invigorating to breathe in the fresh country air; how soothing to sit or lie down beneath the benevolent protection of the stately shade trees; how infinitely refreshing to dip one's hand or feet into the rivers and streams . . . She had taken everything for granted. Now, she thought of the radiant warmth of the sun, the beauty of the glorious blue sky, and the golden chain tree—her favorite—with its exquisite blossoms of gold and white—and she wondered if ever again she would be able to enjoy them as she had before.

Never had she regarded it a luxury to move from one place to another, independently, without the intervention, guidance and assistance of another. Now, virtually all of her movements were guarded or directed by another. For the first time in her brief life, she understood what it was to be helpless and dependent. She began to view even the slightest movement which she initiated and completed by herself as a personal victory. Having devoted no prior thought whatsoever to injury or illness, she had in no way been prepared for the frustration, humiliation and despair which so often characterize the life of one who had enjoyed perfect health and freedom and who is now forced to contend with life as a helpless invalid.

Although she had never felt sorry for herself before, she felt sorry now. And she felt perfectly justified in arguing with God about all which had taken place. After all, was He not responsible for her circumstances? Had he not permitted her to suffer so? And had not her parents, for as long as she could remember; described this God as loving, merciful, and kind? She felt betrayed by Him—whoever and whatever He was—for she could not imagine what she—a child of seven—could possibly have done to upset Him and so deserve such a fate. And so, although she had use for Him before, she did not approach Him now. Rather, recalling the words of Mr. James on that rainy Sunday afternoon at the Tin Church, she turned to her beloved friend and cherished guide, Jesus, who was as real to her as any human being, and she asked Him to help her to become well again.

Regarding Him as her very best friend in the whole world, she confided in Him—fearlessly expressing her tender hopes and fears, her doubts and dreams, her deepest desires. It was to Him, then, that she prayed. Because she trusted Him wholly and implicitly, she was certain that He would come to her rescue. And because she desired to be well again more than anything else in the entire world, she knew that He would assist her in so doing. However difficult—even impossible—the task which lay ahead of her might appear—she could, she would—with the help of her best friend in the whole world emerge triumphant. She would do everything in her power to recover the healthy, joyous life she had known prior to the illness. To regain that which she believed was rightfully hers—this was now her goal.

CHAPTER 6

Recovery

—◡—

FOR MANY MONTHS FOLLOWING KATHERINE'S illness, Dr. Risely was a frequent visitor to the Davies household. Several times a week, he would ride his beautiful russet pony, Mr. Jeeps, up the side of the mountain to call upon the child, who had so courageously fought for her life.

"How is my brave little girl?" he would inquire cheerfully, in his broad, country accent, his face beaming with kindly concern and good humor, as he pulled up a chair by her bedside and took her tiny, feeble hand in his. It would depend wholly upon her mood as to the manner in which Katherine would respond to his inquiry. Sometimes she would smile warmly, as though delighted by his presence. In other instances, she would remain silent, full of self-pity, and turn and face the other way. On still other occasions, she would stare blankly as though she did not quite recognize him and would remain sullen and unresponsive.

But if the good doctor was aware of her many and varied moods and expressions, he seldom reacted overtly or seemed to pay them much notice. And never did he take offense! His vast medical experience allowed him to grasp, as did no one else, the severity of the internal struggle taking place within the child—the bitterness and frustration; loneliness and alienation; doubt and fear with which she was now contending as an invalid.

It had been as a result of the illness that Katherine was now helpless and bedridden. Both her heart and digestive tract had been severely and permanently impaired during the many lengthy hours during which she had endured the raging fever. Now, she was simply too weak and exhausted to move her limbs, and they grew stiff and sore from disuse. Furthermore, because she was unable to digest any solid food at all, her body was not receiving sufficient nourishment to sustain her. For some time, the situation remained precarious as she managed to survive solely on the few liquids and strained fruits she was able to consume and digest successfully.

Whenever Katherine was ready to succumb to sorrow or self-pity, Dr. Risely intervened, circumventing her tantrums and her tears. Perhaps it was as a result of the personal anguish he had so recently endured in conjunction with the tragic death of his own young daughter, that he was so tender, patient and sympathetic. Whatever the reason, he was the kindest, most compassionate gentleman Katherine had ever met. Within as brief and painless period of time as possible, she learned to trust and love him implicitly.

Regardless of the severity of her limitations, or the extent to which she became weary or discouraged, Dr. Risely refused to allow her to indulge in self-pity. He seemed familiar with the destructive aspects of this emotion. "I know it's not easy. But you will win. You're getting better and better. Just wait and see if I'm right," he would inform his young patient. "Why, you'll be up and about in no time at all. You'll be walking once again and better than ever. Just you watch," he promised.

It was his forthrightness, his enthusiasm, and his gentle encouragement which most appealed to Katherine. And she chose to believe his words of comfort. Accordingly, she obeyed his instructions explicitly. As far as she was concerned, no matter how weak or ill she felt at the present time, no matter how improbable, even impossible it might appear, if Dr. Risely claimed that she would walk one day soon, why then, somehow, in some way, she would!

But Katherine found it convenient to forget that Dr. Risely had also consistently advised her to be patient. "One step at a time, little girl. Don't be in such a confounded hurry to make great strides. A babe must crawl before she can walk and walk before she can run, right miss? Just slow down that restless brain of yours for a while, and proceed slowly. Build up your strength." And Katherine was forced to acknowledge (at least inwardly) the wisdom of his words.

However, even with Dr. Risely's comforting presence and good advice, coupled with her own powerful will to succeed, the road to recovery was far from easy. Nor was it pleasant. She suffered many minor setbacks. Each time she happened to catch a glimpse of herself in the mirror, each time she attempted to sit up in bed or to move her arms or legs in the old way; each time she made an effort to consume the tiniest morsel of solid food; each time she tried to describe to anyone else her hopes and fears and dreams— she was reminded of the difficult path ahead. Yet she remained determined to succeed. Nothing could stop her!

One of the most disagreeable aspects in conjunction with the recuperative process was the sympathy and maudlin affection and attention she received from nearly everyone. Friends and relatives alike lavished her with praise and affection and made an enormous fuss over her until she thought she could not endure the flattery a moment longer. Although she knew that they were well-intentioned, and that they sought only to comfort and encourage her, she could determine instantly the shock, apprehension, and disappointment with which they viewed her altered appearance and manner, and the pity which simply could not be disguised under the pleasant smiles and casual manner. She felt the awkwardness and embarrassment with which they attempted to say and do the right thing, and the effort required to camouflage their true thoughts and feelings which were fundamentally, "Poor child. How sad—how perfectly dreadful for such a thing to have happened. I wonder if she will ever fully recover. She is so peculiar now. She was so lovely before . . ."

Before, Katherine would think bitterly to herself. *Before* . . . Had there ever really been a life before the illness? Only dimly now could she recall the happy, carefree days of the past. And yet, how seemingly effortless life had been then and how pleasant! Now, she strained to remember what it felt like to exist without the conscious, persistent struggle—how it felt to be healthy and normal like everyone else.

Among the most difficult moments of this early period were those which arose whenever her parents' close friends Auntie May or Uncle Berry got together with her parents to discuss Katherine's future. Nearly always on these occasions the condescending Auntie May would suggest, in her bold, authoritative manner, that Katherine be sent away to a hospital, sanitarium, or to a special school for invalided children. "My dear Elizabeth," Auntie May would state firmly and decisively, "You must be reasonable. You cannot possibly provide adequate care and attention for this child when you have a husband and family to look after. Katherine would be so much better off in an institution or asylum where she can remain under constant medical supervision. She need not remain there long. Only until her health improves and she no longer requires close supervision."

Hospital! Institution! Katherine was horrified. Why, the mere mention of such a place struck a chord of terror in her heart. Recalling the fearful tales she had heard of such places, she would sob aloud and tremble inside, "Please, God," she would whisper, burying her tear-stained face in her pillow, "don't let them send me away." She had never been separated from her family, and the mere thought made her terribly sad, anxious, and lonely. Life was difficult enough without having to worry about being sent off to some strange place which housed those who were perhaps even more infirm than herself! Auntie May's well-intentioned words of advice induced a feeling of helplessness and despair in the little girl.

A wave of intense joy and relief overcame the child, then, each time her mum replied evenly, without a moment's hesitation, to Auntie May, "Why, we wouldn't think of sending our little girl away—as though we were frightened or ashamed of her. We love her, and we do willingly whatever is necessary to hasten and ensure her recovery." Katherine would nearly weep with gratitude. Nonetheless, she lived in constant dread and fear of that day during which her Mum and Dad might change their minds and heed Auntie May's advice. Fortunately, that day never arrived.

Despite everyone's doubts and disappointments, however, it began to become increasingly evident that Katherine was slowly but surely getting better. After nearly seven months had elapsed, she was able to digest a fair variety of strained fruits and vegetables; she was able to sit up by herself in bed; and could even stand on occasion with the aid of Dr. Risely or her

Mum or Dad. It was in conjunction with the frequent series of instructions issued by Dr. Risely that her health had improved to such an extent. Upon his insistence, she adhered to a strict daily regimen of exercise, diet, and massage. No one but the doctor was aware of the enormous effort this constant discipline required of Katherine, and no one was more aware than he that she was progressing primarily as a result of her powerful will and her enormous determination to succeed.

Whereas another physician might have encouraged Gwilym and Elizabeth to be overly solicitous—to guide, guard, and direct their delicate little girl throughout each and every day—this was not the case with Dr. Risely. Inwardly sentimental, but outwardly brisk and determined, he would not allow them to indulge Katherine as they might have wished. "Leave the child alone," he would reprimand them in his hearty voice. "Give her freedom, some time alone to sort things out and to experiment. Provide an atmosphere in which she can feel free to fail, if need be. Remember, whatever progress she makes will be as a result of her own effort—not yours. And your constant interference cannot assist her in any way. Let her take risks without feeling inhibited or constricted by your presence. You limit the child by exposing her to your own doubts and fears. She feels your reticence, your anxiety, you know. Do not feel that you must constantly supervise her. Relinquish your hold upon her!"

But Katherine could have told Dr. Risely the real reason for which her parents were reluctant to leave her alone. She knew that they were still suspicious and fearful of the changes which had taken place in her personality. Ever since the Williams incident, when her strange ability to "know" had begun to manifest, she was aware that her family regarded her as different or abnormal in some way. Neither they nor Dr. Risely had been able to account for the transformation, but she knew that they in some way associated it with the illness.

"Has her brain been damaged?" She heard her mum tremblingly inquire of Dr. Risley.

"No, of course not, Elizabeth," he had replied in a serious tone. "Is she still delirious, or hysterical perhaps?" Gwilym persisted.

"There is absolutely no indication of either condition. To my knowledge, only her heart and digestive tract have been affected by the fever. She is frail, as one might expect, following such an ordeal, but she is perfectly all right, I assure you. She has made great progress and continues to improve daily."

"Yes, but Doctor, how is it that she knows what is to be?" Gwilym interrupted.

"Or what is in the past?" added Elizabeth.

"Or what we are thinking or feeling?" continued Gwilym.

"I have heard of such things happening before," replied Dr. Risely quietly. There was a far-away expression in his eyes. "However, I have never observed it firsthand. I must say that I do not know the hows or whys. There does not seem to be any scientific explanation of such phenomena. But your Katherine is in good company historically. For throughout recorded history, there have been countless examples of individuals—saints, rulers and religious leaders who have had similar abilities among them Pythagorus, Paracelsus, St. Germain, Francis of Assisi, and Jesus of Nazareth.

"I can only say here and now that you have nothing at all to fear. To my knowledge, Katherine has never spoken unkindly or unfairly of anyone. She has not hurt anyone. Her insight seems to be of benefit to those it concerns. As I see it, you have no cause for worry. Trust the child—let her feel your love and support. Try not to make her feel awkward or self-conscious or frightened or ashamed of her abilities. Treat her as you would a normal child. That is my best advice at the present time. Treat her as though she were exactly like anyone else. Who can say? Perhaps, in time, she will grow out of this phase."

Unfortunately, his words offered little hope or solace to Elizabeth and Gwilym. For Dr. Risely had not known Katherine prior to the illness, and was, therefore, unable to determine just how extensive had been the transformation. Nor was he with her for long enough periods of time to grasp the true scope and nature of her new abilities—which were awesome. Nonetheless, what alternative had they but to accept his advice along with all which had taken place? Inwardly, they would continue to hope and pray that a miracle would occur and that their little girl would once again be "normal."

Sensing their worry and concern, Katherine would feel more detached, more alienated than ever. How desperately she longed to reassure her parents that all was well, that there was nothing really wrong with her. But she did not know how. She wanted to explain that there was nothing to fear—that it was exhilarating in a way and. perfectly natural to know the essence and truth about people and events. But she never seemed able to find the suitable time. She sincerely desired to describe all which had transpired during the latter, critical phases of her illness—the manner in which she had arisen from the body and observed it from afar, her meeting with the angelic beings, the beauty and joy she had experienced at that time—but she simply could not find the appropriate words. *I am the same person deep down inside as I was before—only older—wiser – somehow,* she wanted to cry at the top of her lungs. But she recognized the futility of her situation. She knew that no one would believe her, and that her explanation would be regarded with incredulity and suspicion as simply another of the bizarre and unexpected consequences of the illness. *What's the use of trying to make them understand?* Katherine thought dejectedly. *They never will.* And she was compelled—at least for the present time—to give up any further idea of sharing her experiences with any other human being.

CHAPTER 7

Triumph

‿

FOR NEARLY A FULL YEAR, Katherine patiently adhered to the demanding regimen of diet, exercise, and massage advocated by Dr. Risely. And, for this same year, Katherine worked painstakingly, diligently, toward the goal of someday walking unassisted. Each and every day, morning, noon and night, following the full body massage she received from Mum or Dad or Dr. Risely, she would exercise her limbs—first sitting up in bed, then stretching her arms and legs, maneuvering out of the bed, standing unsteadily, then taking several tentative steps with the aid of her dad and mum. Although she would be completely exhausted following each such effort, she became increasingly confident and convinced that if she were but afforded some time alone, she would succeed in walking all by herself.

Like Dr. Risely, she knew that it was impossible to experiment while under constant surveillance. Although her parents were well-intentioned and supportive, their fear and concern were easily discernible.

"Don't strain, my precious," Elizabeth would murmur in her worried manner.

"Be careful not to hurt yourself, love," Gwilym would cry out at the most inopportune moment.

"Easy now, do be careful," was their persistent advice. Around them she could not help but feel tense and self-conscious.

No, Katherine vowed, *it's impossible to walk while they are nearby watching. I have got to try it when I'm alone—when Mum and Dad aren't around to carry on if I should fall—or fail.* She shuddered at the word. Out of her entire vocabulary it was the one she disliked the most. *I'll not fail—ever,* she promised herself. And with admirable patience and perseverance, she waited for those precious, inevitable moments of solitude when she might be free to perform her experiment.

Now, each time that Dr. Risely called upon her, his eyes sparkled and his lips parted into a warm smile as he exclaimed enthusiastically, "You're getting better and better, young lady. You know that you are stronger in every way, don't you?"

And Katherine would nod happily, her eyes shining, knowing that this was so. "Why, you'll be walking in no time," he would whisper encouragingly in her ear. It seemed downright foolish not to believe him.

Finally, one warm, sunny Thursday afternoon, late in May, the long-anticipated opportunity arose. For the first time in as long as she could remember, Katherine was alone. Dad was at the office, the older children were in school, and Leonard and Olwen were napping. Nearly always had someone sat in attendance by her side, but on this particular occasion, Elizabeth had been required to entertain Mrs. Fiske and Mrs. Taylor who had stopped by unexpectedly for tea and Elizabeth had been unusually flustered and preoccupied ever since. Now Elizabeth was the only one who was anywhere nearby, and Katherine over-heard her humming softly to herself in the kitchen below as she prepared supper. Shivers ran up and down Katherine's spine, as she realized that this was the chance for which she had been waiting. She sat perfectly still for several moments, as she made absolutely certain that her efforts would not be interrupted. Then, slowly, painstakingly, she managed to maneuver her way from under the coverlet.

Perched precariously at the edge of the bed, her face was wrinkled in concentration as she attempted to cultivate sufficient courage and stamina to take the first few steps. Just as she was about to step down onto the floor, she was startled to hear her mum's footsteps ascend the stairway. *Oh, no,* she panicked, maneuvering her way back under the covers as hastily as possible. Her face was flushed, and her heart was beating wildly as a result of the exertion, but she managed to squeeze under the coverlet and appear calm as her mum's voice became clearly audible. Katherine was simultaneously aware of what sounded like soft, melancholy singing coming from some distance away.

Suddenly, she recalled that this was the afternoon during which little Johnny Davis was to be buried. For days, her mum and the neighbors had been lamenting the untimely death of the nine-year-old village boy. Now, Katherine realized that the sounds she heard were the voices of the members of the funeral procession en route to the burial ground. "Katherine," Elizabeth was saying from her position halfway up the staircase, "Little Johnny's funeral is coming by now. I would like to join them for a few minutes, and pay my respects to his Mum and Dad—poor dears. I won't be gone longer than a quarter of an hour. I want you to stay perfectly still until I return. You will be good now, won't you, dear?"

Her heart seemed to stop for a moment or two. A nervous giggle escaped from her throat as she digested the news and felt the full impact of her mum's words. "I'll be fine, Mum. Don't worry at all about me," she called out as nonchalantly as possible. It was difficult to accept her good fortune! The prospect of remaining in the house all by herself was exhilarating and surpassed anything for which she could have hoped or anticipated! In fact, she could hardly refrain from laughing aloud.

"Take your time, Mum. I'm perfectly all right. All is well."

"You're sure, love?"

"Oh, yes, Mum, perfectly."

By now, Katherine knew that her mum had removed her apron, straightened her hair, dabbed some cologne behind her ears, and was prepared to offer her sympathy and support to Johnny's friends and family.

"Goodbye, love," Elizabeth finally called before closing the door behind her. Katherine carefully waited for her mum's footsteps to subside, and then she lost no more time.

With grim determination, she maneuvered her body to the edge of the bed for the second time that day. *If I don't manage it now, I don't know when I will have another opportunity,* she thought, ruefully calculating the number of days, weeks, even months that might elapse before she was afforded another such opportunity. *I simply must succeed,* she told herself.

Slowly lowering her feet onto the floor, she managed to steady her trembling body until she was standing firmly and unaided next to the bed. Having established her balance, she was now ready to begin. She took several steps all by herself. Then, her arms groping wildly for any piece of furniture or object that might lend support, she continued to take first one step, then another, and another, until after several moments had elapsed, she had passed the mahogany chest and the dressing table and was nearly two-thirds of the way across the room. All of a sudden, however, her body felt extremely heavy—much too heavy to support any longer, and her head felt light—as though it were no longer securely attached to the rest of her. The room began to spin dizzyingly, nauseatingly around her. Although she struggled to maintain her balance, she could not, and finally she tumbled to the floor.

Thankfully, within a few minutes the room soon ceased to spin, and she recouped a sufficient amount of strength and confidence to resume her efforts. This time, she decided to conserve her energy and to simply crawl over to the bedroom door and through the hallway leading to the stairway.

Finally arriving at the top of the stairs, she paused for several moments as she attempted to determine the most efficient means of descending the staircase. It was necessary to get to the first floor, for in her mind, she had firmly established her destination as the "golden chain tree" that grew in the garden at the back of the house. The chain tree had always been a source of joy and fascination to her—for it was, by far, the most beautiful tree she had ever seen. As a little girl, she had delighted in lying beneath it and inhaling the gentle fragrance of its blossoms. It had been a deeply satisfying and peaceful presence and she had always felt comforted when nearby. For months now, she had yearned to see it—to touch it and to experience its graciousness, its benevolent support. Frequently, while lying in bed with her eyes closed, it had made her happy to visualize the chain tree—with its radiant golden blossoms, like sparks of sunlight among the pale green leaves which fell into cascades of muted color—its glorious, indescribable fragrance—its gentle, graceful silhouette. It seemed an eternity since she had last experienced its comfort and beauty.

Now, still on her knees at the top of the stairs, her jaw squared and her lips firmly clenched together, she vowed to succeed. Next, seated on the first step, she began to "bump" her way down the stairs one by one—finally landing at the bottom. Here, she rested for several minutes. Her heart was beating so wildly and uncontrollably she thought that it would burst from her chest, and she was wet with perspiration. Closing her eyes and taking several deep breaths, she soon managed to half-walk, half-crawl to the kitchen, finally succeeding in maneuvering her body to the back door which led to the garden.

As she drew closer to her destination, she grew increasingly impatient as though she could not wait a single moment longer to see the sky, to feel the soft grass beneath her feet, to bask in the wonderful warmth of the sun's rays. Reluctant to lose any further time, she devoted virtually all of her remaining strength to the final phase of her experiment. Flinging the door open, she gulped the fresh air as though she could not get enough of it. Somehow, joy put strength into her feeble limbs, and Katherine ran toward her beloved tree. As she drew close, she could not help but gasp—for it was even more beautiful than she had remembered. The entire garden seemed alive somehow—filled with a vibrancy, brilliance, and intensity of color that she had never before noticed. She was breathless and intoxicated. Ecstasy overcame her as she stood beneath the tree—a tiny figure enfolded by the blur of golden and white blossoms, emerald green grass, the pale turquoise of the sky above and the deep violet of the mountain peaks in the distance.

As she extended her hand to caress one of the low-hanging blossoms she was suddenly startled to feel the earth sway under her feet. The vast panorama which surrounded her now abruptly appeared somehow to merge together into a great sea of indistinguishable colors and shapes. Dizziness overcame her, and although she struggled with all her might to combat it, she was helpless. It was too late. Within moments, she had fallen to the ground, unconscious, her frail body crumpling into a small heap, beneath the beloved chain tree.

"Dona, Dona, my love. Please wake up," Katherine was awakened by the sound of her mum's frantic voice. It seemed to be coming from quite some distance away. "Come on, my precious. It's Mummy. Do wake up, Dona." Elizabeth was calling her by the nickname she reserved only for the most critical of circumstances. Her voice seemed to be getting closer.

Whatever has happened? Am I dreaming? wondered Katherine drowsily to herself.

"Come on, love," Elizabeth was searching her face for any sign of recovery, and gently stroking Katherine's forehead. Her mum's voice was still thin and dim, and when she opened her eyes, Elizabeth's face was swirling above her in a dizzying mist.

"Where am I?" Katherine asked aloud. Opening her eyes and blinking several times, the "mist" evaporated, and Katherine saw that she was still outside in the garden, but somehow entwined in her mum's arms. With a gasp of delight, she suddenly recalled the chain tree and the events that had taken place before she had fainted. Now, she struggled to locate the tree within her range of vision from the angle at which she lay. She squirmed in her mum's lap.

"Now wait just a minute, young lady. And just what do you think you're doing? Haven't you had enough excitement for one afternoon?" Elizabeth admonished. But Katherine only smiled. Enough excitement! Why, this was only the beginning! She had done it! She had succeeded! All by herself—without the aid of anyone else—she had walked! From here on, she could do anything—everything that she set her mind to do!

Elizabeth was carefully studying her daughter's face. Love and pride mingled with fear and relief, as she hugged her strong-willed child close to her. "My darling, why?" was all she said. There was a brief silence as Katherine gazed with customary forthrightness into her mum's eyes.

"I had to Mummy," was Katherine's simple response. She knew that deep down inside, her mum not only understood, but even sympathized with her. Tactfully changing the subject, she stated in a weak voice, "I'm fine now, Mum, honestly. If you just help me up, I'll be perfectly all right."

But, in fact, she was far too exhausted to expend any more energy. Without further discussion, Elizabeth arose, gently lifted the child to her breast, and carried her into the house. Never had Katherine felt happier, more fulfilled and at peace inside.

"I love you, Mummy," she whispered in Elizabeth's ear, as her mum tucked her into bed. She did not notice the tears of love and relief that had filled her mum's eyes, as she stooped down to kiss her on the cheek.

"I love you, too, child," Elizabeth murmured softly, and they were the last words Katherine heard before falling into a deep sleep. "I love you more than you can possibly understand, my brave little girl," Elizabeth said to herself, as she softly closed the bedroom door behind her.

CHAPTER 8

Convalescence

NOT LONG AFTER THE WALKING episode, it was decided that Katherine would continue to convalesce in Yeovil, Somerset, at the beautiful country home of her godparents Aunt Mariah and Uncle Charles. As the child adored her aunt and uncle, and as Dr. Risely had advocated a change of pace, it was agreed that she would leave at once and remain for as long as she wished.

"You will see that a change of scenery and companionship will do Katherine a world of good," Dr. Risely had advised Gwilym and Elizabeth. "I am certain that you will perceive a noticeable improvement in her attitude and behavior upon her return."

For many months, Mariah had implored them to allow her to be of assistance and take care of little Katherine in Yeovil, but they had obstinately refused, reluctant to believe that their daughter might recover satisfactorily anywhere but home. Recently, however, following her attempt to reach the golden chain tree, Katherine had seemed bored, listless, and restless. It was as though she required some outward stimulus or external catalyst that would help her to view life differently, to regard it as more than a constant series of painful events requiring enormous discipline and effort. As Katherine sank into a state of despair, her parents suddenly seemed to concede that a change might benefit their daughter after all.

Mariah was overjoyed to learn of their decision. "I'll take care of all the details. Don't you worry about anything," she informed Gwilym. A pleasant, maternal looking woman with neat gray hair tied into a gentle knot at the nape of her neck and wide blue eyes, she had no children of her own. She had always felt a particular fondness for her precocious little niece. Katherine's gentle nature and sunny disposition greatly appealed to her, and frankly, Katherine was everything she would have wished for in a daughter of her own. Although Mariah was disappointed and saddened at the changes that had taken place in her niece, she felt certain that she could assist the child in recovering much of her old spirit, curiosity and vitality.

"Good Lord, doesn't that child laugh anymore?" Mariah had inquired of Elizabeth.

"Not much," was Elizabeth's unhappy but truthful response.

"Well as far as I'm concerned, she takes life far too seriously for a child her age."

"I quite agree, but since the illness, her attitude toward all of us and the world as a whole, I should say, has altered completely. You see, she behaves as an adult, and views life as a great burden."

"Well now, fancy that. A child of eight. We shall certainly have to change her way of thinking, won't we?"

"I surely hope that you can help her," Elizabeth's voice quivered with emotion.

"I am certain that I can," declared Mariah, in her brisk, no-nonsense manner.

The life of an invalid was one that she would never have anticipated for the active, cheerful little girl. Nevertheless, what could one do? She had been forced to watch helplessly as the transformation took place. She and Katherine had always shared a close relationship—for both were of an inquiring turn of mind, easy-going disposition and sensitive nature. Outside of her parents and Dr. Risely, Mariah was the only person whom Katherine trusted implicitly. She knew that her Aunt had intuitively grasped the nature of the ordeal through which she had passed, and that she understood the loneliness, confusion, and frustration she had experienced in conjunction with her illness. And while Gwilym and Elizabeth had done everything in their power to ensure her happiness and comfort, Mariah sensed more than anything else that Katherine needed time away from her home and family to reflect upon the events that had taken place, to regain her shattered confidence, and to acquire a genuine desire to go on living.

"Charles, mightn't Katherine Sedonia spend some time with us?" Mariah had implored of her husband, a solidly built, jovial man with red cheeks, a hearty laugh and a blunt, straightforward manner. He was seldom able to refuse his wife anything, for she so rarely made any requests.

"Harrumph," he cleared his throat, looked up from the evening newspaper in which he had been engrossed, and studied his wife's countenance for several moments. Lost in thought, he absent-mindedly lit his pipe, took a few contented puffs, leaned back in the large overstuffed chair, and finally spoke, "I think it's a fine idea. Fine idea. You know how much that child means to me—I've always enjoyed having her around. Of course, Katherine is welcome to visit—anytime you wish—for however long you wish her to remain with us."

"Really, Charles?" Mariah could hardly suppress her delight.

"Really," he replied with a grin.

"Oh Charles, thank you," was all she could say.

"Thank me? Whatever for? Now let's have none of that nonsense. It will do us both a world of good to have a child on the premises. She'll liven this place up a bit."

And so it was settled. No one had been more surprised than Mariah to learn of Gwilym's willingness to let Katherine spend time with her in Yeovil. "Katherine can stay for as long as you and she find it desirable," Gwilym had informed his sister-in-law. "Just keep in close contact with us so that we may know how our little girl is progressing."

"Of course, Gwilym," Mariah responded graciously. "And please bring Elizabeth and the children to visit all of us."

"With pleasure . . . Just take good care of our baby."

"You know we will," Mariah had promised. Her face was full of tenderness and compassion, and Gwilym felt certain that his daughter would be in good hands.

And so it came to pass that Katherine went to live with her Aunt Mariah and Uncle Charles in Yeovil, Somerset. For as long as anyone could remember, Charles had been the overseer of Major Hennage's huge estate, and, as such, had been provided with a beautiful cottage residence of his own on the premises. The Major owned nearly one hundred acres of land consisting of rolling woodlands, meadows, fertile farmland, and orchards. Almost fifty years old, Charles and Mariah had spent nearly all their adult lives in the Majors' employ. Having always been treated with kindness and respect, they were content to remain here for the rest of their lives. All their needs had been fulfilled. They had everything they desired—everything, that is, but the one thing they wanted above all else—and which Major Hennage was not able to provide—a child of their own.

It was in Yeovil that Katherine, for the first time since her illness, experienced some slight degree of happiness and the feeling that the future held promise after all. The lovely cottage tucked away in the country suited her perfectly, as did the companionship of her generous and easy-going aunt and uncle. Although they petted and admired her like the relatives at home, their manner was sincere and straightforward, and their praise and encouragement were genuine. To her infinite relief and satisfaction, she did not detect any trace of hypocrisy or self-consciousness in their behavior toward her. She felt that they truly loved her and sought only to make her comfortable and happy. It was with joy that she realized that they were among the very few who felt no awkwardness or constraint around her. Never did they criticize her or discourage her from speaking "the truth." Candid and down-to-earth, they permitted her to be herself, and for the first time in a very long time, Katherine felt as though she belonged.

Oddly enough, many months were to elapse before Katherine felt even a trace of homesickness. During this period away from home and family, she acquired both strength and confidence. As her hair grew out, she resumed a more normal appearance and was able to discard the funny crocheted hat she had worn for so long. Her thin cheeks acquired a rosy color; her eyes sparkled with warmth and intelligence. Even her body grew slightly rounder and healthier, for she was now able to digest a wide variety of the fresh fruits and vegetables that grew in abundance in the surrounding orchards and gardens and which Mariah prepared especially for her.

Here, in Yeovil, although she was frequently alone, she was seldom lonely. For she was virtually always accompanied by the cows, sheep, and horses that grazed peacefully in the meadows; the gardeners and other workers on the estate; and the rambunctious children of the staff who regarded the property as their own. Their simple friendship touched her deeply, and the easy, playful manner in which they all treated her was a source of unimaginable pleasure. The awkwardness and wariness that she had experienced for so long now evaporated, and she began to truly believe that she would never again be regarded as "peculiar" or "abnormal."

During this time, she learned once again not only to enjoy life but to value it. Throughout the illness and the early phases of her convalescence, Katherine had been strangely detached and alienated from all that had taken place around her. At that time, she had little interest or desire in continuing on. It had seemed to senseless, so futile to struggle merely to survive when life held such little promise and offered so flimsy a reward for one's effort. Although she had tried with all of her might, she had been unable to think of even one human being of whom she knew—even those who had perfect health and wealth—who was truly happy. And if no one was happy, well, just what was the point of living?

But somehow, in some inexplicable manner, the beauty of Major Hennage's estate, the simple peace and quietude of her surroundings affected her deeply and offered her sufficient evidence of life's worthwhileness and purposefulness. Deeply moved by the persistent beauty, she felt something stir deep inside her—the awakening of an inner response—that seemed to afford her the assurance that she, in some unfathomable way, was profoundly linked to everyone and everything in the universe. She was more acutely aware than ever before of the power of nature, sensing that it, in some mysterious way, was linked to the answers about life that she had been asking ever since she could remember.

She could not possibly have put these feelings into words. She only felt that underlying—and even responsible for—the glorious stillness and serenity of Major Hennage's meadows and orchards, was an active, dynamic intelligence. She was certain that, despite the appearance of things, nothing in the world was haphazard or arbitrary, and that the exquisite peace could not possibly have arisen out of inactivity, disorder, or chaos. Rather, this peace was the culmination of an enormous and unceasing power, order, and movement. Intuitively, she was aware of the mighty power responsible for everything that existed.

Katherine's favorite spot was a lovely meadow located only a few hundred feet away from her aunt's cottage. It was, by far, the most tranquil and beautiful place she had ever visited. Naturally isolated from the rest of the property, it was surrounded by a small lake, great orchards containing fruit trees of many varieties, vast, hilly fields of amber and emerald which were dotted by the graceful silhouettes of sheep and horses. And although Katherine had lived amidst great beauty in Gwaelod-y-garth, she had never seen anything quite so lovely or as perfect as "her meadow" as she came to regard it.

Not a day passed by during which she failed to spend time here absorbing the wonderful atmosphere. The delicate fragrance of the fruit trees in blossom; the vivid colors of the apples, pears, plums, cherries, raspberries, blackberries, and assorted wildflowers that grew in abundance; the stillness and beauty of the lake; the simple grandeur of the stately oak, elm, and maple trees; and the wonderful carpet of spring-green grass—all were of sublime and indescribable beauty. It was not the mere surface beauty with which she was intoxicated, however. Rather, it was the extraordinary and exquisite peacefulness of the spot which uplifted her spirit. There was no adequate way she could describe her feelings in a manner that would have meant anything to anyone else. She only knew that never before had she experienced such profound and unutterable peace, such complete contentment. For the first time in her life, she neither needed nor desired anything at all. She was perfectly satisfied at peace and fulfilled. After the long, painful months of recuperation, she finally felt "at home"—as though she, like the flowers and trees, the hills and meadows, the birds and animals that surrounded her, truly belonged on the earth, and that, at last, "God's in His heaven. All's right with the world." For the first time since her illness, Katherine came to regard life as a kind of gift or privilege.

By the end of her tenth month in Yeovil, then, Katherine was ready to return home. During the period away, she had accomplished much in the way of growing up, of overcoming the fear, resentment, and frustration that had been brought about by the illness, and of becoming accustomed to the idea of living a normal and fulfilling life. From this time on, she felt certain that she could make a joyous and rewarding experience of her life. Furthermore, she was now prepared to assume whatever responsibilities awaited her. In short, she was ready to relinquish her hold on the past and to expend her time and energy instead to the creation of the future.

CHAPTER 9

The Remarkable Mrs. Dunham

BY THE TIME OF HER return home to Gwaelod-y-garth, Katherine was healthier and happier than she had been since the illness. Her family was overjoyed to observe such a marked improvement in both her manner and appearance. Although she was still terribly frail and delicate, she looked perfectly "normal." Furthermore, she was able to move about independently and with relative ease and efficiency.

Nearly nine years old now, she was an attractive and intelligent child. It was apparent, however, that despite the subsequent progress she had made, she would never again be the cheerful, outgoing creature she had been prior to the illness. Whereas she had been full of joy and vitality, she was now solemn and fragile. Whereas she had once been friendly, extraverted, even gregarious, she was now timid, shy, withdrawn, and self-conscious. It was in the company of her robust, high-spirited brothers and sisters that she felt most awkward, for their heartiness, spontaneity, and utter lack of inhibition served as painful reminders of her own limitations and vulnerabilities—both physical and psychological.

Still very much an invalid in some ways, Katherine grew tired easily, and required frequent intervals of rest throughout the day as well as a great amount of sleep. She was unable to digest much food and, more often than not, threw back up what little she did manage to get down. Also, she was highly strung, hypersensitive, and terribly nervous—unable to withstand even the slightest shock or pressure. So delicate was she, in fact, that she was not permitted to return to school. Not long after she had come home from Yeovil, she had been sent to the County Primary School.

Weak and painfully thin, and bearing the ridicule of her classmates, the child had worked herself into a frenzy and had subsequently collapsed before the entire class. Another attempt was made with similarly disastrous results, and it was finally deemed advisable by her parents, Dr. Risely, and the superintendent of the school, Mr. Marwell, that she continue all future studies at home with the aid of a tutor.

"I know of many highly qualified tutors from whom Katherine might derive great benefit," volunteered Mr. Marwell.

Unfortunately, Katherine was not to derive great benefit from the services of a tutor, for she vehemently protested against and resisted all efforts on the part of her parents to secure a private teacher. At the mere mention of the possible visitation of such a person to the Davies house, Katherine would "collapse" and when one particularly well-educated but condescending young gentleman appeared to render his services, Katherine was dreadfully ill and refused to budge from her bed. Her parents were helpless under the circumstances. Despite their repeated entreaties, their daughter remained adamant in her refusal. It was in this manner that she managed to evade the Welsh educational system altogether.

Ironically, Katherine had always delighted in learning. Prior to the illness, she had enjoyed school and been an excellent student. No one, then, was more surprised than she at the outcome of these recent experiences, and of the manner in which she had responded to the steady stream of tutors her parents had hired on her behalf. Yet, it was for some powerful but unknown reason that she felt compelled to avoid all formal education.

Not now, later, a voice inside her seemed to say, *later on in life, you will study formally to the extent to which you desire. But not just now.* And she felt it necessary to obey this inner voice. She felt certain that it would not mislead her.

"I'm afraid that her heart simply cannot withstand the strain," Dr. Risely advised Gwilym and Elizabeth each time they decided to try sending Katherine to school once again.

"You had best give up the notion of any formal education whatsoever for Katherine. She's just not meant for it. You need not worry, either, for I am quite certain that she will catch up later on in life." And so, Katherine was free to learn and discover and explore in her own manner at her own pace.

It was by means of careful observation that Katherine acquired most of her information and understanding. Still spending a large portion of her time in bed or lying on the sofa in the lounge, Katherine amused herself by carefully examining the countenances, expressions, and gestures of those around her. She would pay close attention to the conversations that took place in her home among friends and family—noting the subtle differences in manner, dialect, vocabulary, phraseology, vocal quality, and inflection that characterized each individual. Since the Davies' home was seldom quiet, and friends and neighbors were nearly always dropping by for tea or a brief visit, Katherine had ample opportunity to survey human nature—at least on a small scale. An excellent listener and observer, she would pay close attention and carefully examine all such interaction.

Fascinated by the gossip as well as by the vast range of social, political, and cultural issues that were discussed, she absorbed the facts and figures described as well as the manner in which they were conveyed. Following each such togetherness, Katherine would carefully dissect and analyze the conversation and then the role of each participant. Attitudes and motives, the real meaning behind the words, the selection of specific words and phrases, arguments and their rebuttals as well as the conclusions and resolutions drawn, all would be scrupulously and scientifically examined, assessed, and finally catalogued in her mind in order of their possible future usefulness. Blessed with an excellent memory, she enjoyed memorizing verbatim those sentences and phrases she found especially clever, witty, or insightful. Possessing a keen ear, she made the conscious effort to imitate the individuals who spoke in the most elegant and refined manner.

Similarly, Katherine assimilated the information from the books and periodicals her dad sometimes read aloud to the family. Many of her days were spent in reflection, and much of her time alone was spent imitating either those around her or the characters about whom she had heard and in employing her imagination to invent hypothetical situations in which all these characters interacted. So adept was she at capturing the essence of each "character" that she frequently convulsed her brothers and sisters with the devastating accuracy of her impressions and imitations.

It was not long before her thirteenth birthday that Katherine came into contact with a woman who deeply influenced her and who was responsible for altering many of the perceptions and misconceptions she had about herself and her abilities. Late one Saturday afternoon in March 1912, Katherine and her cousin, little Della (named after Katherine's eldest sister), were leisurely strolling through Taff's Well when they happened to notice a placard outside the town hall advertising a free magic lantern demonstration.

"Come on let's go," whispered Della, the younger of the two, excitedly.

"Do you really think we should?" replied Katherine, the more cautious of the two.

"Of course. After all, it's free. Come on," little Della pleaded, tugging at Katherine's sleeve.

"Oh, all right, then," Katherine agreed, and the two girls entered the large, gray stone building.

On their way in to the main auditorium, however, their attention was diverted to yet another placard that advertised "Mrs. Dunham, Fortune-teller Extraordinaire, Demonstration at 4:00 p.m."

"I've never seen a real fortune-teller before, have you?" Katherine exclaimed.

"Oh, no, never. You know my Mum would never allow me to. She's very suspicious about that sort of thing. She says that no decent person should have anything to do with fortune-tellers, gypsies, or witches 'cuz they are the Devil's agents."

"Well, fortunately, neither of our Mums are with us now. Want to go see her? That sign says that her demonstration of "clairvoyance"—whatever that is—is over there in the next room," and Katherine pointed to one of the small lecture halls adjacent to the main auditorium.

"I really don't know if we should, Katherine," Della's voice quivered with fear.

"Let's just see what she does. We needn't stay long."

"Promise?"

"Promise."

"Oh, all right, then," muttered Della. And the two girls managed to slip into the back of the hall without being noticed. Mrs. Dunham was already speaking as they settled as noiselessly as possible into their seats.

"Your work has always meant a great deal to you," Mrs. Dunham was saying to an intense black-haired young gentleman in the sixth row. "You are a fine musician, and you have worked very hard to achieve your current success. Therefore, you must not be discouraged or think of giving up now. You will discover that within two months' time, your present financial difficulties will be completely resolved. An offer will come your way with which you will be most satisfied. Do not blame your wife for interfering. She was only trying to assist you. She is still in London with relatives and is waiting your correspondence. Do not disappoint her. You will soon join her in London, and there, both of you will be pleasantly surprised by the attention which will come your way. Take heart, sir. You will soon realize that there are no mistakes, and that everything which has taken place has been essential for your growth. Thank you, and God bless."

It was obvious that the young man to whom Mrs. Dunham had been speaking was a total stranger, and that he was dumbfounded by the accuracy of her message. His face was flushed, and his mouth was open. "Everything that you have said is true," he cried out hoarsely before the entire audience. "My circumstances are precisely as you have indicated. You are extraordinary. Thank you so very much."

"Thank you, sir," she replied graciously, with a smile. And she turned to address another gentleman.

At this juncture, Katherine took the opportunity to study Mrs. Dunham. It was evident by her accent, delicate features, coifed hair, and the fastidious manner in which she was dressed that this "fortune-teller" was both cultured and refined. Furthermore, she looked perfectly normal and completely unlike any of the witches or gypsies about whom her mum had warned her. In fact, she looked more like a Sunday school teacher and was one of the loveliest, most genteel, and well-groomed women Katherine had seen in the area. Katherine had been amazed at the fact that this cultured woman possessed abilities that were similar to her own. Like Katherine, Mrs. Dunham "knew"—what had been, what was, and what would take place in the future. Furthermore, Katherine had been pleased to observe that Mrs. Dunham had not uttered a single unkind or insincere remark, and that she was neither critical nor pessimistic. Evidently she utilized her gift to guide and assist those in need of advice, and Katherine felt instinctively that those members of the audience to whom she was drawn were those who were in the greatest need of help.

She and Della remained at the demonstration for over an hour, deeply impressed by Mrs. Dunham's persistent insight. Finally, shortly before the program's scheduled conclusion, the fortune-teller spoke to Katherine.

"You, my dear. May I speak with you?" she smiled warmly at the two young girls in the last row.

Katherine felt her cheeks turn crimson, and her heart began to pound wildly, "Yes, oh yes, please do," she stammered in embarrassment.

"Do you know, young lady, that you possess a fine mind, and that you will use it to your own advantage as well as to the advantage of others? Do not regret the fact that you have not as yet received a formal education and that you do not know how to read or write. There is a very good reason for your inability to attend school. You will acquire these skills when the time is right, but it will be awhile yet before this time has arrived. In the meantime, your health will continue to improve, and you will derive far more satisfaction from life than you have for quite some time. Do not allow yourself to feel discouraged. You are doing beautifully—and so is your little cousin," Mrs. Dunham smiled warmly at little Della, who blushed immediately and hid her face in Katherine's shoulder. The clairvoyant returned to Katherine and concluded, "You, my dear, will succeed in achieving everything that your heart desires. God bless you."

Katherine was speechless and could only stare and nod dumbly. "Thank you, my dear, for being such a good listener," said Mrs. Dunham, smiling kindly. Then she turned to address a buxom, silvered-haired lady sitting several rows in front of the girls.

"Thank you," Katherine murmured, so softly that only little Della was able to hear her. Although she struggled to appear perfectly calm, inwardly she was trembling with joy and excitement. Mrs. Dunham was the first person she had ever met who possessed abilities similar to her own, and there was nothing the least bit spooky, strange, or abnormal about her. Since becoming ill it was her desire to appear as much like "everyone else" as possible. After her encounter with Mrs. Dunham she felt proud and privileged to be "different," and reluctant to regard her powers with doubt, fear, or suspicion. As a result of her chance meeting with Mrs. Dunham, then, she would never again feel completely isolated or alone in her uniqueness.

One evening, following a rather rare elaborate family dinner at "The Cottage," in the middle of March and only a week or two after she had come into contact with Mrs. Dunham, Katherine overheard a conversation between her parents and Uncle Thomas.

"They say she's the largest passenger ship afloat. I met a gentleman who works for the White Star Line who has only praise for her," Thomas was explaining.

"And I have heard that she's to be the fastest vessel afloat," added Elizabeth.

"They say that there's never been one like the *Titanic* before," Gwilym concurred. "In fact, it is said that she's unsinkable."

"Indeed, indeed," Thomas corroborated. "That is precisely why I regard it as such a privilege to be a passenger on the *Titanic's* maiden voyage across the Atlantic. I reserved my cabin some months ago, you know, and I will be sailing along with more than two thousand others," he boasted.

"Is that so?" replied Elizabeth, impressed by the large number of people the ship could comfortably accommodate.

"I do envy you the experience, Thomas. What an adventure! You will have to tell us all about it upon your return," said Gwilym, good-naturedly.

"You bet," smiled Thomas with boyish enthusiasm. "It is a history-making event, without doubt, and I assure you, I can hardly wait."

Now Katherine had listened to the exchange, politely feigning interest in the subject matter. But frankly, she would never have volunteered her own thoughts or opinions. Yet suddenly, for no apparent purpose whatever, she felt compelled to speak. Embarrassed, she heard herself utter words which, in light of what had been said that evening seemed not only improbable but impossible.

"Excuse me, uncle," she interrupted in her full, adult voice, "but I am afraid that the *Titanic* will sink." There was a sudden hush at the table, as each one digested her words. Staring at his niece in astonishment, Uncle Thomas was too surprised to say anything.

"Eh, what's that you say?" he finally managed to croak out hoarsely.

Deliberately ignoring her mother's efforts to curtail her end of the conversation, she continued, "You must not sail on board the *Titanic*, uncle. Please cancel your passage as soon as possible. I am telling you that you will regret it if you do not heed this warning. I repeat, the *Titanic* will sink in mid-April, on her maiden voyage. There are many who will die as a result—those who have not been so fortunate to receive such a warning."

Although she knew that her parents disapproved of any demonstration of her abilities, she had been helpless to prevent the words from flowing forth. Glancing over in their direction, she saw that her mother's face was flushed, and that her father's lips were pursed. Fortunately, she suddenly remembered Mrs. Dunham and took heart from the fact that she was not the only one with such unusual powers of perception.

Now where, in God's name, did the child ever get such a peculiar idea? wondered Thomas to himself. He was both perplexed and annoyed by her prediction. He was loathe to admit—even to himself—the sudden inexplicable fear and uneasiness he had experienced upon receiving this message. He had said little in response, only an occasional "indeed, indeed." Inwardly, he was attempting to determine why it was that the child's words rang true. Conversation at the table limped along for a while. The subject had been swiftly and tactfully changed, and Katherine mentioned nothing further to anyone about the *Titanic* or the nature of her prediction.

Several weeks later, however, she was relieved to learn that her uncle had heeded her warning after all. Postponing his journey across the ocean, he decided to remain home and travel at some later date. *Thank goodness,*

Katherine thought to herself in relief upon the receipt of the news. She did not know why, but she felt as though a great burden had been lifted from her shoulders.

It was not until she heard the news from her father on April 15, 1912, that she understood why she had been so relieved, for the *Titanic*—believed to be the largest, greatest passenger ship afloat—on her maiden voyage had collided at full speed with an iceberg off the coast of Newfoundland and had sunk. Over fifteen hundred lives had been lost in the accident. For some time everyone spoke of the tragedy, and Katherine was sharply aware of the role she had played in saving the life of her Uncle Thomas. She realized that had he failed to heed her advice, he would not be alive today.

Yet much to her disappointment and dismay, even after this extraordinary display of clairvoyance, her family still chose to ignore her abilities. Katherine sensed that they were more frightened and suspicious than ever. It was a dilemma, for she herself had come to trust and depend upon her ability to know. No one, including Uncle Thomas, ever spoke of the incident again, and Katherine was left with a feeling of sadness and disappointment. Nonetheless, as a result of the experience, she grew increasingly confident and certain that her abilities might one day be employed for the benefit of others. Like Mrs. Dunham, she would assist those in need of guidance. In the meantime, she would respect the wishes of her parents and struggle to appear to be as "normal" as possible. Still preferring to believe that it was only a matter of time before they would learn to appreciate her uniqueness, she would temporarily comply with their instructions to conceal her abilities as best she could.

Despite the reservations of her family, then, her special abilities were no longer responsible for making her awkward or self-conscious. Although she was different from others, she was rather pleased with this difference. No longer did she expend time and energy challenging the source of her insight; rather, she learned both to trust and value it.

That there was nothing spooky or in any way distasteful about her gift was apparent. It was a matter of simply knowing, perceiving far more than the average person. Often she would hear herself reciting facts and figures of which she had no prior knowledge. That this information was readily available she understood; from what source it was derived she had not the slightest idea. She only knew that it was nearly always accurate. Recognizing the suspicion with which she was regarded by others, however, she seldom volunteered advice or information unless expressly asked for such. Exercising formidable control then, she adhered to her parent's strict advice that she refrain from "interfering" in anyone's life. For their sake, she attempted to appear as much like everyone else as possible.

The remainder of her childhood, then, and much of her adolescence, was spent in convalescence and in overcoming the harsh effects of the early illness. In addition, her time and attention were devoted toward helping her Mum and Dad at home in whatever capacity she was able. Most frequently, this assistance assumed the form of looking after the younger children—feeding, bathing, clothing them, etc. By 1913, Elizabeth had given birth to three more babies, Morfydd, Glyndwr, and Megan. Katherine adored Megan and she regarded her as the most beautiful baby in the world. There were now nine children—ranging from six months to twenty-three years—in the Davies household, and Elizabeth's hands were full. Had Gwilym's business not been doing so poorly, they could have afforded to hire additional help, but, as it was, they were required to do without any outside assistance. By now, as Della and Cora were both busy outside the home learning a trade, much of the household responsibility fell upon Katherine's shoulders. Nonetheless, she never minded caring for little Megan or the other babies. "Dear, beautiful little Megan," she would whisper tenderly in the infant's ear. "I love you." And Megan's eyes would crinkle and her lips expand into a brilliant smile, as though fully comprehending her sister's words.

In the meantime, the strange ability to "know" that had manifested following Katherine's illness continued to surface throughout these years. Much to the worry and dismay of her family, Katherine continued to expose fraud, detect hypocrisy, advertise the subtle, hidden meanings behind external statements and events, and to predict the future. Katherine's ability had not disappeared as Elizabeth had hoped it would—in fact, it had become sharper, more refined, and both she and Gwilym, who were fearful of its cause and effect, did everything in their power to discourage Katherine from demonstrating it. During a time in which the prevailing law of the land incorporated both the Witchcraft Act of 1735 and the Vagrancy Act of 1824 under which fortune-tellers, witches, palmists, and all "persons pretending or professing to tell fortunes" were ruled to be "rogues and vagabonds" and could, therefore, be tried, convicted, and imprisoned under such law for these practices, their doubts and fears were justified. They consciously chose, then, to ignore their daughter's prophesies and insight. They frowned and abruptly changed the conversation whenever Katherine exhibited her powers of perception. Although she was hurt by their attitude, she never fought to defend herself. Sadly, she wondered when that time would arrive when her family would no longer be intimidated or embarrassed and would simply allow her to be herself.

It's so silly to be frightened, as Mummy and Daddy are. It's far more natural to know than not to know, she would think to herself, but she knew that she could not make them understand. She herself was not at all frightened or ashamed of her unique abilities.

CHAPTER 10

Mr. Mesmer: I Can and I Will

BY HER FIFTEENTH BIRTHDAY, KATHERINE was a strikingly pretty girl with a lovely, slender figure, creamy complexion, and soft, pleasant features that seemed to glow with an inner radiance and a sharp intelligence. Those who had known the sister for whom Katherine had been named were startled by their close physical resemblance. For Katherine was very much like the little girl who had died before her. Only recently had Katherine blossomed— becoming far more confident and extroverted than she had been since her illness and near death experience. In addition, she displayed a charm and vivacity that were singularly captivating. Katherine's deep, penetrating hazel eyes tilted up at the corners and usually sparkled with warmth and humor but could, on occasion, seem shy and full of wonder. A comical, upturned nose, a square jaw, and decided chin, plenty of rich wavy light brown hair, and a sweet smile along with an easy, playful manner contributed to her considerable charm and appeal.

Ironically, although few young women could have led a more sheltered existence, Katherine appeared unusually poised and sophisticated—in possession of a wisdom and maturity which belied her fifteen years. Despite her lack of formal education, she had a biting wit and lively, playful disposition that made her a great favorite among her friends. Needless to say, she never—even at this relatively early age—lacked her share of gentlemen admirers.

Already, she had enjoyed the sincere affections and attentions of a steady stream of young admirers. But it was not until Will Griffiths appeared—with his tall, slim figure, coal black hair, brilliant turquoise eyes, and even, virile features—that Katherine began to grasp just what it might be like to fall in love with someone. Never had she encountered anyone so handsome. She felt her cheeks turn crimson, and her heart beat wildly, uncontrollably each time he drew near.

To her annoyance, Katherine discovered that she was not the only girl in Gwaelod-y-garth who found Will irresistible. In fact, nearly every female her age—including Rosalind Goddard, Georgine Bryant, and Maravanuie Edmunds—shared her infatuation. Yet everyone seemed to feel that Will was partial to Katherine, for his eyes sparkled with admiration and his lips always curved into a warm smile upon seeing her, and he always seemed to make a special effort to approach her at church or in town. Their conversations were nearly always brief, but Katherine felt certain that Will would soon invite her out.

Then, one day, while strolling in Taff's Well, she spotted Will window shopping across the street. Her heart sank as she saw that he was holding hands with another girl! As if this wasn't enough to upset her, she noticed that they were absorbed in conversation and seemed to be having a wonderful time together. Katherine knew Will had not noticed her, and leaning against the corner of the structure by which she stood, she struggled to discern who the girl was. With mounting disappointment and frustration, she suddenly realized that the girl was none other than the irrepressible, man-crazy Lilly Roberts, a well-known flirt, and Katherine had to concede that Lilly looked simply ravishing in what appeared to be a brand new outfit of pale, shimmering pink.

No wonder Will couldn't resist her, Katherine thought miserably to herself, slinking stealthily out of view. And looking down at her own plain, worn frock, she could not help but feel, *I'll bet Will would have asked me to go out if I'd been wearing a dress as pretty as Lilly's, instead of my old, dowdy rags,* she sighed wistfully. It had been such a long time since she had owned anything new! Mostly, she had worn her sister Cora's outgrown gowns, and she knew them to be far from flattering to her, for Cora's coloring and complexion were entirely different from her own.

Soon after the chance discovery, Katherine learned through gossip that Will and Lilly were seeing each other often and were, in fact, an item. Terribly upset, she wondered if she would ever see her Will again. In the midst of her depression, she paid little attention to anything or anyone else.

Early one Saturday afternoon in late October, Elizabeth was ironing while Gwilym was carelessly sorting through the large pile of mail that had just been delivered, and Katherine was day-dreaming as she half-heartedly folded the freshly washed laundry. For several moments the kitchen was perfectly still, as each was absorbed in the task at hand. Suddenly, Katherine's attention was diverted to the small yellow booklet entitled *Mr. Mesmer's Teachings - What You Should Know*, which her dad had picked up and in which he now appeared to be thoroughly engrossed. In fact, he had been unconsciously nodding in agreement with the contents of this booklet for several minutes.

Observing him, Katherine could finally no longer contain her curiosity, "Come on, Dad. Don't keep it all to yourself. Read a bit aloud to Mum and me. We want to know what's got you so excited!" She winked at Elizabeth, but Gwilym did not take any notice. "Come on, Dad, please!" she persisted.

Briefly sighing, then clearing his throat, he reluctantly closed the book and placed it in his lap. "Well," he began, staring at his inquisitive daughter, "it seems that this small book consists of the teachings of a rather remarkable man—an Austrian physician and the father of what is known today as hypnosis—named Franz Anton Mesmer who lived—let's see, now—ah, yes—from 1734 to 1815. This most curious and highly controversial gentleman seems to have possessed the ability to heal literally thousands of men and women from all walks of life—including members of the ruling classes—of all manner of so-called incurable physical and mental disorders. Apparently, he was able to effect these cures by means of a unique method he formulated called 'mesmerism.'"

"Whatever does that mean?" Katherine interrupted.

"Well, first of all, it states here," and Gwilym pointed to a paragraph on one of the early pages of the manuscript, "that this Mr. Mesmer is responsible for discovering the psychological root of many physical illnesses and for attributing man's mind—his thoughts, beliefs, and attitudes to both the cause and cure of disease."

"Really, Dad?" Katherine was dubious.

"Ummm," Gwilym nodded. "I've only read a small portion of this booklet, he continued, "but basically it appears that this Mr. Mesmer holds man himself responsible and accountable for the physical and mental disorders he experiences, maintaining that these are merely the consequences of his negative and destructive thoughts and his own belief or fear that he will become ill. He regards the human mind as a highly powerful instrument and one that plays a crucial role in determining not only one's health, but one's success and joy as well, in other words, man's mind is largely responsible for the circumstances in which he finds himself. By controlling the patient's mind, therefore, and teaching it to operate in a healthy, constructive manner, one is able not only to "cure" one's maladies, but to prevent future difficulties. Furthermore, Mesmer emphasizes the importance of the elements of belief and imagination in conjunction with the patient's recovery.

"It says here," Gwilym pointed to yet another paragraph, "that to the extent to which a patient believes he may be cured, expects to be cured, he is cured. To the degree to which a patient believes in illness and his inability to recover, he remains ill. When a patient's mind is full of hope and confidence, his chances for improvement and full recovery are far greater than when his mind is full of doubt and fear."

"All this certainly sounds reasonable," volunteered Elizabeth, who had, by now, completely abandoned her ironing and was listening intently from her seat at the kitchen table. Gwilym seemed to take no notice of her comment, however, and continued.

"Having concluded, therefore, that it is the imagination as well as the nature, quality, and intensity of man's habitual thoughts that are responsible for the circumstances in which he finds himself, then it must be man's negative, destructive, and disharmonious thinking that brings about his unhappiness and illnesses. So often he experiences illness in conjunction with anxiety, sadness, frustration, or anger—with equal frequency does he enjoy good health in conjunction with poise, success, and serenity. Mr. Mesmer has, therefore, devised a method of curing his patients by affecting their thoughts or imaginations, by means of administering to them a series of powerful curative suggestions, inducing in them the belief that they will recover. Through this process of induction or 'Mesmerism,' the patient's imagination is affected so that he is enabled to believe that he will get well. And when he believes that he is getting better, he is getting better. Do you see?"

"In other words," Katherine replied slowly, "if a physician can successfully affect the patient's imagination so that he believes he will get well, he will get well."

"Exactly," said Gwilym, with a smile. "And the physician induces this belief by means of cultivating and securing the patient's trust and confidence and then by subsequently continuing to address the patient's subconscious mind, informing it that he will recover."

"Fascinating," Elizabeth remarked lost in thought. "And so," she spoke slowly as though thinking aloud, "Mr. Mesmer believes that one's thoughts are responsible for one's circumstances. That one's thoughts—both good and evil—are real and manifest in accordance with the intensity and conviction with which they are created."

"Why, isn't that exactly what Jesus said in the New Testament? That 'As a man thinketh, so is he?'" Katherine interrupted excitedly. Gwilym and Elizabeth nodded simultaneously. "I don't think that I have ever interpreted it that way," said Elizabeth slowly.

"Nor I, to tell the truth," admitted Gwilym.

"Well, I for one find Mr. Mesmer's teachings very interesting indeed," Katherine stated with considerable enthusiasm. "Go on, Dad. Read it aloud—the entire booklet."

"Yes dear, do read on," Elizabeth urged her husband. Unable to refuse, Gwilym spent the remainder of the afternoon reading the small book aloud to his wife and daughter. So engrossed were the three of them that it was nearly dinner time when they finally reluctantly disbanded. Not until they heard little Glyn and Megan giggle conspiratorially did they remember that neither they nor the children had eaten since mid-day.

"I'd better get supper on the table, hadn't I?" said Elizabeth, and the discussion over Mr. Mesmer's theories was, at least for the present time, concluded.

The author of the pamphlet that had come in the mail was anonymous, and Katherine and her family subsequently learned that many of Mesmer's teachings were not, in fact, Mesmer's at all but rather those compiled, interpreted, and presented by various well-intentioned students and admirers. Nonetheless, they found the subject matter intriguing. Katherine, who had for so long been weak and invalided, was particularly affected by his ideas.

"If you persuade yourself that you can do a certain thing, provided this thing be possible, you will do it, however difficult it may be. If, on the contrary, you imagine that you cannot do the simplest thing in the world, it is impossible for you to do it, and molehills become for you unscalable mountains," the author of the pamphlet had written.

Of special significance to Katherine was Mesmer's statement, "If certain people are ill mentally and physically, it is that they have first imagined themselves to be ill mentally and physically. You can control and direct your imagination. To do so, it is enough to know that this is possible, and secondly, the means by which you do so is autosuggestion. Whereas you constantly give yourselves unconscious suggestions, all you have to do is to give yourselves conscious ones. In short, tell yourselves you can, and you can. If the unconscious accepts this suggestion and transforms it into an autosuggestion, the thing or things are realized in every particular."

For weeks following the arrival of Mr. Mesmer's booklet, Katherine reviewed and analyzed the principles contained therein. *I know,* she concluded, *that Mr. Mesmer is right—that man's thoughts are responsible for his circumstances—that my own personal thoughts are responsible for the manner in which I live. And if my life has thus far been manufactured by my own thought, I can, therefore, consciously transform my life by means of my thought. I believe that I am capable of constructing and patterning the remainder of my life so that all which I truly wish may manifest. I am certain that Mr. Mesmer's principles are workable,* she would think excitedly. *We are responsible for our circumstances and lives.*

Deeply influenced by the theories attributed to Mr. Mesmer, Katherine sought to prove their validity and practical value by applying them to her own life. *I've everything to gain and nothing to lose*, she maintained, as she set about implementing the notion, *tell yourself you can and you can*. It took only a short while to determine the most effective means of putting her newly acquired information to the test.

I am going to use Mr. Mesmer's teachings to achieve that which I most desire—and that, at the present time, is definitely Will Griffiths, she decided earnestly, the image of Will's face vivid in her mind.

"I want Will back," she declared boldly, with conviction. "And I am certain that the methods advocated by Mr. Mesmer will serve me well in so doing. Tell yourself you can, and you can," she repeated aloud. "I can, and I WILL!" she vowed. *Somehow I am going to earn enough money to buy a beautiful new dress—the loveliest Will has ever seen—one that will make Lilly Roberts' costume dowdy by comparison. I will look so elegant that Will won't be able to take his eyes off of me. And he will never even glance at Lilly again. I just know I can get Will back. I know I can. I can, and I will*, she promised herself one more time. And she set out to prove that this was so.

CHAPTER 11

A Business Venture

With amazingly little difficulty, she stumbled upon a business venture that she felt certain would provide the sum of money necessary to obtain a new dress with which to impress Will Griffiths. For years, her family had received through the mail numberless mail order catalogs from which one might purchase all manner of food and articles ranging from such items as woolen under-garments to draperies. One afternoon while reading aloud from one such catalog, Gwilym described the process whereby an individual might be employed by such a company. The prospective employee would order merchandise through the catalog, agree to sell it on behalf of the company, and receive, for one's work, a percentage of the profit derived from the sales. Katherine listened with bated breath as her dad listed the various items one might sell and the profit to be made by a potential employee. *I can do that!* she felt like shouting to any and every one. But she remained calm as she attempted to calculate the duration of time it would take her to earn enough money to buy a new dress.

Employing Mr. Mesmer's method of positive thinking, Katherine managed to persuade her dad to assist her in her first business endeavor. It was decided that Gwilym would stand as guarantor should she fail to sell in accordance with the company's expectations. With her dad's endorsement, then, she was able to order four dozen pairs of woolen stockings. Her remuneration was dependent upon the number of stockings she could sell. For each dozen sold, she would receive one shilling. And she knew that she could purchase a perfectly lovely dress for nine or ten shillings!

Several weeks elapsed between the time that Katherine ordered the stockings and their arrival. During this period, she refused to indulge in fruitless impatience or discouragement. Instead, she devoted hours at a time toward the achievement of her goal by implementing Mr. Mesmer's technique of visualization whereby she continually "saw," imagined, and believed the desired outcome as already achieved. She would imagine, then genuinely believe that she had already sold the forty-eight pairs of stockings, had bought a beautiful new dress, and succeeded in winning the heart of Will Griffiths. With her eyes closed, she would visualize Will by her side, as they contentedly strolled together through Taff's Well. There would be a wonderful expression of warmth, tenderness, and admiration for her in Will's eyes, and she, in turn, would be smiling happily at him. Refusing to succumb to doubt, fear, or despair, Katherine "saw" her dream fulfilled. She allowed nothing—no one—to interfere with her goal.

Finally—after what seemed an eternity, but which was, in fact, only two and a half weeks after she had placed her order—two enormous cardboard boxes arrived. It was a bitterly cold, blustery November afternoon, but Katherine was far too excited to pay much notice to the weather. In fact, she could hardly contain herself, so anxious was she to get on with the experiment and attempt to sell the merchandise in accordance with the techniques advocated by Mr. Mesmer.

Unwilling to lose any time at all, she bundled up in her heavy woolen overcoat, crocheted hat and mittens and rubber boots, gathered one of the bulky cardboard boxes and held it awkwardly to her breast, and then calmly announced before her startled family, "Good-bye, I am off to sell my stockings." She did not wait to receive either their blessings or good wishes. Before they had any chance at all to reply, in fact, she had vanished through the kitchen door.

"Well, have you ever seen anything like it?" Elizabeth remarked in a husky voice, marveling at the decisiveness and determination of her daughter.

"I do hope that she won't be disappointed. She has so diligently applied the advice of Mr. Mesmer," Gwilym observed.

"Somehow, I do not feel that she will be disappointed," said Elizabeth with a soft, knowing smile. "Regardless of the outcome, I am certain that our Katherine will have learned a great deal as a result of this experiment."

"I couldn't agree with you more wholeheartedly," Gwilym replied, returning his wife's smile. "I personally shall be most interested in learning the results of this experiment."

No one was more eager than Katherine to determine the practical validity of Mr. Mesmer's principles. In accordance with the instructions provided in the pamphlet, then, she began telling herself that she would succeed—that, in fact, success was already hers. Bristling with confidence and optimism, she was now prepared to approach her very first customer. Upon her arrival at the small stone cottage in which Mr. and Mrs. Wilfred Blair resided, she first stood a short distance away from their front door, closed her eyes, concentrated, and then conducted an imaginary conversation with Mrs. Blair. She said aloud, "I have excellent goods. You need my woolen stockings. You want them, and you shall, therefore, buy several pairs from me. The stockings are already yours. And success is already mine!" Having performed this ritual three times, she took a deep breath, sighed aloud, made her way to the front door, and rang the bell. "Come on, Mr. Mesmer. Don't fail me now," she muttered under her breath, while waiting for a response.

For several moments, there was not even the hint of a sound from within the cottage, and Katherine began to fear that no one was at home. Disappointed, she was about to depart, when she suddenly heard some faint footsteps and a rustling noise from within. "Oh, my," she whispered in sudden anticipation of the interview to follow. She struggled to maintain her composure. A nervous smile played about her lips, and her eyes glistened with a new purposefulness and intensity.

"Good day, Mrs. Blair," she heard herself say to the plump, good-natured little lady who now stood in the doorway.

"Why, good-day to you, child," replied Mrs. Blair, wondering for what purpose the girl had come. It was only a matter of a few seconds before she noticed the large ungainly cardboard box in Katherine's arms. "Whatever is in there?" she inquired.

Katherine felt herself go hot, and then cold. Gulping, she plunged into the routine she had practiced and memorized beforehand. "Well, Mrs. Blair, it so happens that I have some lovely woolen stockings in this box. They are pure wool, come in a variety of colors, and are, I assure you, of the very highest quality. I thought that you and your husband might be interested in purchasing several pairs from me. They cost one shilling per pair, and are a real bargain at that price."

Katherine smiled now, genuinely grateful that she had been able to speak at all. Inside, however, she was still trembling with fear, as she studied Mrs. Blair's countenance which appeared unusually serious. *Tell yourself you can, and you can*, Katherine continued to repeat silently to herself while Mrs. Blair considered Katherine's proposal. Katherine refused to feel anything but certainty that success was already hers.

"The stockings are ever so warm and cozy. Would you like to see a pair?" Katherine inquired now with far more confidence than she felt.

"Why, yes, child, indeed I would," replied Mrs. Blair. And reaching into the box, Katherine managed to extract several pairs in navy blue. She handed them to Mrs. Blair.

"Just slip your hands through them, and feel their texture," Katherine advised.

"Well, Katherine, it seems to me that you are quite a little saleswoman at that," smiled Mrs. Blair, after carefully examining the stockings and discovering their quality. "I do believe that I could use several pairs. Perhaps Wilfred could use one or two pairs also. Have you any in brown?"

"Oh, I do, indeed," replied Katherine, unable to hide the note of joy in her voice. And she extracted several more pairs of stockings in a deep chestnut color.

"How much did you say they were?"

"One shilling a pair," answered Katherine wishing with all her heart that they were less costly.

"Well, even at a shilling, they appear to be a bargain. I will take all four pairs."

"Oh, how lovely. Thank you, Mrs. Blair," Katherine murmured excitedly. Mrs. Blair could hardly repress her laughter. Never had she seen anyone so delighted, so obviously thrilled as young Katherine Davies was at this moment.

"You know, my dear, I believe I had better take two more pairs of stockings. How about one more of each color?"

"Oh, why yes, of course, Mrs. Blair," Katherine could hardly believe her good fortune as she reached one last time into the cardboard box. "That will be six shillings altogether, Mrs. Blair," she murmured bashfully.

"Of course, my dear. Here you are," and Mrs. Blair counted out and then placed the exact amount of change into her palm. So surprised was she at the easiness of the transaction that Katherine could do nothing but stare at the currency in her hand for several seconds.

"Oh, thank you so very much, Mrs. Blair. I shall never forget your kindness. And I do hope that you and your husband will positively love your stockings, and that they bring you great happiness always. Thank you, thank you again."

"Nonsense, child. Don't be silly. The stockings are, as you have indicated, high quality, and you, my dear, are an excellent saleswoman. Thank you, my dear, for coming by this afternoon." And, feeling like hugging her neighbor, Katherine finally took her leave.

"Thank you, Mr. Mesmer," she cried aloud, as soon as she was far enough away so that no one would hear her. She felt like throwing her cap into the air and shouting "Hip, hip, hurray!" so pleased and excited was she. How sweet was even this small taste of success! She could not wait to try her technique on the rest of her neighbors. *Why, at this rate, I will be a wealthy woman in no time at all*, she thought, as she scurried on to the next cottage.

"Tell yourself you can, and you can," she repeated perhaps one hundred times that afternoon, certain that she had stumbled upon a great formula for success. It was bitterly cold outside. The sky had turned a dull gray color, and a light snow had begun to fall. But Katherine was oblivious to the weather. It was as though time was suspended and nothing but the selling of her stockings mattered at all to her. She seemed to float through the remainder of the afternoon. Mr. and Mrs. Baker purchased four pairs of stockings, Philip and Rosemary Joslin bought two, the Stitfalls had bought four, and Alf Sherwood had bought six, etc. By 3:00 p.m., Katherine had sold the entire contents of the first cardboard box and had been required to return home to retrieve the other box. By 5:00 p.m., she had sold all forty-eight pairs of stockings! She could hardly believe her good fortune! Never had she been so exhilarated! And describing the events of the day to her family later on that evening, Katherine knew that she had discovered a formula for successful living that would serve her for the rest of her days. Not since the days prior to her illness had Gwilym and Elizabeth seen their daughter so happy.

During subsequent weeks, Katherine ordered, received, and sold literally hundreds of pairs of woolen stockings throughout Gwaelod-y-garth and Taff's Well. Within six weeks, she had earned enough money to purchase the beautiful sapphire blue velvet frock she had spotted at Anderson and Company. The dress was the loveliest one she had ever seen, and it set off her creamy complexion, slender figure, and rich light brown hair perfectly. She knew that poor Lilly Roberts—in all her pale pink finery—could not possibly compete with her now. She looked and felt wonderful in the new dress.

As she had hoped—and expected—in accordance with the principles advocated by Mr. Mesmer, Will Griffiths was overwhelmed by her appearance. More attentive and appreciative than ever before, it was evident that he was just as smitten by her as she had been with him. She was victorious! For quite some time, the two were an item, and Katherine could hardly suppress her gratitude to Mr. Mesmer. For months, even years following this episode, Katherine remained inordinately fond of the beautiful sapphire velvet dress which had played such a crucial role in bringing about her happiness with Will. The garment served as a vivid and pleasant reminder of the power of one's thought.

Some years later, Katherine recounted the history of her success to a friend:

I earned the money with which to buy my lovely outfit. And as a result I got my man back. And also, I acquired a great deal of self-confidence. Not only could I sell, but I had discovered a wonderful system—and that was the greatest result of the experiment—that enabled me to direct and manage my life and feel as though I were master of my destiny.

If I could sell the stockings, and if I could buy the outfit, then I knew that I could also conquer my illness which was really weakness more than anything else at this stage of my life. I knew that it was within my power to control and pattern my life. And so, to a very great extent, I have been indebted to Mr. Mesmer for providing me with data that had enabled me to perceive my potential. I have incorporated both mind-power as well as self-hypnosis into my life. I am presently employing his system. The statement "As a man thinketh, so is he" is a fact to me. Through numerous experiments and experiences, I have learned that "thinking it is it." This is a most powerful tool to have at one's disposal.

Katherine continued to sell the mail-order merchandise for many months following her initial triumph. Having achieved success in such important areas as business and love, she acquired a certain amount of pride in her abilities and enormous confidence in the teachings of Mr. Mesmer.

Furthermore, in conjunction with Mr. Mesmer's theories and techniques, she became increasingly curious and determined to know far more about the nature of the human mind and man himself. Intuitively, she had always suspected—and now Mr. Mesmer had afforded her proof—that man was something far greater than he either appeared or imagined himself to be, and that he possessed untapped, perhaps unlimited, potentialities.

CHAPTER 12

Iris Comes to Visit

NOT LONG AFTER THE PAMPHLET attributed to Mr. Mesmer had been amply digested, dissected, and absorbed by the Davies, and only a month or two after fifteen-year-old Katherine had successfully concluded her experiment, the family—and Katherine, in particular—was exposed to yet another powerful influence—this one in the form of an outspoken, twenty-one-year-old woman named Iris Sedgwick.

Iris bore the dubious distinction of being the plainest girl Katherine had ever seen. Yet, if Iris was the least attractive young woman Katherine had ever known, she was simultaneously the most intelligent and articulate—and certainly the most sophisticated! The daughter of a prominent local official and friend of Gwilym's from Bristol, Iris was pregnant and unwed. Upon Iris's father's insistence, she had come to stay with the Davies until her child was born. None of these facts made much of an impression upon Katherine. She was far more interested in Iris's dynamic personality—her candor, self-possession, and utter lack of hypocrisy. She had never known anyone—male or female—so forthright, assertive, and independent, and she truly admired these qualities. Intuitively, Katherine grasped that Iris was one of the few people she had ever known who genuinely cared nothing at all about maintaining proper appearances and pleasing or impressing others. Had Iris not dearly loved her parents and desired to protect them from the shame and stigma of having a daughter who was about to become an unwed mother, she would never have consented to stay with the Davies for the duration of her pregnancy. High-spirited, rebellious, and free-thinking,

Iris had long ago abandoned formalized religion as well as conventional morality. Prior to her pregnancy, she had been an uncommonly successful and outspoken businesswoman.

For some reason, Iris took an instant liking to Katherine, recognizing at once her charm, intelligence, and potential. And because she herself had learned to use her abilities to advantage, she felt certain that Katherine could do the same. "You are very clever, and very pretty, and it's obvious that you have a flair for business," Iris informed her. Katherine had told her all about Mesmerism and the manner in which she had by now sold literally hundreds of pairs of woolen stockings.

"Really?" Katherine asked modestly.

"Oh, yes, indeed. In fact, I am certain that you possess all the qualities necessary to achieve success in the business world. Why not give it a go? Make something of yourself? Surely, you don't wish to remain here in Gwaelod-y-garth all your life and do nothing but raise a passel of children—like your own mother. You could begin as an apprentice in a trade; after all, it's wartime. I am sure that there are any number of businesses in Cardiff in need of help. I know that you would be able to land quite a decent position."

She noticed the dubious expression in Katherine's eyes. "It's true, it would be far easier to get a position if you could read and write. But you can attend night school and easily acquire those skills. Having been exposed to Mesmer's theories, you are already aware that you can do anything you wish—succeed in any area you desire. Do not permit any false concepts or opinions to stand in your way. You are not too young to begin building your future. Why not go to Cardiff and try your wings? You'll succeed, I know you will," said Iris with an encouraging smile, patting her friend's shoulder in sisterly fashion.

Iris's words had a powerful effect upon Katherine. Young and impressionable, she had been, up until the present time, terribly sheltered and naive and certainly out of touch with anyone as sophisticated and perceptive as this young woman from Bristol. Katherine was suddenly reminded of the fact that she had always wished to return to Cardiff one day. She was also aware of the insightfulness of Iris's observations, for she was attractive and intelligent. And had she not proven her strength of character, her ability to overcome whatever obstacles loomed before her? Why, by the age of fifteen had she not "miraculously" managed to survive a devastating illness, to walk once again when it was feared that she might never do so, to value life, to lose her best beau to another woman and then win him back again, to become an expert saleswoman? She had become aware of the necessity of assuming responsibility for one's life.

Carefully considering Iris's well-intentioned advice, Katherine arrived at the conclusion that this worldly young woman was correct. *I'll bet that I can get a good job and earn a lot of money,* she would think to herself. *And I do believe that the time has finally arrived when it would be advantageous to be able to read and write. I would like to try my wings,* she thought to herself. *Perhaps I will put Mr. Mesmer's theories into practice once again.*

Throughout the five months that Iris remained with the Davies at The Cottage, she encouraged Katherine to think independently and to rely upon no one but herself. It was Iris who urged Katherine to discount the attitudes and platitudes of others and to be herself. In the meantime, Katherine grew increasingly confident, energetic, and courageous. For she genuinely desired to succeed on her own. By the time that Iris had given birth to a strapping ten-pound baby boy and was ready to leave the Davies household permanently, Katherine was ready to venture forth into the world. Turning sixteen next month, she had decided that it was time then to seek suitable employment in Cardiff. Without enlisting either the aid or advice of a single living person, she patterned and planned the future. Armed with Mesmer's formula and Iris's substantial praise, she found it convenient to ignore the obvious obstacles and limitations which might preclude the achievement of her goals. Rather, she chose to believe that she could accomplish whatever she set out to achieve. Despite her delicacy, fragility, nervousness, and illiteracy, she was certain that she would succeed.

Every once in a while during this period, Katherine would experience moments of fear, remorse, doubt, or frustration. But for the most part, she was relentless in her determination to "get on with it." No doubt she would

succeed at all costs. That the world itself was in a state of chaos and constant change; that a great war—the war to end all wars—was ongoing;
that thousands upon thousands of men were dying in combat each day
while others were terribly ill, homeless, or starving—none of these factors
were of any real interest or significance to the sixteen-year-old girl from the
tiny village of Gwaelod-y-garth in Southern Wales. Like her mum, she was
single-minded and resolute. Nothing could dissuade her. She was conscious
only that the times were changing, that people were not nearly so stuffy
or stodgy and set in their ways as they had been in the past, that life held
glorious promise for her personally, and that Cardiff was a lovely place in
which to live and would be an exciting city in which to work, and that she
would accomplish great things one day soon. Boldly, then, she faced the
future. Against all odds, with all the audacity and ambition of a sixteen year
old, Katherine made plans to find employment in nearby Cardiff. Not for a
single instant did she believe that she might fail.

CHAPTER 13

First Job

⤜

DURING THE WAR YEARS (1914–1918), it was not at all uncommon for a young person of little means or education to apprentice in a trade. If, for example, a young man desired to become a tailor or a carpenter, he would first volunteer his services or even pay a fee in order to acquire the necessary training and skill from one who was already well-established in the profession. Assisting and observing the tradesman, the apprentice would receive whatever experience and instruction would enable him to become an expert in his field of endeavor. The training period might last anywhere from twelve months to five years, and would be terminated when the apprentice had achieved the desired level of proficiency. After successfully completing the rigorous training, the apprentice would become a journeyman working for a master for wages, or he might set up as a master himself.

As one might imagine, Katherine was neither pleased to discover nor willing to accept such conditions of employment—wherein she would be required to pay a fee in order to receive training as an apprentice. Her family was in desperate need of money right now—the family's earnings had been drastically reduced as Gwilym's digestive disorders continued to worsen and kept him from being able to work—so she simply could not afford to take anything but a paying position! She cared not at all what others did, had done, or would do. It was essential that she earn decent wages! Furthermore, it had never even remotely occurred to her that, if accepted as an apprentice, she would be required to commute to Cardiff and back six days a week without recompense. *No*, she concluded, *I cannot afford to serve as an apprentice*

93

for any length of time; I am going to have to get an assistantship. I don't care what others say—that it's impossible to land a paying position right off—with no prior experience. I know I shall get one—I must get one, she promised herself. Fortified by the memory of Iris' encouraging words and the techniques of Mr. Mesmer that had so effectively served her in the past, she felt certain that her abilities would be of value to someone in Cardiff. She had heard much gossip recently that implied that many of Cardiff's finest shops and businesses had been forced to close temporarily due to the lack of competent help. The War effort had demanded the full cooperation of the vast majority of the United Kingdom's working citizenry. Only those too old, infirm, or unable to serve the government had remained in private business.

Under these exceptional circumstances, then, Katherine was certain that she could somehow manage to persuade an employer to pay her and train her simultaneously. It was with this intention that she set out by rail for Cardiff one early August morning in 1915. Equally unfamiliar and inexperienced in all areas of business, she very wisely decided to apply for any and every position for which she might possibly be suited.

Having a number of errands to perform in Cardiff, Elizabeth accompanied her daughter as far as the train station. Arriving in town at half past eight, the two soon parted and went their separate ways, agreeing to meet for lunch and to compare their experiences by one o'clock that afternoon.

"Best of luck, my love," Elizabeth called to Katherine one last time, as her daughter turned to wave—a sweet, tentative smile upon her face. "Poor dear, it can't be an easy task that lies ahead," Elizabeth murmured sympathetically, wishing somehow that she could help her child.

But her daughter was not in need of either sympathy or pity. For months now she had been preparing for this day, paying homage to Mr. Mesmer's methods by strictly adhering to them. Although her heart was beating wildly and her breathing was a bit irregular, she assured herself that it was perfectly natural and quite forgivable to feel frightened and nervous under the circumstances. Furthermore, she was heartened by the realization that she at least appeared well-groomed and poised in the classically tailored wine-colored costume she had recently purchased from Powell's Department

Store. The admiring glances cast in her direction from several handsome young gentlemen assured her that she looked well. *Thank goodness I had enough sense to buy a new suit, otherwise I would not stand a chance of getting a position*, she thought to herself, as she observed the beautifully attired men and women who filled the busy streets of Cardiff.

Walking briskly with an outward efficiency and ease which belied her inner anxiety, she looked the very essence of a successful young career woman. Her pace began to slow down discernibly, however, as she drew near the commercial heart of the city. Here, she paused frequently outside the various shops and businesses in desperate search of "help wanted" signs or any outward indication that assistance might be needed. She was disappointed to discover, after proceeding in this manner for five or six blocks, that there were not nearly as many opportunities available as she had hoped for or imagined. Nonetheless, she refused to be disheartened. Rather, hastily recalling Mr. Mesmer and past obstacles that had been overcome, she became more determined, more confident than ever to secure a well-paying position.

After applying at both a chemist's shop and a green-grocer's, she continued to stroll through the commercial district, eventually entering by chance, an elegant shopping arcade in High Street. "How exciting to work in such a shop," she sighed, staring rather wistfully at the extraordinary array of expensive merchandize displayed in the great glass windows. Elaborate evening gowns were the featured item of one shop; bathing and sports attire in another; china in another; baby linens; umbrellas; men's hats in still others—all were represented.

Situated alongside a ladies' millinery shop and opposite a delicatessen was an elegant jewelry shop that boasted, in golden letters the words, "First Class Jewelers: L. Crouch and Company." It was not the name of the shop that attracted Katherine's attention but, rather, it was a small placard tastefully placed in the shop's window that caused her heart to skip a beat. The sign read: *ASSISTANT NEEDED, Experience Preferable, Inquire Within.* Immediately Katherine seized upon the opportunity, mumbling, "Tell yourself you can, and you can," straightening a few scattered wisps of hair with her hands, biting her lips to give them color, and taking a deep breath. And before she had time for further reflection, she glided gracefully into the shop.

Although she was frankly intimidated by the plush interior, she successfully assumed an attitude of unshakeable calm and sophisticated nonchalance.

"Excuse me," she murmured in her most winning, cultured voice, to a paunchy, middle-aged man with thinning hair and pungent breath who appeared to be the store manager.

"Yes?" he replied coldly.

"Uh, my name is Katherine Davies. I—uh, I have had some experience in the business world, and I am here in response to the advertisement in your window—you know, the one that says, 'Assistant Needed.'"

"Indeed," was the man's icy reply. It was evident that he had no interest whatsoever in her or the reason for which she had approached him.

"Well, sir," Katherine continued undaunted. "I do feel that I would be an asset to your firm. You see, although I have had relatively little business experience, I learn quickly and am willing to work very hard. In short, sir, I do believe I am just the one you're looking for."

There was a firm, no-nonsense quality about her that appealed to the gentleman. He was now scrutinizing her carefully, and there was a combination of amusement and respect for her in his eyes. "Is that so?" he replied. "You are the one we're looking for, eh?"

"I believe so," Katherine did not hesitate. And inexplicably feeling that she had somehow won this gentleman over, she approached the subject of a salary. "I think you should know, sir, that I cannot afford to work for less than ten shillings a week plus transportation to and from Cardiff. You see, I live in Gwaelod-y-garth."

"Gwaelod-y-garth, eh?" was all he said, and he studied her features one last time. She was startled to see him turn away abruptly and stalk over to the telephone in the backroom. *How rude he is*, she thought angrily to herself, but as her overtures had not yet been rejected, she decided to wait a few more minutes. No one was more surprised than she to discover that the gentleman was now speaking to Mr. Crouch himself—the owner of the shop—on her behalf. Within several moments the man returned to the showroom with the results of his conversation with the owner.

"Mr. Crouch has agreed to interview you at his St. Mary's Street shop within the half hour. Be there!" he advised sternly with no trace of humor. "It's not far from here—only a matter of a few blocks." And he proceeded to provide her with directions to the shop on St. Mary's Street.

"Thank you very much for your intervention on my behalf," she said, genuinely grateful and now quite sorry that she had thought him rude before. The peculiar man did not take any further notice of her, however, and she was soon on her way.

How positively thrilling! Katherine thought to herself, as she considered her good fortune thus far that day. The mere prospect of a position in such an elegant shop was exhilarating! Furthermore, she was thoroughly convinced that she could somehow win over Mr. Crouch and persuade him to hire her. Inching her way through the heavy midday crowds, she contemplated the manner in which she should approach Mr. Crouch. Should she appear poised and citified? Sincere and hard-working? Bold and confident? Quiet and dignified? She was not certain. Then, it suddenly occurred to her that Mr. Crouch must be a millionaire, and that she had never even seen, let alone met, a millionaire before. Hastily surveying her appearance in the reflection of a glass window she happened to pass by, she derived some little comfort from the fact that she at least looked good, and that Mr. Crouch would find her attractively, if not expensively, attired.

Perhaps five hundred feet from her destination, Katherine paused, took several gulps of air, and applied Mr. Mesmer's formula—silently repeating, *The assistantship is already mine. I am already working as an assistant for L. Crouch and Company. Success is mine now.* Boldly, then, she completed the remainder of the brief journey, arriving at L. Crouch's St. Mary's Street shop at half past twelve.

It was immediately apparent that the St. Mary's Street shop was even more elegant than the one she had visited in the Arcade. The plush, deep violet carpeting, the paneled walls, and elaborate mahogany display cabinets along with a vast array of beautiful jewelry, porcelain figurines, china, and silver bespoke a highly successful and lucrative business. Frankly, L. Crouch had more stock than any jewelry shop she had seen in wartime Cardiff, and Katherine wondered fleetingly what kind of man Mr. Crouch was. Intuitively, she respected him for being clever enough to maintain such a large inventory. *How has he been able to do it?* she puzzled. She did not have to wait long for an answer to her queries. Upon meeting Mr. Crouch, she was aware immediately that he was the shrewdest, most powerful, and ingenious man she had ever known. If anyone could defy the economic lethargy and limitation of domestic commerce during the War years, it was he.

Drawing upon her own resources and her innate ability as an actress, Katherine mustered every ounce of charm and poise she possessed, entered the display room, and approached the elderly, aristocratic looking gentleman who was poring over some invoices and whom she knew instantly to be L. Crouch. Tall and powerfully built, his eyes partly encircled by golden pince-nez, high cheekbones, and a shock of pure white hair, he was exquisitely attired in what Katherine knew was the most expensive suit she had ever seen. Although her heart was fluttering in fear and anticipation, she maintained her composure, cleared her throat, and in as a mature and refined voice as she could manage, introduced herself, "Excuse me, sir. But are you Mr. Crouch—the owner and proprietor of this shop?"

Several moments elapsed before the gentleman looked up from his papers and peered at her. His intense turquoise eyes were unlike any she had seen before and seemed to penetrate, to pierce right through the facade of casual sophistication and composure she had assumed in the hope of impressing him. It was obvious to her that he was not one to be easily deceived or impressed by anyone. By the time that he replied to her question, it was apparent that he had already determined much about her character and disposition and that he had drawn certain conclusions regarding her potential value to him.

"Yes," he stated in a firm business-like manner, "I am he."

She hesitated before addressing him further, and he seized this opportunity to scrutinize her more carefully. *Pleasant-looking child. Seems intelligent, of a sensitive nature, obviously poor—judging by the cut of her clothing.*

Seems eager to learn, hard-working. Yes, I'd say she's got potential, Mr. Crouch thought to himself, while Katherine formulated in her mind the most tactful, least offensive method of bringing up the subject of her possible employment. Deciding that forthrightness would be most advantageous, she plunged in.

"I have just come from your High Street shop wherein the manager has informed me that you would like to interview me personally. I believe that he has already informed you of my background and of the fact that I am interested in acquiring the position of 'assistant.' Furthermore, I believe that he has told you of the conditions that must be met in order for me to accept such a position. These include a minimum salary of ten shillings per week and the cost of my railway fare roundtrip from Gwaelod-y-garth to Cardiff."

His face was perfectly expressionless as she spoke, and she had no means of discerning his reaction. There was a brief silence, as he processed her words. Although she felt awkward under his steady scrutiny, she neither flinched nor faltered. Rather, she met his gaze with equal strength and steadfastness, refusing to feel intimidated.

"Let me see if I am to understand you correctly, Miss—uh—Miss . . ."

"Davies," Katherine supplied.

"Yes, Miss Davies," he continued, unperturbed. "From what I have gathered, you are interested in working as an assistant in my High Street Shop. And yet, although you are inexperienced, you expect to be paid ten shillings a week for your services—and railway fare to and from your home as well?"

"Yes, sir, exactly," she replied evenly, without hesitation.

"But do you not realize that it is customary for one of your limited education and experience to pay *me*—the employer—for the opportunity to learn a trade, to acquire experience?"

"Pay *you*, sir? I should not think, Mr. Crouch," she said simply, with meaning, as her gaze took in the costly and luxurious accoutrements of the shop, "that you are in as desperate need of ten shillings as I am."

"But what could you possibly have to offer us?" Mr. Crouch continued, ignoring her innuendo. "You have no skills, no experience, and yet you are desirous of serving us in so responsible a position as a jeweler's assistant whereby you would be required on a daily basis to handle numerous, virtually priceless jewels, antiques, and other objets d'art as well as a sophisticated clientele. Furthermore, my dear, I do not wish to offend you, but it would be essential for you to possess a suitable wardrobe—one which bespeaks refinement and breeding. My customers expect such an appearance of my employees. In light of these elements, I am afraid, young woman, that I do not see how I might use you."

Although she was terribly hurt and disappointed by his words, she summoned up her courage and spoke proudly, almost defiantly, "Mr. Crouch, my dad has been taken ill recently and is unable to work. Therefore, my family is in desperate need of money, and it is my firm intention to earn enough to help them meet their obligations. I have prayed for employment, and although it may not be from you that I acquire a position, I know that I shall get one. In the advertisement you specifically state 'experience preferable,' not 'experience necessary.' It is for that reason that I chose to apply and felt that I was qualified. I am intelligent, quick to learn, and willing to work very hard. Although I have been an invalid, I am now strong and healthy, and I plan to do whatever is necessary to ensure my family's well-being. I have prayed, sir, and I know that my prayers shall be answered," she concluded quietly, the conviction evident in her voice. And although she was, by now, trembling inside, she appeared calm and in perfect control.

"You have prayed, eh?" replied the gentleman in a gruff voice. But Katherine noticed that there was a subtle difference in his manner, and that he was somewhat softer than before. She also saw a twinkle in his eyes which she had not previously detected.

"Yes, sir," she repeated. "I have prayed."

The answer pleased the old gentleman; he gave a short laugh, and then suddenly turned away to address a pretty red-haired woman who Katherine guessed was in her early thirties, and who had entered through the back room and had apparently overheard a good portion of the interview.

"Well, Mrs. Pfyfe, what have you to say? Have you any idea as to what we should do with this young lady?" he inquired in his gruff voice.

Smiling graciously at Katherine, Mrs. Pfyfe proceeded to speak, "I personally am willing to assist this young lady in whatever manner I am able. She looks intelligent and capable, and I'll bet she's a real worker, too." She smiled warmly in response to Katherine's grateful expression. "I think she deserves a chance, sir."

"Oh, you do, do you?" was Mr. Crouch's retort. But Katherine saw that he had high regard for Mrs. Pfyfe, and that her words had no little influence upon him.

"Have you had any prior experience at all, young lady?"

"Yes, sir," she replied boldly, and proceeded to describe the manner in which she had sold literally hundreds of pairs of woolen stockings in Gwaelod-y-garth.

"Indeed, indeed," was all the old gentleman muttered, under his breath. "And you have no education at all?"

"None, sir," Katherine admitted, wishing more than ever that she had learned to read and write.

"I see. I see," he murmured, then closed his eyes briefly to reflect upon the situation. During the short silence, Mrs. Pfyfe nodded and smiled encouragingly at the outspoken young girl.

"Well, my dear," said Mr. Crouch finally. "If you will agree to attend night school at my expense, I will hire you to work at the High Street shop—providing also that you begin your training in the office under Mr. Wilkin's supervision. Once you have proven yourself, you will be promoted to an assistant. Your salary will be ten shillings a week, in addition to which you will receive your train fare. Do you accept my offer?"

"Oh, I do, sir, indeed I do," she replied breathlessly, her voice quavering and her eyes filling with tears of gratitude and excitement.

"Good. Then, you shall begin tomorrow morning at nine o'clock on the button."

"Oh, Mr. Crouch, thank you, sir. Thank you very much. You won't be sorry. I shall make you proud of me, sir."

"Now, now," the old gentleman said awkwardly. "Let's hear no more of that." He shook hands with her, put his finger under her chin, turned up her face, examined it gravely, and let it go, saying, "You will do just fine, my dear, I am certain of it."

And having concluded the interview, he dismissed her with a nod, "And now, good day, Miss Davies." He walked into the backroom, but Katherine was too stunned to do anything but stand and stare.

"Don't worry about a thing," advised Mrs. Pfyfe in a soothing voice. "I will teach you whatever you need to know. As inspector for the firm, I visit the High Street shop nearly every day, and will be available to you always, my dear." Katherine felt like crying in gratitude. She immediately adored this woman, and although she had no idea as to why Mrs. Pfyfe had taken such an obvious liking to her, she knew that she had somehow acquired a powerful ally.

Glancing at her watch, she saw that it was nearly one o'clock and time to meet her mum on Queens Street. As she raced through the traffic and crowded city streets, she could not stop smiling. Her body felt as though it were aglow. She could hardly believe her good fortune. How had she managed it? How had it been possible for a poor illiterate country girl to win such a desirable salaried position for such a prestigious firm? Frankly, she was mystified. Silently, she uttered thanks to God for answering her prayers.

Upon learning of her daughter's success, Elizabeth was not sure whether to laugh or cry, so bittersweet was the realization that her frail little girl was now grown up enough to earn a salary and hold down a full-time position in the city. Yet so excited was Katherine that it was impossible for Elizabeth to refrain from sharing at least some of her daughter's enthusiasm. Her face animated and her eyes sparkling with joy and excitement, Katherine spoke with such breathless rapidity that Elizabeth could hardly understand her. Affectionately embracing the strong-willed girl, Elizabeth immediately declared that a celebration was in order. "Come on, let's have a day of fun," she suggested, a sly twinkle in her eye. And so, the two of them spent the remainder of the day in the city where they dined at a lovely restaurant, shopped, enjoyed high tea at the Continental Market, strolled through several museums, and, finally, attended a concert. Happy, but exhausted, by the end of the day, they reluctantly caught the eight o'clock train and returned home.

It was only after she had shared the news with the rest of the family and was preparing for bed that she was struck by the full impact of all which had taken place. Why, she had acquired a job! She was expected to appear at L. Crouch & Company promptly at nine o'clock tomorrow morning! And to remain in the shop from nine o'clock to seven o'clock at night. Five days a week and one half day on Saturday! "Oh, my," she sighed aloud, as a feeling of dizziness and nausea overcame her. Now that the months of planning and anticipation were over, she realized that she had devoted absolutely no thought or preparation to the manner in which she would conduct her life once the job had been obtained. Much as a young girl might look forward to her wedding day with no thought of her life to follow, so Katherine had no idea as to what to expect from here on.

Overwhelmed by doubt and fear, she tossed and turned in bed, unable to sleep as a thousand disagreeable thoughts tumbled through her weary brain. Was she truly intelligent enough to learn all that was necessary to keep her position? How would she get along with Mr. Wilkins and the other employees? Would she be able to perform whatever duties were expected of her? Or would she make a fool of herself and fail? Miserably, she realized that she could not hope to answer these questions now. Only time would tell. But, in the meantime, she could not prevent these disturbing thoughts from arising, and she hardly slept throughout the night. It was not until nearly four o'clock in the morning that she finally sank into a heavy sleep which brought her no refreshment.

Afraid that her mum might fail to awaken her at the appropriate time, Katherine arose at six. No one was stirring upstairs, the house was freezing cold, and Katherine could not clearly discern whether she was shivering from fear or from the cold. In the cold grey dawn, everything seemed strange and dim and still. Tremblingly, she washed and dressed—all the while adhering strictly to Mr. Mesmer's advice, "Tell yourself you can, and you can. I can," she vowed, "and I will." Although she was aware of the tempting odors of breakfast cooking in the kitchen, she was far too nervous and upset to eat anything. There was a dreadful gnawing sensation in her stomach that she could not seem to overcome. She could think of little other than the day ahead of her. Frightened and ill, she only prayed that she would somehow survive the experience and that the day would pass as quickly and as painlessly as possible.

CHAPTER 14

A Working Girl

◦

HAVING BID HER FAMILY FAREWELL, Katherine made her way down the narrow winding road which snaked its way through the hills, and led down the mountain to the train station.

Normally, Katherine would not have minded making the two-mile journey on foot, but today it left her with too much time to think about this day that would not reach its conclusion until seven o'clock that evening! Furthermore, the doubts and fear that had plagued her throughout the night continued to torment her now. Would she be able to perform her job satisfactorily? Would she learn quickly enough to please Mr. Crouch? Had Mrs. Pfyfe really meant what she had said about helping her? Arriving at the depot, Katherine felt singularly out of place among the confident, well-seasoned, impeccably groomed and sophisticated men and women waiting for the next train to Cardiff. Trying her best both to feel and appear calm and unruffled, she wondered if she would ever appear as blasé and complacent as they. It was with a distinct feeling of annoyance that she felt her heart thundering in her chest. *Grow up*, she rebuked herself, thoroughly disgusted at her childish fears and apprehensions.

The train ride was pleasant and uneventful, and Katherine's attention was happily diverted, at least temporarily, to the observation of her fellow passengers—and to a tall slender youth of perhaps seventeen or eighteen, with gentle, refined features, brown curly hair, and pale blue eyes framed by thick, black lashes. His hands were long, delicate, and nervous, and Katherine felt that he must be an artist. She was content to pass the time concocting in her imagination wonderfully romantic adventures in which the young man served as the hero.

When the train finally arrived at the Queens Street Station in Cardiff at half past eight, Katherine was jolted back to the painful reality of her situation. Upon alighting, she briskly maneuvered her way through the cobblestone streets in her high-heeled shoes, arriving at Mr. Crouch's shop nearly twenty-five minutes early! Had someone been observing her, he would have thought her movements decidedly strange; for, upon arriving, she went into the doorway, peered in the window, stood perfectly motionless for a minute, suddenly dived into the street, and walked away as rapidly as she had come. This maneuver she repeated several times. Perhaps she should return home. Perhaps she could acquire a better position elsewhere. Perhaps she was not suited for the jewelry trade. On and on her mind raced in this manner, until, at nearly ten minutes before nine o'clock, she decided once and for all that she had made a mistake—that the job was all wrong for her—and that it would be advisable to turn around and return home at once! Her family would understand.

Unfortunately, at the precise moment of her intended departure, who should appear but the manager of the shop with whom she had spoken yesterday and who had telephoned Mr. Crouch in her behalf! For a single instant, she seriously considered running away, but she caught herself and then smiled wanly at Mr. Wilkins. Thin-lipped with a pasty white complexion and dull expression, he smiled vaguely in Katherine's direction, tipped his hat and muttered an unconvincing, "Good morning."

As he carefully unlocked the shop door, Katherine still toyed with the idea of slipping away, but she abandoned this notion once and for all as Mr. Wilkins graciously held the door open for her, and gestured her in. Once inside, she knew that there was no further hope of escape.

After she had removed her coat and placed it carefully on the rack in the back room, she checked her appearance in the floor-length mirror in the display room, and then tentatively approached Mr. Wilkins.

"I am ready, sir. Where shall I begin?" she asked softly. Although she stood directly before him, he did not take any notice of her at all. Puzzled, she spoke up once more.

"Excuse me, Mr. Wilkins. But I am ready to begin. What would you like me to do?"

He was evidently absorbed in the task of repairing a gentleman's gold watch. Not wishing to disturb him any further, Katherine remained silent and motionless for some moments, as she watched his nimble fingers. Finally, after many minutes had elapsed, she began to grow bored and to fidget, and she interrupted once again.

"Mr. Wilkins, I should very much like to get on with my tasks. Mr. Crouch said that you would train me, sir," she said meekly.

"Oh, he did, did he?" Mr. Wilkins roared. And Katherine was so startled, her feet virtually clattered on the floor. Backing away from the repair desk at which Mr. Wilkins was seated, she discovered a cleaning rag, and began to polish the display cabinets. "Wipe those window panes—they're all steamed up," barked the manager.

Nearly jumping in surprise, she dropped her rag, retrieved it, then made her way to the enormous display windows that faced the Arcade and began to wipe them. Patiently, she rubbed them until they shone, taking pride in a job well done. She had little time to reflect, however, for the moment that she had completed this task, Mr. Wilkins issued another brusque command. "Now, take a feather duster and dust all the counters and cabinets in the shop."

Although she was beginning to feel more like a hired domestic than an assistant, she willingly complied. After all, it was her first day on the job, and she wished to create a good impression. *Perhaps if I show him that I can perform these simple tasks efficiently, he will entrust me with greater responsibility,* she thought hopefully. It soon became obvious, however, that Mr. Wilkins regarded her as both a nuisance and an unwelcome presence, and that he had no intention of training her at all. Throughout the seemingly endless morning, he was uncommunicative and thoroughly engrossed in the process of repairing the large drawer full of jewelry.

"Sweep the floor of the back room," he had mumbled after she had dusted, and so, her first morning as an assistant had passed in this manner.

One can imagine her surprise then when Mr. Wilkins insisted that she accommodate the first customer of the day—a heavy garrulous, matronly looking woman, who was intent upon purchasing an ornate silver brooch she had seen in the display window.

"But, sir," Katherine implored, "I don't know what to do. I've never sold jewelry before. Can't you show me, sir—just this once—so I can see how it's done?" There was an empty sinking feeling in her stomach.

"There is no time like the present. Learn by doing it yourself. It's easy enough, Lord knows. Go on, now, and don't waste any more of my valuable time." And so, miserably, Katherine attended to the woman.

"That one, dear, I'd like that brooch," the lady pointed to a heavy, metallic-looking pin in the shape of a scarab. "Can you get it out for me?" she inquired.

"I'll try," Katherine stammered, not at all sure as to how to extract it from the elaborate window case. "Uh, Mr. Wilkins, can you assist me over here?" Katherine called out feebly, but she saw that it was no use. Another customer had entered the shop, and he evidently demanded the manager's full attention, for the two were engrossed in conversation. In the meantime, Katherine was struck by an idea.

"Let me check and see if there are any other brooches like this one in one of the drawers." Scurrying about in a frenzy of activity, she finally located a drawer in which could be found two other scarab pins. "Here you are, Madam," she cried out gleefully to her first customer. "See, they are identical to the one in the window." And the woman examined each brooch in turn, holding each one toward the light, then away from the light, close to her, then a distance away from her, until Katherine was so bored and impatient she longed to walk away and leave the woman to her own devices. Finally, when she thought she could not tolerate the woman a moment longer, her customer spoke. "No, I'm afraid neither of these will do. I must have the one in the window."

Gritting her teeth, Katherine looked longingly in Mr. Wilkin's direction one more time, but saw that he was still absorbed in conversation. Then, with a shrug of despair, she approached the window and somehow managed to unlock the case with relatively little difficulty. Unfortunately, however, the brooch was clasped in a most unusual fashion to the plate glass shelf, and could not be removed. *I wonder*, Katherine thought to herself, *what will happen if I apply a bit of pressure over here. . . .* She never had the opportunity to complete this thought, for the manner in which she had chosen to extract the pin somehow caused a great crack to appear in the glass shelf. Aghast, she was by now virtually in tears. Plucking the brooch from the case, she handed it to her customer, excused herself, and then approached Mr. Wilkins one final time. "Please, sir," she whispered, "help me."

But the unfeeling gentleman simply muttered, "Can't you see I'm a busy man? I am supposed to be running this shop, not assisting the assistant. Go on, now, and finish your sale." And Katherine returned to her customer, determined to leave Mr. Wilkins and the shop forever as soon as the transaction had been completed.

"Yes, this one is perfect," the large woman was beaming. "I'll take it." And to the very best of her abilities, Katherine completed the sale and placed the brooch in a handsome, velvet lined box.

"Thank you, my dear. Thank you for being so patient," the woman smiled at her, and Katherine felt better. As soon as she remembered the crack in the glass shelf and Mr. Wilkin's rude behavior, however, she was reduced once again to a state of despair. About to collect her belongings and leave the shop permanently, Katherine was startled to hear the cheerful voice of Mrs. Pfyfe call out from the back-room.

"Good day, everyone, good day." Never had Katherine been so grateful for the presence of another human being—particularly one so kind-hearted and sympathetic as Mrs. Pfyfe.

"Well, well, well, how is our new assistant doing?" Mrs. Pfyfe asked in her hearty manner. Katherine could not help but respond with a shy smile. "Tell me all about your morning, my dear. Is there anything I can do for you?"

And although Katherine would have loved to pour her heart out to the kindly woman, a certain pride and reluctance to "tattle" precluded her from so doing. But Mrs. Pfyfe was intuitive, and sensed immediately that something was very wrong.

"What's the matter, child? Has that selfish Mr. Wilkins refused to help you?" she asked. Miserably, Katherine nodded.

"I am afraid he has provided me with no training at all, and I have been required to dust and sweep and wait on customers without having the slightest notion as to how to act. Oh, it's been dreadful, Mrs. Pfyfe, perfectly dreadful." And she proceeded to provide the visitor with a detailed account of what had transpired that morning—culminating in the huge crack in the display case for which she had been responsible.

"Holy Mother Mary!" Mrs. Pfyfe gasped at the sight of the damaged shelf. Without further ado, Mrs. Pfyfe marched purposefully to the back room where Mr. Wilkins was completing some paperwork, and addressed him angrily, "How dare you treat a brand new employee in such a manner?" she began heatedly, then continued in a voice too low for Katherine to hear. Katherine never did discover exactly what took place that day in the back room. She only knew that following this confrontation, Mr. Wilkins was an altogether different man—pleasant, cooperative, and responsive. She could not believe nor could she account for the changes that took place in his attitude and in his treatment of her. Henceforth, he willingly shared whatever information and assistance she might require. In addition, Mrs. Pfyfe promised to come by the shop for several hours every day and even volunteered to teach Katherine to read and write, so that she would not have to attend night school after all. Katherine was simply flabbergasted by her good fortune! And she was amazed by Mrs. Pfyfe's kindness and generosity. She could not imagine what she had done to earn so thoughtful and considerate a friend and ally.

The remainder of the day passed quickly and uneventfully. By one o'clock she had been famished and purchased some "faggots and peas"—which was a dish made of the pig cut-off meats, peas, and bread crumbs—from the nearby grocery shop. During the brief lunch period, she had delighted in window-shopping in the Arcade. It made her feel so grown up and worldly to know that she was a working girl. The brief meal revived her spirits and gave her strength for the rest of the day. When she returned, there were many more customers upon which to wait and, to her surprise, she found it quite easy and pleasant to serve them. Because Mr. Wilkins was far more cooperative, she was able to avoid making any further catastrophic mistakes. And, to her surprise and relief, she had been able to bluff and maneuver her way out of many potentially disagreeable and embarrassing circumstances. By the end of the day, she had sold nearly two hundred pounds worth of jewelry, waited on perhaps twenty-five customers, dusted and polished the numerous display cabinets and cases until they gleamed, had accidentally overturned a display shelf full of diamonds, asked a constant stream of questions of Mr. Wilkins, familiarized herself with the shop's inventory, and polished an untold number of silver and brass items. By closing time, she was thoroughly exhausted—not so much as a result of excessive physical activity, but rather due to the intense strain upon her delicate nervous system. Weary but proud of herself, she bade Mr. Wilkins a good evening, and hurried to the train station in order to catch the seven-thirty train home to Gwaelod-y-garth.

It took her half an hour to get from Cardiff to the train station in Gwaelod-y-garth. It took her another forty minutes to make her way on foot up the steep mountain. Although she was really far too tired to eat the delicious evening meal Elizabeth had prepared in her honor, Katherine did not wish to hurt her feelings and obliged her by sampling a few mouthfuls of each course and by describing to her excited family the events of the day. The children were enthralled by her account of Mrs. Pfyfe's intervention and outraged by the ungentlemanly conduct of Mr. Wilkins during the earlier part of the day. They were rather jealous that she had been able to roam freely about through the Arcade, and they all coveted mouth-watering faggots and peas she had managed to consume for lunch. Throughout the evening meal, Katherine was hardly able to keep her eyes open, and she failed to notice the worried glances exchanged between her Mum and Dad. Excusing herself prematurely, she wearily climbed the stairs to her bedroom, washed, changed into her bedclothes, and prepared for bed.

With a great sigh of relief, she climbed into bed and snuggled under the coverlets. She noticed with gratitude the hot brick her mum had thoughtfully placed under the blanket. *How kind she is*, Katherine thought to herself. Once gloriously comfortable under the warm covers, Katherine analyzed the events of the day as objectively as possible. It was with a sense of pride and satisfaction that she realized that she had survived. *How fortunate that dear Mrs. Pfyfe came to my rescue, just when I was about to leave forever*, she mused.

Rolling over onto her stomach now, and ready to fall asleep for the night, she thanked both God and her dear friend, Jesus, for the day that had come to an end, wondering fleetingly what the next day held in store. She could not help but derive considerable comfort from the conviction that nothing could prove so difficult as this first day of work had been. Whatever tomorrow might bring, however challenging, she was prepared. Softly sighing, then stretching and yawning one last time, she cast aside the fears and concerns of the day once and for all. Praying silently for God's guidance throughout the night, her lips curved unconsciously into a confident smile. Nothing could harm her, nothing could stop her now. She had survived the worst. There was nothing she could not handle successfully. Bravely, even eagerly, then, she was prepared to embrace all that tomorrow might bring.

CHAPTER 15

On the Job

~~~~~~

As KATHERINE HAD PREDICTED, THE subsequent days passed far more smoothly and pleasantly than the initial ones. Finding herself in a position of authority and responsibility without any prior training or knowledge, she had no choice but to learn by trial and error. Although Mrs. Pfyfe was of great assistance at the beginning, Katherine quickly learned to be almost entirely self-sufficient. To her enormous relief, her mistakes were few and far between. Accordingly, her self-esteem and confidence increased daily.

It was not long before Katherine discovered the reason for the cool behavior Mr. Wilkins had exhibited initially. Unbeknownst to anyone else, he was devoting a substantial portion of each working day toward the establishment of his own independent jewelry repair business, informing no one of the fact that he was conducting his own personal business under Mr. Crouch's roof! Quite understandably, he was frightened of being discovered. It was for this reason that he kept his distance from everyone. In time, however, he grew to trust Katherine, realizing she had no intention of betraying him. In truth, she was far too preoccupied with her own success to give him much thought.

To her great joy and relief, Katherine never was required to work in the office as Mr. Crouch had promised upon hiring her. It was discovered early on that she possessed a genuine flair for selling and for efficiently and tactfully handling Mr. Crouch's demanding clientele. Furthermore, she was an excellent saleswoman, and sales increased rather dramatically during the brief period in which she had been in Mr. Crouch's employ. Neat, punctual, and hard-working, and never one to shirk her responsibilities, she soon became a highly valued employee. Furthermore, as a result of Mrs. Pfyfe's intervention on her behalf, Katherine never was required to attend night school. Instead, the generous Irish woman volunteered to teach her to read and write. With utmost patience and consideration did she work with the young girl. Rarely did a day elapse wherein at least several hours were not devoted to such lessons. Furthermore, so eager was Katherine to learn by now that she requested and received additional tutoring from her dad as well. Thanks to a quick mind, eager heart, and gracious spirit, it did not take her long at all to master these skills. Within a matter of several months, she was reading and writing efficiently and at a level of proficiency that enabled her to perform all facets of her job with ease. Both Gwilym and Elizabeth took particular pride in their daughter's accomplishments, and they were frankly relieved to learn that Katherine was now self-sufficient and perfectly equipped to pursue the career of her choice.

By the end of three months' time, Katherine had made herself indispensable to the firm. Although her days were long and demanding, she seldom complained. Although difficulties frequently arose, she somehow managed to transcend them by employing wit and charm. Furthermore, she was both clever and resourceful. Everyone liked her. She had a way with the customers, and she had succeeded in winning over even those who were cranky and critical. Aware of her success, she wasted no time in requesting a raise in pay from Mr. Crouch. To her delight and astonishment, he gave her no argument.

"You have earned it, my dear." he said, respect and admiration for her evident in his voice. "I have always prided myself upon my keen ability to judge character. And I must admit that I have judged yours correctly."

"Thank you, sir," Katherine had murmured tremulously, blushing from ear to ear. But despite his words of encouragement, Katherine knew intuitively that she had received the increase in pay primarily as a result of Mrs. Pfyfe's kind words on her behalf.

Why Mrs. Pfyfe had taken such a strong liking to and interest in her, she never discovered. The older woman seemed both amused by and sympathetic with Katherine. And Katherine only knew that regardless of her purpose or motive, the woman had selflessly devoted time and effort toward her advancement. The bond between them was strengthened and ripened into a warm friendship, following a weekend they spent together during which Mrs. Pfyfe had graciously accepted Katherine's invitation to meet her family. Feeling indebted to the Irish woman who had been so kind to their daughter, Gwilym and Elizabeth fell in love with Mrs. Pfyfe immediately, embracing her as a member of the family. Eagerly reciprocating their warmth and hospitality, Mrs. Pfyfe paid frequent visits to The Cottage. And feeling a greater degree of responsibility to them for having known the Davies, Mrs. Pfyfe was more devoted to Katherine's welfare than ever. In the meantime, Katherine could hardly contain her joy and enthusiasm over the curious manner in which the quality of her life had improved.

The days and weeks passed pleasantly and uneventfully, as Katherine gradually achieved mastery over all facets of the business. Frequently, during the less busy moments, she observed Mr. Wilkins as he fastidiously cut and polished rare and expensive gems and stones and repaired priceless family jewels and heirlooms. She watched eagerly as he counted up the daily receipts and debits, filled out invoices, collected fees from Mr. Crouch's debtors, took inventory, and reordered new merchandise. Assisting him whenever possible, she memorized all pertinent data and assimilated all useful information. In short, she did everything in her power that might enable her to assume greater responsibility and ensure her of an even greater income sometime in the near future.

It was only a matter of four or five months after she had been hired by Mr. Crouch that Katherine made a startling discovery—one that was to prove of great personal profit. While Mr. Wilkins continued to conduct his repair business on the side, Katherine was busily establishing her own source of additional income at the shop. One day, after seven or eight rather large boxes of merchandise were delivered to the shop, Katherine realized that there was simply no space available to accommodate these goods. *What could Mr. Crouch have been thinking of to have these boxes sent here?* she wondered. Then, suddenly, she noticed a letter that was attached to one of the boxes signed by Mr. Crouch personally and advising her to place the merchandise in the storeroom upstairs.

"Storeroom?" she repeated aloud. *Storeroom?* she puzzled. *What store-room?* No one had ever mentioned the existence of such a room before. She was about to inquire as to the possible meaning of Mr. Crouch's message, but something inside made her stop and think. *Perhaps I'll just slip up the back stairs and see what is up there,* she thought to herself. Stealthily, and unobserved by Mr. Wilkins, she crept up the stairs. Lo and behold she discovered a door that was obscured by a small cabinet laden with empty cardboard boxes. Removing the boxes one by one and then pushing aside the cabinet, she turned the knob. Much to her amazement, the door opened easily; she was not prepared for what was inside.

The room was large, and rather draughty, and in it was assembled the largest assortment of valuable items she had ever seen. She gasped, then giggled nervously, then simply stared in awe at the array of merchandise hidden in this obscure spot. She felt as though she had stumbled into a pirate's lair filled with stolen booty! She was not at all certain whether she should leave at once or linger and count the horde. Deciding upon the latter course of action, she briefly investigated the contents of each box, attempting to calculate as quickly as possible the relative value of its contents. Beautiful Georgian silver tea services of exquisite design, delicate china that was translucent when held to the light, rare porcelain bowls and vases, priceless crystal and lamps, silver and brass candlesticks—Katherine could not contain her delight and admiration for these objects. As she caressed a delicate carved statuette, it suddenly occurred to her that no one but she—and Mr. Crouch—knew of the existence of this room. And, intuitively, she was certain that even Mr. Crouch had no idea how much merchandise had actually been placed here. She had heard that Mr. Crouch had bought out several other jewelry shops in the area and she could only assume that it was from these stores that such treasures had come. Casually inquiring of Mr. Wilkins and Mrs. Pfyfe what had become of the merchandise her employer had obtained upon the purchase of the other shops, she was pleased to learn that they knew nothing whatever of its whereabouts. From henceforth, she, like

Mr. Wilkins before her, plunged into business for herself, selling various pieces of merchandise from the storeroom for her own personal profit. Not wishing to be unfair or greedy, she applied the "one for you, one for me" principle, making quite a sizable sum of money within a very short period of time. This additional income, along with her sisters' small contributions from their part-time employment as teacher aids in a local school, enabled her to repay many of her parents' debts. Due to health problems, Gwilym had been forced to quit his job.

Although she felt occasional pangs of guilt and remorse, these were few and far between, and she certainly never experienced a sufficient amount of either to curtail her subterfuge. Everything was proceeding satisfactorily. Her family was greatly benefiting. There was no possibility of her getting caught, for no inventory existed on the objects in the storeroom. Far too intelligent to refrain from exercising caution, however, she did not indulge in this activity more than once a week. Having won the respect and admiration of Mr. Crouch and her superiors she did not intend to jeopardize their high regard. Only during wartime could it have been possible for someone of Katherine's limited training and education to advance so rapidly in position and salary. For, in addition to her new source of income, she had requested and received yet another raise and a promotion to a full assistantship.

It had taken her a surprisingly short period of time to adjust to the life of a "working girl." Although she found the weekday schedule rigorous and demanding, she genuinely thrived in the constant activity and the continuous acquisition of information. She had always delighted in learning, and her job and the city itself afforded her the continuous opportunity to study human nature. Furthermore, she had grown in confidence and poise. If truth be known, she had become quite proud and rather conceited, for nearly everyone—at home and at work—admired her, saying all manner of pretty and agreeable things to her regarding her abilities and appearance.

She had met and established friendships with several girls her age who were also employed in the Arcade, and they, too, seemed to find Katherine's charm and self-confidence irresistible.

"However do you succeed in managing Mr. Crouch?" cooed Margaret Homsby, feigning a shudder at the mere thought of the irascible old gentleman who was well known, at least by reputation, by virtually everyone who worked in the Arcade.

"Oh, it's not difficult. I just call upon my dear friend, Mr. Mesmer," replied Katherine, with a sly twinkle in her eye.

"Who is Mr. Mesmer?" inquired Charlotte Bigelow, sniffing suspiciously. She worked at Goldilocks and Company Hairdressers.

"Oh, just an old friend who has been responsible for every bit of success I have known," Katherine replied mysteriously.

"Come on, Katherine," Charlotte implored.

"Yes, do tell us all about the gentleman," begged Margaret.

"You really want to know about him?" teased Katherine.

"Yes!" the two responded impatiently and in unison.

"Well, then, all right." And to the delight of her companions, she proceeded to describe her introduction to the work of Anton Mesmer, who had so profoundly influenced her. "Tell yourself that you will succeed and you will succeed!" Katherine concluded, after sharing her own personal adventures. "That is my formula for success."

"I shall have to try it at once," declared Margaret. "Lord knows, I should like a raise in pay."

"Ditto, I'm sure," added Charlotte. And the two, impressed, shared this information with other acquaintances, until, as a result of this conversation, Katherine's reputation as one who was clever and wise beyond her years expanded to the young people throughout the area.

By the end of nine months, feeling perfectly secure in her position and confident in her abilities as a valued employee at L. Crouch and Company, she once again approached her employer for yet another raise in pay, concluding her proposal with an ultimatum, "I am afraid that I will have to receive a higher salary if you wish to retain my services."

"You shall have to receive a raise in order to remain as my employee?" he repeated in an odd voice. "My dear, I am not accustomed to receiving such ultimatums from my sales assistants. Do you know, child, that you are the most demanding employee I have? I fear that you are too ambitious for me and my humble shop. I am afraid that I cannot satisfy your request," he said slowly, with meaning.

"Oh, but, sir," Katherine interjected tremblingly. "I did not mean . . ."

He continued, calmly studying her carefully, "This is the third time you have approached me in this manner in nine months. You have been well paid for your work. No, my dear, I am certain that you will fare better elsewhere. Perhaps you will be better appreciated by another employer. Young and talented—and outspoken, I might add—you will have no difficulty acquiring another similar position. Of this I am certain."

"But, sir . . .," she began once again, feeling faint. But, waving his hands in a gesture of dismissal, Mr. Crouch concluded the interview. And, to Katherine's amazement—for she had never anticipated such an outcome—she was now suddenly to be numbered among the city's unemployed. It was only after she had left Mr. Crouch's office that she realized the full impact of what had happened. She had been dismissed—after nine month's hard work and loyalty and training! All because she had requested more money! For the time being, she was unaware that she would never again be able to draw money from the sale of items in the stock room. Later on, when she did realize this to be the case, she was crushed. *Oh, what have I done! Silly, silly girl. To have forfeited such a grand opportunity to earn real money!* she berated herself, moaning pitiably. Had Mr. Crouch been less headstrong and decisive, she might have addressed him once more. However, having witnessed in the past, how boldly, firmly, and decisively he had rebuffed the attempts of others such as sales people, competitors, and solicitors that had tried to influence or intimidate him in the past, she knew all too well that it was highly unlikely that he would reverse his decision. *No,* she decided ruefully, *I will have to search for another position.*

Fortunately, Mr. Crouch had been correct in his assessment of her marketability. By week's end she was hired by another jewelry firm, J. Samuels, almost immediately, at double the salary she had been earning at L. Crouch. Her sister Cora was in Cardiff doing some shopping when she passed by this shop and noticed the advertisement for help posted on the door and notified her at once. Upon meeting the owner, J. Samuels, Katherine was convinced that he was shrewd enough to recognize her potential. She saw immediately that he was impressed by the fact that she had been employed by so prestigious an outfit as L. Crouch. She could not help but note that his large brown eyes bulged when she divulged her former salary; nevertheless, he unflinchingly offered her double the salary on the spot. Without hesitation, she accepted the offer.

"You will begin on Monday morning—at nine o'clock sharp," the man with dark curly hair, sharp features, and a deep voice informed her. And, with a feeling of profound relief, she left, thanking the man and God for her good fortune. She was beginning to view both her dismissal and the new position as a blessing in disguise.

After collecting her few belongings from the shop and bidding Mrs. Pfyfe and Mr. Wilkins a tearful goodbye, Katherine was ready to begin anew. Frankly, she was prepared for a challenge, and although the new shop was not nearly as attractive or elegant as Mr. Crouch's, she was excited by the prospect of learning and growing in new directions. Upon her arrival at J. Samuels' on Monday morning at ten minutes before nine, Katherine was surprised to note that Mr. Samuels himself, the owner and proprietor, was not present. It was evident that the care and management of the shop was under the jurisdiction of an immense, disagreeable looking woman with a large, round, moist face, small nondescript eyes that were set closely together, a wide nose, red cheeks, long black braids wrapped around her head, and a loud, impossibly shrill voice that made Katherine cringe and long to put her hands over her ears.

Unfortunately, it took Katherine little more than a quarter of an hour to discover that literally nothing about this new shop appealed to her and that, if there were any such thing as a mistake, she had made one. Firstly, the shop was far drearier and dingier than she had remembered it. Secondly, the quality both of the merchandise and clientele were vastly inferior to those of L. Crouch. Thirdly, her fellow employees were impossibly rude and coarse, and did everything in their power to make her circumstances unpleasant. How she longed for the gracious, comforting presence of

Mrs. Pfyfe, half expecting that woman to appear any moment to rescue her from the depressing environment. But Mrs. Pfyfe did not appear, and Katherine was forced to contend with the consequences.

Eyeing Katherine suspiciously—her slender, graceful figure and stylish attire—the woman made no attempt to be anything more than civil. "So you're our new girl, eh?" the woman snarled.

"I am the new assistant," replied Katherine evenly, looking the woman directly in the eyes.

"Well, then, 'new assistant' I believe it's time for you to begin assisting. I've got just the task for you." And she turned and walked away, leaving Katherine standing all alone in the center of the display room. Several moments elapsed before the woman appeared, flushed and wet with perspiration, carrying both a bucket and a mop in her fat hands. "Here you are, dearie. The floors sure can use a good scrubbing!" Katherine was too surprised to do anything but stare at the woman. She thought that she must have heard the woman wrong!

"Come on, dearie. We haven't got all day, you know. Here you are," and she shoved the mop and bucket into Katherine's hands. Katherine felt her cheeks begin to get hot and her heart hammer, as she attempted to repress her anger.

"I am afraid you must be mistaken, madam," she said softly, but firmly. "I was hired as an assistant, not as a housekeeper. "Let's not get high and mighty, miss. The fact is that you are the last one to be hired by Mr. Samuels, and, therefore, you have certain responsibilities that I and the other employees," she winked maliciously at a sallow, yellow-haired assistant who was poring over some paperwork behind the display case, "have 'outgrown' shall we say? If you catch my drift, miss."

"I do believe I have 'caught your drift,'" replied Katherine with an outward calmness and composure that belied her inner state altogether. And, feeling both contempt and disdain for the woman, her position, and the shop itself, she decided that she could not endure this environment for even a moment longer. With a forced smile and deliberate nonchalance, she handed first the bucket, then the mop, back to the manager before the woman had the opportunity to comprehend what was taking place.

"Here you are, dearie," said Katherine, while the woman stood transfixed to her spot. "And a good day to you all," Katherine called out to the other employees who were standing and gawking nearby. And, without further fuss or explanation, Katherine left J. Samuels forever, once again joining the ranks of the unemployed.

Despite the distasteful experience, Katherine did not allow herself to become discouraged. She knew another opportunity would come her way—if she were only patient and persevering. And she was both of these. "If only I could return to L. Crouch," she would sigh wistfully. But she knew that this was out of the question. Her pride would not allow her to beg for a position. And so, she continued to search—this time finding the task far more difficult than it had been before.

Finally, after several months of steadily looking for work, Katherine was hired by Howard Gibson, a jewelry shop owner, in the nearby town of Pontypridd, which was a bit closer to home than Cardiff. It was while accompanying her mum to the home of her Aunt Martha that she learned of this job opportunity. Walking leisurely through the center of town, it had been Elizabeth whose attention was drawn to a sign posted in the window of Gibson's stating "help wanted."

"Look, Katherine," Elizabeth whispered breathlessly, as she grabbed her daughter by the elbow.

"Apply within," Katherine read aloud. "It's certainly worth a try," Katherine smiled mischievously. And, before Elizabeth had a chance to utter another word, her daughter had darted into the shop with customary impulsiveness.

Shaking her head disapprovingly, Elizabeth wondered, *when will that child mend her willful ways?* But she was forced to smile as she thought of Katherine's indomitable will and spirit and her refusal to succumb to defeat. Window-shopping while Katherine investigated the possibility of a position, Elizabeth could not help but reflect upon the manner in which her daughter had blossomed over the past years. *She's all grown up*, she mused wistfully.

At that precise moment, her grown up daughter came bounding through the busy pavement, crying gleefully, "I got it! It's mine. I begin on Monday!"

"Congratulations, love. I'm so glad for you. What a stroke of good fortune!" observed Elizabeth warmly. And Katherine could not have been more in agreement.

The remainder of the walk was devoted to a description of what had transpired in the shop and to the discussion of her new position, and the rest of the afternoon was spent in Pontypridd in the company of her mum and her dear Aunt Martha—a plump, good-natured, but garrulous and gossipy woman. So full of joy was Katherine that even Martha's detailed description of her heart and kidney ailments did nothing to dispel her optimism and enthusiasm. In fact, she could not recall any time in the past when she had found Aunt Martha's company so pleasant.

Gibson's was clean, comfortable, and cozy. Catering strictly to the middle classes, it offered Katherine a welcome change of atmosphere from J. Samuels. And, although she was deeply grateful to have any job at all, still she could not help but long for a more responsible position in a more prestigious firm. It was only a matter of a week or two before she realized that she was both overly qualified and underpaid. In fact, she began to seriously wonder if Mrs. Pfyfe, who constantly pressed her to return to L. Crouch, was not correct after all. "Come on back to us, dear. I know that Mr. Crouch will take you back if you beg him to do so." But Katherine was far too stubborn and proud to beg, and she was not at all convinced that L. Crouch was the correct place for her either. Energetic and ambitious, she decided to remain at Gibson's for the present time and to keep her eyes open in case any opportunity should arise. In the meantime, she would serve Mr. Gibson to the best of her abilities.

By this time, Katherine had met many working people her age, and had enjoyed the attentions of several eligible young bachelors. It was the dashing young department store heir, Michael James, however, who was of greatest interest to her. For he was everything she admired in a man. Tall and slender, with handsome, aristocratic features and a refined manner, he was clever, sensitive, and articulate. Only his moodiness and his infrequent outbursts of temper were of any real concern to her, for they frightened and upset her, and she did not know how to handle him on these occasions. She only knew that his explosions were usually initiated by family or business difficulties, and that following the death of his father, he had been required to assume great responsibilities both at home and in business. At his tender age, he had been ill prepared for so great a burden. And he had been afforded little opportunity to enjoy life. His moments with Katherine were among the very few lighthearted and truly happy ones he had known. It was with her that he was able to express himself most freely; it was through their association that he learned to enjoy life. Although his marriage proposals were frequent and sincere, and although she loved him dearly, she sensed somehow that he was not the right partner for her. Nor could she help but feel suspicious and rather frightened of him, for his behavior was charming but erratic. Nonetheless, she continued to find him a romantic figure, and a gentle, sympathetic soul.

Her responsibilities at Gibson's were simple enough—in fact, too simple for her taste—for the shop attracted few customers and had little to offer in the way of merchandise or ambience. In truth, Katherine was bored and longed for a challenge, such as those that she had faced initially at L. Crouch. Small and stuffy, the shop was either too hot or too cold for her comfort, and there was seldom enough fresh air circulating to keep her from feeling drowsy and discontent. Frequently, throughout the seemingly endless afternoons, she left the main entrance to the business open and would herself stroll in the courtyard leading to the main street in order to exercise her limbs and catch a glimpse of the outside world. Not infrequently various friends or acquaintances would stop by to say hello or to exchange pleasantries. But, throughout the long day, Katherine had perhaps too much time to engage in daydreaming of a successful career, making a name for herself, and perhaps eventually marrying a handsome, charming, and wealthy man—and, of course, living happily ever after.

CHAPTER 16

Percy Hayward

AMONG HER DUTIES AT GIBSON'S were both the opening of the shop in the morning and the closing up of the shop at night. As neither task was difficult nor demanding, she never minded coming in a few minutes earlier or leaving later than the other employees. In fact, she rather enjoyed being alone in the shop on these occasions for it made her feel very grown up and independent to be entrusted with so great a responsibility. Only when she was required to stay later than half past seven did she feel uneasy. For, by this time, it was nearly always dark, and she had, since early childhood, been afraid of the dark.

One evening in the spring of 1917, she was engrossed in the process of locking the shop's front door when she was suddenly overcome by a strange, disconcerting feeling. Shivering, she tried to dismiss the feeling, but could not. She distinctly felt as though she were being watched by someone else. Upon looking around the courtyard, however, she saw that she was alone. There was no sound. No one was lurking about. Most of the other shops and businesses in the area closed at precisely seven o'clock, and there was no sign of life in the early evening stillness. Only the sound of traffic could be heard in the distance.

Silly girl, she admonished herself. *You're behaving like a child*. And, as she extracted the key from the door, she pooh-pooed the funny feeling, attributing it to her vivid imagination and highly strung nervous system. Cautiously finding her way to the courtyard gate, however, she could not completely dismiss the strange feeling. Then, fumblingly, as she tested the gate one last time to make sure it was properly bolted, she suddenly became uncomfortably aware of the presence of someone else. It was still dusk, and for several moments she could not utter a sound as she was overshadowed by the figure of a tall, slender gentleman. Her mouth was dry, and she felt her knees going weak under her. She hardly dared glance up at the stranger who she now knew was keeping an eye on her. *Oh, dear God, please protect me from harm and danger!* she silently prayed. Attempting to remain as calm as possible, she slowly turned and began to walk toward Taff Street. As she turned, however, she was unable to avoid physical contact with the tall man who was now blocking her path. Moving swiftly with remarkable grace and agility, he intercepted her movement.

Although by now she was trembling with fear, she managed to address him with admirable calm and poise, "Would you mind stepping aside?" she said boldly. Her voice was confident and poised.

"Why, yes, as a matter of fact, I would mind," replied the man pleasantly, his white teeth gleaming and his bold eyes laughing at her. "You see," he continued breezily, "although you don't know it yet, you are going to marry me."

Katherine thought her ears must be deceiving her. Had she heard him rightly? For an instant there was a silence so acute it seemed that neither of them were breathing. Then, as life and feeling and comprehension began to flow back into her, she gazed directly into his crystal gray eyes. "

"Indeed?" she replied coldly. Privately, she thought that he must be some sort of madman. Praying that he was only a harmless lunatic, she struggled to maintain her composure and to simultaneously maneuver away from him. Cleverly managing to evade him, she hurried toward the street. But as she approached the town's center, she noticed that he was still close by.

"Won't you slow down?" he cajoled. "I'd like to speak with you."

"About what?" she replied coolly.

"I feel as though I already know you. Don't you think we could be friends?" he persisted. Although she did her best to ignore him, she found it virtually impossible to do so.

"I work in the tailoring shop across the road from you. I have been watching you ever since you began working at Gibson's. I do hope that you'll forgive my impertinence, but, you see, I have known for some time that you and I are destined to be man and wife."

"Is that so?" Katherine thought defiantly, regarding the prospect as nothing short of preposterous. Although it was on the tip of her tongue to sharply rebuke the young man and insist that he leave her alone once and for all, she held herself in check, attempting to ignore him and walking more rapidly and purposefully in the direction of the train station instead. Her restraint was lost on him, however, and he remained unperturbed by her side. Chattering away good-naturedly, he refused to be dismayed by her total lack of interest or response. Irritation and antagonism had arisen in her heart, however, and she yearned to speak tart words. Instead, she continued to ignore him as she made her way through the evening crowds. *This man is impossible*, she thought to herself, gritting her teeth. *He must be mad.*

Finally arriving at the depot and feeling more comfortable among the crowds of people, Katherine was on the verge of telling him off forever, when she happened to glance up at him and notice that his eyes were kind and intelligent and twinkling with humor. He smiled a friendly boyish grin, and she could not help but return his smile. *Perhaps he is not so bad after all*, she admitted grudgingly to herself. Studying his features more carefully now, she saw that he really was quite handsome. And, aside from his insistence that they were to become man and wife, his conversation was rather witty and engaging.

"I have been aware of you ever since you came to work at Gibson's. I have observed and admired you from afar. I simply had to meet you," he stated simply, in the way of an excuse for his forwardness. "My name is Percy Hayward, and I know that we shall be seeing one another often. And do mark my words. I have never been more certain of anything. You and I are destined to be husband and wife," he informed her as he assisted her onto the train. Although she made no reply, she smiled once more. And, like a young boy, Percy had grinned eagerly at her response.

"You will forgive me, won't you?"

She nodded.

"You'll hold no grudge, then?" he implored from the platform, as the train began to crawl slowly away.

"No, I won't," she answered, still smiling.

"Good. Then I shall see you tomorrow, if you won't mind," he called out.

"I shan't mind," she replied shyly.

"Good night, then," the joy was evident in his manner, as he removed the hat he had been wearing and waved it enthusiastically in her direction. This was the last she saw of him, as the train gathered momentum and moved swiftly toward home. Leaning back in her seat, she sighed and smiled dreamily. She took a peculiar satisfaction in attempting to recall in detail her encounter with Percy Hayward. *He's handsome, quick-witted, and persistent. A girl could do worse for a husband, I suppose,* she mused, remembering his repeated assurances that they would marry. Feeling a faint blush creep over her cheeks, she recalled the impudent way in which he had stared at her. *As if he felt he owned me,* she thought. Then, she suddenly remembered that his eyes were a beautiful, deep gray color and that she had never before known anyone with gray eyes. Furthermore, there was something exciting and stimulating about him—something vital and electric. Still, as she reviewed her behavior, she decided that her reticence, her coolness had been perfectly justified. Certainly, she would be more pleasant, more responsive toward him when she saw him tomorrow.

"Tomorrow," she said aloud, feeling a nervous giggle rise to her throat, then suddenly realized with surprise that she could hardly wait to see Percy Hayward again . . . A nervous tingling, embarrassment, and an exciting pleasure overcame her. She could hardly wait until tomorrow.

Percy had fallen in love with Katherine at first sight. Although this was not the way with her, she quickly became quite fond of him—fonder of him than of anyone else. But never was she "in love" with him. Perhaps she was too preoccupied with her career and its advancement or too intent upon making a name for herself, and too much interested in experiencing as much of life as she could, to devote her time, attention, and affection solely to one individual. Whatever the reason, she was not able to reciprocate the passionate intensity with which Percy loved her. Nonetheless, she enjoyed his companionship and found his an enjoyable and exciting personality.

When they were together publicly, she could see how the eyes of other women followed him and how they fluttered at his attentions. The realization that other women were attracted to him made her feel proud to be seen by his side. She found his charm captivating, his boyish enthusiasm for life contagious. His biting wit and sense of humor she found singularly entertaining for she had never met anyone like him. Although he was only a year older than she, he was more worldly, more sophisticated than any young man she had ever known before. His sensitivity, his ambition, the elegant manner in which he dressed and carried himself, his devotion to her, his enthusiasm for life all pleased and impressed her. But, although she saw him frequently, she continually insisted upon dating other men as well, and she repeatedly refused his proposals of marriage. Although he was terribly disappointed each time she refused him, he was unwavering in his confidence that she would, one day soon, change her mind and agree to become his wife. In the meantime, Katherine was nothing less than amazed by his perseverance. She had continued to see Michael, and had repeatedly refused his proposals as well. It was with astonishment that she learned some ten months after she had met Percy that Michael had committed suicide. Gentle, kind, ambitious, and so anxious to please, Michael had been her very close friend as well as her beau. It took her quite some time to recover from the shock of his death.

Grieving over the loss of Michael's unexpected and untimely death, Katherine became distracted and distraught. She was not as attentive to Percy as she could have been. Percy had many friends both male and female, however, one woman in particular seemed to charm him and occupy much of his time. When sightings of the twosome about the town began increasing in frequency, she suspected that Percy was seeing another woman. When contemplating this situation she was startled by her feelings of jealousy and possessiveness and came to realize just how much she had come to care for him.

It was not until after Percy had enlisted and had been away for several months that she came to realize how attached to him she had become. She missed him terribly. Although perhaps not deeply in love with him, there was no denying that she truly cared. Absence had indeed made the heart grow fonder, and it was after another particularly long absence that Katherine finally consented to his proposal. Following a brief summer holiday spent together on Barry Island, Katherine had at long last agreed with Percy's long-held conviction that the two were destined to become husband and wife.

Needless to say, Percy was overwhelmed by this stroke of good fortune. With all his heart, he believed Katherine his ideal mate. There was nothing he would not do for her. Whatever was in his power to give her, he would. He would do everything he could to make her happy. "There's something very special about her," he had told his friends and family. "She's like no one I have ever met before." No one could have been prouder or happier than he on their wedding day.

They were married on October 17, 1919, by a Justice of the Peace. In light of Katherine's unorthodox views and experiences, it was her desire for a comfortable, small civil ceremony. Invitations were limited to family members and intimate friends. Although Percy truly desired to be fair and open-minded, it was much to his consternation and dismay that Katherine had insisted upon rewriting the traditional wedding vows to conform to her own independent and unconventional viewpoints. She had found the concept of "obeying" a husband antiquated and unacceptable. She would never willingly agree to obey anyone, let alone a husband! Furthermore, she attached little commonsense value to the clause that stated, "Till death do us part," for she simply could not regard the contract to which she agreed at the age of nineteen to be permanent and irrevocable. "Who knows what lies ahead?" she had admitted to a barely comprehending Percy.

But Percy was far too deeply in love to quibble with her unusual requests. He was aware that she was an "original," and that he could not possibly compare her with any other woman. Nor could he assert himself and demand that she conform to the rules and regulations—the conventions—that applied to nearly everyone else. Deep down inside he knew that she would never comply with any demands that he might impose upon her. She was far too opinionated and headstrong. And Percy had learned early in their courtship that so long as she had her own way, life could be very pleasant, but when she didn't, life was quite disagreeable.

Unhappily, Percy came down with a severe case of influenza shortly before the wedding, and was far too ill to go on their honeymoon. Instead, the first week of their marriage was spent embarrassingly at the home of his parents wherein Katherine patiently nursed him and attempted to cheer him up.

Only a month following the ceremony, Katherine discovered, to her horror, that she was pregnant. She was shocked and overwhelmed by this discovery. It was not that she didn't want children someday, although she might. But she had always believed—or at least, hoped—that her children would be born into a prosperous, comfortable environment at a time when she felt ready, and willing, to care for them. Certainly, the small income consisting of her salary combined with Percy's was insufficient to comfortably support the two of them—let alone the addition of a child. Furthermore, she still harbored dreams of success and a burning ambition. She had never even really wanted to get married! She had succumbed to Percy's charms and persistence. And now, she was pregnant!

Sick and miserable in the early stages of pregnancy, she fell into a state of despair. Above all else, she had yearned to be free, independent, and self-sufficient. And now, carrying Percy's child, she felt tied and responsible both to the baby she carried and to its father. She felt that she had so much to accomplish in this life! Now, she was helpless—a victim—unwillingly responsible for yet another life!

In the midst of her despondency, Percy received an offer to become manager of Alexander's Bespoke Tailoring, a custom-tailoring firm in the small, rural mining town of Mt. Ash. As the salary was higher than he had been thus far receiving in Pontypridd, he could not afford to refuse the offer. And the two were required to leave friends and family and travel north twenty miles to mid-Glamorgan in February 1919—only four months after they had been married.

Both faced the change bravely and optimistically. Yet neither one had anticipated the conditions they found. For Mt. Ash was a small, desolate mining town buried in the Rhondda Valley and unlike any place in which either of them had lived. Although they were determined to make the best of their circumstances, both secretly despised and despaired at the ugliness, the rawness, and provincialism of the town and its inhabitants. Grim and gray, there was nothing much to Mt. Ash save for the few shops and businesses on Oxford Street and a pleasant middle-class residential area not far from the town's center. Upon first seeing the sprawling, charcoal gray structure that was to serve as her home, Katherine could not help but marvel at how closely it compared with her own conception of what a prison must be like.

For a brief time she succumbed to self-pity, bitterly wondering why she had ever married Percy, why God had allowed her to become pregnant, and why she had ever agreed to come to this barren, God-forsaken place. During this period, she felt desperate enough to do almost anything, and was not infrequently tempted to simply run away from her new home. Giving up her position at Gibson's due to the move and dealing with a difficult pregnancy left Katherine feeling acutely bored, irritable, and listless by turns and she longed to turn back the clock to that time when the future had held the promise of fun and excitement and glory! Not since she had been invalided as a child had she felt such loneliness, isolation, and alienation.

In time, however, she grew accustomed to her circumstances. Percy was relatively content in his position at Alexander's; they had been befriended by the pleasant and kindly shop owners in town, and their quarters had been decorated tastefully and cheerfully. In fact, the majority of Katherine's time and energies had been dedicated to the task of making the hideous apartment into a pleasant, tastefully furnished home. Having nothing better to do, Katherine learned many new skills and read many pamphlets about decorating and devoted many hours to painting, plastering, and wall-papering until the factory-like accommodations had been transformed into a cozy, happy place.

It was not until the fifth month of her pregnancy that Katherine became aware of the fact that she actually truly did want the child she had been carrying all this time. Stumbling and falling on the stairway leading upstairs, she had felt a sickening dart of pain in her ribs as she landed, and had instantly feared for the life of the child within her. Dazed and frightened, she found herself praying fervently for the child's well-being, and she had felt the magical response of the child to her prayers. It was as though a deep and powerful bond of love had been established between the two of them, and from henceforth, Katherine carried the child joyfully, eagerly awaiting its birth.

Thus, the remainder of her pregnancy was not a burden. With gratitude and a distinct sense of being blessed, she carried the baby. And Percy had never been happier! No father had more eagerly, enthusiastically awaited the birth of his first child.

As Katherine and Percy gradually grew accustomed to married life, to Mt. Ash, to their new accommodations, and looked forward to the birth of their first child, they received the news from Katherine's mum that her dad had become seriously ill as a result of perforated ulcers whose poisons had burst and spread throughout his body. Currently, he was in the process of recovering from a series of operations that had been performed by the finest surgeons available in the Cardiff community. In fact, he had been in and out of the hospital on four different occasions during the past year. As Gwilym's condition steadily worsened, it was predicted by the attending physicians that he could not possibly live much longer—that he was, in fact, a dying man.

Understandably, poor Elizabeth had found the doctor's prognoses difficult to accept—and with both Gwilym and the children at home to care for—she was literally at her wit's end. It was obvious to Katherine that her mum needed assistance, and she was willing to assist. However, as it would have been awkward to leave Percy and her home at this time, Katherine implored her parents to visit her in Mt. Ash.

Oh, please do come. We should so love to have you here with us. We are so lonely. It would be a privilege to care for Dad. Stay for as long as you like— we've plenty of space. There is, in fact, an empty apartment adjacent to our quarters. Your visit would benefit us all—of this I am certain, Katherine had written. The mere thought of her invalided father made her long to be with him. He had always been especially fond of her and thoroughly enjoyed her calming presence. Perhaps she could help him to recover, to at least ease his pain. Hastening to post the letter at once, she could only hope that her parents would see fit to accept her invitation.

CHAPTER 17

Catherine Sedonia's Appearance

OF ALL HIS CHILDREN, IT was to Katherine to whom Gwilym turned when most in need. It was she with whom he felt the closest—she to whom he could confide his innermost thoughts and feelings without fear of judgment, misunderstanding, or reprisal. Both highly sensitive and intuitive, they were able to communicate on the deepest, most profound levels with little conscious effort or application. Words were seldom necessary or even advantageous, for that matter. Theirs was a system almost telepathic—inevitably potent and virtually infallible. Rarely did they fail to understand one another.

It is no wonder, then, that Gwilym found it expedient to accept Katherine's invitation to remain at Mt. Ash for the duration of his illness, which had been diagnosed as severe digestive disorder and perforated ulcers. He had always derived comfort from his daughter's presence, and he genuinely looked forward to remaining under her gentle care and supervision. Furthermore, he knew that a change of atmosphere would greatly benefit his wife who had grown pale and thin and terribly nervous as his condition had steadily deteriorated. Elizabeth, too, would derive strength and solace from her daughter.

It took only a brief time to resolve matters in Gwaelod-y-garth and to relocate to Mt. Ash. Entrusting their home and babies to the care of Cora, they were free to move. Shortly before leaving the village, Gwilym invested the tiny savings he had managed to accumulate through the years into a small piece of property which he felt certain possessed commercial value and would provide income for Elizabeth once he had passed on.

It was impossible to be unaffected by the changes that had taken place in Gwilym's appearance. The once handsome, animated features were now pitifully plain and inert, as though the life force were gradually being withdrawn from them. The tall lean figure was now withered and bent due to many months of excruciating pain. He seemed to have aged twenty years. All color had left his face, and his skin was a sallow, unpleasant color and almost translucent in texture. Only the expression of his eyes was at all familiar to Katherine, for in them could be detected nobility of character, strength, determination, kindliness, and humor. She knew that while his eyes held such an expression, there was hope that Gwilym had not given up the battle. Fervently, she prayed that her dad would continue to refrain from succumbing to illness or death.

She enjoyed waiting upon her parents, and she knew immediately that the decision to invite them to Mt. Ash had been nothing short of an inspiration; for, just as she had hoped and anticipated, Gwilym seemed to improve in this atmosphere. By the end of his first month in her home, he was far stronger and healthier. Unfortunately, just as all were ready to congratulate themselves upon his improvement, he suffered a relapse. And just as steadily as his health had begun to improve, it now worsened. It was painful to watch the rapid disintegration. It was even more difficult to stand by and watch the suffering—and to feel the helplessness, the frustration of being unable to assist him. If only there was a way—any way—in which to help! In the meantime, Katherine, now entering into the final weeks of pregnancy, was weak and ill and anxious. It had by no means been easy nursing dad, consoling mum, caring for Percy, and maintaining the large household. She was depressed and exhausted, and she could not wait to give birth to the child which it seemed she had been carrying inside her forever.

Thankfully, the child was born even earlier than anticipated. Little Graham Claude Hayward arrived on June 9, 1919. Following a twenty-four-hour labor noteworthy only for its seemingly limitless pain and duration, Katherine experienced the most profound feeling of peace and joy and gratitude she had ever known. For the first time in her adult life, she felt convinced that there must be a God after all. As she held the tiny, exquisite little being to her bosom, tears of thankful acknowledgment and appreciation to the Mighty Power responsible for its existence, streamed unheeded down her face. This child who had been nurtured in her belly was now a separate and complete human being who one day might be a doctor, or magistrate, a tradesman, or perhaps even Prime Minister. Infinite possibilities for success awaited her child—of this she felt certain!

In the midst of the excitement and joy surrounding the child's birth, Gwilym's condition continued to worsen. And as Katherine slowly recovered, much of the responsibility of running the home and business, planning family meals, activities, and get-togethers fell upon the shoulders of Percy and Elizabeth. Percy now working in the shop found most of his time occupied in caring for his home, wife, and new son, while poor Elizabeth was now nursing both her husband and her daughter. Elizabeth's nervous system could hardly stand the strain of looking after Gwilym. Furthermore, she could not endure the thought of continuing to live without her beloved husband. As it became increasingly apparent that Gwilym would not live much longer, Elizabeth became disconsolate, guilt-ridden, fearful, anxious, and remorseful. "If only I had been more patient, more loving, more forgiving," she wailed, irrationally imagining that some failure of hers had been responsible for her husband's illness. With each day that elapsed, she grew more depressed and despondent.

By mid-September, the attending physician was heartily recommending that Elizabeth take a short holiday.

"It is my feeling that your mother will suffer a nervous breakdown if she does not allow herself time away from her husband and this atmosphere. Were I you, I would insist that she go away at once," the doctor advised Katherine.

"Is her condition as serious as all that?" inquired Katherine worriedly.

"Now, it's not worth worrying about. But she does need some time alone—away from this atmosphere and away from all of you."

"I understand," she replied, suddenly struck by the thought that her mother might derive considerable benefit and refreshment from a visit to her sister Della's home in Ynyssia. Now married, Della and her husband George and their newborn son lived in a comfortable home in the nearby town.

"Yes," she reflected aloud, "it's just the place for mum. She'll do well with Della, and I know Della will do everything in her power to ensure her comfort." Upon the insistence of both her physician and her daughter, Elizabeth could no longer refrain from complying. Telephoning Della, she announced her expected arrival in Ynyssia the following weekend. As Katherine had hoped, Della was delighted at the prospect. Elizabeth's luggage was packed, and it was no time before she was prepared for the journey.

During this tense and difficult period, Katherine became increasingly reflective and determined to discover the answers to the questions which had disturbed her since childhood. *Why*, she wondered over and over again. *Why the suffering? the pain? the sorrow? What has Father done to warrant such treatment? He is so kind, gentle and forgiving. And what can Mother have done to have earned so much grief and despair?* And having been informed by at least five local physicians that her dad's death was imminent, she wondered what that term *death* signified—what changes would take place in her dad and would she meet up with him again? It troubled her that Gwilym now seemed to prefer death to the wracking pain he had for so long experienced. *Is he afraid to die?* she could not help but wonder. She herself did not feel afraid of death. *But what is this life all about? Is there some purpose for my— for our—existence?*

She wanted to know Who or What was responsible for this world. Having sensed the existence of an awesome Power or Intelligence since childhood, she now found herself addressing It—with sincerity and humility and with great longing to know the truth. "Give me proof, God, proof of Your presence," she cried aloud with passionate conviction, with an intensity and yearning she had never before experienced. "Reveal Yourself to me. I want to know You. Show me, God, that You exist, and I will serve You faithfully every day for the rest of my life. I suspect that You exist, but let me KNOW this to be so. LET ME KNOW YOU!" she sobbed, from the depth of her being. Never had she been filled with such a deep and powerful yearning—her mind and body literally ached to know the truth. "I want to know You," she declared boldly, passionately, simultaneously trembling inside and out.

Studying her newborn child—so pure and perfect—she could not help but long to know the Power responsible for its existence. "From whither has it come?" she would marvel, awestruck by the infant's tiny perfection, his radiant presence. *He's Love Itself,* she thought, gazing at her son's smiling countenance. *God must be Loving and yet, how can He—why does He—permit such suffering? For what purpose are we here on earth, God? Why am I here? Why? Why? Why?*

It was shortly before Elizabeth's scheduled departure for Ynyssia that Katherine received a most curious response to her persistent questions. This response arrived in a most unusual and unexpected manner. In fact, she could not have been more startled or pleased with the results of her fervent prayers.

At nearly 4:30 a.m. on a Tuesday morning early in October, Katherine was abruptly awakened from a deep sleep by a rustling sound in the room and the strange but very vivid sensation of a Presence—other than she or Percy—nearby. *Am I still asleep?* Katherine wondered, turning over from her stomach onto her back, and opening her eyes. *I don't think I'm dreaming,* she thought to herself. She lay very still for several moments, as she tried to find an explanation for the strange feeling which had come over her. *Something peculiar is happening,* she said to herself. A sudden chill swept over her entire body, and she pulled the blanket up to her chin. She was about to nudge Percy, who was sleeping soundly next to her, but she never got the chance. For suddenly next to her—standing by the side of the bed—was the most exquisitely beautiful child she had ever seen. Katherine gasped, audibly, and her eyes widened. It was obvious that this strange "figure" was in no way ordinary. Not only was she lovely to look at—but she looked vaguely, disturbingly familiar as though Katherine should know her. The girl smiled beatifically, and as if she were fully aware of what Katherine was thinking.

Mesmerized by the mysterious figure, Katherine caught herself. *I must be dreaming*, she thought closing her eyes, and then opening them once again to see if the manifestation had disappeared. But the extraordinary figure was still there, and Katherine noticed that she was radiant, incandescent—shining and pulsating with a glorious light. There was no question that the girl who had appeared before her was magical—her expression was the most serenely beautiful, gentle, and loving Katherine had ever seen. It suddenly occurred to her that the child could not be of the earth—that she was from some other place, some other time. Then, with a gasp and a muffled cry of amazement Katherine suddenly recognized her. Recollecting the portrait that had hung in a prominent position in the foyer of her mum's home ever since she could remember, she realized that it was Catherine Sedonia—the sister who had died in Pennsylvania at the age of seven and for whom she had been named—who now stood before her. The features were unmistakable—the large, luminous eyes with their wonderful expression, rich honey-colored hair and radiant smile—could belong to no one else.

You're Catherine, aren't you? Katherine silently asked the shimmering figure. The figure smiled in response. And although she did not speak, her very appearance suggested the answer to Katherine's persistent query, "Is there life after death?" Katherine now knew, beyond a shadow of a doubt, that life was continuous, and that following the death of the physical body, one continued to exist in a realm far more glorious than that of earth. The girl seemed to understand all of Katherine's thoughts. *I love you. Thank you. Thank you for coming in answer to my prayers*, said Katherine silently. Once again, her sister smiled lovingly in response. And Katherine sensed that as love had brought them together, it would never keep them apart. A powerful bond existed between them that could never be severed.

Now, as Katherine began to think along these lines, she observed that the figure of her sister was completely solid. Every feature was as it had been in the portrait. Her eyes, the texture of her skin, every line and detail of her face indicated that this form was "real" in every sense of the word. *Oh, this must be a figment of my imagination.* She tried to make sense of the extraordinary manifestation. *Oh, if only Percy could see her,* she thought wistfully, wondering if she should make an effort to awaken him before the figure disappeared altogether. It seemed that the figure that had been standing by her side for at least three or four minutes was now dissolving, or evaporating, into the floor. Katherine's mouth fell open and her eyes widened in astonishment as she observed this phenomenon.

As she released a soft sigh, she was startled by sudden movement on Percy's side of the bed. *Oh, thank God, he is awake!* she thought, silently, praying that he would have the opportunity to see the figure which was now dissolving before her very eyes.

"Oh, my God, I thought it was a dream, but it really is here, isn't it?" Percy croaked out hoarsely. "What on earth is it? At first, I thought it was you, but then I realized you were here by my side? Who is that?" he whispered in a frightened voice.

"Catherine Sedonia," replied Katherine. The form smiled in silent acknowledgment and continued to dissolve into the floor. It took only a few more minutes for it to disappear completely. And now, where Catherine Sedonia had stood gracefully, beautifully several minutes before, there was nothing—no sign or trace of her.

"My God," Percy murmured over and over. "My God. Can it really have been your sister?"

"Yes," breathed Katherine. "There is no doubt."

"I've never seen anything like it before in my life," stated Percy, still trembling in fear.

"Nor have I," murmured Katherine delightedly. "Don't you see, Percy?"

"See what?"

"This is the proof which I have been seeking."

"Proof of what?"

"Proof of God's existence. You see, if there is life beyond the grave, it proves that we are immortal, eternal in nature, and that there is a power that sustains and supports life in other spheres beyond this one. There is a God, after all. Life continues beyond the grave, Percy. Don't you see the significance of such a discovery?"

"Perhaps, perhaps," muttered Percy, still far too surprised to really comprehend the long-range ramifications of the visitation they had received this morning.

"We have been greatly blessed by my sister's presence here today," said Katherine seriously. "Do you realize that we have witnessed what others might call a 'miracle'? I shall never forget this experience as long as I live," she said, with unusual gravity.

"I am certain that I shan't forget it!" Percy exclaimed. "Who would ever have thought such a thing possible?"

"Not many," replied Katherine in a serious voice. "And there are too many that would doubt the probability or possibility of such an experience. Therefore, I believe that it would be advisable to speak to no one—not even Mum or Dad—of what has taken place here this morning; agreed?"

"Oh, all right. Agreed," replied Percy, relieved to temporarily dismiss the entire subject. "Well, then," proposed Katherine, "what do you suppose we go back to sleep and discuss the situation in the morning after our breakfast?"

"That's a good idea," said Percy yawning. And surprisingly, despite their excitement, neither had difficulty falling back to asleep.

CHAPTER 18

The Spiritualist Church

ON FRIDAY—ONLY A FEW DAYS after Catherine Sedonia's appearance—Elizabeth left for Ynyssia. Eager to forget her sorrow for even a short while, Elizabeth gratefully responded to the affection and attention of her eldest daughter and family.

"Dr. Roberts was right after all," she sighed to Della on Saturday morning after her arrival. "I haven't felt so relaxed in months."

"That is exactly how we want you to feel—perfectly relaxed, refreshed and—"

"And revitalized," continued George, with a grin and a merry twinkle in his eye. "We want to make a new woman of you, Elizabeth, and we insist that you do absolutely nothing in our home or on these premises but rest. Understood, madam?"

"Understood," replied Elizabeth, with a glimmer of her old spirit and humor.

"Good. Then we shall get along beautifully," teased George. "Now remember, Mother Elizabeth, you are to behave yourself and to do nothing whatever but rest and pretend that you are on a wonderful holiday."

"I shan't have to pretend, George," said Elizabeth gratefully. "But I do want you to know that I am most appreciative of you two taking me in at such short notice."

"Don't be idiotic, Mother. You're always welcome. Now kindly shut up, and take a turn about the garden. It's quite lovely out there, if I do say so myself."

"All right, Della. I believe I will oblige you. The garden must be so colorful this time of year." And Elizabeth obliged her children by strolling in the garden, taking particular delight in inhaling the wonderfully brisk and aromatic autumn air and carefully examining each blossom, leaf, and shrub which grew there. It was not until mid-day Sunday that Elizabeth felt homesick and utterly compelled to return to Mt. Ash—and to her husband's bedside.

"Don't be ridiculous, Mother. Dad is fine. Katherine or Percy would have telephoned otherwise. Now stop worrying, and enjoy yourself. You're here on doctor's orders, don't forget."

I won't, said Elizabeth to herself. *I must stop all this worrying. Silly nonsense. Of course, my Katherine would have notified me if anything were wrong.* Nonetheless, she could not help but miss her husband. It had not been often in their married life that they had been separated for any length of time. In fact, the only time Elizabeth could recall was when Gwilym had left America and attempted to set up a home for her and their children in England. *And that must be some twenty years ago,* thought Elizabeth, her eyes becoming misty.

She was far too restless to remain in the house on Sunday night. The baby was unusually noisy. Furthermore, it had aggravated her to observe Della, George, and their friends playing cards on the Sabbath day, and Elizabeth felt that she had to escape the din. She needed peace and quietude, the opportunity to reflect upon all that had taken place.

"Where is the nearest church?" she inquired of her son-in-law.

"Right down the main road, perhaps a quarter of a mile," replied George. "But surely, Mother, you are not going to leave the house this evening? It's raining cats and dogs outside."

"No, it's not, dear. It's just a soft drizzle now. And I really do feel the need for that kind of comfort," smiled Elizabeth wanly.

"Oh, really, Mother, you can't be serious?" added Della, with a worried expression in her voice.

"Don't worry. I would just like to attend an evening service, sort things out in my mind."

"I understand, Mother," said George softly. "The church isn't far. You'll see it on the right side of the road. In fact, you can't miss it," he smiled.

"Do be careful, Mother," advised Della.

"You sound like me, child. Don't worry. Don't worry at all. I shall return in no time. But do not be alarmed if I am late—I believe that I shall remain for both services, tonight. I am in need of communion with our Creator."

"All right, Mother," replied Della, looking to her husband for guidance, but he did not take note of her. As soon as Elizabeth had carefully dressed for the weather, she was off.

"I do hope she won't get lost," sighed Della to her husband.

"Not a chance, dear," said George easily. "She'll be just fine." And the two returned to the congenial game of whist they had begun earlier that evening.

In the meantime, the intensity of the rain had increased almost as soon as Elizabeth had set foot forward outside. The wind howled eerily, and the sky was fierce and threatening. *Oh, dear*, thought Elizabeth uneasily, *Perhaps I am behaving foolishly. Perhaps I would be better off at home.* But for some reason, she found herself hurrying along the slippery country road in the direction of the church.

Despite the heavy rain, the night air smelled deliciously brisk and fresh, and after several moments, Elizabeth's nervous excitement began to dissolve, and a wonderful feeling of calmness overcame her. An unconscious smile played about her lips as she happily inhaled the vibrant night air. For an instant, she suddenly felt young and happy and carefree again—as though the rain were somehow washing away all concerns and responsibilities. She laughed aloud in release of some of the tension that had been accumulating in her for such a long time. Then she caught herself, *Silly woman. You're behaving like a schoolgirl.* She glanced around furtively to make certain that no one had been present to witness her strange behavior. The rain suddenly began to taper off and soon thereafter the road quickly became wrapped in a thick blanket of fog. She could see almost nothing in front of her. The world seemed remarkably still. *If I don't see the church soon, I believe I'll turn around and head back for home,* she thought to herself, a sudden chill crawling up her spine. She was unaccustomed to walking alone by night. Rarely had she ventured forth after half past six even at home unless accompanied by Gwilym or one of the children or neighbors. *Now why wasn't I sensible enough to listen to Della and George and curl up nice and warm by the fire?* she rebuked herself.

But moments later, she was glad that she had ignored the advice of her daughter and son-in-law. For before her eyes there loomed a light—several lights—and the simple, homey stone structure she recognized as the church that Della had described to her. *Thank Goodness, I found it!* she sighed in relief, shaking the wetness from her coat and bonnet, and stamping her boots dry before entering the building. She did not catch the name of the church. Although a placard had been placed on the front lawn in plain view, it had been far too dark and misty for Elizabeth to notice it. Frankly, she had been too preoccupied with her own doubts and apprehensions to pay much notice to her surroundings. She only knew that the church was small and pleasant, and that the congregation was very small by city standards. There were, perhaps, only twenty others who sat beside her in the oak pews.

Now, despite her doubts and reservations, she was genuinely happy that she had come. She felt a congenial and soothing warmth come over her, as soon as she was settled in her seat, and she listened to the minister's sermon with a sense of pleasant anticipation. A regular churchgoer in Gwaelod-y-garth, Elizabeth was rather surprised but not disturbed by the content of the minister's sermon, for he devoted an unusually long period of time to a discussion of life after death and communication between the spheres. But, frankly, Elizabeth was still too preoccupied with her own personal difficulties to try to interpret the significance of everything that the minister said. She only knew that she had not felt so peaceful in a very long time, and that he seemed to answer many of the questions that had been plaguing her for months.

Following his talk and a brief interval, the minister announced that he was now ready to deliver messages to members of the congregation from departed friends or loved ones. *What on earth does he mean?*

wondered Elizabeth, trying to make sense of his words. She had never heard a minister speak in this manner before. *There is something very unusual about this place*, she observed. Heretofore she had been unable to accurately pinpoint the difference between this church and the Independent Congregational at home. It was only when the minister began to convey "messages" that she began to recognize that she had never seen or experienced anything like this before. The congregation was advised to sing several hymns and Elizabeth sang loudly and optimistically, *Bringing in the Sheaves*. She had always derived enormous comfort from song.

After a brief silence, the minister spoke. "I am looking for an Elizabeth Coleman. Are you here, Elizabeth?"

She could hardly believe her ears. Surely he could not mean her! How could he possibly have known that she was in the congregation? Why she was a total stranger! And how had he discovered her maiden name?

"I am informed that you are in the back of the room. If you are here, please raise your hand, Elizabeth," the minister continued.

Elizabeth waved her hand and nodded. "I am here," she replied in a surprised voice.

"Thank you," he said politely. "Would you like me to speak with you this evening?"

Despite the fierce pounding of her heart, Elizabeth found herself nodding in answer to his question. "Yes, I would," she finally murmured shyly. There was a moment or two of silence, and Elizabeth shifted uncomfortably in her seat, painfully aware that the eyes of the entire congregation were now upon her.

"My dear Elizabeth," the minister began. "Here with us this evening are your father, James, and your mother, Catherine Coleman." Elizabeth gasped at this statement, but the minister continued unperturbed.

"Your mother tells me that she was known as the angel of the village in which she resided, for she nursed, assisted, and brought comfort to the sick and needy."

"Yes, that is so exactly," murmured Elizabeth, hardly daring to breathe.

"Your father informs me that he was a minister of the Wesleyan Church in Blackwoods, South Wales, and that there is a plaque dedicated to him in the lobby of the building."

"Yes, yes!" cried Elizabeth excitedly. "That is exactly so!"

"Good," said the minister with a pleasant smile, as though he thoroughly understood Elizabeth's reaction. "Your mother and father have a most urgent message to convey to you this evening. But first they wish me to tell you a little about Spiritualism."

"About what?" Elizabeth asked nervously. She had heard of Spiritualism before, but it had only been spoken of in hushed tones, and she knew that no decent, God-fearing Christian should have anything to do with it.

"I'm afraid I don't quite understand," she stammered. "What has Spiritualism to do with all this?" Several members of the audience turned their heads in her direction, while others laughed at her response.

"My dear, Spiritualism has everything to do with 'all this.' You see, this is a Spiritualist Church, and we are a Spiritualist congregation," answered the minister in a kindly voice, his eyes twinkling.

"No, that's not possible. My daughter, Della, would never have advised me to attend a Spiritualist Church," Elizabeth protested.

"Nevertheless," continued the minister, "that is precisely where you are. And may I offer these words of advice, madam? There are no mistakes. It was in the Divine Pattern that you come here this evening. Please calm yourself, and hear the message your parents wish to impart to you though me. And let me say firstly, that you have nothing to fear."

Elizabeth smiled weakly, far too flustered and surprised to protest any further.

"Spiritualism is a science, philosophy, and religion of continuous life, based upon the demonstrated fact of communication, by means of mediumship, with those who live in the Spirit World. I, as a medium, act as an intermediary for communications between the material world and the spirit world. As you may have already guessed, I am capable of making contact with discarnate and other nonhuman entities. You see, madam, there is no death. Life continues on the other side.

"Those who are dead (so-called) have merely discarded their physical bodies as a snake sheds its skin or as you might discard your overcoat. They then enter into an entirely different sphere of life to which we refer as the 'Astral World.' Death is not the end. Rather, it is a beginning. It is a new birth into a spiritual body, wherein the individuality, the essential character and nature of each being, is preserved, without impairment of memory. Unfortunately, I do not have the time now to discuss our philosophy in more depth. Suffice it to say, that I am in communication with your deceased parents, and they wish you to know the following: Firstly, they wish to assure you that they are far more alive than you are at the present time or than they were while existing in a physical body. Secondly, and most importantly, they want you to know that your husband, Gwilym, who is expected to leave the body at any moment, will not die. He will recover from his present illness and remain in the body for many more years. There is much work yet for him to do. Upon the conclusion of your short holiday in our community, you will return to your daughter's home. Not far—only a block or two away—from her house you will discover a small schoolhouse that now serves as a Spiritualist Church. Here, you will find the medium who will direct you to a healer who will assume responsibility for saving your dear husband's life. This healer will appear to be a humble person, of low origin and little education and no breeding, but you will quickly discover his true nature and witness the miracles he is able to achieve. I reiterate, despite all evidence to the contrary, your husband will survive.

"Furthermore, following his illness, your husband will begin the work for which he has come to earth. He will heal—assuage the pain and suffering— of countless human beings. I am delighted to tell you that you too, madam, have the healing gift, and shall not only assist your husband but work alongside him. In the meantime, it would be advisable to return to your husband and locate the healer as soon as possible. God bless you, my dear. God keep you and your loved ones in Peace. That is all."

Elizabeth was numb. It seemed as though her heart had stopped beating and her mind was frighteningly still. Never had she heard anything like this before! Far more disturbing than the minister's words, however, was the distinct awareness that her deceased father and mother were nearby. In fact, although she might not have been able to prove or explain it to anyone else, she had felt them there—right by her side.

I swear, she thought to herself, *that Mum patted me on the back of my head—like she used to in the old days. Who will ever believe such a thing has occurred? What will Gwilym say about all this? And Katherine will surely think the whole thing preposterous—and her mother a lunatic! Oh well, it can't be helped. I shall have to tell them at home.*

Her mind darted from subject to subject for the remainder of the minister's demonstration. *How did he do it? How did he know? Had Mum and Dad really spoken through him, or had he somehow made it all up? It must be a hoax, a subtle form of deception,* she concluded—then remembered that the minister could not possibly have known that her mother was called angel of the village, or that Gwilym was dying, through chicanery of any sort. Shuddering in fear of the unknown, she could not help but feel that the minister's message had not only been valid and truthful but the result of a sincere attempt on the part of her parents to let her know that they were still very much alive. *Ah, well, I'll leave this matter to God,* she decided. *I'll seek His guidance, and then I will know just what to make of all that the minister has said to me this evening.*

Over and over again his words echoed in her mind despite her efforts to dismiss them: "Your husband Gwilym, who is expected to die at any moment, will not die. He will recover and remain in the body for many more years." *Is it possible?* she wondered, tears suddenly filling her eyes, as the promise of hope grew stronger. *Is it truly possible, Lord, that my Gwilym will be spared—that he will remain with me awhile longer? If you spare him, God, I will never stop thanking you.*

Somehow managing to collect herself enough to shake the minister's hand and thank him for the message at the end of the service, she left the church still in a daze. She hardly noticed that the fog had cleared and that the air was now fresh and clear. It was only by chance that she happened to look up, and under the gentle illumination of a gas lantern, notice the sign that bore the name of the building from which she had, just departed.

"Ynyssia Christian Spiritualist Church." she read aloud in amazement. Then, chuckling in amusement, she wondered how it had come to pass that she, a Wesleyan from birth, had stumbled into such a place. She was certain that the church that Della had described must be somewhere farther along the same road. Still marveling at the unusual turn the evening had taken, she hurried toward Della's home along the same pathway she had followed earlier.

Elizabeth decided to reveal nothing of her experience to Della and George. It was to Della's great astonishment, then, that her mother's bags were packed and her mother ready to return to Mt. Ash the following morning.

"You can't be serious. Why, you've only just arrived!" Della protested. "What is going on, Mother?" she inquired suspiciously.

"Nothing at all, my dear. Only I feel absolutely certain that I have achieved all that I set out to accomplish here. I feel wonderful, and I wish to return home to your father. It's as simple as that!"

"Is it?" Della wondered aloud. Her mother's face was flushed with excitement, and her eyes were unusually bright. *She's up to something*, Della thought to herself, but knew her mother far too well to pry. She knew that if her mother did not wish to share her secret, no one could extract it from her.

"All right, Mother," Della sighed. "George will drive you to the railway station."

"Thank you, my love. And don't worry. All is well. I promise you," said Elizabeth, after she had embraced her eldest daughter. "I'll telephone you later on to let you know that I've arrived safely." And within the hour, she was on her way back to Mt. Ash.

CHAPTER 19

The Healer

IT HAD NOT BEEN ANYWHERE near as difficult as she had anticipated to describe all that had taken place the previous evening to her husband and daughter. Not for a moment had she imagined that they would be receptive to such ideas. Ironically, during her absence, Gwilym had received a book by Spiritualist Stainton Moses as a gift from one of his former business associates and had read it from cover to cover. And, unbeknownst to Elizabeth, Katherine and Percy had recently seen Catherine Sedonia materialize in their bedroom.

All three felt it advisable to locate the healer of which the minister in Ynyssia had spoken. Although suspicious, even dubious, of the message conveyed to Elizabeth, each felt that there was nothing to lose and everything to gain by adhering to the minister's advice. The first words of hope they had received in months, each felt profound joy and relief that such an opportunity had arisen—that there might be hope after all.

"If it's the work of the Devil himself, let's have it! I don't care!" Katherine cried out boldly, with feeling. "I'm all for trying anything that might help save Dad's life. Go on, mum, find the healer. I'll do everything in my power to help. You know I will!" she said passionately. She could not endure her dad's suffering a single moment longer. It had been agonizing to witness the daily struggle for life, the battle against excruciating pain, and to see the once virile face so sadly altered, the once active body so weak and wasted, the fertile, powerful mind so dull and unresponsive.

Elizabeth had returned to Mt. Ash early Monday afternoon. Early Tuesday morning, she and Katherine, with baby Graham, set out to find the healer. Just as he had indicated, there was indeed a Spiritualist Society that met in a schoolhouse only one and one half blocks away from Katherine's home. Amazingly, they had experienced no difficulty whatever in locating it. An elderly woman with a knot of thick gray hair, large features and a deep, masculine voice advised them to return that evening. "We're having a public meeting tonight at half past seven sharp. I believe that you will be able to acquire whatever information you are seeking at that time. Do come," she smiled encouragingly,

Although they had hoped to acquire their information without attending such a meeting, they found themselves with no alternative but to accept the woman's invitation. Having informed no one but Gwilym as to their intended destination, the two found their way to the classroom in which the prayer meeting was to be held. Sincerely hoping that none of their friends or acquaintances had observed them entering such a place, they discreetly chose seats in the back, hardly daring to make contact with anyone else in the congregation lest they mistakenly be construed as "Spiritualists." Noticing that the majority of the twenty-five or so members were poorly dressed and obviously of the lower class, Katherine wondered why on earth she had agreed to come. She knew that she and her mother were the objects of considerable attention and speculation among those seated nearby, for they were by far the most sophisticated and well-groomed people there. She had no further time for reflection, however, for almost as soon as they had been seated, the minister of the church assumed his position behind the podium at the front of the room and began to speak. With neither poise nor polish to recommend him, he and his sermon were of little interest to Katherine, and she began once again to regret the decision to come.

Her heart sank as she viewed the bleak little room and those around her. *Poor illiterate blokes*, she thought to herself, studying the intense, eager faces. *I guess they don't know any better than to come to a place like this.*

"Come on, Mum," she whispered suddenly. "Let's get out of here. I think we're wasting our time. I think we've made a mistake."

"I don't, let's stay," was all Elizabeth said firmly, her statement accompanied by a perfunctory grin.

"Oh, all right," mumbled Katherine, still uncertain as to why she had ever been silly enough to agree to come here. At this juncture, the minister concluded his address and introduced a guest speaker: a well-known medium who would demonstrate her gifts of clairvoyance to the congregation.

For an instant, Katherine was reminded of her experience with Mrs. Dunham so many years ago, and she listened intently to the medium's prophesies and predictions. The woman was articulate, and Katherine could not help but be impressed by the obvious accuracy of the information imparted by her to various members of the congregation. *They can't be faking it*, she thought to herself, as each one to whom she spoke corroborated the data conveyed by the medium. *Obviously what she is saying is of value to them.* For over half an hour, Katherine listened to the medium. Judging from the enthusiastic reception of the congregation to her words, Katherine saw that the medium was remarkably accurate. Not expecting the medium to address herself or her mum, she glanced at her mum and was about to nudge her and advise her once again to leave the place when she heard the medium's rich, contralto voice address her. She froze in her seat and felt her cheeks turn crimson.

"You, my dear. May I speak with you this evening?" Miserably, Katherine nodded.

"Good," said the woman. "Let me begin by saying that I know that you are uncomfortable in—even disgusted by—these surroundings," she began, and Katherine gasped audibly. "You feel that you are out of place, that you do not belong here," the woman continued. "But there you are wrong, my dear. For you do indeed belong here, among us."

She smiled sympathetically in response to Katherine's stunned expression. "Although you think that you have come here tonight for the express purpose of acquiring the name and address of the healer who will save your father's life, there is another very important purpose for which you have come, and this is to receive information regarding your own future. Are you following what I am saying?" Katherine nodded, amazed by the woman's words.

The medium continued, "You, my dear, will one day soon, be doing precisely what I am doing at this moment—demonstrating to others through your own gifts of healing and clairvoyance that there is no death, that life is continuous, and that communication takes place between those who are so-called dead and those who exist in the physical body. Throughout the remainder of your life—and you will live unto a ripe, old age—you will be deeply involved, in fact, dedicated to, this work. You will travel all over the earth—to every corner of the globe to dispense that information that will soon be at your disposal. To whomever is willing and receptive, you will teach that life is continuous; that all life is energy existing at different rates of vibration and on many different levels simultaneously; that all life is One Life; and that All Things Are Possible."

"You are wrong. I will never be a medium," Katherine could not help but blurt out.

But the woman smiled knowingly and said, "That is exactly how I responded upon receiving such information." She continued, unperturbed, "The healer whose name and address I shall divulge to you this evening will be a great teacher for you and your family. Through him, you will discover the true purpose for which you have come to the earth. Know that all your father has suffered has been both purposeful and worthwhile. If for no other reason, his illness has been responsible for your presence here this evening. Both you and your father have the potential whereby you will be able to serve, heal, and enlighten your fellow human beings. Your father will soon recover from his illness and begin to heal others. If you and your mother will see me privately after this meeting, I shall be delighted to provide you with the name and address of the healer you are seeking, the man who will assume responsibility for your father's recovery. May God's blessing be upon you and sustain you always!"

Katherine sat in silence for several minutes, too stunned either to speak or to move. Although the message had seemed improbable—indeed impossible—she somehow, inexplicitly felt on a very deep level that the medium's words were true. *I will be doing what she does. Dad is going to recover. The healer will be a great teacher to me and my family.* She was overwhelmed by the enormity of the message. *How could this woman—a total stranger— have known so much? Been the purveyor of such intimate knowledge?* Glancing at her mother, she saw that Elizabeth was equally surprised and moved by the communication. Carefully reviewing the message throughout the remainder of the meeting, Katherine could not help but feel that an important contact had been met, that it had been her "destiny" to come here this evening.

Immediately following the meeting, they acquired from the medium the name and address of the Spiritualist healer who was to save Gwilym's life. His name was Mr. Fletcher. Thanking the woman profusely, they took their leave and headed for home on foot. Each was uncharacteristically silent. Both were lost in thought. How peculiar life was and what an interesting turn it had taken recently! Both had difficulty accepting all that had taken place. Yet neither was willing to negate or ignore the unusual events that had transpired. With all their hearts and souls, they prayed that Gwilym's life would be spared—that the medium would prove correct in her prophesies. They continued in silence until they arrived home.

Perhaps this Mr. Fletcher is capable of performing miracles. God knows that a miracle is precisely what Dad needs—what we all need, thought Katherine ruefully. *Well, I suppose only time will tell,* she mused. *But, in the meantime, I believe that I shall accept the medium's advice and adhere to the concept that "all things are possible." I rather like that!* Somehow, it was surprisingly easy to adopt this viewpoint. And, henceforth, Katherine, knowing that it would require a miracle to save her father's life, began to expect one. Furthermore, she could not help but hope and pray that this "miracle" would manifest in the form of the Spiritualist healer known as Mr. Fletcher.

CHAPTER 20

The Visit of Mr. Fletcher

ᖇ

KATHERINE AND ELIZABETH HAD WASTED no time in contacting the healer. Early Tuesday morning, with the instructions they had received the previous evening in hand, the two found their way on foot to the small, thatched cottage that belonged to Mr. Fletcher. Still fearful of being discovered by any of their friends at the home of a "Spiritualist," Katherine and her mother traveled by back roads and side streets, and upon arriving at his home, behaved as discreetly as they knew how. Still, they felt terribly awkward and self-conscious.

"I do hope that we aren't making a grave mistake," murmured Elizabeth before ringing the front bell.

"Nonsense!" replied Katherine, with far more bravado than she felt.

To their disappointment, however, no one seemed to be at home, and they were forced to leave a short note explaining their circumstances and the purpose for which they had paid such a call.

If you are willing and able to be of assistance to my dad, Katherine had written, *please call upon us at our home this evening at half past seven and arrive at our back door.* The note continued to include her telephone number and street address. They concluded their visit and returned home.

At half past seven on the dot, Mr. Fletcher was at the back door. With a mixture of guilt and shame, Katherine recalled that she had explicitly advised the healer to employ the back entrance of her home. Again, she saw no purpose in allowing any of her neighbors to know that she was cohorting with "Spiritualists." It was with relief that she observed that Mr. Fletcher had not taken notice of her rude behavior. There was an ethereal quality about him, and an attitude that seemed to suggest that he had risen "above" all pettiness, artifice, and class distinction. Katherine sensed that all of this man's passion, all personal ambition, and desire had been, at enormous personal expense, transmuted into something far greater, whereby he was able to serve without personal motive or for personal aggrandizement. *That's it!* she thought to herself. *He is selfless, entirely without the desire for personal gain.* She was overwhelmed. Never before had she met anyone of this mettle!

Any doubts or fears that Katherine may have had concerning Mr. Fletcher's ability to heal her father were dispelled immediately upon meeting him. It was obvious that, despite his humble background and lack of formal education, he was a very special human being. In fact, she had never known anyone like him. Modest and unassuming, he emanated love and gentle wisdom. There was something delightfully warm and engaging about his manner, as though he regarded life itself as a means toward an end—a temporary playmate with whom he did not wish to become too seriously involved. His lovely blue eyes shone with spiritual light and good humor, and Katherine thought that she had never met anyone so serene and truly content. He seemed to radiate peace and goodwill. His Welsh accent was soft and pleasant to the ear, and he spoke with sincerity and an eloquence and refinement that belied his station in life. One could not help but succumb to his simple charm.

To her surprise, Mr. Fletcher had not wished to know anything but the most sketchy information about her dad's illness. Without much ado, he asked to be taken to Gwilym's room at once. As Katherine escorted him up the stairs, she saw that he was absorbed in thought. *A most unusual man,* she thought to herself.

"Here we are," she said aloud in a cheerful voice, pointing to a pleasant-looking room with plenty of windows and lacy white curtains. Here, her dad lay writhing in agony upon the bed. She saw the expression in her father's eyes change as he gazed upon Mr. Fletcher's remarkable countenance, and Katherine knew at once that her dad was going to live after all.

Suppressing a cry of joy, Katherine watched intently as Mr. Fletcher approached Gwilym's bedside and took the "dying" man's hand in his own. He held Gwilym's hand for several minutes, closed his eyes, and uttered a brief prayer, "Dear Lord, let Thy Blessing be upon this man and family. Let Thy will, oh God, be done."

He remained silent for several moments, then issued to his patient the following injunction, "You must take no more medication. The drugs that have been prescribed can only postpone your recovery." Gazing directly into Gwilym's eyes, he was pleased to discover the courage and humor that lay behind them.

"I will do as you say," Gwilym croaked out in a weak voice. But there was a smile upon his lips. It was obvious that he trusted Mr. Fletcher implicitly. Elizabeth had gasped audibly upon hearing the healer's order to discontinue all medication, for she knew that the drugs helped to reduce what she knew to be excruciating physical pain. Yet, for no logical reason, she too trusted the healer and felt certain that Gwilym would respond to his influence.

"Please turn over on your stomach now," the healer advised Gwilym. Slowly, attempting to conceal the pain inherent in such movement, the patient complied. "Are you comfortable?" the healer inquired.

Gwilym's head bobbed automatically in response. Mr. Fletcher then washed his hands in the wash basin and, after removal of Gwilym's shirt, he began to massage Gwilym's spine. Beginning to the right of the spinal column, Mr. Fletcher made small circular movements with his fingers in a clockwise direction. Slowly at first, but with remarkable dexterity and increasing rapidity, his fingers traveled up and down Gwilym's spinal column. From the neck to the waist, the healer's hands gently massaged the entire back in a systematic fashion. At frequent intervals, he would remove his hands from Gwilym's body—as though they had absorbed as much sickness as possible—and shake them in mid-air as though he were shaking from them all the sickness they had absorbed just as one might shake out a dirty rug or towel, and then resume the pattern of massage.

Mr. Fletcher's hands were exquisite. They appeared to Katherine to be specially designed instruments through which healing could take place. There was something exhilarating, fulfilling about watching those hands in motion. Although she lacked the vocabulary to describe all that was taking place, she sensed that Mr. Fletcher drew his powers from a Source with which she herself was unfamiliar.

After turning Gwilym over and applying the same technique of massage to the front of his body, he opened all the windows in the room and allowed the fresh evening air to circulate freely. Extracting a white serviette from the small brief case he had brought with him, he held it facing the center of the room, then began to swing it back and forth and, finally, rhythmically into a circular pattern—first around Gwilym alone, then around all four of them—Gwilym, Elizabeth, Katherine, and Percy. His movements were slow and gentle initially, but within several minutes, they were rapid and vigorous.

Katherine was fascinated by the healer's movements. She had never seen anything like this before. She was aware that subtle changes had taken place in all of them from the moment Mr. Fletcher had set foot into her home. For one thing, Katherine had begun to feel better immediately. Secondly, the atmosphere in the entire house, but in Gwilym's room in particular, had altered dramatically. It was as though someone had suddenly turned on all the lights in the house at once. And although a brilliant golden light suffused the entire bedroom enfolding each of them, the area including and surrounding Gwilym's bed was literally flooded with light. Closing her eyes, Katherine felt exactly as though she were standing in the mid-afternoon sunlight. A glorious feeling of peacefulness pervaded the entire household, and Katherine could not help but sense the Presence of some unknown Power. Amazingly, no one was the least bit frightened or suspicious of the phenomena. All tension, all frustration and hostility seemed to dissolve in this atmosphere.

When, finally, Mr. Fletcher seemed to have completed all he set out to achieve in what was determined to be the first of many sessions he would hold with Gwilym, he turned and addressed the foursome "All life consists of energy operating at different rates of vibration. The rate at which a particular thing vibrates determines the level at which it operates and the form that it assumes. Throughout our subsequent meetings, you will witness much that will amaze you, much that is inexplicable in terms of the limited consciousness, information, and awareness you possess at the present time. Yet, in time, you will be able to perceive far more than meets the physical human eye. You will receive explanations for much that has puzzled you throughout your lives. Therefore, refrain from making judgments or drawing conclusions about anything you have witnessed or experienced this evening or that you will experience during our subsequent meetings. Remain receptive. Keep an open mind, and remember that as it is said in the Bible, 'All things are possible.'" And, with these words accompanied by a brisk smile, he picked up his brief case and strode toward the door.

Hastily recovering her composure, for she had been deeply moved by all that had taken place, Katherine returned his smile and said softly, with deep meaning, "Thank you, Mr. Fletcher. I know that I speak for all of us when I say thank you. And now, if you are ready to leave, I shall be delighted to escort you to the front door."

Words could not capture the surprise, joy, elation, and feeling of well-being that each one had experienced in conjunction with the visit of Mr. Fletcher. Although he had been among them for little more than an hour, there could be no denying, no ignoring the influence of this gentle, great-hearted man. One had but to look at the change in Gwilym's appearance in order to determine how extensive was the power of which Mr. Fletcher was in possession. *What is the nature of this power?* Katherine wondered. *From what source—in what manner—has he acquired the gift of healing, the gift of peace?* She continued to puzzle over these and countless other questions during the coming days.

With each subsequent interaction with the healer, the Davies grew increasingly comfortable and familiar with his manner and the techniques he employed. However mysterious or unconventional his methods might appear, no one could negate their efficacy. In fact, within four days, a total transformation had taken place in Gwilym. His eyes had lost their dullness and listlessness and acquired an animated expression and a sparkle delightful to behold. His face had acquired a fresh, rosy color that was in marked contrast to the pallor and waxen quality that had characterized his appearance for months. And his body acquired a strength and vitality it had not displayed in years. For those who had witnessed on a daily basis Gwilym's steady deterioration, the swift recovery was nothing short of miraculous, particularly in light of the fact that the countless physicians and other members of the medical profession who had attended upon him during the past several months had assured them that Gwilym's death was forthcoming and inevitable.

Mr. Fletcher continued to call upon Gwilym daily for nearly two weeks. During each of their meetings, he repeated the procedure that he had employed initially—beginning with prayer, continuing with massage over the spine and then over the entire body, removing the negativity and shaking the illness from his hands, and circulating the serviette in a clockwise motion, which, he declared, helped to cleanse the atmosphere and elevate the vibration of energy in the room. Sensing their genuine interest and curiosity, Mr. Fletcher made no effort to keep his methods a secret. On the contrary, he seemed to derive considerable satisfaction from sharing that information from which he felt certain they would benefit.

"Most illnesses," stated Mr. Fletcher, in his gentle voice, "spring from maladies of the mind and disharmonies of the soul. They are, in other words, the products of disease, disquiet, sadness, fear, and frustration. Man's thoughts and words reflect this disease and this disharmony. Man's thoughts are very powerful—and are, to a great degree, responsible for the circumstances in which he finds himself. He generally thinks ill—of others and himself—before he finds himself ill physically. Man is very much the product of his habitual thought patterns. He must constantly train himself to look above the dark things of life and to rise above destructive thoughts and depressed feelings and to think positively, and hopefully. He must first think good health in order to experience it.

"Why, that is precisely what Mr. Mesmer taught," Katherine recalled excitedly, finding much of what Mr. Fletcher believed familiar and easy to accept.

Far more than any verbal message conveyed by the healer, however, Katherine was impressed by the extraordinary healing abilities he demonstrated with such apparent ease and seeming effortlessness. To their amazement, she and the others had been able literally to perceive—in the form of a radiant white light—the energy that literally flowed from the healer into the patient like a current of electricity. They had never seen anything like it before! This energy—with its accompanying peace, power, and uplifting—offered indisputable proof to each one involved in the dramatic experiment of the existence of a benevolent Power far greater than any human being.

It was not until after he had administered Gwilym's final healing treatment that Mr. Fletcher provided them with the information for which they had wholeheartedly yearned from the moment that he had entered their lives. "Anyone who truly loves and longs to serve his fellow human beings has the ability to heal," he told them. "Who has not heard of the remarkable healings, the miracles that have taken place as a result of one's love of God or as a result of the love of one human being for another? Love is the greatest power on earth—indeed, throughout the cosmos. But it is not this subject of which I wish to speak to you at the present time. Rather, I would like you to know, that from here on Gwilym's recovery is in your hands. I have achieved all that is in my power to accomplish. Through your love of him, through your sincere desire to see him happy and healthy, you will be able to complete the healing process which I have initiated. It gives me great pleasure—indeed, it is a great privilege—to inform each of you that you are endowed with the ability to heal. It may come as a surprise to you, but your abilities are far greater than my own."

It was at this juncture that Katherine gasped audibly in disbelief. But Mr. Fletcher only smiled and continued to deliver the message that he obviously felt compelled to impart. "Each one of you is mediumistic—meaning that your psychic senses are so acute that they register the presence of beings belonging to the nonphysical world. You are able to interpret the wishes and information that such beings desire to impart to people still in the body in this physical world. With training, you will be able to efficiently manifest these gifts."

"What gifts do we have?" interrupted Katherine. "And how shall we go about 'developing them'?"

"Already your Spirit Guides and teachers are awaiting the opportunity to instruct you as to how to proceed henceforth. They recommend that all four—you, your husband, mother, and father—sit together as soon as Gwilym has recovered sufficiently to do so comfortably, of course, and attune to them."

"What does that mean?" inquired Katherine suspiciously.

Again Mr. Fletcher smiled understandingly, "You must elevate your thoughts from the mundane vibration of the physical world to the higher vibration of the spiritual realms beyond the earth. You may attune to the Higher Intelligences through prayer, song, aspiration, and meditation or contemplation of the Divine Life. By elevating your own thoughts, you enable the process of communication to take place between you and those in the realms beyond this one. Those in spirit must lower their rate of vibration as you raise yours in order for communication between the spheres to take place."

"What are Spirit Guides?" Elizabeth asked haltingly, as though ashamed of her ignorance.

"The guides and teachers of whom I speak are those beings who no longer inhabit the physical body of earth, who have progressed onward into the spiritual spheres of life in which a physical body is no longer necessary, and who have advanced—who are sufficiently enlightened—to be able to share with those on earth who are receptive the wisdom and understanding of Life which they have acquired. Although they have lived on the earth at one time or another, they have experienced the transition known as death and continue to exist on an altogether different plane of existence—one of a much higher vibration. Many of these guides and teachers have spent previous lifetimes working with you in a similar capacity and are familiar, therefore, with the purpose for which you have taken on a physical body in this present incarnation. Your own physical bodies are highly sensitive instruments—able to receive and perceive the communications transmitted from worlds beyond. This ability to serve as a medium or 'channel' between the spheres is both a blessing and a responsibility, and it is hoped that you will employ this blessing for the benefit of others. I realize that much that I have said to you today may be difficult for you either to grasp or to believe. Yet, in time, you will fully comprehend and embrace all that I have shared with you. Of this, I have no doubt.

"It is sufficient for you to be aware at the present time that your teachers are requesting that you sit together as a group for the dual purpose of communicating with them and for developing your own mediumistic abilities. You are advised to approach such potential communication with sincerity, humility, and high endeavor. Before each such effort, you must place yourselves into God's keeping, for there is potential danger to those who are not of noble mind or purpose, and approach such communications for personal gain or self-aggrandizement. You are further advised that under no circumstances must you attempt such communications whilst you are under the influence of drug or alcohol. Your minds—and bodies—must be kept clean and pure—for these are the instruments employed by the Spirit Beings, and like attracts like.

"Hold your development circle in a clean, quiet place. Seek Divine Guidance, make sure that you are wearing loose, comfortable clothing, sing a hymn or two, and sit in subdued lighting so that you are able to relax easily. Meditate—concentrate your thoughts upon God. And then, wait for results. Your efforts will be rewarded. Communications will take place, but it is essential that you are patient. Neither you nor your Spirit Guides can hasten the process. You may perceive no results for weeks—possibly, even months. Yet you must be diligent, patient, consistent in your efforts. Do not lose heart. Your teachers are anxiously awaiting the opportunity to work together with you.

"And now, I believe that I have accomplished the purpose for which I have stepped into your lives. It is now time to step out. I am delighted to have been the purveyor of such happy tidings. I am given to understand that all further questions you may have will be answered at a later date by those who are far more knowledgeable than I and better equipped to respond. In gratitude to you all, and with best wishes, I bid you all farewell."

"Am I correct in assuming that we shall not see you anymore? That you will not treat my father ever again?" Katherine blurted out, upset and disappointed by the thought.

"You are correct, my dear," he replied kindly but firmly. "You see, my work here is finished, and your own is just beginning. I can do no more. There is no further need of my services."

Despite his words, Katherine could not help but feel sad. He had seemed the source of so much significant information, and she had hoped that he would address the issues and respond to the questions that had puzzled her since early childhood. *Apparently, that is not to be,* she thought wistfully.

"Will you accept payment for your services?" inquired Gwilym gently, anxious to express his gratitude in a tangible form. But the healer was adamant in his refusal.

"Absolutely not," he insisted. "I cannot possibly accept payment for what is God's work. My reward is the joy and gratitude written upon your faces. How grateful, indeed how privileged I am to have awakened each of you to your own Potential—to have helped you to become receptive to the great Spiritual Force that will manifest Its Love, Its Wisdom, and Power through you—its "channels" or "conduits"—from henceforth. May God bless each of you always. You may greatly help your fellow human beings. There is great work for you to do."

For an instant, there was a faraway expression in his eyes, as though he were seeing into the future. Before they had the opportunity to react to his words or to ask any further questions, he seemed to vanish into thin air. They were too stunned to attempt to follow him, to try to escort him out of their home. In fact, it was several minutes before any of them was able to speak. And when Katherine finally did recover her senses sufficiently to talk, all she could say was, "Well, have you ever seen anything like it before?" The others could only shake their heads in wonderment.

As Mr. Fletcher had indicated, he conducted no further healing for Gwilym and the Davies never saw him again. Having completed his "assignment," it was obvious that no further contact was necessary. He had been proven correct almost immediately in his analysis that he was no longer needed and that Katherine, Percy, and Elizabeth would complete the healing process that he had initiated. For Gwilym's health continued to improve, and he seemed to grow stronger and healthier every day. Within a week after Mr. Fletcher's departure, Gwilym was sitting up in bed; within two weeks he was walking around the bedroom. What is more, a silence, a glorious peacefulness had settled over the household to which each responded with gratitude and joy.

The influence of Mr. Fletcher upon their lives was profound. They had been transformed by their brief association with this kindly, humble man through whom miracles were accomplished. He had made them aware—both directly and indirectly—of the existence of a great and Holy Presence for Whom miracles were nothing more than child's play. They had been in contact—in communion—with this Presence ever since Mr. Fletcher's arrival. They had experienced the Love, the Elation, the Electricity emanating from this Power. They had felt the atmosphere of Gwilym's room and the house as a whole change completely, had seen the energy, and felt the heat pour forth from Mr. Fletcher's healing hands; had seen Gwilym's mind and body transformed; had experienced the disappearance of their worries; and had felt minor aches and pains dissolve under the influence of the Power that worked through Mr. Fletcher.

Although they had formerly suspected the existence of such a Presence, they were now assured of its existence. They did not know in what way this Presence operated, nor were they aware of its true nature or origin. They were only gratefully aware that it had been responsible for saving Gwilym's life. It was with great excitement and curiosity that they anticipated that time when they would receive information that would enhance their understanding and satisfy their already insatiable curiosity.

In retrospect, it seemed that Mr. Fletcher had only whetted their intellectual and spiritual appetites. He had said so very much of importance, but so much of what he had said seemed startling and incomprehensible at the time. It began to dawn upon Katherine that as "babes in the wood," they had not been spiritually sophisticated enough to correctly interpret many of Mr. Fletcher's statements.

At first, they had believed that Mr. Fletcher would be their teacher. But now, in the aftermath of his visit, they were aware that he had served as both a catalyst and a messenger. His responsibility had been to relate the news that they would soon be the recipients of startling information—information that would supersede all else in importance—information for which they had been waiting all of their lives.

In accordance with the wishes of their Spirit Guides and Teachers, and with the instructions advanced by Mr. Fletcher, it was agreed upon that they would soon establish communications between the spheres. On one hand, such a plan seemed absurd, preposterous, ludicrous, and impossible. On the other, had not they discovered that miracles occurred, that all things were possible? Thrilled and excited, curious and challenged, anxious and a bit frightened, they were determined, nonetheless, to implement the advice administered by the kindly healer.

Spirit Guides and Teachers, mused Katherine. *I wonder what they are like. How will they communicate to us? When and why do they wish to share their knowledge with us?* Rather impatiently, she awaited the time when her questions would be answered, when her father would feel well enough to participate in the extraordinary experiment.

"Come on, Dad. Get well soon," she would silently persuade him. "Let's get on with it." What she did not know was that her father, mother, and husband were equally anxious to get on with the experiment. All were secretly anticipating the communications that they had been assured would take place. Communications with a remarkable Source of Wisdom and Knowledge . . . a Source whose existence they had hitherto only remotely suspected—and of whom they had only recently become aware.

CHAPTER 21

The Spirit Beings

⌐

ELIZABETH AND KATHERINE CONTINUED THE healing massages with Gwilym after Mr. Fletcher's departure. In just short of a month's time, Gwilym was feeling as well as he did prior to the onset of the digestive disorders and ulcers. It was not long after Mr. Fletcher's departure, on a bitterly cold and snowy December evening, that Katherine and her family decided to sit together for the purpose of establishing communications with their Spirit Guides. Outside, the night air was unusually still. The sky appeared as a deep gray canopy above the powdery carpet of snow that covered the peaceful streets of Mt. Ash. Gas street lamps and firelight glowed through many of the windows, and these, along with wisps of smoke that wafted from various chimneys, were the only signs of life on Oxford Street. The nondescript houses and businesses had been transformed into snowy, charming, and quaint fairytale castles and cottages. There was a magical quality in the atmosphere, and the city resembled an enchanted, timeless village of white peaks and valleys.

Content to be indoors on such an evening, Katherine had taken great pains to ensure that the house was as warm and cozy as possible. The lounge—in which they were to conduct their experiment—had been carefully arranged, and a small wooden table surrounded by four large upholstered chairs had been placed in the center of the room. A fire blazed merrily in the fireplace, and the lights had been dimmed so that the sole illumination in the room was derived from several silk-shaded lamps. Freshly cut winter flowers and boughs of holly and other evergreen shrubs adorned the mantel in a tall crystal vase. The window had been left open a fraction of an inch so that fresh air might circulate freely throughout the room.

Having eaten a light supper several hours before, they had bathed and changed their clothing, and were now ready to proceed in accordance with the instructions rendered by Mr. Fletcher. Only shortly before the experiment was about to commence did Percy suddenly, unexpectedly blurt out his reluctance to participate.

"I regret that I shall have to pass up this opportunity," he told the astonished group. "I don't feel it's right for me somehow," he continued. "To tell the truth, I expect I'm a bit frightened. You know, as a result of the way I was raised as a Christian. I suppose I'm wary and rather suspicious about the consequences of tampering with spirits. However, please do not allow me to interfere with your own plans. I shall be delighted to learn of the outcome of your efforts here tonight. But, frankly, I personally should feel far more comfortable upstairs in my library where I can better hear Graham if he needs tending to whilst you are engaged in this undertaking."

"Oh, but Percy," Katherine protested. "It was requested that we sit as a foursome. Do you not recall Mr. Fletcher's specific instructions?" Her disappointment was obvious.

"Now, Katherine," Gwilym gently berated his daughter. "Percy must do as he sees fit. He cannot be coerced. We shall have to proceed without him. I am certain that our 'Spirit Teachers' will understand his feelings on this subject."

"Oh, well," Katherine grumbled. "I suppose you are right. All right, Percy, we shall see you later on then, and report the results of our work together. Wish us luck."

"You know I do," said Percy, with a boyish grin, as he escaped with obvious relief from the lounge.

"I trust that the rest of us are going to remain here?" Katherine inquired in a serious tone of voice after her husband had fled.

"Of course, love," replied Elizabeth reassuringly,

"Indeed. Why, we would be letting Mr. Fletcher down if we didn't conduct our little experiment, wouldn't we?" noted Gwilym. "Let's begin."

"You're sure, Dad?"

"Absolutely. The purity of Mr. Fletcher's motive and purpose cannot be negated. I am ready to proceed on the basis of his recommendation alone."

"All right, then," said Katherine, "here we go. First of all, let us agree that we shall take turns checking on the baby. Let us sit quietly for a short while." At this juncture, all three loosened their clothing, settled comfortably in their chairs, and began breathing quietly and deeply, as Mr. Fletcher had advised.

For a few minutes, the room was strangely silent and very still as the trio accustomed themselves to the atmosphere. When all that could be heard was the slight whistling of the wind from the outside and the sound of their breathing, Gwilym broke the silence by addressing his wife and daughter in his rich, mellifluous voice, "I feel that it is time now to begin this evening's work. Let us commence by seeking Divine Guidance and Protection. But first, let us sing together 'The Lord's Prayer.'"

Unwilling to disturb the atmosphere of peace that had already been established, the three sang softly and with deep feeling. Immediately following the singing of this hymn, Gwilym spoke once again, "Dear Lord, we place ourselves in Thy keeping. We seek Thy guidance, Thy protection, and Thy direction. Let nothing harm us, and let us serve Thee faithfully. Let Thy will, oh God, be done through each of us this evening and always. Amen."

"Amen," Katherine and her mother repeated after him.

"Let us once again enter the silence," advised Gwilym, and within moments the room was filled with an awesome stillness, as each became wholly absorbed in his or her own deeply personal thoughts.

Communications will take place. But it is essential that you are patient. Neither you nor your Spirit Guides can hasten the process. You may not perceive any tangible results for weeks—perhaps even months. Yet you must be diligent, patient, consistent in your efforts . . ." Mr. Fletcher's words echoed in Katherine's mind.

Will anything happen tonight? she wondered. Although she could not be absolutely certain, it seemed to her that the ambience of the room had altered dramatically since they had begun. She felt a tingling sensation radiate throughout her face and hands, and a chill ran up and down her spine. It suddenly occurred to her that she and her family were not alone. Although there was no physical sign or evidence of an additional presence, Katherine was convinced that someone or something—she was not sure which—had joined them. It was an unsettling—but not in any way unpleasant—feeling, quite unlike anything she had ever experienced before. Silently, she placed herself in God's keeping one more time, sincerely hoping that in ignorance, she and the others were not jeopardizing their safety and well-being in any way.

As they continued to meditate in silence, Katherine became increasingly aware of the presence of another being. Although she could not define or describe it, she felt intuitively its benevolent power. Somehow she was not the least bit frightened. Rather, a wonderful feeling of calmness and peacefulness seemed to settle over her and the entire room now. Opening her eyes briefly, she saw that both her Mum and Dad were comfortably seated and that their expressions were of serenity and contentment. Pleased that all was going well, she closed her eyes once again. Almost immediately, she felt a great surge of energy penetrate her entire being. The feeling was exhilarating, but it was also simultaneously hauntingly, disturbingly familiar—as if she had experienced it before, long ago, in the dim past, but she could not recall when, where, or how.

Before departing from their home, Mr. Fletcher had provided them with explicit instructions pertaining to their group work. Included among these instructions was the request that each person at the table place his or her hands lightly upon the tabletop. Furthermore, the healer had intimated that communications would take place initially on a very rudimentary level during which time, attempts would be made by the Spirit Guides to ascertain the most effective and efficient means of communicating in the future. Initially, however, the primitive method would be slow and tedious and would incorporate the following procedure: The family was to recite the alphabet aloud. As they did so, the Spirit Guides would raise or lower the table in conjunction with each letter that formed the specific words and phrases they wished to spell out. For example, when the family arrived at the letter K in their recitation of the alphabet, the table would be either raised or lowered to indicate that this was the appropriate letter with which to spell out, letter by letter, then word by word, the message that the Spirit Guides wished to convey. In order, then, to spell out the name Katherine, the table would first rise when the family repeated the letter K; it would fall when they arrived at the letter A; it would rise again when they came to the letter T; it would fall again at H; and so on until Katherine's name had been spelled out perfectly and the communication was regarded as complete. As one might imagine, this procedure required maximum concentration, patience, and perseverance on the part of those hoping to communicate on either side of life. Nonetheless, Katherine and her parents were prepared to proceed no matter how tedious and elementary the situation might appear. They had been prepared for possible disappointment and failure.

It was only a matter of 10 or 15 minutes following the meditational silence and the singing of several more hymns before the communication between the spheres began in earnest. Because Mr. Fletcher had advised them to expect few, if any, tangible results during their early sittings, they were startled to feel the abrupt, violent movement of the table as it lurched forward, then rocked back and forth. At the first sign of movement, Katherine opened her eyes in astonishment and met the equally astonished eyes of her dad and mum.

"Oh, my God!" she cried aloud.

"Stay calm, daughter," advised Gwilym in a quiet, steady voice. And despite the impassive expression on his face, Katherine knew that he also was struggling to maintain his composure. Despite her mother's apparent calm, Katherine knew that she, too, was terrified. Her heart in her stomach, Katherine said nothing further. Mesmerized, she was conscious only of the vibrating of the table beneath her trembling hands. Up and down, sideways, and back the table moved—seemingly of its own accord. Certainly, no human intervention was responsible for its movement. First the table began to edge its way ever so gently away from the center of the room; then it gyrated up and down, rising and falling in a series of staccato movements; finally, it rose and fell in an easy, rhythmic pattern. This display continued for several minutes as Katherine and the others watched in astonishment.

"Is this a sign that our Spirit Guides are here with us at this time?" Gwilym asked in a weak voice. Immediately the table floated up into the air from its position in the center of the room, as if in response.

"Are you ready to begin communications with us?" inquired Katherine in a low voice. The table, which had remained floating in the air several feet above the floor, began to slowly descend. "Shall we recite the alphabet?" asked Elizabeth, with great presence of mind. The table rocked back and forth enthusiastically.

"I think that means that we should proceed," concluded Katherine.

She was suddenly struck by an idea. "I wonder," she said slowly, "if our teachers can understand our mental questions. I'll bet it isn't even necessary to speak aloud." Immediately the table began to rise once again.

"Incredible," breathed Elizabeth.

"Yes," agreed Katherine. "They can read our thoughts. Nonetheless, I should like to ask our Teachers a question aloud—one that has been troubling me ever since Mr. Fletcher advised us to sit together in this manner." Katherine continued, "Just what is the purpose of our communications?"

She then began to recite the alphabet—A, B, C, D, E, F, G, H . . . The others joined her, speaking as slowly and haltingly as children proceeding in this manner for the very first time. Letter by letter, the answer was spelled out to form the words: **To remove the fear of death by proving to you that life is continuous**.

"Oh, my," murmured Elizabeth.

"Will this method of communication be harmful in any way to anyone on either side of life?" Gwilym asked.

The table tilted twice in response, signifying a "no."

"Will such communications assist our spiritual progress?" inquired Elizabeth shakily.

Emphatically the table tilted once signifying a "yes."

"Will we receive further evidence of your existence?" was Katherine's next query. Once again the table was in motion, tilting once indicating an affirmative reply.

The questions and answers continued for nearly four hours. Far from feeling weary or exhausted, Katherine and the others felt exhilarated and pleased with the results of their initial effort. After the first hour or so, the communications process had become much easier and far more efficient as Katherine and Gwilym began to receive inspirationally the replies to their questions and comments frequently requiring only one or two letters to determine the entire word, or one or two words to be spelled out of a sentence, in order to fully grasp the complete message or concept the Spirit Beings wished to convey. If any discrepancy or misunderstanding occurred, one member of the trio would inquire of the Teachers as to whether they had construed the information correctly. Then, the table would tilt either once in a "yes" answer or twice for a "no."

The Spirit Beings thus far remained unidentifiable. After several hours had elapsed, however, one disclosed his identity. This communicator from the spirit world was none other than Percy's brother, Andrew, who had died at the tender age of 18 on the battlefield in Flanders during the first World War. Percy had frequently spoken of his handsome, happy-go-lucky older brother. And now, obviously eager to make contact with Percy, Andrew was taking this opportunity to share the news that he was still very much "alive."

I am Andrew Hayward, he first "told" the group. He then spelled out a brief message: **I am here to prove that there is no death. Life is continuous. Proceed in the manner you have thus far employed this evening. You will witness phenomena that will convince you beyond a shadow of a doubt of the reality of life beyond the grave.**

Katherine felt goose bumps as she first deciphered, then assimilated the words transmitted by Andrew.

"There is no death," she repeated before the group. "How I wish Percy were here to speak with Andrew," she said regretfully. At the exact instant she had completed this sentence, Percy appeared at the top of the staircase.

"What is going on down there? Do you realize it's nearly midnight, and that you have been at it since nearly a quarter past seven?"

"Why, hullo Percy," was Katherine's deliberately casual reply. "We have just been speaking with your brother, Andrew, who, by the way, seems most eager to speak with you." Her voice was expressionless, her manner matter-of-fact.

"What's that you say?!" she heard her husband exclaim in surprise. And he literally leaped down the stairs. Within seconds, he was standing by the empty chair that was to have been his and eyeing the group with suspicion. "I do hope you are all feeling perfectly well," he stated, studying each one carefully as if to ascertain that they were of sound mind and body.

"Oh, we are just fine, dear," replied Elizabeth cheerfully. "But I am afraid, Son, that you have missed quite a bit of excitement."

"Indeed," murmured Percy coolly.

"Yes, son, Mother's quite right. It has been a most extraordinary evening. We have been in communication with our Spirit Guides since approximately eight o'clock," continued Gwilym, rather enjoying his son-in-law's discomfiture.

"And you, Katherine, have you thoroughly enjoyed yourself as well? Have you derived benefit from this pleasant diversion?" Percy addressed his wife condescendingly.

"Why yes, dear, on both counts. It has been a most rewarding experiment," was Katherine's bemused reply.

"Well, I think that it is time for you all to conclude your little experiment and to go to bed," insisted Percy, with as much authority as he could muster. "I myself am going to bed at once." And detecting no sign of movement or cooperation on the part of Katherine or her parents, Percy began to walk toward the staircase. "Goodnight, then," he called out, as he began to ascend the stairs. He soon vanished from view. They were all astounded therefore when, within seconds, he was back downstairs and seated at the table with the rest of the family, his face ashen, his features frozen.

"At last we are a foursome," said Katherine aloud.

"It was uncanny," said Percy in a hoarse voice, shaking his head in bewilderment. "I was unable to take another step. So help me, God, it seemed exactly as though someone or something was obstructing my way, preventing me from leaving this room." He was clearly shaken by the experience. But the rest of the group was not surprised. Katherine exchanged a knowing smile with her parents, as Percy settled in his chair, still puzzling over what had just transpired.

"All is well, Percy, I promise. There is nothing to fear. Just sit quietly, as Mr. Fletcher advised us. Wonderful things will happen now that you have joined us," she said happily, "now that we are a foursome. I feel certain of it." Her enthusiasm was infectious, and soon, all four were sitting quietly with their eyes closed, eagerly awaiting the next phase of the experiment.

They were not disappointed for the activity resumed almost immediately.

"What's this?!" cried Percy in horror as the table began to move up and down, back and forth quite forcefully. "Is this some sort of prank? Who is responsible for the movement of this table? I demand to know," he growled imperiously.

"It is no prank, I assure you, love. It is the work of our Spirit Guides," replied Katherine calmly.

"Is that so?" asked Percy rather testily. "Prove it."

"All right, I will," she said easily. "Every one of us but you shall move our chairs away from the table and keep our hands folded together in our laps. You will see, Percy, that we are in no way responsible for the table's movement. It is the work of our Spirit Guides. We are not alone here!" And sure enough, the very instant that the three of them had shifted into their new position several feet away from the table, it began to vibrate. Obstinately refusing to believe that it was moving without human intervention and determined to discover the source of its motion, Percy drew his own chair closer to the table and placed his hands lightly upon its surface.

"Now let's see you travel," he muttered, addressing the inanimate object as though it were comprehending. A moment later, he regretted his words, for "travel" is precisely what the table did, as though in perfect compliance with his injunction. "Oh, my God!" he croaked, as he watched the table literally "fly" through the air—as though propelled by some mighty power—hit the ceiling with such force that it created a gaping hole in it, and remained afloat for several seconds. Too stunned to utter a syllable, Percy watched in rapt attention. He was now absolutely convinced that the table's movement could not possibly be attributed to any human being in the room. Stupefied, the entire family watched in complete silence as the table hovered precariously above them and finally descended slowly and gracefully back into its original position on the floor in the center of the room.

"Well, are you convinced that we are not alone?" Katherine asked her husband, who had turned a pasty white.

"I am indeed," stated Percy weakly.

"And are you quite ready now to receive the communications of your dear brother, Andrew?"

"I do believe I am," he stammered, still visibly affected by all that had just taken place.

After several minutes of silence during which time the four resumed their original positions at the table, Andrew reintroduced himself and issued a special welcome to his younger brother, imploring him to keep an open mind. Andrew seemed thoroughly acquainted but not very sympathetic with Percy's attitude toward his "death." **Although I died in battle, I did not suffer at all**, were the words that Andrew spelled out to the group. **The transition from this plane of life to the next was both pleasant and peaceful—mercifully so. I have never—even once—regretted leaving the physical body or wished again to be in the physical form. Life here is glorious, and the possibilities for further growth and development are limitless. Do not, therefore, expend either time or energy regretting my departure from the physical plane. I am supremely happy now—far happier than I ever was on Earth.**

Please try to understand that our work together this evening has been experimental. In subsequent meetings, it will not be necessary to communicate in this primitive manner. Your spirit teachers will be able to impart their information through Percy. Percy is what spiritualists refer to as a deep

trance medium. His physical body and physiological constitution enable him to serve as a channel through whom the Spirit Beings may effectively communicate. The teachers will induce in him a trance or sleep state. While he is unconscious, his vehicle—his mind and body—will be utilized by the teachers and serve as the instruments through which communications will take place. This process with be painless and will feel perfectly natural to Percy.

Your efforts here tonight have been most successful and greatly appreciated, but it is time now to conclude our work together. Please keep in mind that those who guide and instruct you from the world of spirit have requested your togetherness for many reasons. Not only will your own gifts of mediumship be cultivated and developed as a result, but your awareness and conscious understanding shall be greatly expanded and enhanced. Although I personally am not a teacher, I have been permitted to address you all this evening in order to assure you that life is continuous, and that all people continue to survive beyond the death of the mortal body. From this moment on, you will be under the care and tutelage of your own teachers in spirit. With my love and blessings, I thank you for your cooperation and bid you all a good night.

There were tears in Percy's eyes for some time after Andrew had departed. Despite his prior skepticism, he had been deeply moved by his brother's visitation. It was at this juncture that the group—exhilarated but exhausted—decided to disband for the evening. Each had been overwhelmed by the results of the experiment. A discussion ensued and it was nearly 4:00 a.m. by the time they actually put out the fire, turned out the lights, and found their way out of the lounge and up the stairs to their respective bedrooms.

Outside the air was still and clear and fresh with the beginning of the new day. The snow had stopped falling from the sky and had formed a thick blanket of dazzling white over the entire community. Trees and shrubs, fences and gates were encrusted with snowflakes, and icicles delicately adorned the roofs and doorways. "It looks like a fairy world," observed Katherine with delight, viewing the street below from her bedroom window.

"Hmmmmm," was Percy's noncommittal reply. He seemed lost in thought.

"Can it be possible," he wondered silently, "that I have truly spoken with Andrew this evening? That my brother actually exists in another world altogether? That life exists beyond the grave?" Now, as he prepared for bed, it seemed impossible—even preposterous—that he and his family had been involved in communications with Spirit Beings. *I could go to the Devil for participating in such an activity*! he thought uneasily. But somehow, he did not seriously regard this as a possibility. *No, I don't suppose there is any such place as hell anyway. But I shall certainly have to ask our Teachers about that . . . What really took place in the lounge this evening? Did I imagine my conversation with Andrew? No, I simply cannot have imagined any of the highly unusual situations that occurred here this evening. Oh, well, I suppose I must wait to discover the answers to my questions and reserve judgment until a later date after I have experienced further contact with our Spirit Guides, The experiment should prove to be very interesting—most interesting, indeed. I wonder what will take place during our next such togetherness . . .*

CHAPTER 22

Dr. Evans

As Katherine completed her toiletries and prepared for bed, she was equally absorbed in thought. Her fingers trembled as she buttoned her nightdress, and there was a faraway expression in her eyes. *I shall never—as long as I live—forget what took place this evening. Can it really be only a short time ago we had the good fortune of meeting Mr. Fletcher? How that man has transformed our lives! Nothing, not one of us will ever by the same as a result. I can hardly wait to discover what will transpire during our next meeting with the Spirit Beings . . .*

As she crawled into bed, Katherine realized with a smile that she was still trembling with fear and excitement. As she glanced over toward Percy, whose eyes were still open, she noticed that he, too, was preoccupied.

"What do you suppose is the purpose of it all?" he asked softly, biting his lip in frustration.

"I couldn't possibly begin to guess," was his wife's straightforward reply. "I expect that only time—and further contact—will tell. Good night, love."

"Goodnight, Katherine."

Unhappily, although she was exhausted, she was far too nervous and excited to fall asleep. Tossing and turning, she was unable to concentrate upon anything but the unique events that had unfolded ever since she and her mother had attended the meeting at the Spiritualist Church. *No one would believe any of this in a million years!* she giggled softly to herself. At least no one in their right mind would believe such things. Would I—could I—have believed such things actually occurred six or even three months ago—and without the extraordinary evidence I have received? I don't know—I just don't know. . ."

Her mind continued to race in a hundred different directions at once. Finally, realizing the futility of her efforts to fall asleep, she silently slipped out of bed and found her way to the closet to find her dressing gown. It was quite chilly in the room, and as Katherine was about to retrieve her slippers, she was startled to hear movement from the bed. To her amazement, Percy was now sitting up, feeling every bit as wide awake as she.

"Did you sleep at all?" she asked her husband.

"Not a wink," was his reply.

"Well, what should we do?" whispered Katherine, not wishing to awaken her parents or the baby sleeping peacefully in the room next door.

"Come on," said Percy suddenly, as if struck by an idea. He jumped out of bed, yanked his bathrobe from the closet, grabbed her arm, and pulled her out of the room, whispering. "We're going to have another go."

"We are!" Katherine squealed, knowing exactly what he meant. They would continue the communications which had begun earlier that evening.

"Shhhh!" admonished Percy, "We don't want to disturb the rest. Let's go into the spare bedroom." Katherine nodded, and the two tip-toed in silence across the hall into the spare bedroom that they frequently used as a sitting room.

It was early morning now, and the sky had begun to assume a rosy glow. Topaz and amethyst, melting into pale pink, a blush of crimson, and the tiniest tinge of turquoise formed the kaleidoscope of exquisite colors Katherine could see now through the curtain lace of the large bay sitting room window. With the memory of her recent experience still vivid in her mind, the sky now seemed a reflection of her joy and anticipation.

She helped Percy carry the small Pembroke table from the corner of the room to the center and place several high-back chairs around it. Illuminated only by a gas lamp, the room was chilly and dark. But they dared not light a fire for fear of waking the others. So they comforted themselves instead by wrapping a woolen blanket around them.

As soon as they were comfortably seated, they sought God's guidance and protection, and then remained receptive to the influence of "the highest and the best."

"Hum something softly," Katherine felt inspired to say, and they began by humming first "The Lord's Prayer," and then "A Mighty Fortress is our God."

"Let us now enter into a silence," she suggested. The atmosphere in the room changed at once, as though a cloud or layer of light were settling down in their midst.

Suddenly, Katherine became acutely aware of a sharp change in the pattern of Percy's breathing. Whereas he usually breathed rather rapidly and shallowly, he was now breathing very slowly and deeply. Furthermore, his exhalations were accompanied by a slight whistling sound. Tentatively opening her eyes to see if he was all right, she was dumbfounded by the transformation that had taken place in his appearance. His features had somehow been transfigured, and the expression on his face was unlike any she had ever seen him display before! Stifling a gasp of horror, she reminded herself that there was nothing to fear, that they had placed themselves in God's keeping, and that no harm could possibly come to either one of them. But when the man at the opposite end of the table—this stranger who was no longer her Percy—began to speak she literally jumped out of her chair.

Good evening—or shall I say good morning? the voice was saying. **Please allow me to introduce myself. I am Dr. Evan Evans, your husband's spirit guide and teacher. Whilst living on the earth plane during my most recent incarnation, I was a physician residing in the city of Swansea. Should you feel inclined to verify this information, you may do so readily by visiting that city's hall of records. There, you may acquire specific biographical data regarding my previous life as a human being. It is because I have for so long—during many lifetimes, in fact—worked with your husband as his guide and teacher that I find it convenient to work with him now in this manner. We are most comfortable—he and I—and**

have completed rigorous training to achieve the results you are experiencing at this moment.

At this juncture, Katherine was startled to see that the sitting room door was ajar and that her parents had been standing in awe listening to every single word that had been uttered by Dr. Evans.

Ah, do come in and join us, Dr. Evans welcomed them warmly.

"Uh . . . why . . . we . . . uh . . . we were unable to sleep," stammered Elizabeth in confusion.

"And we . . . uh . . . heard voices," continued Gwilym.

"They seemed to be coming from in here, so we . . . uh . . . thought . . . that we had better . . . uh . . . come in here and check," concluded Elizabeth. "I do hope that we are not interrupting . . ."

Not at all, replied Dr. Evans. As a matter of fact, you are most welcome. **Please pull up some chairs, make yourselves comfortable, and we shall continue together.**

So astonished were they by the change that had taken place in Percy, that they could hardly keep their eyes off of him. They somehow managed to maneuver two more chairs to the table, but it was evident that their movements were automatic. Their faces were expressionless, and their gaze was riveted to the stranger sitting at the table. Never had they seen anything like this! Not only was the expression on Percy's face entirely different, but his physical mannerisms as well as his voice and dialect bore not even the slightest resemblance to their son-in-law's.

And now, once again, I wish you all a good morning, said Dr. Evans in his melodious Welsh dialect once Elizabeth and Gwilym were comfortably seated. **You will soon discover that there are no mistakes, and that your presence here is by no means accidental. Now, you see, your small group is complete once again.**

Katherine and her parents exchanged surprised glances. *Has this meeting— which appears to be spontaneous—actually been conceived of and patterned by the Spirit Teachers?* Katherine could not help but wonder.

As though reading her mind, Dr. Evans addressed this question matter-of-factly. **You seem surprised by the events that have taken place here.**

Yet, I would assure you that our meeting has been very carefully planned for quite some time. Long before any of you—the real you, that is—was encased in a body of flesh, desired to render a service to humanity by means of your next incarnation. And so, you selected physical forms that were specially designed and constructed to serve as vehicles—instruments—that would enable you to perform this service. The "service" of which I speak is multifaceted and multidimensional, to say the very least. But, suffice it to say here and now that it incorporates the concept of bridging this world with the worlds beyond, bringing humanity the awareness that they are not alone, that there coexist simultaneously countless spheres of life that interpenetrate one another, that life continues after death, and that each human's soul is immortal.

Henceforth, you will begin a period of instruction whereby you will acquire from us, your spirit guides and teachers, that information that will form the nucleus and foundation for all of your subsequent work and that will assist you in accomplishing the service that you set out to render so long ago and for which you have taken on a physical body. Furthermore, during this period, you will be given many of the answers to questions that have puzzled you virtually all of your lives.

At this time, you are encouraged to set aside several hours each evening for the purpose of receiving such instruction. Please try to adhere to a fairly rigid schedule, meeting in a consistent manner, and at the same time each evening. You are further advised to set aside a special room or at least a portion of a room for our work together, allowing nothing to disturb its atmosphere. By so doing, you are improving the conditions under which our communications may take place. In order for us to most effectively and efficiently communicate with you it will be necessary to establish and maintain an atmosphere of peace and harmony—of unity and accord. You see, because we function at a rate of vibration significantly higher than your own, you must elevate your own vibration and we must lower ours in order to achieve our goal. It is in accordance with the quality of your thoughts, prayers, and aspirations that your rate of vibration is either quickened or retarded. It is the degree of purity, love, unselfishness, and sincerity that determine the caliber and, subsequently, the vibration of your thoughts.

First and foremost, before each of our meetings, it is essential for you to safeguard yourselves from any potential danger by linking in prayer with the source of life—that power that many call God. Music is also very helpful in raising your group's vibration so that you may wish to sing well-loved and inspiring hymns. Then, it would be advantageous for you to attune—by means of your thoughts and aspirations—to the enlightened forces—those advanced souls and highly evolved spiritual beings who exist in realms beyond the Earth. These illumined and radiant ones voluntarily draw close to the Earth to inspire those members of the human race who, like you, are receptive to their influence and who are assisting humankind in its spiritual evolution. These souls ignite in the hearts of humankind the desire to discover the truths of life and live in peace and brotherhood and with feelings of love for and goodwill toward one another. Most importantly, they come to help humans awaken to their true potential—which is far greater than anything of which the average human being can conceive. In time, humans will come to recognize their own divinity, and to draw upon the incalculable wealth, beauty, and wisdom that are a part of the glorious kingdom that resides deep, deep within them. As some of your greatest philosophers have taught 'Man know thyself, and thou shalt know God and the universe' is also the advice rendered by these advanced beings.

'The Kingdom of God is within you' advises the great teacher Jesus. And so, while your scientists, physicians, psychologists, and psychiatrists probe the mysteries of the human mind and body and conduct their investigations, these enlightened ones in the spirit world are deeply concerned with the evolution and progress of humankind. Invisibly, they govern and direct humanity and are behind all institutions, artists, and leaders working to better the conditions of all people throughout the world. It is the spirit of love that has awakened in the heart that draws the soul into this group service. The illumined souls are drawing closer. It is their selfless desire to help humanity to clear away the mists of materialism and debris of folly, to live harmoniously, and to establish peace and true unity and fellowship on Earth.

Each of you must learn to conduct your daily lives in compliance with spiritual law—which is comprised succinctly in the words of the Nazarene, 'Thou shalt love the Lord thy God with all thy heart and with all thy soul and with all thy mind, and thy neighbor as thyself. Seek ye first the Kingdom of God, then all things shall be added unto you.' In short, love one another.

A 'channel' or 'medium' is one who is endowed with specially constructed and designed physical and etheric bodies and a sensitive nervous system that readily enables him or her to receive images and/or impressions from other worlds—to actually see the inhabitants of these worlds or to hear their voices. Each one of you is able to act as a channel or conduit between two worlds, to receive the thought vibrations of those living in the world of spirit, and to transmit them to your fellow human beings. There are many diverse purposes for mediumship as well as many various forms of mediumship. As some human beings are endowed with the gift of painting, or writing, or acting, so each of you has been endowed with the sacred gift of mediumship. And, just as the artist, author, or actor must undergo training, discipline, and the unfoldment of their gifts, so is this also the case with the medium. Our work together has been devised to hasten the unfoldment of your mediumistic abilities.

Throughout the coming months, we will continue to meet in this manner. I am but one of many Spirit Guides who wish to share with you the knowledge and wisdom we have thus far acquired on our side of life. Henceforth, you will be encouraged to participate more actively—to ask questions, to request more detailed information, to advance your own viewpoints, to contest or take issue with what we say, if you are so inclined. We shall make every effort to accommodate your needs and interests. It is essential that you remain consistently aware, however, that it may not always be possible for us to provide you with as complete a response to your inquiries as you might wish. You see, at this juncture in time, you have not been sufficiently prepared—emotionally, intellectually, spiritually—to either comprehend the full meaning or import of all we might convey. Furthermore, it is difficult for us to accurately employ such limited, such inadequate symbols as 'words' to describe, or to translate as it were, fourth, fifth, sixth, and seventh dimensional realities into third dimensional technologies. We can only beseech you, therefore, to remain patient, receptive, and open-minded. Refrain from making judgments during the early phases of our work together. We shall make every effort to clarify and define our meanings. Believe me, it is a great pleasure and privilege to share with you such information. We look forward to our subsequent meetings.

And now, as the hour is so late—or early, if you prefer—we deem it advisable to conclude our meeting. You must take good care of your minds and physical bodies—making certain always that they are properly nourished and rested. Please make certain that Percy is properly cared for—it will take him several minutes to fully recover from this experience and to return to normal consciousness. He has been in what is called a 'trance state' while I have spoken through him. Therefore, his personality has not been functioning here with you. His soul has been withdrawn to a higher state. Always insist that Percy rest following such a demonstration, although I promise you that you need not be concerned that the process entails any ill effects. For I and the other guides are carefully monitoring and attending to his needs all the while. Let me assure you that we have made great progress this evening. It gives me immense pleasure to announce that our experiment has been a success. You will be astounded by the easy and fluid manner in which your lessons will proceed from hereon. We look forward to seeing you all tomorrow evening. God bless and illuminate you. Sleep well, my dears, sleep well.

Within seconds, all traces of Dr. Evans had disappeared, and Percy had once again joined the group. As soon as Dr. Evans had vanished, Percy's features resumed their customary expression, his body its normal posture. As though awakening from a night's sleep, he opened his eyes, blinked for several moments as though he were not quite sure where he was, then yawned and stretched. It was not until his gaze took in the surprised faces of his wife and parents-in-law that it began to dawn upon him that something unusual had taken place.

"What has happened here?" he demanded, trying to recall why he and his family were gathered in the sitting room.

"I wonder if you would believe us if we told YOU," Katherine muttered. And she proceeded to describe as best she could the manner in which he had been "transformed" into Dr. Evans, the unexpected arrival of Elizabeth and Gwilym, and the contents of the message imparted by Dr. Evans. Percy was genuinely mystified. Nonplussed, he could not imagine how he had entered into a trance state.

"It is simply not possible," he protested in confusion. As Gwilym and Elizabeth corroborated all that Katherine had said, however, he gradually began to accept their explanation of what had taken place.

"How extraordinary," he kept repeating, more to himself than to anyone else. "I don't recall even a single word of what was said, or anything whatever about this 'Dr. Evans.' Apparently, I am to derive my instruction from all of you. You must, therefore, record Dr. Evans' words, and then pass them on to me."

"Gladly," agreed the others.

"Well, I don't know about the rest of you," said Katherine wearily, rising from her seat, "but I am thoroughly exhausted. Are you aware that it's nearly dawn? Let's call it a day, shall we?"

"I quite agree," replied Elizabeth with a yawn. And the four made their way back to their respective bedrooms. They were unusually silent—each one lost in thought.

Contact had been established. Miraculously, the Davies and the Haywards had entered into communications with beings from another time, another place, another dimension altogether—beings of a finer substance, a higher vibration, a different outlook, a deeper understanding, and a greater capacity for love than any human being they had known. The "Enlightened Forces" Dr. Evans had called them—great souls who were drawing closer to the earth than ever before to assist humankind in discovering the very purpose for its existence on the planet earth.

Yet the communications had only just begun. The nature and content of the information to be obtained in subsequent sessions they had no possible way of determining. In an odd, compelling way, they felt as though a vast eternal mystery was unfolding before their very eyes and that they were simultaneously both witnesses and participants in the unraveling of this mystery.

An immense, intense volume of information most assuredly awaited them. They did not doubt that they would soon receive the answers to questions that had puzzled and perplexed them and all thinking people since time immemorial. *Who am I? From whence came I? Whither shall I go after death?* At long last they would know the reason for which they lived.

Yet the outcome of the experiment with the Spirit Beings—its purpose and ramifications—remained a mystery. Why, after all, had they been singled out to be the recipients of such information? They could not even begin to guess. They would have to be patient, and persistent, in order to uncover the underlying plan or pattern behind the unusual experiment. Only time would tell.

In the meantime, they would refrain from drawing any conclusions, making any judgments. *One day at a time*, thought Katherine to herself. *I'll not anticipate or project what is to be, or what I imagine should be. Rather, I shall remain as open and objective as I can, and simply observe the drama as it unfolds.*

She stopped by the baby's room to make certain that he had not been awakened. They would take turns occasionally to slip out of the room to check on little Graham. He was sleeping soundly and looked exquisitely peaceful as he lay among the pastel sheets, pillows, and coverlets. "You are a miracle child," she whispered in little Graham's ear. "How I love you." And she kissed him gently on the forehead. Closing the door, she proceeded onward to her own bedroom wherein she discarded her robe, mumbled a half-hearted 'good night' to Percy, and tumbled into bed beside him for the second time that night. Neither one of them had any difficulty whatsoever falling asleep this time.

Outside a lark sang blithely on a snowy bough of an elm tree that stood nearby. The early morning sun—dazzling in its full fuchsia, crimson, and golden glory—had risen to its morning height and seemed to derive considerable delight from the effect it was having upon the snow-laden earth below. And embracing the new day, the town of Mt. Ash was slowly coming to life. The air was already filled with the noise of automobiles, horse drawn carriages, footsteps crunching on the snowy pavements, dogs barking, and cheerful morning voices. Yet, despite the flurry of activity outside, Katherine remained undisturbed—lost in the blessed peacefulness of a well-earned slumber.

Had she but remotely suspected the joy that was coming every minute nearer and nearer, it is doubtful that she would have stayed in bed a single moment longer than necessary. Rather, she would have chosen to wait in a state of joyous anticipation, sharing her feelings of excitement and exhilaration with those she loved. Not privy to such news at this time, however, Katherine slept on peacefully oblivious to past, present, and future. Her features were serene, her face placid upon the pillow, and her slender body at ease.

The merest suggestion of a smile played upon her lips indicating that perhaps, on some inner, deeper level, she was aware after all of what was to be. In the meantime, the rest of the world was unaffected. For the citizens of Mt. Ash, it was a morning not unlike every other morning. No visions, no visitations, or transforming words delivered by Spirit Beings for them. For everyone but Katherine and her family, in fact, it was business as usual . . . and the beginning of a day not unlike any other day.

CHAPTER 23

The Lessons

IT WAS ONLY A MATTER of a few hours after falling asleep that Katherine and the others were required to awaken for the day. Exhausted, they were also deeply disappointed and dissatisfied to have to contend with the mundane round of daily activities after having shared such a startling and exhilarating experience the previous evening. Furthermore, they could hardly wait until nighttime when the communications between the spheres would resume.

As the hours had flown the evening before, this new day seemed to drag on aimlessly, endlessly, and utterly without purpose. It was as though time had been suspended—each moment lasting an age, each hour an eternity. Bored and impatient, with an unbecoming scowl upon her face, Katherine cast frequent glances toward the old clock on the mantle in the lounge, grimly wishing with all her might that she could somehow hasten the movement of its hands. Nor was it easy to concentrate upon her daily tasks and responsibilities for in the midst of her excitement and anticipation for what was to follow she was required to care for little Graham, look after her father and mother, clean the house, prepare the meals, and assist Percy in the business. It was of some comfort to recognize that Percy and the others were equally bored and restless. She noticed that her husband's gaze was firmly fixed upon the clock that hung on the wall of the shop.

"Will this day ever come to an end?" she muttered in disgust to her mother following luncheon, as the two cleared the dirty dishes from the kitchen table.

"Patience, my child, patience," was Elizabeth's unsatisfying response. Yet she, too, seemed out of sorts and unusually flustered and preoccupied. Only Gwilym seemed himself, calm, at ease, and generally unaffected by the turbulence around him.

How can he be so cool and collected? Katherine wondered, admiration mingled with envy as she observed him resting comfortably in his favorite chair, thoroughly engrossed in one of his books, oblivious to the world around him. Momentarily studying his features, she derived considerable satisfaction from the fact that he looked healthier and happier than he had for years. *Thank God that he is well at last,* she thought to herself. And smiling for the first time that day, she left the room and returned to the kitchen to begin preparations for the evening meal.

Finally, at long last, the business day came to an end. At five minutes before six o'clock, Percy abruptly turned off the lights and bolted the doors to the shop. By six o'clock exactly all were seated at the dining table, solemnly engaged in consuming the light supper Katherine had prepared. By quarter past seven, Katherine had cleared the table and tucked little Graham in bed for the night. At half past seven on the dot, all four were seated around the small wooden table in the lounge, ready to commence the evening's work.

For the second time that day, all traces of the impatient scowl and the bored expression had disappeared from Katherine's face. Her eyes were now gleaming in anticipation of what soon would take place. Color flooded her cheeks and her lips had parted into a wide, girlish grin.

"Do you realize that you're positively beaming, my dear?" Percy whispered to her from across the table. "I do believe that this work must agree with you," he teased.

"Oh, hush, Percy. Don't be silly," she snapped, her eyes rolling heavenward in impatience. "Come on everybody. Let's get on with it, shall we? Let's do what we have come here to do."

"All right, love," smiled Percy sympathetically. He could not recall when last he had seen his wife so intense or determined. Soon all four had loosened their clothing, settled comfortably in their seats, and were breathing slowly, deeply, and rhythmically as Mr. Fletcher had advised.

"Let us now seek Guidance and Protection," Gwilym advised. And after a brief prayer and the singing of "The Lord's Prayer" and "Holy, Holy, Holy," they were once again actively engaged in the task of establishing communications with the Spirit Guides. Within moments, the atmosphere had become still and thick—the silence profound. Deeper and deeper was their intrusion into the silence until each had felt contact, then communion with a Power far greater than any of them had ever experienced before. A feeling of perfect peace, then ecstasy overcame Katherine, and for a moment she did not know whether to laugh or cry in response. So acute, so exquisite was the sensation that she did not want to interfere with it—modify it—in any way. Rather she longed to suspend it for as long as possible, hoping deep down inside that it might last forever.

She had no idea how many minutes had elapsed before she became conscious once again of the presence of the others. Somehow "time" had seemed incongruous, superfluous in this atmosphere. Yet, suddenly she became conscious of the change that had taken place in Percy's breathing. Her heart skipped a beat. Stifling a cry of terror, she opened her eyes and observed the awesome procedure whereby Percy's features were being transfigured into those of Dr. Evans.

"Words cannot begin to describe this process," marveled Katherine, wondering how she might ever explain it to anyone else. It appeared as though an intense wave of energy were flooding, overcoming, Percy's body, affecting every part of him. From the crown of his head to the trunk of his body, through his arms and hands and fingers; through his legs and feet and toes, this energy filled him, dramatically altering completely the nature and character of his movements and appearance. His nerves and muscles twitched and flickered in response to the force moving through him. Expanding, contracting, and finally expanding once again. Percy's body finally settled in repose—now under the certain and secure guidance and operation of Dr. Evan Evans.

Does one ever grow comfortable or become accustomed to witnessing such phenomena? Katherine asked herself. But she had no further time for deliberation for Dr. Evans began at once to address the group.

Good evening, dear friends, good evening and welcome. How pleasant and gratifying it is to be amongst you once again. Before we begin this evening's activity, I would like all of you very much to carefully observe the following.

Pausing for a moment, Dr. Evans delicately maneuvered his chair away from the table, arose from his seat, and began to stroll slowly and deliberately around the lounge—as though intending to convince the group that he was no longer Percy at all and was, instead, another individual altogether. Katherine's mouth fell open in astonishment as she observed her husband's body moving and reacting in a manner not only uncharacteristic but alien to his "normal" pattern. Both Dr. Evans' gait and manner were highly distinctive, and he moved with the grace and unconscious poise of an aristocrat. He appeared to be an elderly gentleman of considerable refinement and breeding, and Katherine surmised that he was approximately sixty years of age. Although it appeared he employed a walking stick, it was for fashion's sake rather than for health purposes that he found it useful. His spine was erect; his posture enviable; his manner indisputably elegant. There was an old-fashioned charm and gentility to his demeanor that were winsome.

Good evening, he said graciously to the group, striking a pose with his invisible walking stick and nonchalantly doffing an imaginary bowler.

"Good evening to you, sir," returned Katherine, a nervous giggle rising to her throat.

"Absolutely astonishing," breathed Elizabeth, as the remarkable figure continued to glide imperiously through the room. Finally, after nearly five minutes of such activity, Dr. Evans resumed his position at the table and addressed the group.

I trust that you have derived some benefit from my little demonstration; that you have received sufficient evidence that I am what and who I claim to be, that I am a being separate and distinct from your husband? Do you now understand that I am able to utilize Percy's mind and body for that purpose which has previously been described to you?

"Oh, yes indeed," all three murmured simultaneously, unable to remove their eyes from his form.

Good, said Dr. Evans, smiling. **Then let us proceed with this evening's instruction which you might regard as the very first in your series of lessons. This evening's session will be brief, for it is obvious that you are all very tired and in need of a good night's sleep.**

Katherine's face fell at this. For she had waited all day for the meeting and had hoped that it would last for many hours. She had so many questions. There was so much to learn! Could not Dr. Evans sense her earnestness, her eagerness, her impatience to "get on with it"? There was a compassionate smile on Dr. Evans' face, although he fully understood her feelings.

You must not feel disappointed, my dear, he said in a warm, sympathetic voice. **We will share countless sessions together that I assure you will not come to an end until you have acquired your complete training and both you and we are fully satisfied with its results.**

Your very first lesson is that of mindfulness—carefully observing and paying attention to you, your life, your thoughts, your feelings, your world, and those with whom you share this world—whether they be human, animal, vegetable, or mineral. Recognize and identify the special gifts and abilities you have to share with others. Recognize and identify the gifts they share with you. Give these gifts freely and generously without thought of what you may receive in return.

Be mindful of your surroundings and environment and strive to create harmony and beauty wherever and whenever possible. Be mindful of the needs of others not just in your small community but of those all over the world. You are both teachers and students of all with whom you come into contact. Life on earth is a school in which you learn to spiritually evolve. Never lose sight of this—your higher purpose and destiny.

And so began the first of many lessons, in which Dr. Evans educated them about God, humans' purpose in life, and even death. The subsequent days passed with surprising rapidity. In no way memorable, it seemed that each day served merely as a prelude or preamble to that evening's work. Yet on an inner, deeper level, all seemed to grasp that with each new day came the opportunity to put into practical application the lessons learned by night—the opportunity to attain a truer, clearer, and deeper understanding of the information conveyed by the Guides.

They always eagerly absorbed Dr. Evans' lessons, which never seemed to be enough. In truth, they lived for the daily communion with the Spirit Teachers. And initially, they strove to hasten through the day—attempting to get through their daily tasks and responsibilities as quickly and efficiently as possible and at the same time trying to keep in mind Dr. Evans typically sound advice.

"We cannot emphasize enough the fact that you are spiritual beings. Neither the mind nor the physical body nor any of the qualities or attributes or names or labels by which the ordinary human being is typically identified. The real you is not your physical body any more than you are the clothing that you wear. Your body can be likened to a well-used overcoat that is discarded at the transition known as death. In truth, there is no death, only change. As when the caterpillar leaves the chrysalis to become the beautiful butterfly, so the real you continues to survive in glorious realms beyond. At death, you will lay aside the physical body as you would an outworn and useless garment.

You have no idea of the vastness that exists inside you. All the wonders you perceive in the outer world can be found to a far greater degree within. For within each human being exists the seed of God, the divine spark. We prefer to call it man's true or higher self.

We would state that everything in the world is made of divine consciousness and that this consciousness lives in the innermost core of an individual. In other words, God dwells within you as your own self.

Although man is by nature divine, he, by means of his mind, deludes himself into believing that he is small, weak, and ineffectual when, in fact, he has at his disposal unlimited power and potential. God is all-pervasive, eternal, and perfect. He is in all things, within and without. Everything is God.

"Excuse me," interrupted Katherine, too curious and stimulated to restrain herself any further. "You have said that man is God Himself— that man has no existence apart from Him, and that it is illusion for man to believe himself separate from God. Firstly, I would ask what is God? Secondly, why has He created man? Thirdly, if we are God, why do we human beings experience imperfection, limitation, and suffering?"

"Yes," breathed Gwilym, "Why? Is God Himself as imperfect as we humans? Why has it not been possible for Him to establish and maintain perfection here on earth? What is it all about, Dr. Evans?" he asked earnestly. Only Elizabeth was silent, seemingly absorbed in thought.

"Firstly, you ask what is God and I am forced to concede that even we who dwell in the land of light, in realms supernatural, and in the blessed company of greater souls than you can possibly imagine do not know the answer to this question—one that I assure you has puzzled every being who has ever existed. Yet, on the basis of my own personal research and those views commonly shared by those who are most knowledgeable and enlightened, I would describe God as that supreme universal creative power that embodies all manifestations and which is the source—the originator, sustainer, and destroyer of all that is, has been, and ever will be. It is the supreme energy that pervades and permeates the universe during its processes of involution and evolution. It is the power of consciousness, the mighty impulse, the infinite vibration, and the ceaseless force from which springs everything that is, has been, and ever will be. This force infuses life into the physical senses, and is the unmoving foundation of all actions, inward and outward. It is the power that animates the senses and is the origin of the processes of creation, existence, and dissolution. In short, we would maintain that the entire universe is nothing but conscious energy, and that everything in the universe is this conscious energy, this consciousness expressed in different forms. In other words, all forms of life are God expressing through these forms.

"As to the purpose for man's existence on Earth, we would suggest the following: We would say that human beings incarnate in a body of flesh in order to evolve spiritually. By overcoming limitations, tests, and adversities presented by living life in a dense physical body and planet, their true nature and destiny are to achieve conscious, willing union with their father-mother God from whose heart they have been breathed forth. When the soul has

attained completed mastery over matter—over the pull of the Earth—and understood wholly that all life is one and that all is God, humankind is liberated from the bondage of rebirth on the physical plane of life.

It was only after several weeks had elapsed (during which time they had become accustomed to the remarkable manner and message of the Spirit Guides) that they began to truly digest, absorb, and assimilate the information they were receiving. By the end of the first month of communications, Katherine realized with delight and amazement that never before in her life had she been able to embrace a body of information so joyously, spontaneously, and enthusiastically. As far as formalized religion went, no philosophy had impressed her so deeply or had come so close to providing a satisfactory explanation for the questions that had puzzled her for as long as she could remember. Even with the extraordinary out-of-body experience she had at the age of seven that had enabled her to know that there is no death, she had received no other answers to profound questions as to the whys and wherefores of life and death. As Gwilym's healer, Mr. Fletcher had informed Katherine and her family they were uniquely qualified and specially gifted to warrant the instruction of their Spirit Guides. She was profoundly moved by the love with which these explanations were rendered. For it had been immediately apparent that Those attempting to transmit such information were motivated by a generosity of spirit, greatness of purpose, and beauty of character that she had not previously encountered in an individual. She could not help but feel overwhelmed by their largesse and by their abiding purity and love.

During these early stages, Katherine gleaned that the primary purpose for the communications was to educate them and as many human beings as possible so that these informed souls might individually and collectively work to protect, respect, love, and appreciate the Earth and prevent any further desecration or destruction. In light of the recent horrors brought about by World War I and with further international violence imminent, the Guides were intent upon persuading all those ready and willing to hear them and their human channels that future war could be circumvented if a sufficient number of men and women understood the significance of life on

Earth and the True Potential of human beings and could convince their fellow beings to employ methods other than violence, brutality, and destruction to resolve the petty differences, conflicts, and difficulties that separated man from his brother and one nation from another.

It was only after they had become both comfortable and familiar with such viewpoints, that the four were introduced to yet other Spirit Guides and Teachers who wished either to corroborate or elaborate upon the concepts presented by Dr. Evans. One very special Guide, named Hassan, claimed to be an Egyptian who had previously lived and taught on the Earth at the time of the Old Kingdom over 3,200 years ago. Hassan could recall vividly the architecture, culture, political, and entertainment figures of his day and was as eloquent in his fashion as Dr. Evans was in his. Like Dr. Evans, Hassan took Percy over completely so that Percy's voice, mannerisms, and features were transfigured entirely when he addressed the group. Hassan was a very tall, statuesque, and powerfully built man who moved slowly and deliberately and whose mannerisms in no way resembled either Percy's or Dr. Evans. He spoke softly and succinctly. In contrast with Dr. Evan's lilting, almost lyrical cadence, Hassan's speech was clipped and formal.

With apparent ease and simplicity, Hassan treated such complex philosophical subjects as the continuity of life after death; the nature of good and evil; freewill and destiny; reincarnation; the law of cause and effect; the heavenly life; the power of thought; and the nature of the changes that would inevitably be taking place on Earth. Amplifying and sometimes simplifying or even reiterating Dr. Evans' words, Hassan also sought to elucidate the myriad questions and issues pertaining to man's earthly existence.

"We would like you to understand that every soul on Earth is in the care of a guardian angel who has been appointed to watch over your actions and reactions to life. The guardian angel is a protecting and inspiring energy force that has never incarnated upon the Earth and that has evolved along another path to reach the angelic kingdom. He does not function at the same level or in the same way as human beings. This angel directs you toward those

opportunities that will enhance your spiritual growth and toward opportunities to pay off karmic debts or earn good karma. He seems impersonal, he supervises the learning of certain lessons, and watches over birth, marriage, and death. Your guardian angel never leaves you but remains with you from the moment you enter into mortal life until you leave it, and possibly even beyond this.

"We bring to your conscious awareness the presence of these angels not so that you may learn to rely upon them or that you may seek their assistance, but rather so that you may perceive their loving, comforting, and supporting presence and thereby become more fully acquainted with the nature of your creator and the infinite and incomprehensible love with which you are regarded. The gentle emissaries from the spirit realms serve only to advance your own spiritual progress, to awaken the soul to spiritual truth, and to remind you constantly of your creator."

Although Katherine may have felt inclined to challenge Hassan's words on an intellectual level and was rather tempted to blurt out, "On what basis is this so?" she intuitively grasped—with the "mind within the heart"—that his words were true. Furthermore, she sensed the urgency with which Hassan and the other Spirit Guides spoke. It had become perfectly clear to her and her family now, in the aftermath of the First World War, that scientific and technological advancement had greatly enhanced man's capacity for unprecedented destruction and even paved the way for the possible annihilation of the planet.

Ever a pragmatist, Katherine was not interested in far-fetched theory—no matter how high-sounding or greatly touted. She was, rather, concerned with the information that one might practically apply toward the improvement in quality of one's daily life and the lives of others could increase her understanding of life's purpose and meaning. Furthermore, to the extent one was able, she would examine and explore the teachings imparted by the Spirit Beings in as a systematic, objective, and scientific manner as possible. It was obvious from the first, however, that much of the material described or depicted by the Spirit Beings was of an intangible and unverifiable nature in accordance with conventional scientific methodology. Nonetheless, by establishing her own form of experimentation, Katherine was able to ascertain the validity of the information she received. For example, she began to experience her higher self, her potentially greatest self, and paused to listen to its guidance and support. Each morning Katherine would attune herself to her Creator and attempt to directly make contact with her Spirit Guide throughout the day as difficulties or challenges arose. She asked her Guide to help her form the decisions that would be of greatest benefit to her and those around her and to be as fair and open minded as she could be—discounting ego, personal aggrandizement, and gratification. By strictly adhering to the instructions outlined by the Guides, she would evaluate their efficacy in the context of her own daily life. "By their fruits ye shall know them," she vowed.

None of the four were in any way disappointed or disturbed by the information that was being imparted on a daily basis. Ironically, although it seems as if they were hearing the information for the first time from the Spirit Guides, much of what was said was not unfamiliar. On a subtle level, it became increasingly obvious that they had learned all this before—perhaps many dim, distant ages ago. It was as though their memories were being reignited and refreshed. Neither the vast quantity nor quality of the material offended them in any way. On the contrary, they found it helpful and uplifting. Within a very brief period of time, they discovered the material to be imminently practical. In fact, they were beginning to realize that the data would, as the Spirit Guides had indicated, provide the solid philosophical foundation upon which they would construct the rest of their lives. It was as a result of the constant testing, questioning, and measuring, and to which Katherine subjected the data that she would ultimately value, utilize, and trust it so deeply.

Certainly, Katherine was never embarrassed or intimidated, and freely asked questions of the various Teachers and Guides. Poor Hassan and Dr. Evans had quickly grown accustomed to her constant demands for "clarification," "definition," and "edification." With admirable patience and calm did they provide detailed examples and explanations in response to Katherine's perpetual whys, wherefores, and "on what basis." For they were well aware of their students' need to acquire as solid a grasp and as deep an understanding as possible in order to render the service for which they had all come together. The group's ultimate success would be determined by the extent to which they believed in what they were doing. It was essential, therefore, that they recognize and accept the information as the truth. Any doubt would hamper all future efforts.

CHAPTER 24

Moving Forward

———

THERE WERE MANY EVENINGS DURING which very little was spoken, but during which the foursome was given the opportunity to experience the exhilaration, the power, and beauty of the inner worlds. On these occasions, they would be guided into meditation by one of the Guides and remain in this wonderfully peaceful state for many hours. Afterward, each member of the group would discover with amazement that they had seen and experienced the same things.

In one instance, they saw beautiful, serene, radiant beings of light standing in a circle of pure white light, chanting and praying for peace on Earth and the hearts and minds of humanity. They seemed to be filled with a wondrous white light and to radiate this light to and throughout the cosmos. On another occasion, they ascended a beautiful snowcapped, rainbow colored mountain unlike any they had ever seen. As they climbed to the top, they were joined by glorious angelic beings who radiated love, kindness, and goodwill. These angelic beings were ethereal and diffused with light and the energy of pure love. Periodically they stopped and paused to breathe in the breath of God and to share the depth, vibrancy, "aliveness," and dimensions of the beautiful foliage and creatures they encountered as they made their way up the mountain. They were able to step into the future and to travel in the past. They were introduced by their Spirit Guides to many of the greatest Masters, Inventors, and Teachers of the past. Each of these "encounters" were exhilarating, extraordinary, and beyond words to describe. The skies were a vivid cerulean blue and the waters clear and bounding with life. The animals were regarded with respect and appreciated as friends and "brothers and sisters" of humanity. Humans were living in attunement with the earth and the whole of life—being good and respectful stewards of the planet. The trees were ripe with fruit, vibrant and robust. The earth itself was a glorious living, breathing organism. It was simultaneously both powerful and fragile. They saw in the future a different world. A world of peace, grace, joy, and beauty. No wars blighting the planet. No violence. No brutality. Only serenity and a deep abiding and magical peace.

There were other evenings during which they were witnesses to physical phenomena—the likes of which they had never seen or heard of before or even thought possible. On these occasions, the Guides chose to demonstrate to the physical senses of the group the existence of life beyond the physical plane. Through every conceivable manner of phenomena—apports, levitation, materialization, passing matter through matter, spirit lights, and transfiguration—the Spirit Beings demonstrated life's continuity and the concept that all life is energy operating at various rates of vibration. Furthermore, the group was introduced to a young female black Spirit Guide named Bright Eyes; a gentle, soft-spoken nun called Marie-Therese; a beautiful and noble and wise Native American Teacher named White Eagle; along with many former family members, friends, teachers and acquaintances the group had known on Earth but who had passed through the transition known as death and were now residing on the other side. One of the most remarkable visitations was from Catherine Sedonia, the girl who had died before Katherine was born. She was overjoyed to communicate with her beloved family. Catherine was euphoric to be reunited with those that she had so dearly loved.

Throughout the weeks and months Katherine was meditating two or three times each day as she attuned to her Creator and Spirit Guides. It was obvious that she and her life had been transformed. She would never be the same. Of this she was certain. She could never revert to her former attitudes and behavior; neither could she imagine life without the Spirit Beings who had become her closest, her dearest friends and confidants. *What would life be like without them?* She wondered occasionally. And yet, she knew that this period would not last forever. "Six months is the time allocated for your instruction," Dr. Evans had informed them at the inception of their work together. She could not imagine what would take place following their period of instruction. *Will we still maintain communications with our Guides?* she wondered. She was not afraid, only curious as to the manner in which her life would be conducted from hereon. It had been explained that the instruction was the foundation of all future work. But what would be the nature of this future work?

Finally—it did not seem possible—the lessons came to an end. After numerous demonstrations of physical phenomena and dialogue with many Spirit Beings; after receiving answers to many of the questions that had for so long perplexed them; after experiencing joy and fulfillment beyond anything they had ever known before; after six full months of daily communications with the Spirit Beings had elapsed, Dr. Evans announced, that the end had come (had Katherine actually perceived a twinge of remorse in his wonderful voice?).

"My dear friends, I am pleased to announce that you have at the present time received the information that will form the foundation for your future work. You will have no further need of our instruction. It is time now for you to successfully implement and apply all you have learned in your daily lives. Soon, you will be sharing your understanding as well as your own unique gifts with your fellow men who are so desperately in need of the information and gifts you have to offer. We will always be nearby to inspire and assist you in whatever manner we may. We shall certainly share many more joyous meetings together, I assure you. But these will be of a somewhat different nature than those of the past six months. The purpose for which we have come together at this juncture has been achieved. The work that we have shared has been successful. You are on your way.

"You are not alone now, nor will you ever be alone. May you ever be aware of the constant presence, peace, and love of your Creator. This is the wish and blessing of all those who guide you from the realms supernal. We pray for your eternal happiness and peace. So be it."

And in this manner were the six months of daily communications between the spheres concluded. That those in both worlds had greatly

benefited from the experience none could doubt. Each one who had participated had recognized the power and impact—and overall significance—of
the sharing that had taken place. None would ever again doubt either the
purposefulness of life on the Earth or the existence of life beyond the grave
and other planes altogether.

Had they received merely oral instruction from the Spirit Guides, it is
unlikely they would have accepted the information as readily as they did.
It was the physical evidence in the form of phenomena of all types that
convinced them beyond a shadow of a doubt of the existence of the realms
beyond the Earth. For they knew of no connivance, chicanery, or "magic"
that could have been responsible for all they witnessed with their own eyes.
They had experienced the direct wonder of the unseen world, and in so doing had realized that the laws that govern that invisible world also govern
the Earthly world. To Katherine it was the appearance of these Beings, the
very fact of their existence that served as the catalyst to her continuous quest
for the truth about the existence of all forms of life and if other forms of
life existed, that was the primary lesson to be learned. And if They existed,
how many other worlds were there beyond the Earth? How many different
Beings existed in the cosmos? If man's soul was immortal, from whence did
he originate? Whither would he go after death? How quickly after "death"
would he once again resume the mortal yoke? There could be no doubt that
her consciousness had been greatly expanded, her perceptions and perspective irrefutably and permanently transformed. She knew that she was not
the same young housewife of six months ago; she knew that she would never
again be the same. Life had altered dramatically for her and her loved ones.
There would, could, be no turning back. And as for the future—she could
only wait . . . accept . . . and observe.

It had not been until the final two months of the communications that
Katherine had received the conclusive "proof" she had required, enabling
her to accept fully the information imparted by the Spirit Guides. Only
after witnessing the extraordinary range of physical phenomena was she
able to truly "know," to feel without the slightest remnant of doubt that the
lessons provided by the Spirit Guides had rendered an accurate portrait of

life and had depicted life as it truly was. Furthermore, she realized that any further understanding on her part would have to come later in life. At the present time, she had absorbed as much as she could grasp. Further understanding and illumination, she felt certain, would arrive only after she had matured and experienced more of life and put these simple teachings to the test.

CHAPTER 25

Leonard

NOW, IN THE HEAT OF late July, Katherine thought wistfully of that snowy evening in December during which contact with the Spirit world had first been established. *What a long way we've come since then,* she thought to herself with a smile. *How much we have learned.* Yes, she was thoroughly satisfied with the unique series of events that had transpired. Never, for a single instant, would she regret the time and energy she had devoted for the purpose of receiving a greater understanding. At this particular moment, it seemed as though time were suspended and that everything had a distinct and important role to play in the scheme of things. It was with greater clarity and deeper appreciation that she now viewed the world—both its people and circumstances—around her.

The extraordinary events that had taken place over the past months flashed before her—first in sequential fashion, then in a kaleidoscope of changing images. The levitation of the small wooden table in the lounge—would she ever forget the look of horror mingled with fear and incredulity upon Percy's face as he watched it rise from the floor, hover over the room, and descend into its original position? The transfiguration of Percy's features and mannerisms as Dr. Evans and the other Guides who spoke through him. The full materialization of the form of Katherine's Guide, Bright Eyes; the partial materialization and visitation of numberless friends and relatives (including her sister) from the Other side; the phenomena of apports wherein physical objects were brought by spirit power from a distance to the séance room, often for many miles. She had received a lovely bouquet of flowers in this manner along with the feather from the headdress of a Native American Indian Guide that she kept hidden in her jewelry box. She had witnessed the sofa, along with the overstuffed chairs, lamps, cabinets, and tables levitate and remain suspended in mid-air for hours at a time. Never, as long as she lived, would she forget the unexpected late night visit of her younger brother, Leonard, with whom she was closest, who was, under the specific instruction of Dr. Evans, invited to join the foursome.

In compliance with Dr. Evans' wishes, Leonard had received a brief but illuminating account of what had been taking place in his sister's home every night for the past four months. Looking rather sheepish, tired, and terribly unhappy to have disturbed his family at so late an hour, Leonard had explained apologetically that he had somehow caught the wrong train home from work. Furthermore, he had failed to realize his mistake until the train had drawn close to Mt. Ash. On the spur of the moment, he had decided to seek rest and refuge at his sister's home. "I'm so terribly sorry for barging in on you like this," he apologized profusely, once he had understood that he had interrupted the evening meeting between his family and the Spirit Guides.

"Nonsense, you're not interrupting," Katherine reassured him. "Dr. Evans has been expecting you. He feels you ought to see for yourself what has been taking place here in our home over the past four months. You'd never believe us if we attempted to explain in words, so the Spirit Guides have devised a means for you to experience firsthand the nature of our communications. Until this moment, we have been forbidden to share our experiences with anyone else. You are the first outsider to be admitted into our circle."

"Indeed," Leonard had muttered under his breath, wondering what all the fuss was about, and not at all sure his sister was experiencing perfect mental health. It was not until Elizabeth and Gwilym smilingly came to Katherine's rescue and heartily endorsed her words that Leonard began to consider the situation seriously. "You really do mean what you are saying, don't you? You really do believe that you are in communications with Beings from another world."

"We don't believe it," Gwilym said lightly. "We *know* it to be so. We, your mother and I as well as your sister and your brother-in-law, have been in communications with Spirit Beings every evening for the past four months. And now, although we have pledged secrecy to Those Who guide us from beyond, it is obvious that you are being privileged enough to share this extraordinary experience with us this evening. You cannot begin to imagine how great a privilege it is to be a part of this experiment."

With his family siding against him, Leonard finally acquiesced, reluctantly agreeing to give the experiment a fair trial. "All right, then," he sighed. "Let's go. Where do we hold this meeting?"

"In the lounge," replied Katherine gleefully." "Come on everybody. Let's go. Let Leonard see for himself what takes place every evening in the lounge of the Haywards' home on Oxford Street in Mt. Ash, South Wales!" And in this manner was the unsuspecting Leonard induced to spend the remainder of the evening and a good portion of the morning in the company of the Spirit Guides.

As one might imagine, he had been astounded to observe the transformation that took place when Dr. Evans spoke "through" his brother-in-law. So surprised was he, in fact, that he almost fell out of his chair and was literally speechless for some minutes after Dr. Evans had introduced himself and invited him to ask any question he wished. But Leonard had been able to do little more than sit dumbly with his mouth wide open and his eyes firmly fixed upon Dr. Evans' countenance. Dr. Evans' voice, his dialect, his movement, and mannerisms bore no resemblance whatever to those of Percy!

What the hell is going on here? How can one account for such a change? he wondered silently. As though reading his mind, Dr. Evans explained the nature and purpose of the communications and volunteered a brief description of what actually transpired in order for him to speak through Percy in such a manner. *I cannot accept that explanation. I do not believe what you are telling me*, was Leonard's silent response to the demonstration he was witnessing. Once again, Dr. Evans seemed to be replying to Leonard's thoughts. He spoke gently but firmly.

"What evidence of our existence would you require? If it is at all possible, we should be pleased to oblige you. You see, your family will require your support and approval further down along the line. It is essential that you receive the evidence you require in order to grasp the nature of your family's work. Therefore, whatever you would require in the way of knowledge or proof, we shall be happy to provide."

Rather embarrassed at being so transparent yet suspicious nonetheless, Leonard finally blurted out. "If you really are a Spirit Being, and possess 'heightened powers of awareness,' then you should be able to describe in detail the events that took place in my life today—those that I have described to no human being and of which no human being is aware. Furthermore, I should like you to describe the nature of my business transactions this afternoon and the partner with whom I share my business. This information is what I should like to see you divulge here and now—if you do not find it impossible to do so." He seemed defiant. Katherine detected a malicious twinkle in Leonard's eyes and a positive smirk in his voice.

Come on, Dr. Evans, Katherine pleaded silently with the Spirit Guide. *Don't let us down. Show Leonard what you can do.* There was a brief pause as Dr. Evans digested Leonard's request and the full meaning behind it.

"It is my pleasure to describe before this group the events that transpired today," the Spirit Guide finally replied in a soft voice. And beginning with the precise time of Leonard's awakening that morning, Dr. Evans proceeded to describe in detail all that had taken place throughout the day.

"It's positively extraordinary," breathed Leonard, wondering how Dr. Evans had obtained, such information. Yet the best was yet to come.

For, after Dr. Evans had completed the verbal description, he addressed Leonard once again. "Rather than simply describe your business partner to you, why do I not bring him in our midst? Then we shall all be able to get a good look at him. After all, is not the saying 'one picture is worth a thousand words' apropos? Let us see young Mr. Hewitt." Leonard gasped as the name of the young man who was his business partner was announced. Undoubtedly, these were remarkable goings-on.

Only seconds later, the room began to fill with a vaporous substance—a white, cloudy film seemed to settle in their midst. In the very center of this swirling, eddying mist of vapor could be distinguished the faint figure of the young man whom Dr. Evans had just described as Leonard's business partner, Mr. Hewitt. No one uttered a word as the vapory substance continued to shift and form into varying shapes and patterns. In the meantime, the figure of Mr. Hewitt became more solid and in a short while he was vivid and obviously three-dimensional. Furthermore, there was no discernible difference between Mr. Hewitt and any of the other human beings in the room. All appeared to be solid and three-dimensional.

Leonard stared, utterly transfixed by the appearance of his business associate. As hard as he tried, he could find no explanation for this phenomenon. He could hardly believe that Mr. Hewitt had literally "floated" into their midst! Yet every feature of the man was clear. His eyes, the texture of his skin, every line and detail of his face were there for all to witness. Apart from the visual proof, he appeared as solid when each group member took his hand.

"How is it possible?" Leonard queried aloud, trembling from a combination of fear and excitement.

"Alas, you would not understand what makes this demonstration possible," stated Dr. Evans. "I can only tell you that there is no time or space in reality, and that all life consists of energy operating at different rates of vibration. Nothing, no one, is fixed or immobile or solid despite appearances. Everything is constantly changing, vibrating. Once one acquires mastery over matter, one is able to control the atoms and molecules around him. One learns to harness energy and to transmit and transform it. This is how so-called miracles, such as those described in the Bible, occur. Those great and luminous souls about whom so much has been written were so attuned to the creative power of the universe that they knew how to control the environment. Someday all men will possess these abilities. Man is then the master of his destiny, the captain of his soul."

"Dr. Evans may I attempt to explain Mr. Hewitt's appearance here to-night to my brother? I should like to test my knowledge if you don't mind. And you can correct me if I make any mistakes." Katherine blurted out while Mr. Hewitt remained very much in their presence.

"Go ahead, my child. I should like very much hearing your response," the Spirit Guide replied as though pleased by the progress of a diligent pupil.

"Well," she began, choosing her words carefully. "All human beings possess many subtle bodies in addition to the physical body—these subtler bodies being invisible to the human eye but very real nonetheless. These are often called the etheric body, the astral body, the mental body, the causal, buddhic, and atmic bodies, which are composed of progressively more subtle matter and all of which work in harmony with the physical body. For example, the etheric body is of a fine type of matter and permeates the physical as water does a sponge. The astral body is the model or framework as well as the replica around which the physical body is constructed and from which, in a sense, the physical body flows or develops. Made of a subtle and tenuous substance, it penetrates every nerve, fiber, and cell of the physical organism and is constantly in a state of vibration and pulsation. The astral body is most active when the gross body sleeps, and this is when the astral body may visit another locality, near or far, and communicate with other astral bodies of other living persons or of the so-called dead. This astral travel is also called astral projection by some. How am I doing so far, Dr. Evans?" Katherine turned from her brother to address the Spirit Guide.

"Very well, indeed, my dear. But, do go on."

"All right, then. Are you following me, Leonard?"

"Rather, but it all sounds like a good bit of science fiction to me," he admitted truthfully.

"Believe me, what we have learned to be factual is far more bizarre and unbelievable than any work of science fiction," smiled Katherine. "Now then," she continued, "countless human- beings travel in their astral bodies throughout the astral planes each and every night as their physical form remains in the sleep state. In these astral planes, one meets up or reunites, as it were, with those whom one loves or with whom one shares an affinity or a strong rapport. As a general rule, one does not recall the experience. Yet often, upon awakening in the morning, those who are of a sensitive nature and can attune to the worlds beyond may on occasion consciously recall at least a portion of the experiences of the night. 'I had such a vivid dream last night. It was so real. I dreamt that I was with my Mother. Mother was radiant and happier than I've ever seen her before. She assured me that she was still very much with me and that truly there was no separation between us—only a veil or curtain which obscured clear vision.' This is a fairly common occurrence among those who travel astrally by night. I am given to understand that adepts and highly evolved souls may travel astrally by conscious volition whenever they wish. They can command their astral bodies to go anywhere they desire in order to make observations, investigations, and acquire important information.

"Now to get to the point and the crux of our meeting with Mr. Hewitt this evening," Katherine continued calmly. "The astral body is an exact counterpart of the physical body, but is composed of an ethereal substance of a very high degree of vibration. Under certain conditions it assumes the vapory form of matter and is perceptible to the ordinary physical senses as a 'ghost' or 'apparition.' While a person is asleep, this astral body—in our case, the astral body of Mr. Hewitt—can travel anywhere."

"That is so, precisely. But this evening we must emphasize that it is as a result of our intervention that the astral body of Mr. Hewitt is present amongst you. It is we who have communicated with Mr. Hewitt on the astral level and asked him to make his appearance here this evening."

Dr. Evans had interrupted Katherine's recitation in order to make this point. "And so," concluded Katherine, "while the physical body of your Mr. Hewitt remains at home in bed, his astral body is here in our midst this evening. The communication that is taking place is occurring on the astral plane. Therefore, do not be surprised or dismayed when tomorrow at the office Mr. Hewitt recalls nothing whatever of this experience. This demonstration has been devised merely to assure you that there is far more to life than meets the eye—at least the physical eye, that is. There are countless spheres of life beyond this one and which interpenetrate this one. So now, why not ask of Mr. Hewitt himself any questions which are puzzling you at this moment? Let's see how he responds to his present circumstances!"

And although Leonard appeared completely nonplussed, he half-heartedly directed several questions and comments toward Mr. Hewitt. It was evident that Leonard was not entirely convinced of the true purpose and nature of the display. At one point, he had admitted, "It feels as though I am in a dream. Can this really be taking place?" And his sister and the others good-naturedly assured him once again that he was neither dreaming nor imagining any of it.

Finally, it came time to bid farewell to Mr. Hewitt and to conclude that evening's session. All were exhausted—poor Leonard in particular, and it was decided that he would spend the night in his sister's home.

"You'll awake feeling wide awake and wonderful, and then we shall further discuss this evening's experiment," Katherine had murmured after showing Leonard to his room.

"Lovely, thank you dear," Leonard had replied with a yawn. "See you in the morning, then. Good night, love—and thank you for this evening. I do not know quite what to make of it all yet, but I cannot deny that it has been a remarkable experience."

"Good night, love—and sleep well. We will discuss everything in the morning," said Katherine with a sympathetic smile, as she closed the bedroom door behind her. How vividly she recalled her own astonishment and confusion upon witnessing such a demonstration as this evening's. *Poor Leonard, I do hope that he's not too upset. Well, we can only hope for the best,* she thought to herself, then dismissed the subject entirely as she heard little Graham sobbing in the nursery.

Leonard was shaken. As he prepared for bed, he was not at all certain as to the true interpretation of the amazing events he had witnessed that evening. *By Jove, I wonder if they're all mad!* he thought suddenly, remembering the peculiar gestures and glances that had been exchanged between Katherine, Gwilym, and Elizabeth. *Or worse, perhaps I am going mad,* he tried to recall the events that had led him to his sister's door. *Perhaps I am just overly exhausted. God knows I have been cursed with an overactive imagination!* He could not help but feel that his arrival in Mt. Ash had been no coincidence, but rather something that had been planned or patterned. He shuddered, and a sudden chill pierced through his body. But no matter how he tried to rationalize that evening's experience, he could not dismiss the highly distinctive voice and visage of Dr. Evans. Nor could he hope to forget the swirling mass of vapor in which the form and face of Mr. Hewitt could be clearly seen. He shuddered again as he thought of the all-too-solid and tangible form of Mr. Hewitt and the handshake they had exchanged that had been as "real" as any he had ever known. Having changed into a borrowed pair of Percy's pajamas, he sank wearily into one of the pale blue armchairs near the fireplace and leaned back, waiting for the trembling of his limbs to subside and his mind to stop racing.

Suddenly, he was struck with an idea. "Damn!" he exclaimed excitedly. "If there are Spirit Beings nearby, let's see evidence of you right here and now." He addressed the latter to the empty space. "After all, my sister and her husband—the family—may have been trying to pull the wool over my eyes and perform some kind of trick in the lounge. But now, I am here all alone and know that no trickery can be responsible for your appearance."

Whispering in a hoarse voice, he once more challenged the Spirit Guides to make their presence known. "If you are truly around, let me have my own sort of proof." And, eyeing the two large windows covered with long deep blue draperies and matching valances, he continued firmly, "If you can hear me, you will indicate that this is so by making your presence known, please unravel those draperies stitch-by-stitch."

There was a moment's silence during which he experienced a sudden chill and a feeling of regret for having spoken so abruptly. Then, without any warning at all, the chair in which he was seated began to rise from the floor of its own accord and began to float in a circle around the room. "Oh, my God," he moaned softly—horrified to observe that the chair was rising and falling, rising and falling, that he could do nothing to control its movement. Furthermore, there was no indication that its motion would soon cease.

"I'm sorry," he cried hoarsely. "I do know now that you're truly here with me. But please do make this stop." He was getting both dizzy and nauseous. "Dear God, please make it stop." But the chair showed no sign of responding to Leonard's pleas. Instead, it paused for a moment in mid-air and faced the windows. Now, to his complete astonishment, Leonard watched as the draperies moved as though of their own accord. Stitch-by-stitch, the seams and hem were being unraveled. The valances also were flapping, and Leonard saw that they, too, were being unraveled stitch-by-stitch in compliance with his own request. Soon, the blue fabric, the curtain rods, and ties were thrashing and flapping wildly in no random fashion, very obviously under the careful control and guidance of some unseen force. "Thank you for this demonstration," he managed to croak out to the invisible forces at work. "I have seen enough, I assure you. Please stop, please stop. I beg of you." But in spite of his pleas, the movement continued. Now, the entire room seemed to be in motion. When Leonard was more frightened than he could bear, he screamed out in a voice loud enough for everyone in the house to hear, "Help! Someone please come and help me."

Within moments, Katherine, Elizabeth, Gwilym, and Percy were standing huddled at the doorway of Leonard's room watching horror-struck as Leonard floated above them, his face white and terrified. "Please call them off," Leonard sobbed. "I challenged them, and now they won't leave me alone. I know now that they exist. I need no further proof. Oh, please make them put me down."

"Now calm down, son. Calm down. There has been no harm intended. They were simply offering you the additional proof you required. All you have to do is remain calm and ask them to stop."

"That's all?" Leonard asked in a weak voice.

"That's all," replied Gwilym with a smile.

"Now?"

"Now, son. Whenever you feel ready."

"Oh, I'm ready. Believe me, I'm ready. I've had enough proof of their existence to last me a lifetime. Please, Spirit Guides, stop all this activity and place me and my chair back down upon the floor."

Only a moment elapsed before Leonard received a response to his request. Within an instant the draperies were being re-stitched and tied and being placed back over the windows and Leonard's chair was gently returned to its original position. "I shall never, ever doubt the existence of the Spirit-Guides as long as I live," he assured his family in a quivering voice. "Furthermore, I shall be happy to assist the Guides and all of you in whatever way I can. I assure you, I have never experienced anything like this in all my life. And frankly," he added, "I hope never to experience anything like this again. Once is definitely enough!"

Thankfully, by the time Leonard was ready to catch a morning train to Cardiff, he had almost fully recovered from the experiences of the previous evening. As a result of the evidence he had received, he was, in subsequent months, able to convey to the rest of the family the nature of the six-month period of instruction that had taken place in Mt. Ash and was able himself to fully support and endorse whatever public work the family was to undertake.

It was not long after Leonard's visit to her home that Katherine's eldest sister, Della, underwent a similar demonstration of the Spirit Beings' presence. As a result of a series of "coincidences," Della, who never paid a call upon Katherine without notifying her of the intended visitation, found herself wishing to surprise her younger sister with a visit to Mt. Ash. Like Leonard, Della was introduced to the Spirit Guides. Furthermore, she was introduced to the mediumistic abilities of those members of her family who had been participating in the extraordinary communications. During her brief visit, Katherine, under the influence of Bright Eyes, predicted in detail the events to follow in Della's life—all of which manifested within the next few weeks just as Katherine had foretold. As had been the case with Leonard, Della was convinced of the authenticity and, purposefulness of the communications. She, too, became a firm believer—a powerful supporter of the family's work. In years to come, she and Leonard would defend and endorse the controversial work that the family had undertaken. In spite of public derision and skepticism, these two would serve as staunch supporters and proponents of the work.

CHAPTER 26

Spreading the Word

SHORTLY BEFORE THE FORMAL INSTRUCTION came to its official end, the Spirit Beings provided Katherine and her family a summary of their teaching in the form of a simple prescription for joyous living. A somewhat abbreviated list of these guidelines is as follows:

1. Begin and close each day by acknowledging the creative force and your oneness with it and all life. Acknowledge that God—your Greater Self—will guide and direct your lives.

2. Remember that you are divine—that, in truth, you are neither the mind nor the physical body—but rather you are the unlimited power responsible for and manifesting through the physical form. The Real You is eternal and indestructible.

3. Many times throughout each day pause, relax both mind and body, and detach yourself from the material world. Attune to the creative force and the higher intelligences. Allow the wonderful healing, inspiring, and adjusting energies to flow to and through you. During these moments, "Be still and know that you are God."

4. Live thankfully. Each day presents myriad opportunities for the growth and development your soul requires. Life on earth is a school—and each day you are presented with new lessons. When you pass all your tests and courses, you will graduate and be admitted to a more advanced curriculum.

5. Live joyously and optimistically—knowing that in spite of the appearance of things, all is well and proceeding in accordance with the divine pattern. All is outworking for your blessing, benefit, and the unfoldment of all life.

6. There are no mistakes, and each human being is performing to the very best of his or her abilities at any given moment in time. But all human beings are at varying stages of development. Some are as infants, others are adolescent, some are middle aged, and so on. The old and wise soul recognizes that everything is purposeful; and that one is always in the right place at the right time.

7. Be kind. In your thoughts, words, and actions be kind to your fellow beings. Never judge or condemn, for you cannot know what it is to be in your neighbor's position.

8. Despite seeming evidence to the contrary, know that there is no injustice in life. Regardless of your circumstances you are but working through your karma, reaping what you have sown in the past, or else you are being given an opportunity to learn an important lesson. Look upon your circumstances with gratitude, knowing that each situation is an opportunity to acquire greater spiritual strength and knowledge.

9. Forgive those who have injured you. As the great teacher Jesus, who said, "Father forgive them, for they know not what they do." It is only ignorance that enables one man to hurt another. Try not to hurt any living being.

10. As often as possible think positively, constructively, remembering thoughts are things—that thought creates—and that what you think today will be externalized tomorrow. With each good, Godlike thought, you serve all humankind. With each negative thought, you harm your fellow beings and the world as a whole.

11. Learn to assume responsibility for your actions, thoughts, and words. By means of them, you are constantly contributing to your own future and the future of your world. Remember, "As you sow, so shall you reap."

12. There is no death. There is no hellfire or damnation. Man's soul is immortal; life is eternal. And where there is true love, there can be no separation.

13. Live patiently, adhering once again to the principle advocated by Jesus who stated, "Thy Kingdom come. Thy will be done in earth, as it is in heaven." In other words, resign all to God. "Not my will, O God, but Thy way. Thy will be done on earth as it is being done in Heaven."

14. In times of difficulty, chaos, and despair, pray to your Creator, ask to be shown the way and say "Take over God. Take charge of this situation." Then wait for the incoming of the light that will flood your entire being. Retain faith; do not lose heart, and know that there are no obstacles with which you are presented that you are not strong enough to overcome.

15. Treat the physical body as the temple of the soul; feed, rest, and exercise it and the mind judiciously and lovingly.

16. Know that all past karma, all difficulties and obstacles, can be transmuted through the constant application of love. Love is the greatest power of the universe; it is the resolution to all conflict and illness. Only when we have learned to love one another will all conflict, all disease be permanently eradicated.

17. The whole purpose of your life and the purpose behind every human experience is the growth and unfoldment of your soul. Delve beneath the surface of experience for wisdom and knowledge, and you will hasten the process of growth and unfoldment.

18. "Man, know thyself, and thou shalt know God and the universe." Attune, meditate daily, and discover the vast, untapped reservoir of love, wisdom, joy, and peace deep within you. Be mindful with conscious intention and purpose. Pay attention to all aspects of your life and the world around you.

And so, finally, at the end of six months, the Spirit Beings informed the group that they were now ready to share the knowledge they had acquired with all who were ready to receive it. **"It is time now for the next phase of** your work to begin, wherein you shall share your understanding of life with the public. All arrangements have been made. Your work will be of great value to those of Earth, and because you are rendering such an important service, we shall continue to guide and inspire each of you. We will be in close contact with you throughout your lives. Do not be disappointed or frustrated if there are many who doubt your words—forgive them, pray for their increased understanding and enlightenment. Love each and every one with whom you come into contact. Never ask anyone to accept or believe all that you teach; merely advise them to be receptive and open-minded. Remember, we ask no more of you than that you do your best. Our love, gratitude, and blessings are with you. God bless you always."

Dr. Evans' words had brought tears to Katherine's eyes, and she wondered if she were truly capable of rendering the "service" to humanity that Dr. Evans had described. With all her heart, she hoped that she would be of assistance.

And so, in this manner, were the four diligent pupils sent back into the world. Oddly enough, each felt ready to re-enter the mainstream. Each was ready to do their part.

During the most remarkable six-month period in her life, Katherine had become a teacher, and her real work—the work for which she had come to Earth—was about to begin. She could hardly repress her excitement! She was literally bubbling with joy and enthusiasm. What a turn her life had taken! So many of her questions had been resolved; former perplexities and obstructions cleared away. And now, finally, she was about to embark on the most extraordinary adventure of her life.

Toward the end of the six-month period of communications, the family had been advised by the Guides to share their healing and psychic abilities with those friends and neighbors who would benefit. Accordingly, Katherine and Percy rearranged the lounge in order to accommodate the surprisingly large number of guests who were interested in learning about their work. By word of mouth, news of these meetings spread. Within several weeks' time, their weekly Thursday evening get-togethers had attracted over fifty people! At these meetings, Katherine would briefly address the audience, explain that she, her parents, and Percy were gifted psychics and healers and would introduce her husband who was the primary healer. Percy had been designated by Mr. Fletcher and the Spirit Beings as a gifted healer. Now his healing gifts along with Katherine's psychic abilities were to be shared with the public. Often, she would predict the futures of those who attended the meeting. Both Katherine and Percy would be assisted by Gwilym and Elizabeth, who played important—if less obvious—roles in the process.

"It was your own teacher Jesus who stated, 'He that believeth in me, the works that I do shall he do also; and greater works than these shall he do,'" Katherine solemnly informed the people who gathered around her. "Each one of you has a vast and unlimited potential, for each one of you is God manifesting in human form." As a result of these meetings, remarkable psychic readings and healings took place, and the reputation of the group expanded rapidly.

CHAPTER 27

The Real Work Begins

No one was more surprised than Katherine by the sudden appearance of a rather pleasant-looking gentleman at her door who claimed to be a reporter for one of South Glamorgan's leading newspapers.

"May I introduce myself?" he had inquired politely. "I am Jeremy Woods, chief editor and journalist, and I should like very much to write a piece for my newspaper concerning the work you do from your home every Thursday night."

"Are you referring to our healing and psychic work?" asked Katherine, looking directly into the man's eyes.

"Yes, precisely," he replied evenly.

"How did you come to hear of us?" inquired Katherine suspiciously, wondering at the man's true motive for approaching her in this manner. *For what purpose could he possibly wish to write about us?* she asked herself.

As if reading her thoughts, Mr. Woods smiled. "A close friend and trusted coworker, who has attended several of your meetings, has advised me to contact you. Perhaps you remember her? Mary Gibbons. As a result of the healing performed by your husband, Mary has been cured of a debilitating back ailment that had plagued her since childhood. Although she has approached and received care from countless physicians and spent a small fortune trying to find a cure, it was your husband who healed her and absolved her of her affliction. She views what took place as a 'miracle,' and hopes that others with similar health problems may find their way to your meetings. Mary asked me, as a favor to the many who suffer, to publicize your family's work. And, frankly, I am quite curious myself as to the healing method your husband employs."

"I see," murmured Katherine, finally grasping the purpose for his presence and studying the man's countenance more carefully now. "What can I do for you?"

"Well, if you don't mind," replied Mr. Woods hesitantly, "I would very much like a bit of your time—the opportunity to interview you—get some background material regarding you and your family and how you came to be involved in your present work. I can arrange my schedule to meet your needs," he volunteered shyly.

"Well," stated Katherine thoughtfully, "as long as you are here, why don't we conduct this interview here and now—if that is all right with you?"

"That is precisely what I had hoped you would say," admitted Mr. Woods, with a boyish grin. There was a pleasant twinkle in his eye, and Katherine began to genuinely like him.

"Well, then, won't you come inside, Mr. Woods?" she suggested. "You may begin your interview with me—and then I shall be happy to introduce you to my husband and parents—all of them are deeply involved in the healing and psychic work we do together."

"I should be delighted," declared Mr. Woods. And Katherine spent the remainder of the afternoon describing her psychic abilities and the healing that Gwilym had received from Mr. Fletcher and the events leading to the present time.

"What a story! It hardly seems possible!" Mr. Woods had murmured at least five times throughout his visit.

"Nonetheless," stated Katherine calmly, "not only has it been possible, but it has been so. For the past six months, we have spent every evening—often for five or six hours at a time—in communications with our Spirit Guides. During this period, we have received a remarkable body of information and, furthermore, have been trained to employ our gifts of mediumship and healing."

"Absolutely extraordinary," Mr. Woods had remarked over and over again. "How I shall enjoy writing this piece! No one will believe it!"

"Ah," said Katherine suddenly, and in the most serious tone she had used throughout the afternoon, "I must insist that you present the information I have conveyed to you as factually as possible. You see, people *must* believe it! They must understand that what we have told you here today is the truth—no exaggeration, no embellishment—not a fairy tale but the truth, plain and simple. As we wish to share this truth with all who are ready and willing to listen to us. For those who receive it will benefit greatly. Of this I have no doubt." The latter was spoken with such intensity and conviction that Mr. Woods was unable to remove his eyes from Katherine's animated face.

"I see," he said softly. There was a brief silence as he digested the full significance of all he had seen and heard in the Haywards' home. "I should very much like to see a demonstration of your work, and I would very much like for as many as possible to see a demonstration of your marvelous abilities. If you would permit me, I should like very much to arrange a large public meeting in this community—say, at the Workman's Hall—where several hundred people may be exposed to your . . . er . . . philosophy."

"Why, I don't know," stammered Katherine in surprise. "I hardly know what to say."

"Well, 'yes' would be pleasant," teased Mr. Woods, wondering whatever had induced him to make such an offer. Certainly he had not come here with any intention of doing so. The words had merely flowed forth. He had been compelled to blurt them out!

"I just don't know—I will have to give it some thought," Katherine demurred. But Mr. Woods was insistent.

"Come now," he implored. "You have important messages to convey to the public. And I am merely affording you the opportunity to do so. I must insist upon making all arrangements for your first public meeting. I shall handle all publicity—we should have quite a bit. I shall be glad to handle all the details. You and your family need only show up on the appropriate date at the correct time. I will not listen to any further objection. I will notify you as to the details. And now, I must go. I cannot thank you enough for spending your afternoon with me. I shall never—for as long as I

live—forget all that you have shared with me today. And I am greatly looking forward to your debut."

"But . . . but, Mr. Woods," Katherine protested feebly, "we simply cannot accept." But her protestations were in vain. Mr. Woods merely clasped
her hand warmly in his, wished her a fond farewell, and found his own way
to the front door. "Well now, fancy that!" Katherine had marveled, as she
observed Mr. Woods' brown linen jacket disappear through the door.

"Can you believe it? Whoever would have thought our first public meeting would be arranged as easily as that!" She could hardly repress her excitement—for she knew that Mr. Woods' arrival that afternoon had been no
accident—that his intervention had been carefully and cleverly arranged by
the Spirit Guides. It had been such a brief time since they had begun their
Thursday get-togethers. And, already, preparations were under way for her
first public meeting. As the Guides had predicted, they would be surprised
by the ease and simplicity with which the pattern would be unfolded to
them and they would be carefully guided every step of the way. With genuine gratitude, Katherine recalled Dr. Evans' words, "You could not make a
mistake if you tried. We are ever with you."

"Thank you, Dr. Evans," she said aloud, in case he happened to be
within hearing distance.

Needless to say, Percy and the others were equally astonished by the
speed and efficiency with which the Guides had arranged their first public
meeting.

"If this is only the beginning, where from here?" Percy had mumbled to
his father-in-law.

"I know what you mean," Gwilym had replied, trying to imagine all
that lay in store for them. Already, his life had become an exciting business.
Each day was an adventure! Even though they were no longer in formal
daily contact with Them, he was sure that they would continue to receive
astonishing evidence of the power and presence of the Spirit Beings.

Only one week after Mr. Woods had appeared at her doorstep, placards
and brochures advertising the meeting had been distributed throughout
the Mt. Ash and Aberdare communities and to the neighboring villages as

well. Furthermore, there had been consistent advertisement and coverage in local newspapers. In addition, Mr. Woods had written a flattering and thoughtful essay based on his initial meeting with Katherine. The article had provoked quite a public response. Clearly, Mr. Woods had been a man of his word and had done everything in his power to ensure the success of the Haywards and Davies at their first public meeting.

It was a clear, warm August evening in 1920. The pale moon, a mere silver sliver, was already visible in the early evening sky but almost completely overshadowed by the sun which was now a luminous crimson and golden ball that seemed to dominate the heavens. The sky was all a riot of color ranging from pale primrose to lilac to deep violet. And Katherine reveled in the beauty of the sky from her bedroom window. A gentle breeze stirred the branches of the beech, larch, and scotch fir trees in the yard and cooled the bedroom wonderfully as she dressed and prepared for her first public appearance.

To her amazement, she was not feeling the slightest degree of nervousness. She felt only a sense of fulfillment and fruition—as though finally and for the first time in her life—she was doing what she had come into the world to do. "Mission accomplished," she giggled to herself, contemplating her response to what would take place that evening. Gratitude and a joy which seemed to be bubbling from deep within her and outwardly toward everyone and everything were the other feelings that overcame her as she completed her toiletries and began to dress.

"I'm glad I decided on the apricot-colored gown," she said aloud, viewing with satisfaction the image that she beheld in the full-length mirror. She had selected her clothes for the evening earlier in the day. An apricot-colored purse and hat, identically matched her high-heeled pumps. A string of pearls and simple pearl earrings were the accessories she had chosen to complement the classic, tailored gown. As she continued to gaze at herself, she realized with pleasure that her appearance was simple and understated and indisputably elegant.

Glancing over in Percy's direction, she watched in admiration as he casually completed the final phases of his toiletries. With his tall, lean physique, he wore nearly all clothing with style and elegance and, on this night, he looked particularly handsome and debonair in the beautifully cut navy blue suit that he reserved for only the most special occasions. *Why, he really is a handsome man,* she thought to herself. *And I do believe we are a handsome couple,* she continued, then blushed in embarrassment at the lack of modesty inherent in such thinking. *Oh dear, I'll be getting conceited if I don't watch out,"* she thought, smiling to herself.

"What's the secret love? What are you smiling so mysteriously about?" inquired Percy, noticing her facial expression, which was reflected in his dressing-table mirror.

"No secret at all, my dear—only a genuine appreciation of you and your appearance this evening," she replied honestly. And now, under his wife's admiring glance, it was Percy's turn to blush.

To Katherine's amazement, neither she nor Percy were the slightest bit nervous or apprehensive about the outcome of the meeting. Furthermore, as they rode en route to the Workman's Hall, she saw with surprise that neither her mother nor her father were at all nervous.

"How is it that not one of us has a case of the jitters?" she inquired of her family, marveling at the poise that all of them seemed to be maintaining.

"I suppose we are keeping to the fore of our minds Dr. Evans statement, 'What is fear but thought?' So long as we are aspiring to the highest and the best and performing to the very best of our abilities, what have we to fear? The rest is in God's hands," laughed Gwilym. "You know, although I haven't the slightest notion as to the nature of the reception we shall receive, I know that all is taking place in accordance with God's will. Certainly I shall accept neither praise nor blame personally."

"I think that I shall take Dr. Evans' advice and merely 'observe' the role I perform and the words I speak with detachment and objectivity," murmured, Katherine, wondering as she spoke if, indeed, it would be possible to behave in such a manner.

Although they were not scheduled to begin their demonstration until eight o'clock, they arrived at the Workman's Hall at half past seven. As Katherine alighted from the taxi, she was astonished to observe the large number of people milling about in the street as well as a long queue more than halfway around the block.

"Whatever is going on? What on earth has happened here?" she asked Percy, then realized suddenly that these people—*all* of these people—were waiting to enter the hall wherein they would soon be watching her demonstrate the proof of survival!

"I can't believe it! They're waiting to see us, aren't they?" her eyes were dancing with merriment and excitement as they met Percy's smiling countenance.

"You are now experiencing firsthand the power of advertising," he teased.

"Do you mean that all this," Elizabeth's gaze took in the street now teeming with people, "is a result of the publicity Mr. Woods has provided?"

"Exactly, my dear," replied Gwilym.

"It is amazing, isn't it?" Katherine remarked.

"What isn't amazing these days?" replied Percy, as they found their way into the back of the building in accordance with Mr. Woods' instructions.

"Hey, blokes, where do ya think you goin'? Why ain't you waitin' in line like the rest of us?" several people in line had called out angrily.

"Who do ya think you are?" one young lad had cried out in a nasty voice.

"We think, sir, that we are those whom you have come to see demonstrate the proof of survival here this evening," Gwilym had replied easily in his kind voice, whisking his family away from the confusion.

"Whew!" sighed Katherine upon entering the building. "I sure am glad that we are out of that mess!"

"Good evening," they heard a familiar voice address them and Katherine was relieved to see Mr. Woods waiting for them by the rear entrance. "So happy to see you all. I do hope you are looking forward to this evening's program as much as I am," Mr. Woods smiled. "You all look simply wonderful. Follow me; I shall guide you to the auditorium."

"Lovely, thank you," replied Katherine happily. And at last they were on their way.

"I've never seen anything like it before," whispered Elizabeth once on the stage behind the heavy burgundy velvet draperies that separated her and her family from the audience, as she observed literally hundreds of people pouring into the auditorium. For a single instant Katherine wished that she could be free and return to the lounge wherein so many evenings had been spent listening to the beautiful and comforting words of the Guides. But then she caught herself, realizing that her words might affect those in the audience as deeply as those of the Guides had affected her. "Not my way, O God, but Thy way," Katherine repeated dutifully, as she recalled Dr. Evans' advice.

At precisely eight o'clock the doors to the auditorium were closed. The idle gossip, chatter, and laughter of the audience that had already begun to subside now ceased abruptly. All shifting and fidgeting stopped, and a great hush came over the hall. As the draperies slowly parted, Gwilym took his position at the podium at the center of the stage.

"Good evening, dear friends," he began in his beautiful, melodious voice. He spoke with the poise and presence of one who has appeared in the public eye all his life. "My family and I are here before you this evening to share with you the remarkable discoveries we have been privileged enough to make during the past six months. Although some of you may be shocked by what I am about to tell you, let me assure you that I and my family were equally shocked by the events that have culminated in our appearance here before you this evening. No one who has been raised to believe that he is a Christian or a Catholic can accept easily what I am about to tell you. On the other hand, everything that I am about to share with you can be easily compared with and corroborated by the teachings of the greatest saints and sages and religious leaders of all time—including Jesus, who knew with utter certainty and conviction that he would not, that he could not 'die' with the mere death of his physical body. Some of you may recall that this great teacher spoke frequently of life beyond the grave. And, furthermore, did he not actually appear to his disciples following his 'death'? 'I will not leave you comfortless; I will come to you. Yet a little while, and the world seeth me no more; but ye see me; because I live, ye shall live also. At that day, ye shall know I am in my Father, and ye in me, and I in you.' Jesus had stated. 'Ye have heard how I said unto you, I go away, and come again unto you.' Jesus had further stated. And do not all of you recall Jesus' appearance to Mary Magdalene and the words he spoke to her following his 'death'? 'Touch me not; for I am not yet ascended to my Father; but go to my brethren, and say unto them, I ascended unto my Father and your Father, and to my God, and your God.'

"And, on that same day in the evening, did not the Lord Jesus appear before his disciples and stand in their very midst? To the doubting Thomas who had declared, 'Except I shall see in his hands the print of the nails, and put my finger into the print of the nails, and thrust my hand into his side, I will not believe.' Jesus said, 'Reach hither thy finger, and behold my hands; and reach hither thy hand, and thrust it into my side; and be not faithless, but believing.' And having received this proof, Thomas replied, 'My Lord and my God,' to which his wise and beloved Master responded, 'Thomas, because thou has seen me, thou dost believe; blessed are they that have not seen, and yet believed.'

"There are other statements and descriptions in both the Old and New Testaments that may be used to corroborate everything that we shall say and demonstrate this evening. For example, you will be able to witness the remarkable healing ability of my son-in-law, Percy Hayward. Certainly, you are all aware of the numberless healings and miracles performed by Jesus. The fifth chapter of the gospel of St. John is concerned to a great extent with healing. At the pool of Bethesda in Jerusalem, Jesus asked one who had been infirm—'impotent' for thirty-eight years—'Wilt thou be made whole? Then, rise, take up thy bed, and walk.' And immediately the man was made whole, and took up his bed, and walked. And to the man who had been blind since birth, Jesus anointed the eyes of the blind man and the man received sight.

"And I have not even mentioned the miraculous manner in which Jesus brought back to life Mary's brother Lazarus who had been dead for four days. Although Lazarus had been in the grave for four days, Jesus had cried with a loud voice, 'Lazarus come forth.' And then 'he that was dead came forth, bound hand and foot with grave-clothes; and his face was bound about with a napkin.'

"Furthermore, my dear friends," continued Gwilym, "Jesus stated, 'I am the way, the truth, and the life; no man cometh unto the Father, but by me . . . He that hath seen me hath seen the Father, because I am in the Father and he in me . . . I am the good shepherd; the good shepherd giveth his life for the sheep . . . As long as I am in the world, I am the light of the world . . . I, if I be lifted up from the earth will draw all men unto me. The Father that dwelleth in me, he doeth the works . . . He that believeth in me, the works that I do shall he do also, and greater works than these shall he do. . . Be still and know that I am God.'

"In other words, Jesus came as a great teacher, a leader, and an example to show us, his younger brothers and sisters, the manner in which to live and view our lives. 'You are God,' Jesus tells us. 'In time you and all men shall do all that I can do. The kingdom of God is within you. As God, you too are capable of rendering healing to your fellow beings, you too are capable of achieving miracles.' It is only by living as did Jesus and as Jesus recommended, 'Love one another. Seek ye first the kingdom of God, and His righteousness, and all these things shall be added unto you. Continue ye in my love.' said Jesus, 'that you will know true happiness and perform life-giving miracles.'

"Those great and advanced souls who have lived in accordance with these principles have discovered not only the formula for successful and joyous living, but they have also discovered that they, like Jesus, have the potential to perform miracles. My family and I believe that each one of you has the potential to become master of your life, of your body, of your conditions, and of your circumstances in the world. 'I come that ye might have eternal life,' said Jesus. Gentle Jesus—who poured forth love to all creatures, to all men—is the example all men are to follow. 'Be still and know that I am God'—that *you*, each one of you, is God. Tonight you shall see a demonstration of so-called miraculous powers displayed by my daughter and her husband. We have no doubt that dormant within each of you is the potential to perform 'miracles' of a similar nature.

"During the past six months, I and my loved ones have been in constant communication with Spirit Beings—discarnate Enlightened Souls who dwell in worlds beyond the physical. These Beings—who have all at one time lived in a physical body on the Earth—assure us and wish us to assure you that there is no death. Life is eternal; man's soul is immortal. Man continues to survive beyond the grave. In fact, man is more radiantly and joyously alive following the death of his physical body than while in the body. Tonight we wish to demonstrate the proof of survival—to share with you in some way, the information that has transformed our lives. It is with greater joy than you can possibly imagine that we share our insight with you this evening."

Cheers and a large burst of applause greeted Gwilym's words. But he seemed unaffected. He spoke as though inspired.

And so he is inspired, smiled Katherine, deeply aware of the presence of the Spirit Guides. *How blessed we are,* she thought with profound gratitude. The time flew by. Soon it was Percy's turn to stand at the podium and address the crowd. To Katherine's dismay, he seemed ill-at-ease and stiff in contrast with her father. There was an affected quality to his delivery and manner. *Is it my imagination, or does Percy sound pompous?* she thought to herself. And she noticed that there seemed to be quite some yawning and fidgeting among the audience members.

"Come on, gov'nor," one burly young man had called out, "We didn't come 'ere to get a bloody sermon—we want to see you heal. That's what the advert said—healin', proof of survival. Let's see some of that!"

Elizabeth was aghast at the young man's rudeness, and Katherine saw that Percy's face was flushed with embarrassment. Her heart sank, as she saw Percy lick his lips nervously. *What is he going to do?* she wondered worriedly.

She then heard Percy laugh and say good-naturedly to the young man, "You're quite right. You came here to see a demonstration of healing. So let's get on with it, shall we?"

With an enormous sigh of relief, Katherine watched various volunteers from the audience file on stage one-by-one and receive treatment. The effects of Percy's healing were immediate and extensive in many cases, and as Katherine watched him work, her eyes glistened with pride.

"Cor, you're a bloomin' miracle man," the burly young man had exclaimed before the entire audience, as Percy's healing hands instantly soothed a skin irritation which had bothered the lad for several weeks.

Finally, it was time for Katherine to demonstrate her gifts of clairvoyance. Each had been given the gift of healing and mediumship. Katherine's special gift was clairvoyance as well as eloquence in her ability to communicate. Perfectly calm and unruffled, she approached the podium. Several men in the audience whistled appreciatively, but she took no notice. In her rich, inimitable and highly theatrical voice, she addressed the audience as naturally as if she had been performing in front of them all her life.

"Well now," she began. "I am Katherine Hayward." She paused dramatically, then continued, "And I want all of you to know what I know to be true—and that is, there is no death, the kingdom of heaven is within us all—and all things are possible.

"My father and my husband have already shared with you the extraordinary events that have led to our appearance here tonight. Now I would like to assure you that there is no further motive or purpose for our presence here than to share with you the information we have acquired and which has transformed our mundane lives into a joyous, fulfilling, and beautiful experience. That each one of you may benefit, that each one of you may live more joyously and purposefully—these are the true reasons for our presence here among you.

"And now, I will prove to those who have come to witness evidence of life's continuity, that there is no death. I shall put you in touch with your friends and loved ones who have passed through that transition called 'death' and who are now very much alive in worlds beyond the Earth. As you are neither the mind nor the physical body but rather that power or spirit that motivates the mind and body, the real 'you' continues to exist eternally. So is the case for all human beings. At 'death,' the real you enters a world far more sublime than the Earth plane where it continues to experience life of a different nature than that of Earth. Because I am a trained medium (a conduit for those on the other side), I am able to receive impressions from the worlds beyond this one and act as a sort of telephone between two worlds. I shall now proceed to put you into contact with those who no longer inhabit the earth and who no longer dwell in a physical body."

Pausing for a moment, Katherine closed her eyes, took several deep breaths and then, with a smile, pointed to a young woman with a pale face and shoulder-length golden hair in the third row of the audience. "You, my dear," stated Katherine in a loud, clear voice, "are not at all certain as to the reason for which you have come here this evening. You had other plans, in fact, and canceled them to come. A dinner engagement with a close female friend, named Denise, I believe." The woman gasped audibly.

"Yes, that is true—exactly," she whispered, obviously quite shaken.

"Well, my dear let me assure you that there is a very important purpose for your visit here this night. For your dear son, James, whom you lost less than a year ago, is very eager to communicate with you. He wishes you to stop grieving, to stop mourning his death, and to know that he is still very much alive. Your sadness deeply distresses him. He cannot bear to watch you suffer." Tears filled the young woman's eyes, and she began to sob softly. Embarrassed, she started to cover her face with her arm.

"It's all right, my dear," Katherine murmured gently. "It's all right."

"How do you know of my James?" the woman finally managed to get out.

"He is with me now," replied, Katherine calmly. "He is standing next to me—to my right. He is smiling and asks me to assure you that he is well. He is showing me a scar on his left knee, which he states was the result of a wound inflicted upon him during childhood—when he was eight years old. Apparently, he had fallen off of his bicycle and landed on the sharp edge of a rock. He says that he had never seen you so worried, and that he had to be very brave and assure you that he would be all right. He says you were such a good mother—you cared for him so deeply. You bathed and bandaged the wound with such tenderness. Now he wishes to repay your kindness, your many kindnesses. He begs you to be sad no more, and to live your life fully. He advises you to visit a Spiritualist Church in order that he may speak through a medium to you more often. He says that he often sees his grandmother, Augusta Montgomery, on the other side and that both of them are doing their best to look after you. James says that your husband will find work soon—in the coal mines near Rhondda Fawr–and that there will be money enough to meet all of your expenses."

"Thank you—oh, thank you, my wonderful James—Mrs. Hayward—James!" cried the woman who was deeply moved. "Just one more thing, Mrs. Hayward, if you please, can you tell me what my boy looks like now that he is . . . uh . . . on the Other Side?"

"I would be happy to describe him," replied Katherine, "but he says that he looks exactly the same as he did when last you saw him at home while in the physical form. His hair is black and wavy—and as unruly as ever, he says. His eyes are a deep blue color, almost violet. His face is smooth, his complexion fair and clear. He is a tall, gangling fellow—over six feet tall I should say—and he is dressed in what he says you always called his 'bonnie blue trousers.' As he smiles, I notice that he has only one dimple—in his left cheek. Shall I continue?" asked Katherine.

"No, Mrs. Hayward. I have heard enough. I know that you are in touch with my boy, and that he has lived on. No one but James, my husband, and I know of the scar on his knee or how he got it. Furthermore, I have felt my son's presence very strongly here tonight. I am certain he put his hand on my shoulder. It is the first time in nearly a year that I have felt any happiness at all. Thank you, Mrs. Hayward. I cannot tell you what this experience has meant to me. I shall never forget it. I thank you with all my heart." Great tears trickled down her cheeks, and there was hardly a dry eye in the audience.

"You are welcome, my dear. You will find your life greatly changed from hereon. For your son wishes to keep in close contact with you. Now that you are aware of how to make this contact, you will feel his presence often. That is all I have to tell you, my dear. God bless."

"God bless you, Mrs. Hayward. "

Next, Katherine's attention was drawn to a portly, rather distinguished looking silver-haired gentleman who sat far back in the auditorium. "May I speak with you, sir?" she asked, politely. The man opened his mouth to speak, but no words came out. He was obviously terrified. "May I speak with you, sir?" Katherine inquired once more. The man nodded dumbly, averting his eyes to the ground.

"I have someone—a lovely, fair-haired young lad of approximately thirteen years—who wishes very much to make his presence known to you. His hair curls becomingly around his face; he has a ruddy complexion; round blue eyes that are as clear as glass marbles; is rather short and stocky; has a lovely, sweet smile; and calls himself 'Billy.' Although he is smiling beautifully now, he tells me, sir that you are more likely to recognize him with an unbecoming scowl or an impish grin upon his face. He says, you and he were quite frequently at odds with one another—even though you loved each other dearly. Although in blood you were his uncle, he says you raised him from the age of two when his own parents died in a tragic railroad accident. He remembered very little about his real parents and claims that you were in every way a father, a very good father, to him. He says you are not to worry—not to fear the future. The business matters with which you have been involved during the past six weeks will be resolved to your satisfaction, and you will be making a tidy profit as a result of your endeavors in this area. He says that 'Kitty' will not only be accepted into University but will also be awarded a scholarship that will help to pay her tuition. So anxious is little Billy to convince you of his presence with me this evening, that he is at this moment impressing me very powerfully—so powerfully, in fact, that if you look closely—come here sir, so that you will see clearly—you will see that Billy is with me, influencing me. Can you feel his presence?"

"I feel him amongst us," the man said in a hoarse voice.

"Oh, my God. Oh, my God. It is you, Billy. How I have missed you, my child. How sorely I have missed you, my son. Why have you not come to me sooner? Nothing has been the same without you, lad—without your laughter, your preposterous questions, your delightful conversation. I shall never stop loving you, my Billy boy."

And again, Katherine continued to deliver Billy's message. "And I, dear uncle, shall never stop loving you. Look for me each night before you fall asleep. You need only think of me to connect with me. For I am always nearby. I would not leave you, uncle. You must understand, that where there is true love, there can be no separation. I have learned an awful lot since I have come to this place. There are wonderful halls and temples for learning here. I have received the constant guidance, support, and assistance from wonderful teachers and companions who are very kind and understanding. And you must believe me, uncle, that although I loved you and our home on Earth, I would not wish to return there. It fact, were it not for my love for you and dear Kitty, I would not choose to link with Mother Earth at all. For life on this side is wonderful and very beautiful and fulfilling in every way. There is wonderful scenery; beautiful music and art; exquisite buildings; the opportunity to learn and grow in all areas; and a nobility and gentleness in spirit of the Beings that are unparalleled in the human beings on Earth. Here, the power of one's thought is far greater than on the Earth. For one has but to think something or someone for it to manifest instantly. There are trees here, and fruits and flowers and children and animals—everything that is on Earth—only here they are far happier, more bountiful, and lovelier. The spirit world is solid and real—as real as the Earth life, only infinitely more beautiful.

"You must not think of life and death as being separate, but concentrate instead upon eternal life. I have two requests, uncle. Firstly, that you truly begin to feel that there is no death and that nothing can separate us; and secondly, that you share what you have experienced here this evening with others so that they, too, may come to realize that life continues beyond the grave. That is all for now, uncle. I must go. I love you."

"I love you too, my son," the old man sobbed. "I love you, too."

By now, the man had broken down and was weeping unrestrainedly. The audience sat in stunned silence. They had been deeply moved by the communications that had taken place. Now, they watched in awe as all traces of Billy disappeared and Katherine resumed her normal demeanor.

"Bravo," one man cried from the first row.

"Bravo," many others joined in. "Well done, Mrs. Hayward. Well done."

"Thank you," murmured Katherine modestly. "Your appreciation means a great deal to me. Shall we continue?"

"Yes," the audience roared.

"Good," smiled Katherine. And she spoke with many others introducing to them loved ones who had passed over to the other side.

Not until half past ten did the meeting conclude. The audience had stood and cheered, and had not wanted to leave. But Katherine had been firm. No one could be in doubt of the overwhelming success of their first public effort.

"Can you believe it's over?" she whispered joyously to her father as they made their way into the waiting taxi, teems of people still calling out to them from the sidewalks. Her face was shining with excitement; her eyes glowed with pleasure and the satisfaction of having completed a job well done.

"Well, now, I am glad that's over!" sighed Elizabeth, first kicking off her high-heeled shoes, then yawning and stretching comfortably in the back seat of the taxi.

"Never has time passed more quickly," observed Gwilym. "That crowd was extraordinary. Seemed as though they had been hand-picked."

"Don't think they weren't," was Katherine's retort. "I wouldn't put anything past our Spirit Guides."

"I have to agree with you there, love, concurred Gwilym with a laugh.

"What a night! I shall never forget it as long as I live," sighed Katherine happily. The three chatted gaily for the remainder of the ride home. Only Percy was unusually quiet, lost in thought.

The publicity that followed their first meeting was overwhelmingly favorable, and they were persuaded by Mr. Woods and many of their friends to schedule another such meeting within the month. Furthermore, as a result of the publicity, they received numerous invitations to appear at local clubs, societies, and churches to speak and to demonstrate their healing and mediumistic abilities. Within several months, news of their work had spread throughout South Wales and they were in great demand. Fortunately, one of their elderly and maternal neighbors volunteered to care for Graham during their absences. Soon they found themselves traveling frequently from one city to another appearing as guest lecturers, and granting countless interviews and private sittings.

The pattern that was to continue for the rest of their lives had thus been established. To heal; to share the understanding of life's purpose and meaning that they had received from the Guides; to demonstrate life's continuity; to bring love and hope and the desire to live in peace into the lives of as many as possible—these were now their tasks. Finally, their "real" work had begun.

CHAPTER 28

Percy's Change of Heart

FOR MANY MONTHS FOLLOWING THEIR first public meeting at the Workman's Hall, Katherine was overwhelmed by the extensive public response to her family's work. In fact, nothing could have come as a greater surprise than the instantaneous recognition, success, and demand for their services. No one had been prepared for the deluge of invitations requesting their appearance in all parts of Wales and western England, or for the extensive travel and preparation required to keep these engagements. Within a very brief period of time their lifestyle had been dramatically and irrevocably altered.

Because they refused to charge any fee at all for their services, they were still required to earn a living by day in addition to the "real" work they did by night. It was necessary, therefore, for poor Percy to continue managing the custom tailoring shop during the day and to lecture and heal by night. And Katherine was required to run the household and care for little Graham as well as to demonstrate her mediumistic abilities during the evening hours. By Christmastime, all four—Percy, Katherine, Gwilym, and Elizabeth—were thoroughly exhausted, and privately wondering how such a hectic pace might be maintained.

Shortly after the Christmas holidays, Gwilym and Elizabeth announced their decision to move out of Mt. Ash and to live, instead, on the small piece of property that Gwilym had purchased as an investment shortly before leaving Gwaelod-y-garth. Now that he felt better than ever, he felt it advisable to establish a small psychic research center and congregation wherein he and Elizabeth could teach, heal, and demonstrate the proof of survival in their own simple, unpressured way. Nearly fifty-three years old and still delicate after the recent illness, Gwilym simply was no longer capable of maintaining the busy public schedule of the previous six months. After careful deliberation, he and Elizabeth decided that they could best serve by opening up their own place.

Carefully concealing her own disappointment, Katherine helped her parents pack and sent them on their way. "How empty this house seems without them!" she had sighed aloud following their departure. How often during the days to follow did she have to bite her lip to keep it from quivering, to blink away the tears that rose to the surface of her eyes. *Why must you behave like such a child?* she silently berated herself during these instances. But the truth was that she was lonely.

Yet although she was saddened by their departure, Katherine felt its rightness, its inevitability. From somewhere deep inside her a voice insisted, *You must work alone. You will work alone.*

Don't be idiotic! she chided herself, then silently explained to the "voice" that it would be utterly impossible for her to work alone. *After all, I have a husband and a little boy to care for. How could I possibly work alone?*

You shall see, was the voice's only reply. And Katherine shuddered as a sudden chill overcame her. Feelings of dread and foreboding gnawed at her, and although she tried to laugh aloud at her silliness and to assume a mood of lighthearted gaiety, the ominous feeling would not go away. Thankfully the unpleasant reverie had been interrupted by the irritating jangle of the telephone in the kitchen, and any doubts or fears were temporarily set aside.

For more than six months following the departure of Elizabeth and Gwilym, Katherine's life proceeded smoothly. No major disturbance marred her home life; her loneliness had ceased; little Graham was becoming a fine, handsome little lad; and, as the Spirit Beings had predicted, the public work that had begun so auspiciously continued to flourish. Nearly every night of the week was devoted to the work—healing circles, public meetings, lectures, and demonstrations occupied nearly all of Katherine's free time. For some time, both she and Percy were engrossed and completely fulfilled by their involvement in the work. Imperceptibly at first, but more noticeably in time, however, Percy's attitude toward the work began to change. A handsome, intelligent young man in the prime of his life, he had little time to enjoy life. He had grown bored and frustrated with his role as manager of the tailoring firm.

Having always detested Mt. Ash, he now longed more than ever to get away permanently from the mining town. Unfortunately, his requests to be transferred to another firm had been turned down repeatedly. Furthermore, he was weary of the financial responsibilities inherent in family life that had fallen upon his young shoulders. He was also resentful of the time his wife had been devoting to the work, and despite her fancy words and pretty phrases, he knew that he could never hope to capture her heart or compete for her time and attention. Most importantly of all, however, Percy was deeply saddened and disappointed by the manner in which his own speaking and healing abilities had been received by the public. Although he frequently demonstrated remarkable healings and gave excellent talks, it seemed that his achievements paled beside those of his wife in the public's eye. Of a highly competitive nature, Percy could hardly endure the consistent praise and flattery received by his wife while his own abilities were largely ignored or casually dismissed. He could hardly bear the awful burden of being held in lower public esteem than his wife.

Frankly, Katherine herself had difficulty in determining why she always seemed to receive more praise and attention than her husband, for she genuinely regarded his gifts as greater than her own. His healing ability was matchless. And, after all, had it not been for Percy's mediumship, she would not even be doing the work! Yet, for whatever reason, regardless of the city or village in which they appeared, the crowds were wildly enthusiastic over her and her clairvoyance and only moderately impressed with Percy's healing. She could only attribute her success to her instinctive theatricalism. Showmanship, in fact, seemed to be an integral and inherent aspect of proving survival. Each communication was a drama unto itself. In truth, Katherine's success could be attributed to a number of factors including her striking physical appearance; her indisputable charisma; her easy charm and playful personality; her delightful candor and droll sense of humor; her lively wit; the devastating accuracy of her predictions; and the lucid, straightforward manner in which she communicated with those in the spirit world.

She would have done anything in her power to help Percy—to ease his pain and lessen his burden. But she did not know how. As he grew increasingly frustrated and resentful, he was unwilling to discuss his difficulties and withdrew into his own internal world. The more depressed he was, the more uncommunicative. In time, he became virtually unapproachable. In the meantime, Katherine could only hope and pray that time would somehow heal Percy's wounds and resolve the situation.

Despite his disappointment, Percy continued to work alongside of Katherine, and the two toured all over Wales demonstrating their mediumistic abilities. For nearly three years after the daily communications with the Spirit Beings had ceased, he and Katherine continued to devote a substantial portion of each day to some facet of the work. Unfortunately, however, the situation did not improve as Katherine had hoped. Rather, it had steadily deteriorated until the two were as strangers living under one roof—exchanging pleasantries and maintaining civility, but little else..

In spite of her own personal difficulties, or perhaps as a result of them, Katherine became wholly absorbed in her work, allowing nothing to disrupt or in any way interfere with it. And in this regard, never had she been happier or felt more fulfilled. The satisfaction she derived from sharing what she knew was incomparable. How many she had comforted and healed along the way! How often had she helped to turn bitterness and resentment into understanding and forgiveness! How many had been "saved" from eternal hellfire and damnation as a result of her words? Fear had been transformed into hope; despair into submission to God's Will. To literally thousands of people she conclusively provided evidence of life's purposefulness, continuity, and meaning.

It was after the appearance of an especially unkind and unflattering article in a local newspaper pertaining to a demonstration and a talk that Percy had delivered in Abergavenny that he quietly made his decision.

Without a doubt, it was the most difficult decision he had been required to make in his young life. He was only twenty-five years old.

It was a fine clear evening. The sun had already descended below the horizon and its fiery glow had dissipated into the softest, palest pink. Only the shadow of tiny distant stars and the ghost of the moon could be seen in the half-light, and the atmosphere was unusually still. The warm, fragrant balminess of summer enveloped the streets of Mt. Ash. As she and Percy strolled leisurely arm-in-arm toward their favorite cinema on a rare evening off, Katherine sniffed the sweet night air and wondered why it was she was deriving so little joy from the beauty of the early evening which was normally her favorite time of the day. Furthermore, she could not imagine why there was not a soul stirring on the quiet streets. Although she had been anticipating the evening out, she had a strange, uneasy sensation that something terrible was about to happen, that something was horribly wrong. Rather than feeling soothed by the stillness of the town at twilight, she felt distinctly unnerved by it, and frankly, she could not wait to get to the movie theatre. Attempting to shrug off this feeling of foreboding, she made superficially gay conversation with Percy. But although he made the appropriate responses to her questions and comments, she saw that he was paying very little attention to what was being said. He was unusually silent and preoccupied. And, finally, Katherine gave up any further hope of conversation. The two continued walking in silence.

As they drew close to the cinema, Percy, after having taken a deep breath and sighing softly, spoke in a peculiar voice, "I think that you had better cancel the remainder of our public engagements this week—in fact all future engagements . . . I, we," he stammered. It was evident that this was painful to express. Pausing for a moment to gather courage, he then continued in a weak voice, "We are not going to do the work anymore."

"What?" Katherine could hardly believe her ears. Did Percy really mean what he was saying, or was this some kind of joke? Or was this merely a means of letting off steam? Looking directly into his eyes, she knew that he was deadly serious. Suddenly, as her mind raced in a million different directions, she remembered Percy's recent sadness; the hurt and disappointment he had experienced in conjunction with the unfavorable publicity he had recently received; his lack of enthusiasm toward the healing work that had in the past brought him such joy. Studying his features, she realized with surprise that virtually all the humor and sparkle—the sense of fun and spontaneity—that had characterized his manner in the early days of their courtship and marriage had vanished, and that he was but a shell of his former self. For an instant she felt a pang of deep remorse. *It's been too much for him. But it just isn't fair for someone with Percy's gifts to face such cruel disappointment. Please God, don't let him give up the work. He has so much to give,* Katherine felt like crying aloud. But, in a sudden flash of illumination, she realized that perhaps he had already achieved everything in the way of "the work" that he had been meant to achieve. After all he had been responsible for her introduction to the work; had accomplished remarkable healings; he had been the channel through which wonderful psychic phenomena had taken place. All these thoughts had passed through her mind while Percy had continued in his strained voice.

"Although I thoroughly enjoyed the work in its early stages, you know that I have not enjoyed it for some time, and now frankly, I find it impossible to continue. It has interfered with our home life—hampered our relationship, taken time away from our son—do you not see? We must give it up. We simply must." The latter was said in a desperate voice.

Katherine said nothing for several moments and only stared at him. She was dumbfounded. Finally, calmness returned to her and her mind collected itself. Although her heart was still hammering furiously, she spoke with a conviction and intensity Percy had never seen her display before. "Never—as long as I live—shall I give up the work, Percy. You may do what you feel you must, but I would sooner give up my life than the work that I believe with all my heart and soul that I have come to the Earth to do."

He gulped. Even in the dim light she could see the rosy flush on his cheeks. He started to speak several times, but could not get the words out. Their eyes met, and Katherine continued in a low voice, "I will live with whatever decision you find it necessary to make. But I cannot—I will not—ever forsake my work—not for you, not for anyone, or anything. There is nothing more important, or sacred, to me."

Although he was miserable, Percy could not help but feel moved by her words. Furthermore, he admired her courage and commitment. Knowing that it would be hopeless to say anything more on the subject, he magnanimously decided to spare her from any further upset or pain by closing the subject gently and with as little show of emotion as he could manage. "Just so you know, love. My decision has been made, and there is to be no turning back. From hereon I am giving it up—all of it. Never again will I heal or lecture before the public. Never again will I go into a trance. From here on, my love, I am afraid that you are on your own.

"Do not be afraid, love."

"I most certainly am not afraid," said Katherine simply. "What is to be will be. I wish to God it were otherwise, but if you feel it necessary to give up the work, then that is the way it must be. All is God's will," she repeated Dr. Evans' words with a slight tremor in her voice.

Although Percy's words had brought a chill to her heart and a dull aching in her brain, some level of her was aware of the inevitability of his decision. Neither said anything more on the subject, and so as curiously as it had arisen, it was now permanently concluded. The following day Percy canceled whatever personal interviews and engagements had been scheduled for him. And, true to his word, he would never again exercise or demonstrate his remarkable abilities before the public.

Although she did not show it overtly, no one was more astounded at this sudden turn of events than Katherine. Never—no matter how difficult life had become—had she doubted that she and Percy would work together for the remainder of their lives, as a team. Since the very first time that Dr. Evans had "appeared" Katherine had viewed Percy as her partner and her collaborator as well as her husband. After all, he had been dominant in the work from its inception—in fact, the very means whereby she, her father, and her mother had acquired their training. Now she was forced to think along different lines. Suddenly—and only for an instant—was she reminded of the voice deep inside her that warned her years ago, "You must work alone. You will work alone." It was haunting and fateful. She was nonplussed. Yet she had little choice but to adhere to that somber advice and continue on alone.

CHAPTER 29

A Clean Slate

To Katherine's knowledge, Percy never regretted his decision. Nor did she ever live to regret her own. Life without the work was meaningless, purposeless—definitely not worth the living. She was consciously aware of the service that she rendered through the work, for she was a channel through whom powerful, positive energies were constantly being transmitted—those energies that could ignite in all with whom she came into contact the desire to know and achieve one's true potential. Far more importantly than reaching the mere minds of those with whom she came into contact, she was touching their hearts, awakening and inspiring them and stirring within them the urge to discover the truths of life, to discover who they really and truly were, which was far removed from the physical mind or body that one normally identifies as himself or herself.

Yet, although Katherine continued to derive great joy and fulfillment in conjunction with the work, her life with Percy was growing increasingly unpleasant, frustrating, and challenging. Now that he was no longer interested in the work, he grew impatient with Katherine's intense involvement. It was becoming obvious that they shared little in common. Neither in nature nor in temperament were they similar. And although Percy never again recommended or insisted that Katherine give up the work, it was obvious that he continued to hope that she would. But it was not merely the work that drew them apart.

There were many factors responsible for the rift between them, which grew wider daily. First, Percy was bored. Second, he was frustrated both at work and at home. Third, he began to seek companionship and diversion outside his home which he had never sought before. Fourth, he had discovered the healing and liberating properties of liquor. Fifth, he had begun to feel comfortable and singularly at home in the atmosphere of a pub. While healing and utilizing his mediumistic abilities, Percy had received strict advice from the Spirit Guides concerning the proper health and maintenance of the physical vehicle. And so, for the years during which he had functioned as a medium, he had refrained from drinking, smoking, taking drugs or medicines of any variety, or engaging in any practice that could deplete the body or cause the mind to run along unhealthy channels. The need for a medium to possess a healthy mind and body had been emphasized over and over again by the Spirit Guides.

But Percy, now relieved of the heavy burden of constant restraint and self-discipline, experienced a greater degree of personal freedom than he had known for a very long time. Furthermore, as an escape from the dull routine of his daily life, he now sought pleasure and excitement through other means. He began to spend a considerable amount of his day in the pub across the street from the tailoring shop. Here, he enjoyed the easy companionship of his "mates," the luxury of a glass or two of good ale; several games of "draughts"; and the opportunity to speak extemporaneously to a captive audience on any number of subjects, including liberal politics. In fact, he had quite a local following. And the outgoing and charming Percy Hayward was nearly always surrounded by a group of admirers.

Although Katherine had not minded Percy's visits to the pub initially, nor had she been upset by the common and gregarious tradesmen he had taken as his almost constant companions, she began to be very much disturbed by the fact that, in time, he had begun to drink all through the day and the night. Accordingly, his behavior altered significantly. Under the influence of alcohol, Percy became far more aggressive, acerbic, and argumentative. Furthermore, having always been of a volatile disposition and in possession of a short temper, he was now erratic and unmanageable. Coming home from the pub at any hour of the day, Katherine never knew when he might appear or what to expect from him. Sometimes in his slurring drawling voice, with the pungent smell of whiskey on his breath, he would lavish her and little Graham with praise and affection. On other occasions, he would come home violent and abusive—raving, ranting, and bellowing and threatening his wife and child with absurd forms of punishment and cruelty. Although she did not show it, Katherine would be terrified—not so much for herself but for her child. She knew that Percy loved them both dearly and meant no harm, but under the influence of alcohol Percy was not himself and simply could not be trusted. It was with genuine relief that she regarded his increased absence from home.

Certainly, it was far from easy to maintain her own work during this period for she never knew what would greet her at home following one of her public appearances. She could not endure Percy's verbal abuse or the absurd insults and accusations that he hurled at her. Engrossed and exhilarated by her work, she would, upon seeing him, quickly plummet to the level of despair, wondering how much more of this insulting behavior she could endure.

In time, the behavior that Katherine had come to dread in the privacy of her own home was manifested at the business and in public as well. Percy was frequently sullen, rude, and defensive—thoughtlessly offending customers and coworkers. Furthermore, he grew increasingly neglectful of his responsibilities at the shop—carelessly forgetting to take the inventory, or to reorder stock; failing to keep track of daily and weekly sales and business expenditures; and even borrowing from the till to pay for his drinks and entertainment. Often he would stop at the pub before opening the shop; and, as a result, the shop (which was scheduled to open at nine o'clock on the dot) did not open until ten, or eleven or even noon.

Knowing the vicious nature of the gossip that went on behind his back Katherine tried to apologize and cover for him as best she could. It was she, therefore, who often opened the shop at nine and waited on customers. Although everyone was kind to her face, she knew that they were talking about her behind her back and were pitying her. She also knew that an explosion of some kind was inevitable, that it was only a matter of time before someone at the main headquarters of Percy's firm was informed about

Percy's irresponsible and reckless behavior. Frankly, the burden that had fallen upon her shoulders and the suspense with which she waited for the inevitable was more than she could bear. For the very first time in their relationship, Katherine began to seriously consider the possibility of leaving Percy and going on alone. Of course, she would take little Graham with her. Although he adored his father, she knew that Percy was not, under the present circumstances, fit to rear the child. Secretly, in the far recesses of her mind, she began to plan for that time when she might be forced to take her child and leave home.

What Katherine had come to fear most, actually came about early in March of 1924. Miraculously, up until this time, no one had reported Percy's negligence to the main office. But now that the Christmas holidays were over and business was slow, someone had obviously found the time to notify the operations manager, Charles Hawkins, of the main branch of Alexander's of Percy's irresponsibility and lack of professionalism. Katherine had known Mr. Hawkins for several years, for he periodically called upon Percy to check his progress. He had always liked Katherine as she was hard-working and straight-forward and always kind. Never had she permitted him to leave Mt. Ash without insisting that he share a hot meal or at least a cup of tea with her and Percy. The operations manager had always liked and admired her sincerity and pluckiness. But, frankly, Mr. Hawkins was, for the most part, a grim, taciturn, humorless man who performed his job efficiently and conscientiously. It was abruptly and without any advance warning whatsoever that he appeared at the front door of the shop five minutes before ten o'clock on a Thursday morning. It was with a dreadful sinking feeling that Katherine recognized him. As he paused to examine the arrangement of the display windows, Katherine prayed with all her might that Percy, by some miracle, would somehow manage to return from the pub in time to deal with Mr. Hawkins. But somewhere deep inside, she knew that she was helpless to prevent what was inevitable. Bracing herself for the worst, she silently called upon God to help her.

"Good day, Mrs. Hayward," Mr. Hawkins called out, removing his hat politely as he entered the shop.

"Good day to you, Mr. Hawkins," Katherine said quietly, hardly daring to breathe. As their eyes met, the manager knew instantly that she knew what was coming.

"I regret very much the purpose for which I have come here today," he spoke in a kind but no-nonsense manner. "Is your husband in?"

"I am afraid that he has . . . uh . . . just stepped out . . . to the bank, I believe," she stammered unconvincingly. "Can I be of some assistance to you?"

"I am afraid not, Mrs. Hayward. Perhaps I had better come to the point of my visit?"

"Oh no, Mr. Hawkins," Katherine said, her eyes silently pleading for more time. "Percy should be back any moment now."

"That's not what I have been given to understand, Mrs. Hayward. I have heard that there are mornings when he does not come in until almost noon. Furthermore, it makes no difference whether your husband is present or not, for it has already been decided by those at the head office that he must be dismissed."

For a single instant, Katherine felt a glorious sense of relief—that the worst was over—that what she had anticipated, all that she had dreaded, was actually taking place and would now be resolved. At least the terrible tension and suspense under which she had been living on a daily basis for so many months would finally come to an end. She knew that she could not have continued on for much longer.

"I see," she murmured in response to the Mr. Hawkins announcement. Then softly, but with great feeling, she asked, "Is there nothing I can do to help my husband? Is there no way to save Percy's position with the firm?"

Sadly, the gentleman shook his head. "I am afraid not, Mrs. Hayward. Although he was a young man of great promise, his work over the past several years has suffered greatly. Evidence of his incompetence, his utter lack of responsibility, and lack of loyalty to the firm cannot be overlooked any longer. Furthermore, I fear that he is in no condition to plead his own case. I'm terribly sorry about all this, but I am afraid that you and your family shall have to vacate the premises within the week—the new manager shall be arriving within ten days' time."

"Oh, I see," Katherine said mechanically once again, for want of anything better to say. "We shall be gone one week from tomorrow. But are you absolutely certain that there is no way to save my husband's position? Can't you or someone at the firm give him a second chance? After all, he's only human, and everyone makes mistakes."

"I am afraid not, Mrs. Hayward. If the problem were anything but drink, there might be some lesser punishment, as it were. But where alcohol is concerned, head office has seen far too many lives and businesses utterly ruined. I assure you that none of us relish this decision, Mrs. Hayward. We feel, however, that there is no alternative. And now, if you will excuse me, I will try to find your husband to break the news. I believe I know where I might find him," he said with meaning.

As he walked toward the front door, he turned toward her and paused one last time. Meeting Katherine's eyes, he said again with complete sincerity, "Don't be too unhappy, ma'am. It will all work out in the end—you'll see. I am so very sorry."

Having recovered her poise to an extent, she replied graciously, "I know, sir. I quite understand."

"It will all work out in the end," she repeated Mr. Hawkins words mechanically after he had departed from the shop. Slipping unnoticed into the high-back chair in the office behind the shop, Katherine was too stunned to do anything more than sit dumbly. *It can't be happening. It just can't be happening. This must be a dream*, she kept thinking over and over to herself. For over two hours, she remained in that position—too unnerved to cry or speak. She did not cry until some hours later. When she did, she could not stop. Throughout the day, she waited for Percy to return, but somehow he did not. It was not until evening that Katherine saw him, and she had been forced to confront the full impact and ramifications of Mr. Hawkins news all by herself. "Oh my God, my God, whatever will become of us?" she had moaned pitiably at frequent intervals throughout that seemingly endless day. How she hugged little Graham close to her, covering his body with tears and kisses as she wondered what lay in store for them.

When Percy finally returned that evening, he was a sight to behold. He looked pale and grave, and his eyes were swollen and bloodshot. And despite her own grief, Katherine took pity. Never had she seen anyone look so wretched.

"I've lost my job, love," he whispered. "Mr. Hawkins found me at the pub; he told me I was dismissed, and that I was to have no reference. What shall we do? Where shall we go?"

With far more poise and compassion than she felt, she said very simply, "I know all about it, Percy. Mr. Hawkins stopped by the shop around ten this morning and explained the entire situation to me."

"Oh, my God, Katherine. What shall become of us? What will we do?"

"Calm down, love. We'll think of something, I promise. It will all work out—you'll see." It was the second time that day she had found herself repeating Mr. Hawkins words. The hopelessness and despair faded somewhat from Percy's eyes, and Katherine could see that he was comforted by her words. There were tears in her own eyes as she put her arms around Percy and held him as she had often held her little boy. And stroking his head gently, she murmured, "It will be all right, love. It will be all right."

Within two weeks' time, they had vacated the Mt. Ash apartment, had sold virtually all their possessions in order to repay what Percy had "borrowed" from the firm, and had, as a temporary emergency measure, moved into the home of Percy's parents in nearby Pontypridd. Somehow Katherine had managed to survive this period. She did not know how. Far too dazed to do more than go through the mere notions of daily living, she was numbed to the additional pain and humiliation of explaining to friends and family the reason for her sudden departure from Mt. Ash. By far the most humiliating and difficult experience she had known thus far was moving into Percy's family home, for she knew that Percy's family had never liked her and had instinctively blamed her for their son's failure and unhappiness. To accept charity from those whom she knew disliked and distrusted her was humiliating, yet there had been no other alternative. Katherine's parents lacked the space to put them up, and there was no one else to whom they could turn. *What can God be thinking?* Katherine asked herself, as she adjusted herself to the new surroundings. But at least they had been provided with food and shelter, and Katherine was grateful for these.

Although she had not been at all certain whether or not she could bear living under the same roof with Percy's cantankerous, outspoken father and his unctuous, self- righteous and icily reserved mother, she put into practice the advice rendered by the Spirit Guides, and approached life one day at a time. And so bear it all she did—with remarkable strength and fortitude. *It is extraordinary what one is capable of enduring,* she marveled after several weeks under the Haywards' roof. What was even more remarkable was the manner in which her priorities had shifted within the short period of time. Until the past month, she had been absorbed in her public work and the daily routine of caring for Graham, preparing meals, and performing other household tasks. Now, mere physical survival and a means of earning had become the primary concerns while all other needs and goals were temporarily cast aside.

Within several months, Katherine had become adjusted to life in the home of her in-laws, and she sincerely felt that she was capable of dealing efficiently and tactfully with anyone and anything that happened to come her way! To her utter amazement, she had actually grown fond of Mother and Father Hayward, and they, in turn, had grown to love her. *Whoever would have expected such a strange turn of events?* Katherine had mused. Yet, although her circumstances were more tolerable, they were far from ideal, and she could not wait to leave and establish her own home once again.

While they had originally intended to stay with Mr. and Mrs. Hayward for only a few weeks—until either of them acquired some kind of employment—they soon realized that it would not be nearly as easy to find work as they had thought. They learned quickly that without references, Percy did not stand a chance of being hired at any reputable outfit. In South Wales in the 1920s, one's references were one's passport into any respectable position.

And although Katherine had been fully intending to acquire any means of earning, she discovered shortly after her arrival in Pontypridd that this would be impossible. For she was far too weak and ill, with frequent spells of dizziness and nausea, to undertake any work at the present time. Having attributed her weak state to nervous strain, she was flabbergasted to discover after a visit to a local physician that she was three months pregnant.

How could you, God? However could You allow this to happen? How can I possibly afford to bring another child into the world? she had addressed God angrily. *Was there to be no release, no escape from the constant pain and sorrow?* With far greater weariness than she had ever known before, she wondered what was to become of them all. And she prayed with what was left of her heart to be shown the way.

Her prayers were at least partly answered. For as she entered into the fourth month of pregnancy, she became violently, miserably ill and lost the child she had been carrying. Terribly thin and white, weak and wracked with pain, she, nonetheless, felt only gratitude that she would not have to feed and care for another child at this critical juncture of her life. At this same time, Percy managed to borrow enough money from a neighbor to establish his own grocery shop. Things were looking up. For nearly a month, it appeared as though the business would be successful. Unfortunately, the shop was located in a part of the city that was mostly inhabited by coal miners, and when the miners declared a strike, and were subsequently without income, Percy's shop was robbed of both funds and merchandise, and he was forced to close down. Poor Percy was distraught, for now he could not even hope to repay the kindly friend of the family who had generously lent him the money.

Nearly at his wit's end, Percy decided to take one last plunge into business and to open a stall at the Caerphilly Market where general produce, fresh vegetables, fruit or baked goods as well as arts and crafts, were sold Monday through Saturday from nine in the morning until five thirty in the evening. At this same time, Katherine had recovered sufficiently to take on a job herself. After several weeks of searching, she responded to an ad in the local newspaper. Using her maiden name in order that she might use Percy as her reference, she acquired a position as sales representative for a custom draperies firm performing many of the same tasks she had taken on so many years ago as a young girl selling stockings in Gwaelod-y-garth. This job required her to travel from city to city to sell the company's merchandise door-to-door and also to collect past debts. In the deadly cold of mid-winter, Katherine stoically endured the icy journeys by train and on-foot from customer to customer until she became desperately ill and was, under the insistence of her family, forced to give up the job. She did not relinquish her position, however, until she had managed to erase her own Mum and Dad's name from the company's "active" list which consisted of those individuals who still owed money to the firm. She had smiled with great satisfaction, as she had carefully deleted the names of Gwilym and Elizabeth Davies, who owed twelve pounds, from the firm's files. *At least I've done some good here*, she thought with no little pleasure at the prank.

Following this experience, Katherine assisted Percy at the Caerphilly Market. Detesting every minute of the time spent there, she remained in constant agony over the possibility of being seen and ridiculed by friends and family members who happened to be passing by. After nearly a week, Katherine decided that she had had enough. She simply could not endure any more. And Percy concurred. He, too, was at the end of his rope. Yet neither knew what to do. Without a proper reference, there was no future for them.

After an evening of fervent prayer and deep meditation, Katherine awoke feeling that she had discovered the resolution to their difficulties. "I am going to pay a call on Mr. Hawkins," she informed Percy the following morning. "And I shall go this afternoon." He did not know why, but Percy felt a profound sense of relief at her words. Both knew better than to get their hopes up, however.

"I shall accompany you there, love, all right?" he asked solicitously.

"You may take the train journey to Barry with me, Percy, if you wish, but I truly feel it best that I speak with Mr. Hawkins alone."

"Whatever you say, love."

Arriving in the seaport town of Barry at half-past two in the afternoon, the two paused briefly for tea, then found their way on foot to Mr. Hawkins residence. It was Wednesday—the inspector's day off—and they were certain that they would find him at home. He had often described with pleasure the way in which he had spent his time off—a good portion of which he devoted to reading. He was apparently an avid reader of detective novels. As they approached his front door, Percy took his leave, agreeing to wait for Katherine at a cafe they had passed on the way.

"Good luck, love," Percy had whispered, his body all a tremble and eyes shining in anticipation.

I've come to the end of my rope, God. Please, please take over now, and show me the way, she prayed silently as she mounted the stone steps leading to the large wooden doors of the Hawkins home. Pausing to take a deep breath and to straighten her hat, she rang the doorbell. To her immense joy and relief, it was Mr. Hawkins himself who answered the door at once.

"Why, Mrs. Hayward!" he cried, staring at her in disbelief. "What a surprise! Why, I was just thinking about you and your . . . er . . . husband . . . the other day. Well, well, well! What a surprise!"

"May I come in?"

"Oh, of course, Mrs. Hayward. Do forgive me, but it's just such a surprise. So peculiar," he mumbled to himself, gently guiding her into the lounge. "Please have a seat. May I get you a cup of tea—or a bite to eat?"

"No, thank you," she replied quietly. "Frankly, if you don't mind, I would rather come to the point of my visit."

"Certainly, Mrs. Hayward. You're sure?"

"Yes, I'm sure."

"It must be pretty important, if you have made such a long and tedious a journey." After an awkward silence, he inquired in a kindly voice, "Well, then, Mrs. Hayward, what is it that I can do for you?"

"You can do a great deal for me, sir, if you would be so kind. You see, so very much has taken place in my life since last we were together." Although her voice quivered and her eyes began to fill with tears, she continued resolutely to describe the series of unfortunate events that had occurred during the eleven months following Percy's dismissal from Alexander's and that had culminated in the recent experience at the Caerphilly Market.

"And so, sir," she concluded, "you begin to understand the purpose for which I have come. I have come as a result of an earnest prayer seeking God's guidance. For truly, I am in need of guidance, I have never felt so desperate in my life. Percy and I have tried every conceivable way to earn a living, but without a reference, it is impossible. And Mr. Hawkins, I must tell you that my husband is a changed man—he has not touched a drop of liquor during the entire eleven months of which I have spoken. Furthermore, he behaves responsibly in every way. And there is one thing more, Mr. Hawkins, that I would like you to know. Percy was only twenty years old when he first started working for Alexander's."

"Twenty?" he sputtered. "Why, he informed us that he was twenty-five years old. Why, he was only a boy. . ."

"Exactly, Mr. Hawkins. My husband is only twenty-seven years old at the present time, and is simply too young to spend the remainder of his life being penalized for a mistake he made at such a tender age. Believe me, sir, he has received enough punishment and experienced enough suffering to last a lifetime. And so, sir, I have come here today to ask you to please give my husband another chance at life. In short, it is your reference that I am seeking, sir. Your reference will let my husband and me start afresh, do you see?" she spoke with such sincerity and longing that Mr. Hawkins could not help but feel deeply moved by her account. He opened his mouth to speak, but Katherine interjected before he had a chance.

"If you will provide my husband with a reference, Mr. Hawkins, I personally shall stand as guarantor for his behavior. In other words, I shall assume complete personal responsibility for everything my husband does on the job. Should he ever, for a moment, deviate from the path of normalcy, I should notify you at once and ask you to take your reference back. Please look into my eyes and know that I mean every word I have spoken. I shall never disappoint you, sir. I promise. But please do give us another chance. Please give my Percy a reference."

Now the operations manager was basically a decent, good-hearted man, and he had not been able to bear hearing of Katherine's travails. Furthermore, having always possessed a high regard for her and her obvious intelligence, charm, and ability, he was certain that if given the opportunity, she would go far. Also, he knew that she could be trusted and would be as good as her word. If she had promised to stand as guarantor for Percy, well then, by God, she would assume responsibility for her husband's future actions and behavior. Although Mr. Hawkins was an imminently practical man and although he knew that Katherine's appeal had been directed toward his emotions, he felt it worth his while, at least in this instance, to follow his heart, and to give Percy Hayward another chance.

For several minutes neither spoke and the room was completely silent. During this time, Katherine's mind raced. Had she appeared too eager? Too bold? Common? How had Mr. Hawkins reacted? His features had remained impassive throughout the visit, and she had no way of determining the outcome of her efforts.

Such a lovely girl, pity, Mr. Hawkins could not help but think as he reviewed her story and stared at Katherine's hopeful countenance.

Finally, after what seemed to be an interminable amount of time, Mr. Hawkins rose and placed a paternal hand upon her shoulder. "My dear," he spoke in his well-modulated and refined voice, "I have given your request serious consideration."

"Yes?" asked Katherine hardly daring to breathe.

"And it is my opinion that you should return home now."

"Oh," said Katherine, gulping to fight the tears that were imminent.

"Now, don't misinterpret what I am telling you, Mrs. Hayward. You must let me finish," he advised. "Now then, it is my feeling that you should return home at once and inform your husband that he may apply for any and every position he wishes, for he shall have an appropriate reference."

Too stunned to utter a word, Katherine sat perfectly motionless for several moments. "Thank you, Mr. Hawkins. Oh, thank you so very, very much. You shall never regret this—and I shall never forget your kindness," were the words she finally blurted out when she had recovered her senses. The tears spilled forth, but the normally reserved Katherine did not care. Never had she felt such intense gratitude and relief!

"Now, little lady," Mr. Hawkins was once again speaking in what Katherine thought was the most beautiful voice she had ever heard. "Go your way. Go on home. All is well, I assure you. God bless you, my dear, and

God bless your loved ones." And to her amazement, the dreaded interview was over. The gentleman graciously guided her to the door.

"Thank you, God, oh thank You!" she cried aloud, as soon as she was safely out of the range of Mr. Hawkins hearing. But she could not repress her happiness, and she felt like clapping her hands and jumping up and down with joy. She felt as though she were floating on air, as she approached the cafe in which she was to meet Percy. Feeling as though she were on top of the world, she entered the restaurant and found Percy at an attractively set table near the window. Without her uttering a single syllable, he knew immediately the results of the interview.

"We've got it, don't we, love? We've got our reference!" he shouted glee-fully. Several of the patrons turned to stare at the young man who was car-rying on in such an uncivilized manner, but Percy was happily oblivious. "Oh, my God! Is it true? Is it really true?" he asked, clasping Katherine's hand tightly in his own. She nodded happily.

"Oh, thank God. Thank God," he murmured over and over. "Our wor-ries are over at last! I know that I shall get a decent position right off. Oh, Katherine, do you know what that reference means? It means that we will be able to begin afresh, to start a new life for ourselves and for little Graham . . ."

There were tears in his eyes, and Katherine could see that he was trying not to sob aloud. Finally, the misery, pain, and humiliation of the past year had come to an end. Both were exhilarated, intoxicated by the promise of the future!

"Everything will be different than before," Percy declared boldly, with confidence. "I promise. I really feel as though God has forgiven me for the past and that we are now beginning life all over again—starting with a clean slate, as it were."

"Yes," agreed Katherine, repeating happily, "A clean slate . . ."

CHAPTER 30

Aberdare

MR. HAWKINS WAS AS GOOD as his word. Within several weeks of his meeting with Katherine, he had provided Percy with an appropriate written reference. Within a month's time, Percy had been hired by a prestigious custom tailoring firm named Palmer's whose ubiquitous branch stores dotted the urban landscape throughout southern Wales.

Percy had accepted this offer with alacrity, feeling that it was ideal. Although he had been interviewed for the position in Cardiff, he had been informed by his prospective employer that he was to undergo a managerial training program for several months in Swansea, by the sea. Katherine and Percy had been delighted by this unexpected news, for they had always liked Swansea. Now they were very much looking forward to spending time there. A change in scenery and lifestyle was exactly what they required.

"We're on our way, love," Katherine had declared gleefully upon learning that they were to move.

Nor were they in any way disappointed. In fact, Swansea was everything and more than they could have wished. After the bleak and tedious landscape of Mt. Ash, Swansea offered them a breath of fresh air—literally—for the city was situated near the Bristol channel and boasted wonderfully clean and refreshing ocean air and breezes.

Aside from fresh ocean air, Swansea also boasted lovely scenery, a lively commercial district, beautiful residential areas, excellent shopping, and diverse opportunities for culture and entertainment. Katherine was in her element! After the suffocating atmosphere of the provincial mining town, this large city seemed to radiate freedom and pleasure!

Oddly enough, as much as all four had initially detested the arrangement, Katherine and Percy and Mother and Father Hayward had all been sad when the time had come for Katherine and Percy and little Graham to leave Pontypridd. Within the eleven-month period, and despite the great disparities of age and personality, they had grown to genuinely love and enjoy one another's company. Tears had streamed down Mother Hayward's face as she embraced her son goodbye, gently kissed her daughter- in-law on the forehead, and nearly squeezed the life out of the little uncomprehending Graham. And, there was an undeniable catch in the old man's voice, as he gruffly wished them a safe and pleasant journey to Swansea. Even the un-sentimental Percy felt a slight tug in his heart, as his mother called out one last time before he climbed into the taxi that would take them to the railway station, "Godspeed, love. Don't forget to write as soon as you are settled." And then, suddenly, it was over. The months of utter hopelessness and de-spair, of grief and humiliation, beyond anything they had ever known be-fore had finally come to an end. Thankfully on the train, they bade farewell to Pontypridd and to all it had represented. Finally, the bleakest and most dismal chapter of their young lives had come to an end.

In spite of a temporary housing shortage, they had little difficulty in finding a furnished apartment only three blocks away from the ocean and only fifteen minutes' walk away from Percy's business. Within a surprisingly short period of time—a matter of a few weeks—they were comfortably set-tled in their new home and busily adapting to the new responsibilities and relationships inherent to life in a large city.

Although Katherine would have vastly preferred her own home and furnishings to those which were rented, she still took considerable delight in making the apartment as homey and pleasant as possible. In the back of her mind, however, remained the strong desire to establish a real home and home life for her family. She fervently hoped that Percy would be successful in his new position, for therein, she thought, lay the key to all future hap-piness and stability.

Thankfully, Percy did appear to be enjoying himself. For the first time in years, he was enthusiastic about his responsibilities as well as his coworkers. Not only was his work challenging and gratifying, but his home life and social life were pleasant as well. For both he and Katherine made friends easily in this hospitable community; in fact, everywhere they went—in their own neighborhood, on the city streets, in the shops and arcades and in the galleries—the citizens of Swansea were wonderfully warm and gracious. In addition, Percy's employer had taken quite a liking to his new protégé, and the two men and their wives spent frequent social evenings together—sharing the beauty and cultural events that Swansea offered.

Best of all, as far as Katherine was concerned, Swansea afforded her the opportunity to continue her public work on rather a grand scale. To her great surprise and pleasure, she had no sooner begun planning her first local public lecture and demonstration than a lovely means of promoting and advertising her work was presented her by a kindly gentleman named Mr. Sweet who owned, among many other businesses and commercial properties in the area, the butcher's shop which she visited several times a week. Mr. Sweet was a handsome, refined man in his early forties who had been intrigued by Katherine upon their first encounter that had taken place when the regular butcher had been taken ill, and Mr. Sweet had temporarily stepped in to fill the gap.

From the moment he discovered Mrs. Hayward's vocation, he was intent upon doing everything in his power to ensure her local success; and as Mr. Woods had publicized her work in Mt. Ash, so Mr. Sweet set about the same task in Swansea. A man of wealth and no little influence, he also personally introduced her to many of Swansea's most prominent citizens. Aside from the promotional work he handled on her behalf, Mr. Sweet also insisted upon providing Katherine with her own chapel rent free—a beautiful, graceful structure that happened to exist on one of his own properties. Katherine had no choice but to accept Mr. Sweet's generous offer, and for some time she was inexpressibly content delivering lectures, presenting demonstrations of the proof of survival, and offering many classes and workshops in Mr. Sweet's charming building. It was only when Percy began to exhibit jealousy and suspicion toward Mr. Sweet that Katherine felt compelled to spend less time with her new friend and less time at the chapel. Nonetheless, throughout the entire duration of their stay in Swansea, Mr. Sweet was a kind and generous as well as influential assistant in the propagation and perpetuation of her work.

Their days in Swansea passed swiftly and pleasantly. It was a time of great release and reconstruction. To Katherine's relief, Percy had not touched a drop of alcohol throughout the duration of their stay. Furthermore, he had successfully demonstrated both his ability and his diligence. He had, in fact, received the repeated praise of his employer and the firm itself. As he had promised Katherine, he had started with a clean slate.

Unfortunately, Percy's training period quickly came to an end, and with it the happy days he had known in Swansea. It was with deep disappointment that he received instructions from the head office to take over the management of the branch shop in the mining town of Aberdare, which was only a few miles away from the detested Mt. Ash. Both Katherine and Percy had been stunned by this turn of events, for Percy had specifically requested employment in one of the large city shops. Once the decision had been made by the head office, however, there was virtually no likelihood of it being altered. And the two were forced to make the best of the situation.

"Don't worry, love," Katherine had said, attempting to lessen Percy's disappointment. "Perhaps you shall be transferred elsewhere within a short time."

But even as she spoke, she knew that there was little chance of Percy ever receiving a transfer. Once one was assigned to a particular branch office, one was usually expected to remain there until retirement!

"God, I just don't think I can go back there!" Percy had cried out in genuine dismay, "I don't know how I can bear it, love. To live in that ugly, barren God-forsaken place—don't you see it's Mt. Ash all over again?"

And, although she hated to admit it even to herself, Katherine knew that Percy was right. It was, indeed, Mt. Ash all over again—with its miserable stone-gray streets; the surrounding lands stripped and scarred and also gray; with its slag heaps and endless rows of terraced houses in which the collier's lived; the shabby, dirty little children of the coal miners; and the harsh, flat accents of the grim old men who were too old and weak to work in the mines any longer and who now permanently inhabited the pubs, sitting in the same chairs they had occupied for decades and nattering away all through the night and day. No, she herself could not bear it!

Yet somehow in subsequent days, she found herself curiously detached and remote managing in a mechanical way to perform the necessary tasks and making the appropriate arrangements for the move to Aberdare. And within several weeks' time, she, her husband, and her little boy were settled in their new "home," a small, square white- washed little house that was situated only a few blocks away from the shop.

Although Katherine liked nothing at all about her new home, she held her tongue and determined to make it as pretty and hospitable as possible. For the first time in her married life, she bought furnishings on credit—so eager was she to establish a real home, one that was to her own taste. And, in time, as a result of her efforts, she actually grew quite fond of the place.

Yet although she struggled to make the best of her circumstances as she had so often in the past, she never felt anything but revulsion for the town of Aberdare, and never did she feel as though she belonged there. Not long after they had moved into their new home, Katherine discovered to her horror and utter despair that she was pregnant once again. Having only recently recovered from a miscarriage, Katherine was never more forlorn or frightened, nor could she remember feeling so weak and helpless or so completely drained of energy. Dizzy and nauseous nearly all the time, she could not imagine how she would survive the full duration of the pregnancy. Feeling with all her heart that she could not go on this way, and feeling that no one would be the wiser, she contemplated inducing an abortion.

By the end of her fourth month, she became even more violently, desperately ill than before and the days and months in Aberdare passed by without her being consciously aware of the events that were taking place in the outside world. Finally, to her immense relief, she miscarried. Under doctor's orders, Percy sent her to the resort town on Barry Island to recover. It was the first holiday she had ever taken by herself—she delighted in the placid beauty of the spot and the wonderful, soothing warmth of the sun and the fresh ocean breezes. For the first time in her married life, she felt the singular joy of being alone and responsible for no one else. Unfortunately, even after three weeks on the island, her health had not improved to the extent to which one might have wished. In fact, nearly an entire year was to elapse before Katherine fully regained her strength.

Upon her return home, Katherine resolved to make the best of her circumstances. She resumed her responsibilities despite their distastefulness. She felt gratitude that she was back with her husband and child and hopeful that their lives would somehow be improved.

CHAPTER 31

The Letter

$\backsim$

SHE COULD NOT REMEMBER PRECISELY when or how the change in Percy's behavior had taken place but it began to become increasingly apparent to Katherine—even in her weakened state—that Percy had begun to revert to the disastrous behavior that had culminated in his dismissal and disgrace in Mt. Ash. For a short while, she chose to overlook his brief social visits to the pub or his late nights with his new "mates," cleverly deluding herself into believing that they did not exist, but it began to become perfectly clear that Percy, in order to escape the drudgery of daily life in the dismal mining town, had taken to drink once again.

During Katherine's recuperation, he had spent frequent evenings at the local gentleman's club wherein he became quite popular. Furthermore, he wished to impress his new circle of friends, and chose to entertain them lavishly (by Aberdare standards) by taking them to the best restaurants, bars, and theatres. And although Katherine knew of these goings on, she was helpless to prevent them. It was during this time that it had suddenly occurred to her that Percy was once again "borrowing" money from the shop's till in order to pay for his elaborate evenings out.

Enjoying his turn in the limelight and basking in his new popularity, Percy was far from willing to listen to Katherine's criticisms or advice. "Stop nagging at me," he would snarl viciously whenever Katherine brought up the subject of alcohol, or his all-too-frequent visits to the pub. "Leave me alone," he would shout in an embarrassingly loud voice whenever Katherine dared intimate that he might seek more constructive forms of diversion than the local hotels and restaurants.

Toward the end of their second year in Aberdare, Katherine gave up all hope of ever living normally and happily with her husband. She was helpless to change him or alter his self-destructive behavior. And, as she had known in Mt. Ash, she knew once again that it was only a matter of time before the inevitable explosion occurred.

By late August of 1927, Katherine had endured as much as she could. Her sensitive nature could no longer tolerate the constant stress and strain of life with Percy. That the two had steadily drifted apart seemed schoolgirl hyperbole in comparison with their present relationship. For in fact they had nothing in common but their son. Percy's temper tantrums, his sarcasm, his selfish preoccupation with his social life, and his lack of concern for his family's welfare had, day-by-day, become increasingly unendurable to Katherine. She remained in Percy's home for two fundamental reasons: first, divorce was as yet uncommon and unrespectable behavior for a well brought up middle-class woman and women were expected to endure their lot no matter how difficult; second, she knew that Graham adored his father and should remain together with him for as long as possible. Frankly, it was primarily for little Graham's sake that she remained. Also, in the back of her mind she could not help but feel that Percy might somehow change and become once again the loving, doting husband and father he had been during the early years of their marriage.

It was after Percy had casually mentioned one evening during a rare appearance at dinner that he wished to sell her ornate silver candlesticks, which had been her favorite possessions, that Katherine knew for certain that they were on the brink of disaster. Despite his deliberate nonchalance, Katherine had sensed the desperation, the fear, and worry that formed the undercurrent for his request.

As the situation steadily worsened, Katherine began to devise a plan in order to salvage whatever remnants she could of her married life. This plan began to assume the form of an ultimatum whereby Percy would either alter his behavior or lose his wife and child. Knowing that it was no longer possible to go on living in this manner, she felt that only something as power-ful as such an ultimatum would in any way affect Percy. For she knew that deep inside Percy was well-intentioned and deeply loved both his wife and son. She also knew that in order to effectively implement this ultimatum, it would be best to get little Graham out of the way all together. She was, there-fore, extremely grateful to Mother and Father Hayward who invited Graham to remain with them for the remainder of the summer holiday until the end of September. When he was safely en route to Pontypridd, she knew that the time had finally arrived during which she could confront Percy.

It had been an unusually hot and humid afternoon in August and tiny beads of perspiration had formed on Katherine's brow as she gently guided little Graham to the bus stop. Her eyes glistened with admiration for the lovely little boy in his new cream-colored summer suit, and she firmly held his small hand in her own.

"My dear, brave little boy!" she had murmured, to which unsuspecting Graham had replied, "But I'm only going to visit with Grandmother and Grandfather, and I shan't be gone long, Mother. I don't know why you're making such a fuss." And Katherine had been compelled to smile through her sudden tears. No matter how bad things were at home, Graham had been oblivious. He loved both his Mum and Dad and trusted them implic-itly. She wondered how Graham would react if ever she and Percy divorced. *I'll not think of such things now*, she told herself as, out of the corner of her eye, she saw the motor-coach that would transport her son to Pontypridd. Tears stung her eyes, and she began to wish that she had never accepted Mother Hayward's invitation. *Oh God, I can't let him go! I can't!* she felt like crying at the top of her lungs.

But she only said, "There's the coach, love. You be a good boy, now. Be kind to Grandmother and Grandfather, and telephone your Mum whenever you wish. All right, love?" She hugged him so close that he could hardly breathe, and hid her tear-stained face in his tiny shoulder.

"All right, Mum," said Graham simply, wondering if anything was wrong, Certainly his mum had never acted so funny before when he had gone to visit his grandparents.

Lifting her head from his shoulder, she looked him directly in the eyes, "I love you Graham—more than you will ever know. Whatever happens to us, know that I love you very, very much and always will. All right, baby?"

"All right, Mum," he said in his clear voice. "I love you too, Mummy. And I shall miss you. 'Deed I shall."

"Oh, my little darling!" she murmured, burying him in her arms and covering him with kisses.

As the motor bus screeched to an abrupt halt right in front of them, Katherine guided her little boy to his seat. Kissing him tenderly on the forehead, she took her leave with surprisingly little fanfare. "Be good, love. Let Mummy know if you need anything. All right?"

"All right, Mum."

"Goodbye, love," said Katherine as great tears slid silently down her cheeks. Soon the bus and her little boy vanished from sight merging into a great cloud of dust.

Feeling terribly alone and lonely in the late afternoon stillness, Katherine decided that she simply could not return to her own empty house. On impulse, she decided to make the brief journey by train to Abercumboy where her Mum and Dad now lived. Now, more than ever she felt the need of the reassuring presence and sound advice of Gwilym and Elizabeth. Pouring her heart out to them and informing them of her plan to issue an ultimatum, she waited for their reaction. To her surprise, both were highly supportive and in complete accord with her proposal.

"There are no mistakes," Elizabeth reminded her daughter, "Just follow your heart. You will never go wrong." Katherine left their home feeling more refreshed and optimistic than she had felt in months. She would implement her strategy as soon as possible.

Although it was nearly ten o'clock by the time she arrived at home, she saw immediately that Percy had not been home all day. She could not control herself. She was simply overcome by despair and the tears streamed down her face. Sobbing as though her heart was broken, she suddenly, instinctively knelt upon the floor beside her bed and prayed, as she had as a child. "Please God. I am lost, show me the way, show me the way to go from here." She continued to cry softly to herself for some time. Finally, exhausted, she fell upon her bed and into a deep sleep.

She awoke shortly past midnight cold with sweat, sobbing brokenly. *Leave this house as soon as possible. Get out while you can,* she had distinctly heard a strange voice advise—was it in her dream or while awake that she had heard the voice? Shuddering in fear, she contemplated the significance of the words, then impulsively decided that she would pack up her belongings and leave first thing in the morning. Glancing over at Percy's side of the bed, she stared at the freshly laundered and pressed pillows and sheets and realized that he had never come home. She simply could not remain all alone in this house any longer.

Lying in bed with her eyes open—for she was, by now, wide awake—she began to plan in detail her departure from Aberdare. *I will leave Percy a note explaining my feelings. I will have to make him understand that my absence shall be temporary only if he reforms at once. I shall return to him if and when his behavior has altered.* After deciding that the dining table would be the most noticeable place upon which to leave the note, she suddenly wondered where she would go—where she might hide until Percy came 'round. "Where can I go where Percy will not find me?" she wondered aloud. After some reflection, it occurred to her that her sister Cora's home, in Newport, would be one place in which Percy would never expect to seek or find her. "That's it!" she had cried in excitement. "I shall stay with Cora and Ivar. Percy will never think of looking for me there. He knows that Cora and I aren't as close as we once were, that we had little in common and seldom spent time together."

And reflecting further, Katherine decided, "I shall divulge my whereabouts to no one but Mum and Dad. Perhaps, a little later on—once I'm settled—I will inform Mother Hayward as to my whereabouts, and explain that my departure has been the only means at my disposal of salvaging both Percy's professional and domestic happiness." And continuing to plan her future, she concluded, "In Newport, I shall find employment and earn enough to support both myself and my son." And having resolved these major issues, Katherine drifted once more into a deep sleep.

Awakening promptly at half past six in the morning, Katherine felt comforted by the stream of golden sunlight that poured through her window. As her awareness increased, she realized that Percy had never come home. Although this had happened before, she had somehow thought, or hoped, that she would at least have a chance to see him once more before she left him. Realizing that she was powerless to change the situation, however, she devoted no further time to reflection. Now that she had made her decision, she was anxious to execute it as quickly and efficiently as possible.

After having bathed and dressed, she packed those personal articles and items of clothing of which she was most fond and which were of greatest practical value into a large trunk. Having completed this task, she raced through the house in a whirlwind of activity—cleaning, dusting, and mopping until every room was virtually spotless. It had inexplicably soothed her nerves to leave the house in as neat and orderly a fashion as possible.

By the time she had finished packing, cleaned the house and eaten a light breakfast, it was nearly half past seven. Already the air was thick and heavy. It was surprisingly warm and humid, and she was damp with perspiration as a result of her exertion. Finally, neatly attired in her navy blue and white cotton travel suit, she sat alone at the formal dining table and began to compose a letter to Percy.

My Dear Percy,

I only pray that this letter reaches you in time to save you great unhappiness. Having hoped and prayed and carefully deliberated over our future together, I have arrived at the conclusion that I can no longer remain in this house with you. At least not under the present circumstances. Know that it is in order to salvage what is left of our relationship that I go.

Although I do not wish to accuse you of any intentional wrongdoing or misbehavior, your actions have distressed me deeply. Furthermore, you have hurt and humiliated me in ways I would never have thought possible. It is your drinking that has caused me the greatest anxiety; but only somewhat less important have been your excessive expenditures upon entertainments and diversions that I know that we cannot possibly afford. I can no longer overlook your rude and selfish behavior toward both myself and your son. Unless you and our circumstances alter dramatically, I do not feel it possible to live with you.

In order for me to return to you, you must give up drinking altogether. You must repay all "borrowed" monies, and you must be ready to live peacefully and happily with little Graham and me. With all my heart, I urge you to become once again the loving and gentle man I married. Until you do, I fear we must remain apart.

Please do be sensible, Percy, and make no attempt to locate me, for I assure you that I shall not be found until I wish to make my presence known. Do believe me when I say that I shall keep close scrutiny over your behavior, for I am most anxious to see its improvement. When you have reformed, I promise that I shall return . . . I only pray that you will heed this warning. For the consequences of your actions are grim indeed. I love you, my darling. Never doubt this. But please, for the sake of your family, change your ways. God bless you, Percy. God bless us all.

With love always,

Your Katherine

Upon completing the letter, she sat back in her chair and read it carefully through. Her brow wrinkled in concentration, her cheeks pale, and her lips pursed, she added dashes here and there, inserted, commas and various words and phrases, and crossed out those words that now seemed superfluous. Once she had finished this task, she sat perfectly still for a moment and stared at the letter with a sober, wistful expression which plainly revealed her own ambivalence at having been "forced" to write such a document. After sighing deeply, she picked up the ink pen and hastily scrawled her signature at the bottom of the page. Feeling simultaneous relief and anxiety, she deliberately placed the note at the center of the dining table—in plain view—so that Percy could not help but notice it at once.

Gathering her luggage and placing it by the front door, she decided to take one last, lingering look around her. Her gaze included the beautiful living room suite, lamps, and paintings she had recently purchased as well as the radio and sewing machine that had been her pride and joy. Each piece of furniture—each object—had some meaning, some sentimental value, and reminded her of a particular incident or conversation with either Percy or Graham. A stab of fear and then deep sadness overcame her, and for a moment, she lacked the courage to take one step further.

"God help me," she cried out in anguish, and within moments, both fear and sadness had dissipated, and she was doing all that she believed was necessary to save her family. Tugging at the heavy front door, she picked up her bags and walked out. As she closed the door behind her, she was suddenly jarred by the feeling that the end of an era, the closing of a chapter had somehow taken place. Then she was astonished by her subsequent detachment—for she seemed to be observing her home, herself, her actions as a witness, as though she were a spectator viewing a motion picture. "God help us, show Percy and Graham and me the way from here," she murmured, as she made her way along the gravel pathway that led to the street.

As she drew near the railway station, Katherine could not help but feel, despite her fears and genuine grief, that she was being carefully guided every step of the way. As tears of sadness and apprehension flowed upon her cheeks and onto her white lace collar, she prayed that matters would soon be resolved to her own satisfaction and to the satisfaction of her husband and child, and that all three would be happily reunited.

With renewed strength and optimism, she entered the station, purchased a one-way ticket to Newport and found a seat on the platform outside. Sincerely, she wondered how she could have been so naive as to expect life to become easier as she grew older. Now she knew that life was never intended to be easy—never intended to be anything other than what it was in reality—a school wherein one learned the lessons necessary for one's growth. Nonetheless, she still remained hopeful that things would straighten themselves out, and that life would proceed smoothly once again. Mostly, it was for a new beginning that she hoped—for Percy, Graham and herself. It was with this in mind—the sincere hope for a new beginning— that Katherine sat silently and patiently that unusually warm late August morning waiting for the arrival of the train that would safely transport her to the home of her sister, Cora. What the future held in store, she could not even begin to imagine.

CHAPTER 32

A New Beginning

THE TRAIN JOURNEY WAS SURPRISINGLY pleasant—almost enjoyable, in fact—for it was an immense relief to leave the heavy, oppressive atmosphere of Aberdare behind. The sweet, fragrant country air that rushed in through the open window of her compartment felt delightfully soothing, and Katherine breathed it in appreciatively. Already in a way she felt inexplicably lighter, freer, as though on a deeper level she were aware of the liberty soon to come. After the constant strain and tension of the past week, Katherine was able to relax somewhat, inhaling deep draughts of the fresh air, she observed with total detachment the activity around her.

As a disinterested member of the audience might view the movement and interaction of the actors on stage in a play, Katherine watched the other passengers—most of whom appeared to be on summer holiday—with their careless, ebullient chatter, brightly colored clothing and breezy, outgoing manner. She noticed with total indifference a young couple sitting catty-corner, obviously deeply in love. With wry amusement, she saw the obvious contempt and disapproval for the young couplers' elaborate public displays of affection written upon the face of a thin, elderly woman with narrow, beady eyes, pursed lips, and wrinkled roseleaf cheeks. When Katherine felt the elderly woman's critical gaze fall upon her, she smiled slightly to herself and then deliberately turned to examine the view from her window. But she did not really see the lovely, shifting August landscapes that flashed momentarily into her range of vision as a blur of variegated green and topaz, pale blue, and white.

For suddenly, uninvited, the sharp image of little Graham's face had appeared before her. So startlingly vivid was his presence in her midst that she actually gasped aloud in surprise, causing the elderly lady seated across from her to turn her attention from a stout man with red hair, a large nose, pink complexion, and a long, red moustache with straight, bristly hairs—like the bristles of a broom—and to glare suspiciously at Katherine. Now, huddled in her seat, her eyes fixed unseeingly upon the hills and valleys and the railroad tracks in the distance, Katherine saw the wide, blue eyes, the tiny nose that tilted up at the end, the wavy, soft light brown hair, the rosy cheeks of her little boy. She felt his small, confiding hand slip into hers; she heard the thin, precocious voice; the cheerful, bubbling laughter. For several minutes, she could think of nothing—of no one else. *He is mine as nothing else has ever been before*, she thought to herself, her heart leaping to her throat and lodging there uncomfortably. She yearned—ached—to hold him to her now. The agony of being separated from him for even a short while was almost unbearable. *My God, my God*, she moaned inwardly, *I want my son. I need my son. Please bring him back to me, God, please.*

She soon recovered her senses, however, wondering why she was behaving so foolishly. *Now what is the point of such thinking?* she silently berated herself. *After all, for the present time, I am helpless to alter the situation. Would that I could!* she murmured ruefully. *But I can't right now. I shall have to be patient and allow time to render its own healing balm.* And then, employing great strength of will, she focused her attention on her own immediate future. *I shall have to find a place to live and obviously a means of earning. I can stay with Cora for only a short time—it would be terribly unfair for me to do otherwise—to disrupt their household . . . Once I have found a suitable position, I shall send for Graham immediately. I shall keep him together with me until Percy comes round. Percy . . .* Now her reverie was interrupted as her husband's features loomed sharply before her, and she was helpless to prevent her mind from racing in a hundred different directions. *Where is Percy now? Has he discovered my note? Will he conduct a search for me? Will he contact Mum and Dad? Mother and Father Hayward? Will he take my message to heart and mend his ways?* Mercifully, these questions ceased abruptly as the conductor announced the train's arrival in Newport.

"Thank God I made it," Katherine murmured in relief, as the train grinded to a halt. She hurriedly disembarked, found her way through the crowded railway station, and arrived on busy Mill Street. Managing to get a taxi almost immediately, she was soon en route to the Fields Street home of her sister, Cora. It was only a matter of several minutes after she had settled in the cab that the driver announced that she had arrived at her destination. Hastily glancing at her watch, Katherine saw with astonishment that it was only half past nine in the morning. To her disturbed mind, it had seemed that several days, rather than just a few hours, had elapsed since she had undertaken the journey from Aberdare to Newport. Now, having paid the driver, she clumsily gathered her luggage together, alighted from the car, and paused wearily before approaching the footway that led to Cora's large Victorian home. For an instant, she wished with all of her heart that she could simply return home and forget the whole ordeal. But, remembering that she no longer had a real home anymore, she realized grimly that she had no alternative but to continue on the pathway that led to Cora's front door. She did not hesitate again. Pale and slender, a serious expression upon her face, she boldly banged the brass knocker several times. With a deep sigh, she waited for a response.

She suddenly felt faint, and with great embarrassment, feared that she would collapse at her sister's front door. Thankfully, however, the feeling passed, and Katherine stood her ground. Several moments more elapsed, and Katherine began to fear that no one was home. Just as she was debating whether to try the back door, however, a frazzled-looking blonde-haired woman in her early thirties opened the door a fraction of an inch.

"Just a moment, please," she called out while simultaneously attempting to quiet the baby who was screaming and sputtering in her arms. "Quiet, lovey, please," Katherine heard her coo softly to the child. After the baby had quieted down a bit, the blonde-haired woman opened the door wide enough to notice her visitor's face. For a moment, Cora failed to recognize her sister. It had been several years since the sisters had been together. Cora had been a mother preoccupied with her household and maternal responsibilities. Katherine had matured into a lovely albeit wistful waif-looking woman who had obviously been through different times.

"May I help you?" she began, then realized that the face of her caller was very familiar. "Katherine!" she cried out suddenly. "Katherine, is that you? Oh, dear, I am terribly sorry to keep you waiting. But, frankly, I wasn't expecting anyone and thought it was a solicitor. What a wonderful surprise! Oh, do forgive me, come on in, love."

Fortunately, the baby had calmed down by now, and Katherine's voice could now be heard. "Cora," she asked in an urgent voice, "May I stay with you and Ivar for a short while? I . . . I have left Percy," she stated, getting to the point of her visit immediately.

"Oh, I see," Cora said quietly, carefully studying her sister's face and noticing with sudden fear the pained expression and ashen features. "Of course, you may stay with us for as long as you wish, love," Cora said kindly. "Now come on with me into the lounge. Put your bags down here, and make yourself comfortable," Cora insisted. Meekly, Katherine obeyed these instructions, grateful for her sister's casual, pragmatic acceptance of the news.

"Now then, my love, I want you to sit there quietly and relax for a few minutes while I prepare some tea," said Cora after she had gently guided her sister into a low, inexpressibly comfortable chair of emerald velvet with a matching velvet hassock. "Close your eyes and rest until I return, all right?" Cora asked, gazing directly into her sister's eyes.

"All right," Katherine returned feebly, the slightest trace of a smile upon her lips. Squeezing her sister's arm lovingly, Cora left her alone.

"She's left Percy," Cora whispered dramatically to her husband, while preparing tea in the kitchen. "And she looks god-awful—as though she might pass out any moment. She hasn't told me any of the particulars, but I invited her to stay here with us for as long as she wishes. She seems terribly worried. What should I do? What should I tell her?" asked Cora of her husband, Ivar, who was seated at the kitchen table, finishing his breakfast of fried ham, boiled eggs, and hot rolls.

"I should simply listen to her, my dear. I imagine she's anxious to just talk to someone," he said, with a man's simple wisdom, as he wiped the crumbs from his lips with the linen serviette. "Don't worry, Cora. She'll be fine. If I know your younger sister as I have through the years of family events and get-togethers, she'll manage beautifully. Just offer her sympathy and a good listening ear," continued Ivar, as he rose from the table, and kissed his wife lightly on the cheek. "And now, love, I had better go. I'm running rather late this morning. But first I shall say hello to Katherine. Bye, love."

"Bye, sweet." And Cora, having handed baby Phillip over to his nanny, hurried about, carefully arranging a breakfast tray for her sister. "She looks so thin, so worried and nervous, I'll bet she hasn't had anything decent to eat in days. Why, she looks as though a good, hearty breeze could knock her down. I shall insist that she eat and then take a nap. She shall have the guest room across from Yvonne's bedroom." Cora was so preoccupied with her sister's dilemma that she was hardly conscious of what she was doing. Nor was she aware that she was talking to herself.

In the meantime, Katherine was grateful for the opportunity to rest in solitude. Taking several deep breaths and closing her eyes, she fell into a pleasant sort of half-sleep. She heard from what seemed to be a great distance away the clattering of dishes, the tinkling of silver, and some voices. It seemed that Cora's husband and her five-year-old daughter, Yvonne, were upstairs getting ready respectively to leave the house for the office and school.

"Hurry now or you'll be late," Cora was calling from the bottom of the stairs.

"All right, Mummy," little Yvonne had answered obediently. And suddenly Katherine heard first the dainty little footsteps followed by the heavy footsteps rapidly descending the staircase. For an instant, she detected the distinctive scent of men's cologne in the air.

She was startled out of her half-sleep state by Ivar's sudden appearance in the lounge. "I'm awfully sorry, Katherine. Did I frighten you?" he murmured in embarrassment.

"I'm afraid you did a bit," Katherine smiled weakly. "I guess I was nearer to sleep than awake."

"How are you, love? Cora tells me you've left Percy."

"Yes, it's true," replied Katherine, wondering why she felt that dreadful, sinking feeling in her stomach. "But hopefully, Percy and I will be reunited soon."

"I see," mumbled Ivar. "I'm afraid I can't really talk right now as I'm rather late for the office, Katherine. But hopefully we shall be able to discuss it all over dinner. I do hope you'll be staying here with us for a while. You know, you're always welcome, don't you, dear?"

"Yes, Ivar, thank you," murmured Katherine shyly.

"Good, then. I shall see you later. 'Bye now—I'm off." And he kissed his sister-in-law gently on the cheek. As soon as Ivar had left the room, her heart stopped its fierce pounding and she closed her eyes once again.

Now she heard the excited voice of the little girl, "I'm leaving now, Mummy. Good-bye!"

"Good-bye, Yvonne. Be a good girl today, won't you, my sweet?" Cora's voice had come from the direction of the kitchen.

"I will, Mummy, promise," was Yvonne's confident response. Finally, all conversation died, and the commotion subsided. Then Katherine heard the front door bang shut. Suddenly, the house was blessedly, mercifully silent.

A lazy somnolence lay over the house now, and the lounge was in semi-darkness, for the draperies had been drawn against the early morning sun. In the half-light, Katherine observed her surroundings for the first time, viewing with genuine appreciation the tasteful furnishings, the lovely rose and spring green floral design of the satin draperies, and the matching throw rugs that had been artistically arranged on the highly polished wooden floors. *How well Cora has done for herself,* Katherine thought, vaguely recalling her sister's previous first home that had been much smaller and far less attractively furnished than this one. *Yes,* Katherine continued to reflect, *they are on their way.*

She was reminded of Cora's ambition from childhood onward to become as wealthy as possible, as rapidly as possible. She knew that Ivar felt similarly. Both were employed at the present time, and they had frequently invested in property through the years—refurbishing each home and then selling it for a handsome profit. *No doubt Cora shall have everything she's always wanted,* thought Katherine, marveling at the difference in their natures and temperaments. In fact, the two women shared virtually nothing in common besides their parentage and upbringing. For Cora had always been highly ambitious and materialistic, intent upon acquiring both wealth and social position. She had, of her own choice, become a Catholic, and was now also heavily involved in church affairs—her involvement predicated upon social advancement and prestige rather than spiritual yearning. The acquisition of wealth and social status, church affairs, and the welfare of her son, Phillip, daughter, Yvonne, and husband, Ivar, comprised both purpose and meaning to Cora's life. Never, in a million years, could Cora have been able to grasp the nature or purpose for which Katherine lived. The two were as different as night and day.

Once again, Katherine closed her eyes. But this time she was interrupted by the clattering of cups and saucers and the clinking of silver along with Cora's deliberately cheerful voice, "Come on, darling. Wake up. Time to eat." Cora had appeared in the doorway with an enormous tray of food.

"Oh, Cora, you shouldn't have gone to such trouble," Katherine murmured, gazing in astonishment at the incredible array of pastries, homemade jams and preserves, and delicious looking fruits.

"Don't be silly," Cora admonished, placing the tray on the small table by Katherine's chair. Katherine stared with incredulity at the hot buttered scones, thin slices of bread and butter, clotted cream, finger sandwiches, and the assortment of cakes and biscuits. It was obvious that Cora was used to entertaining!

"Now, love, you must eat—for me. And then you can tell me what has happened, all right?" Katherine nodded miserably, as she helped herself to a cup of tea and forced herself to take a bite of a hot scone literally dripping with butter. Although she did not feel well and was not hungry at all, she felt somewhat revived by the hot tea. For a moment she closed her eyes and felt the liquid's pleasant, soothing warmth penetrate her body. After several moments of silence, during which Katherine feigned interest in the food before her—picking at the biscuits and the fruit—and during which Cora observed her sister with intense interest, Katherine began slowly to describe the events that had culminated in her arrival in Newport that morning.

Katherine had begun haltingly, as though finding it very difficult and painful to speak, but soon her voice and manner assumed an impersonal quality, and she managed to describe in detail the horror and humiliation of life in Mt. Ash, the all-too- brief but happy time in Swansea, the move to Aberdare, and Percy's steady deterioration. With great effort, Katherine struggled to recount matter-of-factly the changes that had recently taken place in Percy—his drinking, his late nights out, his thoughtless and erratic behavior. She described her miscarriage and illness and the deeply rooted fear that what had taken place in Mt. Ash would happen again in Aberdare.

"You see, I know that Percy has been borrowing money from the till at the shop," she confided in a hoarse voice to Cora. It was not until she began to speak of Graham, however, that Katherine suddenly began to convulse and sob aloud. "I'm sorry, Cora," she managed to get out, "but I don't think I can go on."

"It's all right, love, it's all right. You mustn't worry. The worst is over, I assure you." Cora had come over to where Katherine was sitting and tenderly put her arms around her. "Just go ahead and cry, love. Let all the anger and fear out. Lord knows, you've borne enough to make anyone crazy. You've been through a tremendous strain, but you must believe me when I say that you're on your way toward achieving a resolution to these difficulties. I'm sure Percy will come to his senses. And you know that little Graham is in good hands. You will be with him in no time at all. I am certain of it," said Cora in her motherly way. "Worry not, love. All will be well. Just do as Mother has always done. Go to God. Ask to be shown the way. You'll see a way out of this mess. I know you will," Cora spoke in a firm but gentle voice, all the while stroking her sister's hair and holding her to her breast.

"How kind you are," said Katherine looking up, her face white and stained with tears. "Thank you, Cora."

"Now, none of that," said Cora kindly, but matter-of-factly. "Now, love, I shall show you to your room, and I want you to spend the rest of the afternoon resting. Do you understand? And when you have rested sufficiently and bathed and changed into some comfortable clothing, I want you to come downstairs and talk to your heart's content. Ivar and I shall do everything in our power to assist you through this difficult time. Do you follow?" Katherine nodded, squeezing her eyes tightly to keep back her tears.

"Thank you, so much," she whispered, finding her sister's hand and clasping it tightly in her own.

"You're very welcome, love," said Cora softly. And with that, she held Katherine's hand as she might have held that of a child and led her up the staircase and into the guest room. "Here you are, darling. Make yourself comfortable. And do not hesitate to let me know if you are in need of anything. Now I shall leave you alone. Sleep well, love," she murmured, kissing her sister tightly on the forehead. And then Cora left the room, gently closing the door behind her.

Wearily removing the cumbersome dress and slip and stockings, Katherine splashed some cold water over her face and neck and then changed into a thin nightdress. Glancing at the clock on the bureau, she was surprised to see it was half past one. Thoroughly exhausted and emotionally drained, she tumbled into bed, settled under the cool cotton sheets, and fell into a deep and dreamless sleep at the precise moment her head touched the pillow. She awoke several hours later only to discover that she felt no less exhausted or weary. Opening her eyes and glancing around the room, it was some moments before she was able to recall where she was or why she had come here.

"Am I dreaming?" she wondered aloud, unable to determine where reality began and the dream-state ended. For a few seconds, she was a young, carefree girl of sixteen living in beautiful Wynstay House in the midst of the mountains of Gwaelod-y-garth. The beautiful garden; the wildflowers of every imaginable color that grew in abundance; the fragrance of the fruit trees in bloom; the cheerful banter between her brothers and sisters; the comforting presence of Mum and Dad; the sweet breakfast smells of bacon frying and rolls baking permeating the atmosphere—all were intensely vivid and real. It was the tiny voice of Cora's little girl, who had apparently returned home from school that brought her back to reality.

"Whatever that is," Katherine muttered, as she adjusted to her surroundings and began to think. Now, in the still heat of the late afternoon sun, whose rays filtered through the lace curtains, Katherine remained in bed. Her head ached, and she felt weak and dizzy as she recalled with startling clarity the events that had taken place during the past several days. Bravely, she sought to prevent the tears from flowing forth, but as persistent thoughts of home—and of Percy and little Graham—their present whereabouts and circumstances gnawed at her brain, she was soon helpless to prevent an outburst of raw emotion. Suddenly, she let go and began to sob as though her heart were breaking. Her chest heaving, her heart hammering away fiercely and persistently, she lay under the soft sheets as the tears spilled forth onto her cheeks and neck and shoulders. For well over an hour, she cried like this until finally there were no more tears to flow. Feeling empty and drained, she lay perfectly still, cold with sweat, her eyes raw and red and swollen. For some reason, Percy's face kept appearing before her— young, boyish, animated, charming—as it had been during the early days of their courtship, and she recalled clearly the sound of his voice and the words he had spoken during their very first meeting, "Although you don't know it yet, you are going to marry me."

"Indeed?" she had replied haughtily, her every instinct protecting her from this man. She wondered if even then, she had had some foreknowledge, some inkling of what was to be. As though viewing a motion picture, she observed in clear, visual images the outstanding episodes of her adult life: her first meeting with Mr. Crouch, her lessons with Mrs. Pfyfe wherein she first learned to read and write, the jewelry shop in Pontypridd where she had been working when she had met Percy, her marriage, the move to Mt. Ash, the birth of her only child, the incredible early morning materialization of the sister who had lived and died before her, her father's illness, the visit of Mr. Fletcher, the extraordinary six-month period of communications with the Spirit Beings, her first public meeting, her family's public career, the move to Swansea and then to Aberdare, and, then, finally, the recent events that had culminated in her present circumstances.

Now, she was helpless once again to prevent Percy's presence in her midst—his winning self-confidence, boyish charm, and youthful exuberance. How proud, how doting, and happy Percy had been at the birth of his son. She recalled his laughter and his shining eyes as he first beheld the small pink, newly born baby nestling at her breast; she recalled the gleam of love and affection and of genuine admiration in his eyes whenever his gaze had fallen upon her. How genuinely fond of him she had been then. *Why, I am still fond of him!* she thought with a sudden start. *I shall always love Percy*, she realized with surprise.

Would she ever forget Percy's despair after learning that he had been dismissed from his position at Alexander's? The horror and helplessness written upon his face as he described what had taken place, "I've lost my job, love," he had whispered. "Mr. Hawkins found me at the pub—he told me that I was dismissed, and that I was to have no reference." The desperation of his words echoed hollowly in her mind, evoking terror in her heart still . . . Now, simultaneously, she heard the words he had uttered that day in the cafe in Barry following her visit to the home of Mr. Hawkins, "Everything will be different than before, I promise. It's as though we are beginning life all over again—with a clean slate." How prophetic she had thought his words. And how wrong both of them had proven to be.

And lastly, Katherine recalled with startling clarity the fateful twilight walk during which Percy had calmly informed her, "We are not going to do the work anymore." The sudden shock, the searing disappointment, her disbelief, her utter unwillingness to accept those words—all came back to her now. And the memory of the words she had uttered in response, "Do not speak of giving up the work in the plural. Never—as long as I live—shall I give up the work, Percy. You may do what you feel you must, but I would sooner give up my life than the work which I believe with all my heart and soul I have come to the Earth to do."

Now, in the heavy, warm somnolence of the late afternoon, she became vitally aware of the intensity, the passion with which she loved her work.

Undoubtedly, nothing—not even her child—mattered so deeply to her as the work that she had come to Earth to do. She would bear whatever life had to offer—endure whatever suffering and experience were to come her way with courage and wisdom—so long as she could continue to do the work. Nothing else really mattered.

She was astounded by the simplicity of this realization, but it was this understanding that she had sought. For with it came the realization that she could, from hereon, take whatever life had to offer—for everything had meaning and would prove useful to her as a teacher. She felt an exquisite peacefulness creep over her, like an anesthetic, relaxing—almost numbing—her mind and body until she could feel no further pain. From here on, nothing mattered. All was God's Will. Slowly, easily her eyes closed shut, and she was soon fast asleep.

CHAPTER 33

Seeking Employment

—⤴—

IT WAS SUPPERTIME WHEN KATHERINE awoke several hours later; in fact, she had been awakened by the delicious smells of a roast baking in the oven. Sniffing the air hungrily, she dragged herself out of bed, washed her face, combed her hair, and dressed. She was startled to hear the clock in the hallway strike six, and from downstairs she heard Cora and Ivar talking. Hastily, she completed her toiletries. Although she dreaded the idea of being sociable and making polite conversation over dinner, she would not be rude. Not wishing to cause her sister any further upset or worry, she hastily made her way down the stairs.

Much to her relief, dinner was not an unpleasant affair. Despite her own self-consciousness and the well-intentioned advice and worried glances exchanged between Cora and Ivar, Katherine's strength and appetite began to revive and her spirit along with them. While politely pretending interest in the general conversation, Katherine was in fact absorbed in her own thoughts. *However kind and generous they are, I shan't intrude upon the hospitality of Ivar and Cora any longer than absolutely necessary*, she concluded. *I must find my own accommodations. I shall begin looking for a position tomorrow.* By the time the meal had drawn to an end, Katherine had carefully patterned her immediate future and planned the events of the coming day.

"My dear, you seemed a million miles away this evening," Cora had observed solicitously, as they relaxed in the lounge after dinner. "Are you all right?"

"Yes, fine," Katherine assured her. "Only I have been thinking . . . planning . . . that's all. I have decided to begin looking for a job tomorrow."

"Tomorrow? But that's much too soon! I won't have it. You must rest, recoup your strength first," Cora had protested with vehemence and Ivar concurred.

"I think it's premature, Katherine," he had stated, genuine concern evident in his voice and manner. "You've only just arrived here this morning. Can't you wait a few days and settle in?"

"I'm afraid not, dear. The sooner I acquire a position and money, the sooner I get my little boy back," she had murmured with feeling.

"I see," said Ivar, recognizing that it was futile to argue with his strongheaded sister-in-law. "Well, I suppose you must do as you see fit, my dear," he had stated dubiously, "but it just doesn't strike me as sensible."

"Nor me," added Cora, scrutinizing her sister's pale face.

"Nonetheless, I shall arise early tomorrow morning and begin looking for a suitable position," Katherine had persisted in her calm, no-nonsense manner. "And now, if you will excuse me, I shall retire to my bedroom. Thank you for the lovely dinner, your wonderful hospitality, and your kindly concern. I shall be perfectly all right, I assure you. Good night!" And after embracing Cora and kissing Ivar lightly on the cheek, Katherine returned to her bedroom where she formulated in further detail the strategy to be employed the following day, and pulled from her trunk the clothing suitable for the task at hand.

Awakening promptly at six the next morning, she felt refreshed and revived from the sleep she had enjoyed the previous day. Although tears and sadness and longing for her son still filled her eyes, and there was a tightness at her throat that would not go away, she adamantly refused to succumb to any further self-pity. She simply would not allow anything to interfere with the execution of her plan.

By eight o'clock, she had bathed, and dressed and was engaged in eating a delicious breakfast with her sister's family. Already, it was warm, and still feeling weak and dizzy, Katherine could hardly get down the delicious foods her sister had prepared.

"Katherine, you're hardly touching your food," Cora gently admonished. "You must eat something to keep up your strength, dear."

"I'm afraid that I am just not hungry. It's too warm, and I guess I am a bit nervous. After all, it's been eight years since I have worked at a real job—I am not at all certain as to what I'll find out there!"

"You'll do beautifully, love, I know it," Cora said comfortingly. "Just do be careful and don't overdo it. Your health is far more important than any old job. There's no hurry, love, in spite of what you think. For I told you, you're welcome to remain with us for as long as you wish."

"Thank you, dear" Katherine said warmly, "but you already know my feelings on that subject. And now," she said, glancing at her wrist watch, "if you will all wish me well, I shall be on my way."

"Goodbye, love, and good luck," Cora said, firmly clasping Katherine's hand.

"I'm with you one hundred percent," Ivar cried. "Good luck, sis." And on that hopeful note, and with the happy image of the smiling faces of little Philip and Yvonne fixed in her mind, Katherine excused herself from the room, gathered her purse and hat, and was soon on her way toward the commercial district of Newport. It was half past eight. "Precisely according to scheduler," she murmured, satisfied to be proceeding in accordance with her plan.

Past Godfrey Road, she hurried, through Bridge Street, onto High Street, and finally onto busy Commercial Street where Katherine carefully scrutinized the windows of every shop and business in the hope of discovering a placard, some advertisement of help wanted or indicating that her services were requested. Although Newport was not nearly so attractive a city as Swansea, it was far more appealing and exciting than either Mt. Ash or Aberdare had been. And so, as she strolled through the streets, she derived considerable pleasure from her surroundings. She had always liked large cities and much preferred them to the country. And so today, in spite of her own precarious circumstances, she rather enjoyed the sights and sounds of Newport. Furthermore, bittersweet memories of the early days with Mr. Crouch in Cardiff were awakened.

How much has happened since that time, she thought wistfully. *Whoever would have thought then that I should find myself here today?* She was jolted out of her reverie by the loud, impatient honking of the horn of a passing automobile. "Oh dear," she murmured. "I had better stop daydreaming." From here on, she paid strict attention to where she was going, carefully investigating every building she passed for any indication that help was needed.

For several blocks, there were no advertisements at all, and Katherine began to despair. But finally, she discovered a pleasant shopping area wherein several shops (a ladies' dress establishment and a jewelry shop) were requesting help. Unfortunately, however, someone had already been hired to fill the position at the dress shop, and she was found lacking sufficient experience by the manager of the jewelry shop. She continued walking until she found several other shops also requesting help. But was quickly learning that the experience she had acquired more than eight years ago was regarded with little esteem. "Sorry, Miss, but I'm afraid that you're just not qualified," was the discouraging response she heard over and over again throughout the morning.

By noon, she was both worried and exhausted. It was by now hazy and humid and extremely warm outside, and the heat seemed to bounce up in waves from the pavement. Her eyes were stinging and tearing with the noxious fumes from factories and automobiles; her clothes were sticky and uncomfortable, and her face was wet with perspiration. She felt weak and ill. *I can't go on,* she thought in sudden desperation. *I simply can't go on like this.* She felt like crying, but with great self-restraint, she cast the tears aside, and, silently promised herself, *I won't cry now. I'll have a good cry later on at home.*

Her head throbbed, and her feet were swollen and tired and aching. Pausing to rest on a stoop outside a tall building, she took off her shoes and wiggled her toes, sighing in the temporary pleasure this activity afforded her. Not caring what anyone thought of her, she removed her hat and gloves. After resting in this manner for several minutes, and massaged her aching feet, and wondering, *Where do I go from here?,* she happened to glance up at a second story window of the tall gray structure next door wherein a placard boldly proclaimed that this was a Registry Office.

"Apply within" were the words inscribed beneath the name of the business. "Hmmmmmmmmm," mused Katherine, lost in thought as she placed her shoes back on her feet. She was almost entirely oblivious to the discomfort caused by this action. She took several awkward steps, then, using one of the plate glass windows of the brick building as a mirror, Katherine carefully smoothed her dress, repinned her hat, and put her gloves on. "Hmmmmmmm," she murmured aloud. "It's worth a try isn't it? After all, what have I got to lose?"

CHAPTER 34

The George 'N Dragon

⟋⟍

HOLDING HER HEAD HIGH, SHE strode rapidly and purposefully toward the gray office building in which the Registry Office was located. "Let Us Find the Right Job for You," a sign in the lobby of the building stated invitingly, which also bore the information that the Registry Office was to be found on the second floor of the building in Suite 200. "I will gladly let you find the right job for me," Katherine mumbled in response to the message written on the placard, as she mounted the stairway leading to the employment office.

Several moments later she found herself in a pleasant, sunlit office decorated with many fine antiquities and plenty of plants. "May I help you?" a brisk, cheerful feminine voice called out from behind a large, carved Georgian desk.

"Yes, please," Katherine replied politely, trying to locate the owner of the mysterious voice, for she could not see anyone.

"Do have a seat, and I shall be with you in just a moment," the voice continued.

"Thank you," said Katherine, gratefully dropping into one of the handsome, high-backed chairs. She used this opportunity to survey her surroundings and to plan what she would say to the mysterious woman.

"Please forgive me," the voice spoke once again, "but you see, I dropped my pen, and had to go foraging for it." Now, from behind the great desk, the figure of a stately, gray-haired matronly looking woman in her mid-fifties emerged. "So sorry," she apologized. "Now then," she said, resuming her seat, "what can I do for you?"

Her sharp blue eyes carefully studied Katherine's figure—the simply tailored traveling suit; the wavy brown hair; the pretty, expressive features; the penetrating hazel eyes; the courage and strength of will written in her countenance; and the air of sadness that emanated from the attractive woman who sat before her. *Poor dear, she seems to be in some kind of trouble. She's pretty and seems intelligent enough,* the woman thought to herself. She smiled graciously and Katherine returned the smile. *I like her,* decided the older woman. *Yes, I would say that she has possibilities. I wonder if she has any skills?*

"My name is Jilia Edwards, and I am the owner and manager of this Registry," the older woman volunteered.

"I am Katherine Hayward, and I am seeking a position here in Newport. In fact, I only just arrived in Newport yesterday. You see, I have recently . . . uh, lost . . . my husband, and find that I must now assume complete financial responsibility for my eight-year-old son and myself. My husband left me with virtually nothing in the way of money or property. I have had quite a lot of experience in business in the jewelry trade—although this was some years ago. I am most anxious to begin earning as soon as possible. Furthermore, if it is at all possible, I should very much like to find a position that offers accommodations as well. You see, I have nowhere to live." The enormity of her circumstances hit Katherine as she spoke, and her voice choked with pent-up emotion. Although she quickly recovered herself, she knew that Mrs. Edwards had intuitively grasped the desperateness of her plight.

There was a brief silence as Mrs. Edwards digested Katherine's story and then began to peruse her files as though in search of some particular sheet. "My dear girl, I believe I have just what you are looking for. Let me see if I can find the order form. . . Ah, here it is!" She smiled broadly, holding the piece of paper high in the air, as though victorious. She glanced over the form once more, nodding with approval. "Yes, my dear, I really do think you are perfect for the Hurleys."

"The what?" Katherine asked, uncomprehendingly.

"The Hurleys, my dear. A lovely, aristocratic family whose employees I have been supplying for over twenty years. They own and operate a charming hotel and pub called The George 'N Dragon and own a beautiful residence on the grounds as well."

"A hotel?" Katherine repeated in dismay. A dreadful, sinking feeling came over her. "Oh, I am terribly sorry, Mrs. Edwards, but I could not possibly accept a position at a hotel," she stammered awkwardly.

"But why not, my dear?" inquired Mrs. Edwards.

"Well, you see, it's my upbringing. My Mum and Dad always taught us to keep away from public houses. Mum in particular has always regarded hotels rather as 'dens of iniquity.' I just wouldn't—well, I simply couldn't—feel comfortable in such a place. Have you no other position for which I would be suitable?"

"I am afraid not," stated Mrs. Edwards firmly. "I do wish that you would let me continue. For I can't help but feel, that despite your upbringing, the position at the Hurley home is right for you. And I can think of no one more suitable than you for the Hurley home."

"Indeed," murmured Katherine coldly. She had no desire to listen to Mrs. Edwards any further, and she certainly had no intention of working in a hotel. She remained obstinately silent.

But Mrs. Edwards was equally obstinate. The shrewd but kindly woman was convinced that Katherine and the position were perfectly suited for one another. "You must hear me, child, when I tell you that you will not be working at the hotel. Rather, you will be hired as a companion for the young mistress of the Hurley home. Miss Doris who, following the death of her mother, is in dire need of someone to befriend and look after her. And I must say that Master Trevor—that's Miss Doris' older brother—would benefit, greatly from your companionship as well. You would also be required to supervise the domestic staff—a position of responsibility, I assure you," said Mrs. Edwards solemnly.

"I am terribly sorry to disappoint you, Mrs. Edwards—you've been very kind and patient—but I just cannot imagine myself as someone's live-in companion. Why, it sounds as though I would be little more than a personal maid. I just don't think I would be happy there!" Katherine said, beginning to lose patience now, and rather wishing that she had never set foot in Mrs. Edwards' Registry Office.

But Mrs. Edwards seemed unaffected by Katherine's words. She continued unperturbed. "Mrs. Hurley—Trevor and Doris' mum—was a dear, gentle woman—lovely to look at, too. When she died some years ago, the children were heartbroken. I don't think a day elapsed wherein they didn't sorely miss their mum. Mrs. Hurley was everything that Mr. Hurley—Mr. William Hurley, that is—wasn't: genteel, artistic, refined, delicate of health, and very sensitive. Mr. William Hurley is a businessman—clever, extroverted, strong, and pragmatic—and robust and hearty as they come. The children seemed to take after their mum, and when she passed on, they were lost. Mr. Hurley was never able to understand his children. A wide rift arose between the children and their father when Mr. William decided to marry the housekeeper without even consulting them. Now, their dad is planning to move out of the old residence and into his own place with the housekeeper—soon to be the second Mrs. Hurley. Furthermore, they have been very short of domestic staff and Trevor and Doris have been terribly overworked. Their present housekeeper has fallen ill. So you see, the children are in great need of comfort and of guidance, and I have the very powerful conviction that you, my dear, are the one to assist them. You know," Mrs. Edwards' voice broke off suddenly, "it may sound strange, but I swear I feel the influence of the first Mrs. Hurley here with us now. As though she were with us in this room. Isn't that odd?"

Although she had been inclined to walk out of the office and never return, Katherine had felt inexplicably compelled to listen to Mrs. Edwards' account of the Hurleys. And, as Mrs. Edwards had spoken, she too had felt the influence, the presence, of the first Mrs. Hurley. Katherine had the strong sensation that Mrs. Hurley was still looking after her children—albeit from the other side of life.

"Well, what do you say, Mrs. Hayward? Won't you at least meet the Hurleys? After all, you needn't accept the position. But," she added shrewdly, "the position seems to offer everything you require including a generous wage and pleasant accommodations. Furthermore, I am certain that the Hurleys would not mind in the least if you brought your little boy there to live."

Graham! Katherine's heart began to beat rapidly. *My God, perhaps Mrs. Edwards is right. Perhaps I owe it to Graham to at least investigate the possibility of a job. As there seems to be no other position at the moment, nothing else available, perhaps I had better at least meet the Hurleys.* Mrs. Edwards was watching Katherine very closely. Taking full advantage of her obvious confusion, the manager of the Registry Office employed her warmest, most persuasive tone.

"Look, my dear, the Hurley residence is only a five-minute walk from here. Why not at least see the grounds? After all, you have nothing to lose. Won't you go to oblige me?"

"All right," sighed Katherine, conceding defeat. "Give me the directions, and I shall go at once."

"Lovely," breathed Mrs. Edwards.

Mrs. Edwards had not in any way exaggerated the importance of the Hurley estate. Occupying what appeared to be acres of commercial land, the property consisted of a large hotel and a beautiful stone residence. There was a garden that was large and well laid out, stables and a cobblestone courtyard that separated the hotel from the residence. Katherine was delighted by the beauty of the landscape that surrounded her, and she spent several minutes standing in the courtyard and absorbing the pleasant atmosphere. In her excitement, she had failed to notice the sign on the lawn that read "Private Property - No Trespassing."

"May I help you, miss?" a man's severe voice seemed to come from nowhere, startling Katherine to such a degree that she actually jumped. A tall, handsome, well-groomed man who Katherine surmised to be near sixty was standing only a few feet away from her, and had, apparently, been coming from the hotel. Katherine had been too surprised to respond, and, the man repeated, "May I help you?"

"Uh . . . why, no," she finally replied, quite embarrassed at being discovered by anyone while she was on strange property. "I was just having a look around the grounds." Sensing something amiss, the man motioned to the sign that indicated that this was private property.

"Surely, you must have noticed this?" he asked pointing to the sign.

"Why, no," said Katherine, seeing the sign for the first time. "I am afraid I did not notice it at all."

The man seemed to be observing Katherine for the first time. His penetrating gaze took in the smart, tailored outfit, her well-coifed hair, the thoughtful, sensitive expression of her eyes. For several moments, Katherine bore his steady scrutiny in an uncomfortable silence. Finally, the man spoke once again, this time in a curious tone of voice. "You know, I cannot help but feel that there is some motive—a definite purpose—to your visit here this afternoon."

"Oh . . . uh . . . really?" Katherine stammered.

"Yes, really," he responded, a trace of a smile evident on his lips. "You wouldn't, by some chance, be the young woman that Mrs. Edwards was to send by?" he inquired pleasantly.

Feeling a faint blush creep over her face, Katherine was wondering whether to reveal her identity, when she heard herself say, "Why, yes, I've only just come from Mrs. Edwards' office. How did you know?"

"Well," said the gentleman warmly, "let's just say Mrs. Edwards notified me about your intended visit."

"About me?" asked Katherine. "Whatever for? Perhaps I had better explain," she sighed. "You see, Mrs. Edwards—of the Registry Office—was most insistent that I meet the Hurleys, who are, apparently, in need of an individual to act as a lady's companion to Miss Doris Hurley. Although I do not believe that the position is right for me—or me for it—for that matter, I promised Mrs. Edwards that I would at least see the grounds."

"And—," interrupted the man.

"And," concluded Katherine, "here I am, uh, viewing the grounds."

"I see," he murmured, as though amused by her.

"You do?" asked Katherine, puzzled.

"Yes," he replied, politely taking her arm in his and guiding her toward the Hurley residence. Katherine was too surprised to struggle. When they had drawn within perhaps one hundred feet of the front door, Katherine protested. "I fear that I must be on my way, sir."

The man turned and faced her squarely. "Please wait, miss. You see, I am William Hurley—the owner and operator of this property and The George 'N Dragon, and I am very happy to meet you, Miss eh . . ."

"Hayward," Katherine supplied. "Mrs. Katherine Hayward."

"Oh, you are married then, are you?" asked Mr. Hurley.

"I—er—that is to say, I am a widow, sir," Katherine heard herself saying.

"Oh, so sorry. I, too, am a widower. I know how difficult it is to be left behind."

Despite her anxiousness to leave the spot, she found herself inexplicably drawn to Mr. Hurley. There was something in his masculine good looks and vitality—an authoritativeness that appealed to her.

"Mrs. Hayward, after my wife's death, my children, my home, my life was not the same. My son, Trevor, had handled his mother's death as well as might be expected of a twenty-seven-year-old young man who is heir to my estate and has already assumed responsibility of managing most of my business concerns. His sister, Doris, unfortunately, who lacks Trevor's resilience, has not fared so successfully. For she is far more shy, delicate, and reserved than her older brother. We are in great need of someone like you, Mrs. Hayward. I can't help but feel that you could do my daughter a world of good. Won't you consider helping us?" he implored.

"I . . . I am afraid not, Mr. Hurley. A hotel . . . lady's companion . . . I just don't feel I would be suitable. . ."

"Well, then, Mrs. Hayward, mightn't I at least make your visit worthwhile and give you a tour of our property?" His eyes were so kind that Katherine, who did not wish to appear rude, could not help but graciously accept his offer.

"All right, Mr. Hurley, I should enjoy seeing your estate."

Arm-in-arm, they strolled, as Mr. Hurley pointed out the various points of interest.

"What a lovely spot!" Katherine had repeated over and over again. The grounds were most impressive and tasteful.

"Now, then, won't you come inside and meet my children?" the persistent Mr. Hurley pleaded, looking like a sad-eyed little boy. Realizing that there was no way to escape the clever trap devised by Mr. Hurley, Katherine good-naturedly acquiesced.

"What else can a lady do?" she laughed.

"Exactly as I thought," replied Mr. Hurley, with a pleasant sparkle in his eyes. "Come, then." And he escorted her into the enormous entrance hall that was finely proportioned and contained many beautiful ornaments. Each room was larger and grander than the next, and Katherine could not help but admire the genuine elegance and tastefulness of the decor. Mr. Hurley finally escorted her into the dining parlor—a lofty, handsome room with a long gleaming mahogany table and tall carved chairs covered with rich red velvet. Beautiful oil paintings and tapestries adorned the walls; and sparkling crystal and silver gleamed richly against the luxurious velvet draperies. Yet despite the beauty of the room, Katherine could not help but feel the sadness that pervaded it—that permeated the entire house, in fact.

"Now, then, Mrs. Hayward, please have a seat. I shall go and fetch the children, and then we shall have tea."

Within several moments, Mr. Hurley returned and sat opposite her at the long table, which was laden with fresh fruit and flowers, the scent of which filled the room. "Trevor and Doris will be down momentarily," he smiled. Soon a servant appeared with a great silver tea tray set with an exquisite Georgian tea service and delicate gold-rimmed bone china. Following in his wake was a middle-aged maid who also carried a large tray, this one laden with food—scones and biscuits, wafer-like sandwiches of cucumber, watercress, and tomato; sponge, lemon, and raspberry cakes; and all manner of homemade preserves and jams. The two servants made an elaborate display as they supplied Katherine and Mr. Hurley with everything one could possibly wish.

As they sipped their tea and chatted amiably—almost as old friends—they were interrupted by the arrival of a strikingly handsome young man with wavy light brown hair and large blue eyes. "Good day," he said politely, looking directly into Katherine's eyes. She squirmed awkwardly under his gaze. She did not know why she was so acutely aware of his physical presence. "I am Trevor Hurley. How do you do?" he was saying, as he politely extended his hand.

"How do you do?" she replied, hardly able to take her eyes off of him. "I am Katherine Hayward." She proffered her hand in greeting.

"Father has told me the nature of your visit here. I do hope you decide to accept the position," he said boldly. "Father has assured me that you would be the perfect companion for my sister."

Gasping audibly at his forthrightness, Katherine only replied, "Indeed." And although she noticed that Trevor Hurley was brisk and efficient as well as highly intelligent, she thought that he was one of the saddest looking people she had ever known. *He's carrying quite a burden for such a young man*, she thought to herself. But her thoughts were interrupted by the arrival of yet another person. This time, it was Doris Hurley who introduced herself to Katherine. Doris was tall and slender with a pale oval face and dark eyes that were deep in their sockets but wide apart, she had long chestnut-colored hair that she wore parted down the middle and in a bun at the nape of her neck. Katherine thought that Doris was an odd, old-fashioned, and wretched looking girl. Both she and her brother seemed so intense and serious for their ages. *They are positively joyless*, thought Katherine to herself.

"Don't you think you could stay—help us out—for just a short while?" Doris asked of Katherine as soon as she had taken a seat at the table. Katherine nearly choked on the biscuit she had been munching. Glaring at Mr. Hurley, then studying the serious faces of Trevor and Doris, Katherine was about to say "no" once and for all, when Mr. Hurley spoke softly but firmly.

"Money is no object, Mrs. Hayward. You shall have whatever you desire in the way of salary." Katherine simply could not refuse his generous offer.

"All right," said Katherine, placing the biscuit back on her dish. "I see I have no choice, but to at least seriously consider your kind offer. But I think that I must make it perfectly clear that even if I accept it, I can make no promise as to how long I shall remain here with you. I should give it a fair trial that is all!" She spoke vehemently, carefully averting her gaze so that she did not see the triumphant expression in the eyes of all three Hurleys. Furthermore, she did not notice the flicker of disappointment cross Trevor's face when he heard his father address Katherine as "Mrs. Hayward."

"I did not realize that you were married, Mrs. Hayward," Trevor had stated politely.

"I am a widow and I have an eight-year-old son currently staying with my relatives, Mr. Hurley," she lied, feeling her face flush. She did not know exactly why she had lied, other than she wanted no one to know of her present situation with Percy. It just seemed easier than explaining the truth.

"Oh, I see," murmured Trevor, thinking that there was something odd in the tone of her response. "When shall you start with us, Mrs. Hayward?"

"Let us leave it this way," she replied. "Since I do not feel that I can make a decision at this time, let me have the rest of the day to think matters over. I shall let you know my decision first thing tomorrow morning, if that's all right with you."

"Certainly seems fair to me," observed Mr. Hurley.

"And to me," added Doris, smiling.

"We shall look forward to hearing from you early tomorrow morning, then Miss Hayward," agreed Trevor.

"That's 'Mrs.' Hayward," Katherine corrected.

"Oh, yes, of course," Trevor smiled queerly.

"Well, then, I shall take my leave now. Thank you very much for your hospitality—and for the lovely tour of the grounds," said Katherine, rising from the table and extending a gracious hand to Mr. Hurley, and to each of his children. Trevor guided her out. And she was soon on her way back to Cora's home.

Oh dear God, what should I do? she wondered all the way home. She spent the remainder of the day in dialogue with God and herself.

You would earn a good wage; have a pleasant position; decent accommodations, a voice inside her advised.

And if and when I decide to stay, I can have little Graham with me, she thought with relief.

Furthermore, this is one spot that Percy would never think of looking for you, the voice continued.

"It's time," Katherine said, thinking out loud. "Percy would never find me at The George 'N Dragon." I'd be safer there than anywhere else. For Percy knows I would never have anything to do with a hotel or pub."

Although she had discussed the situation and sought the advice of Cora and Ivar at dinner that evening, Katherine knew that the decision was hers to make. No one could really help her. Now, before falling asleep for the night, she knelt in prayer. And as she asked God for guidance, it suddenly occurred to her that the position might not be so bad after all; that if she accepted it, she would be able to leave Cora and Ivar tomorrow; and that The George 'N Dragon was not nearly so unpleasant a place as she had initially thought it would be—in fact, it was quite charming and very attractive.

"The George 'N Dragon . . . hmmmmm," she mumbled, before falling asleep, "it might be just what I'm looking for after all. . ."

CHAPTER 35

A Lady's Maid

_⟶_

DEAR GOD, PLEASE GRANT ME *guidance and the strength to act upon it*, was Katherine's simple prayer. Seated at the edge of her bed, she stared blankly at the telephone for several minutes before she actually picked up the receiver and began to dial the number of The George 'N Dragon.

"I have decided to accept your offer—for at least a short while. I will arrive early this afternoon, if that is all right with you," she informed the delighted Doris Hurley.

"That will be lovely. I am so pleased that you will be working for us," Doris had murmured happily. "We shall look forward to your arrival."

Katherine quickly repacked her luggage and bade farewell to Cora and her family, thanking them for their kindness and hospitality.

She arrived at the George 'N Dragon early that afternoon. "I shall stay for only a short time—as a temporary measure—until you find someone who can permanently fill the position." Katherine had repeated several hours later in the presence of all three Hurleys—Trevor, Doris, and William.

"That is perfectly all right with us," Trevor had responded with a grin. "We are so short-staffed right now, that we shall be grateful to have your assistance for any length of time."

"We do hope that your stay here will be pleasant. We shall do everything in our power to make you happy," added Doris. "Now, let us show you to your apartment. I do hope you will find it suitable."

"Apartment?" Katherine felt like asking, but said nothing for fear of making a fool of herself. But certainly no one had indicated that she was to have her own apartment. This was more than she had bargained for.

"Really a lovely suite of rooms on the second floor. I do hope that you'll like it," Doris was saying.

"I'm certain I shall," smiled Katherine, and she followed Doris up the long, winding staircase, down a long, beautifully decorated hallway past an impressive library, by a series of large bedrooms, and finally into the suite of rooms that were to be Katherine's new home.

"Why it's lovely," Katherine exclaimed upon viewing the spacious living area. It consisted of a parlor, bedroom, and bath—all of which were adjoined, and all of which bespoke undisputed wealth and impeccable taste. The dark polished floor gleamed against the richly woven rugs in the parlor; two long sofas with matching chairs faced one another across a handsome table in front of a marble fireplace. It was everything that Katherine could possibly wish. The bedroom was equally lovely, with its pale yellow walls, lovely floral draperies, and matching bedspread; large window overlooking the garden; exquisite Chippendale cabinet and Georgian tables and consoles; and beautiful oil paintings of flowers and English summer landscapes. Certainly her quarters were like a breath of fresh air in comparison with the rest of the house, with its heavy Victorian furniture and somber colors.

"Please make yourself comfortable," Doris was saying. "Let us know if you are in need of anything at all. Tea will be served in the dining parlor at precisely half past four in the afternoon. Until then, just unpack your things and relax. We shall look forward to seeing you later on, all right?" Katherine nodded, too surprised by the Hurleys' generosity to utter a word. Katherine watched as Doris walked toward the door and slowly closed it behind her.

As soon as Doris had vanished from view, Katherine unpinned her hat, removed her gloves, kicked off her high-heeled slippers, and shed the tailored suit jacket she had been wearing. Her hands on her hips, she carefully examined each one of the rooms, delighting in their practical beauty.

It was not until after she had unpacked most of her belongings and was resting upon the bed that a sudden, intense wave of loneliness engulfed her and she began to cry. Deep sorrow tinged with a powerful yearning (she knew not for what) overcame her, and she sobbed as though her heart were breaking and until it seemed that she could contain no more tears.

"Oh, what am I doing here?" she moaned. "I must get away. I want my son—my little Graham. I need him—and he needs me. God, this can't be happening to me." And for a moment, she was struck by the pleasing notion that perhaps this was all a dream—that none of it was rooted in reality. She opened her eyes and blinked several times as though to ascertain whether or not she had been dreaming. As her gaze took in the unfamiliar decor, however, she realized with a sinking feeling that Trevor, Doris, the house, and the George 'N Dragon were only too real after all. Hardly moving except to wipe her tears or to blow her nose, she remained in bed until nearly 4:00 p.m.

Upon seeing that it was almost time for tea, she reluctantly arose and selected a skirt and blouse from her closet. Although she had no desire to go downstairs or to see any of the Hurleys ever again, for that matter, she realized that it would not be wise to hurt or offend them during the first afternoon in their employ. Applying a touch of rouge and some lipstick, she brushed her shoulder-length hair until it framed her face becomingly. *There*, she thought, glancing at her image in the mirror. *That's the best I can do under the circumstances. At least they won't be able to tell that I've spent the afternoon crying my eyes out.* And after pausing to remove a thread that hung unbecomingly from her skirt, she closed the door and found her way down the long staircase and into the dining parlor.

Tea at the Hurleys' was an elaborate affair, and Katherine was astonished to observe that it was even more elegant today than it had been during the previous afternoon. Great silver and crystal platters of cakes and fruits and biscuits adorned the table; along with crystal vases filled with fresh flowers; imported chocolates and candies; delicate china cups and saucers; and hand-carved silverware. Yet Katherine was far too preoccupied to feign interest in either the food or her companions. She was pleasant but distant, refraining from speaking unless spoken to first and replying to questions and comments politely rather than enthusiastically. Although she desired to make a good impression, she had no intention of calling attention to her presence.

Fortunately for Katherine, it was Mr. Hurley who directed and generally monopolized the conversation, entertaining the group with his lively accounts of the various individuals who had, throughout the years, for one reason or another, visited The George 'N Dragon; his own family history; and the changes that were taking place in Newport.

"We're growing fast and we're growing strong," he told the group proudly. Katherine knew that Mr. Hurley's congenial display was for her benefit, and she suddenly made a conscious attempt to appear deeply interested in all facets of the conversation. Perhaps a half hour had elapsed before Katherine was aware that Trevor had been staring at her. At first she was distinctly annoyed. *Why is he looking at me that way?* she wondered, and she deliberately met his gaze.

Although he self-consciously averted his eyes for a short time, Katherine noticed that they were soon fixed upon her again. She could not possibly have known that there was a mixture of wit and charm as well as sadness about her that both puzzled and bewitched Trevor. He had never met anyone quite like her. It was at this time that Katherine frankly studied each of the Hurleys and drew her own conclusions about Trevor and Doris.

Once again, she was struck by the singular sadness that seemed to afflict both of these lovely young people in spite of their gallant effort to conceal any unhappiness. She was also struck by the genuine love and affection as well as camaraderie shared between brother and sister, and of the constraint that existed between both children and their father. *It cannot simply be Mr. Hurley's impending marriage to the housekeeper that divides them so. I must get to the root of their estrangement*, she thought to herself.

Thankfully, Trevor was called away to attend to an important telephone call, and tea was soon over. It was at this time that Mr. Hurley asked Katherine to join him in the library wherein they could, in detail, discuss her duties and responsibilities as "a member of the staff." Katherine complied, feeling that despite the Hurleys' overwhelming hospitality, she would be regarded as little more than a servant. For nearly two hours, Mr. Hurley described the nature of her work that consisted chiefly (as far as she could discern) of attending to the needs of Miss Doris.

It's just as I had thought. I'm to be little more than a lady's maid to the mistress of this great house, she thought bitterly, as she listened to Mr. Hurley's explanation of the household hierarchy and manner in which the domestic staff of his home functioned. When she was so tired and bored that she felt like screaming, Mr. Hurley smiled graciously and concluded their session together.

"You'll see," he winked encouragingly, "you'll have no trouble adjusting. I can tell that you are clever and ambitious. And I assure you that your abilities will be rewarded."

Katherine had hardly been able to tolerate Mr. Hurley's lengthy descriptions of life on the estate, and when he finally concluded his "talk," she literally fled from the room and raced up the stairs seeking refuge in the solitude of her own quarters. "God, I just don't think I can bear it!" she sobbed into her pillow, great tears rolling onto her cheeks until her pillow was soon quite wet. At this moment, she wanted nothing to do with the Hurleys or their home or business. All she wanted was to be reunited with her husband and child and in her own home!

In light of Katherine's despondence, dinner was a dismal affair, even more so than tea. Katherine managed to get through it. It had been a long time since had she been required to utilize her acting abilities to such an extent! Fortunately, the meal passed quickly, and Katherine excused herself immediately after the family had departed the dining room and were on their way to the drawing room.

Thoroughly exhausted and drained of all emotion, she fell into a deep sleep as darkness, like an anesthetic, numbed, enveloped, and finally overtook her mind and body. Still, she awoke early the following morning feeling refreshed only momentarily as memories of all that had recently taken place came rushing forth into her consciousness. Then, she felt lonelier and more frightened than she had ever felt. She began to shake and whimper. *I must get hold of myself,* she thought then, and through an enormous effort of her will prepared for the day. Thankfully, somehow her first day on the job passed both swiftly and easily, and she found solace in the activity required of her. She was far too busy to dwell morbidly on her own affairs.

Although terribly shy, reserved, and delicate, Doris Hurley was, by virtue of her wealth and breeding, an important woman—a woman of substance and responsibility. Not only did she keep the household running efficiently, but she also assisted her father and brother in the daily operation of the hotel and pub. And although she was fragile, Katherine saw that she was strong-willed and intelligent. As Doris' companion, Katherine automatically became closely involved in all aspects of her life. And, as the Hurleys were a prominent and civic-minded family, Katherine found herself in a position of responsibility within a very short period of time. For as each day elapsed, Doris grew to trust and depend upon her to a greater degree. And, as Doris grew more dependent, so did Trevor and Mr. Hurley.

Within a matter of a few weeks, therefore, Katherine's responsibilities had expanded greatly. Within a month's time, she had become indispensable. She knew that Doris and the others had regarded her presence as a godsend, but still she refused to consider remaining with them on a permanent basis. She would remain only as long as her own personal difficulties made it absolutely necessary. Not a day elapsed during which she had not expected to receive an encouraging message from about Percy. It was to her amazement that no such message had yet arrived. *Something has gone awry. Something dreadful has happened*, she would think morbidly when time permitted.

Finally, nearly six weeks after she had taken the position with the Hurleys, she received a succinct note from Mother Hayward (whom she had finally informed as to her whereabouts but had sworn to secrecy) that read:

Dear Katherine,

I regret to inform you that Percy has been dismissed from Palmer's. He is penniless, without a reference, and without any hope for the future. Immediately following his dismissal, he disappeared from Aberdare. But he finally returned to our home.

Although he suffers from a severe case of depression, we are assisting him as best we can to overcome this sadness.

Do not worry, child. Percy knows nothing of your whereabouts. We will not divulge them until we receive your permission to do so. We are all doing what is necessary for the time being. Percy will pull out of this. Of this, father and I are certain.

In the meantime, Graham is glad to be with his father and is as happy as one might expect under the circumstances. Still, he asks for you every day, so do telephone him when you have the chance. We will have Graham telephone you when Percy is away from the house.

All is well. Do not worry. I pray that God will help us all through this trial.
Mother

Over and over and over again Katherine read the brief letter, as if to make certain her eyes were not deceiving her. It was almost impossible for her to believe that what she had most feared, most dreaded had come to pass, that Percy had lost his position and with it all hope for the future. *I cannot—I will not—go back to him*, she decided after having read the letter for perhaps the tenth time. *That is, I won't go back until he has paid off all prior debts, has acquired suitable references and a good position, and is earning enough to fully support Graham and myself. If he cannot meet all these criteria, then I will never return to him. And, as for the present, I shall assume full responsibility for my own welfare and that of my child. I will send for Graham as soon as I am more fully settled here and as soon as matters are resolved between Percy and me.*

It was not long, perhaps only a day or two after she had received the note from Mother Hayward, that Katherine awoke experiencing great anxiety and the powerful conviction that it was necessary to return to her former house in Aberdare. *I must pick up the rest of my belongings before Percy sells them, or before they are taken away by one of his debtors*, she thought grimly. Leaving a simple note for Doris explaining that she had been called away on a business matter, Katherine hastened out the door of the Hurley home and caught an early morning train back to Aberdare, arriving at her former residence at the precise moment the moving men were lifting her beloved sewing machine into a large lorry.

Nearly all her furniture, lamps, carpets, tables, and chairs, as well as her beautiful silver and crystal, had been carelessly arranged on the gravel walkway and over the front lawn. For several moments, she stood transfixed, as though hardly daring to believe that what she was seeing was actually taking place. *It can't be*, she moaned inwardly. "It won't be," she declared aloud.

Bravely approaching one of the three large, muscular men who were moving her possessions, she said in her most authoritative voice, "Just what is it you think you are doing? I am the owner of these possessions. And you have no right to touch them—let alone move them anywhere."

"I'm sorry, ma'am," said a burly yellow-haired man with a large, bulbous nose, "But we 'ave our orders."

"Your orders?" queried Katherine in a haughty tone. "And from whom have you received your orders?"

"From our boss, ma'am," the man answered wondering why he felt intimidated by this tiny woman.

"Your boss, eh?" she smirked. "And from whom did your boss receive his instructions?"

"I'm afraid I don't know, ma'am," said the man squirming uncomfortably under her steady scrutiny.

"Well, then, may I suggest that you check with your boss before you proceed any further? For I fear unless you do so at once, you and your men will be in grave trouble. These are my possessions, and I must insist that you return them to my house. I shall take what I can with me now, but the rest must be transported back inside." She started toward the house, then turned to face the yellow-haired man and his companions who had heard the entire exchange. With icy formality, she addressed them once more.

"Were I you, I would not proceed a single step further. Good day, gentle-men," and she walked briskly toward the front door. Once inside, Katherine gathered together as many of her belongings as she could, completely filling the trunk and other pieces of luggage that had been left behind. Thanks to the inner directive that had inspired her to make the trip to Aberdare, she managed to salvage the few items of value (both financial and sentimental) that she and Percy had managed to accumulate over the past few years. Those items she could not carry she arranged with her former landlady to store.

Surveying the house in which she had experienced such great sadness one last time, Katherine knew that she would never return. For the first time in her life, it occurred to her that her separation from Percy was no temporary measure, but, rather, permanent. For the very first time since she had agreed to marry Percy Hayward, she realistically faced the possibility of living without him.

"God help me," she murmured helplessly, feeling lost and bewildered as she wondered what the next step was to be. For several minutes she was lost in thought, recalling the various incidents and conversations over the years that had culminated in this moment. Regret mingled with undeniable relief as she realized that a chapter of her life had drawn to a close. *I am free—free to do as I please.* It was the first time in over nine and one-half years she had been able to utter these words. Yet she was well aware that with freedom came a formidable responsibility. After all, it would now be necessary for her to support herself fully—not to mention her child. But she was far from afraid. She had seen and experienced too much pain and suffering to fear the future. She would take life one day at a time.

Now, she recalled Dr. Evans' words spoken so many years before, "There are no obstacles with which you are presented that you are not strong enough to overcome."

He's right, of course, she reflected. *I know that somehow I will over-come all of this and emerge victorious.* And, after taking one long, linger-ing final glance at the home—one final look at the life she was leaving behind forever—she collected her belongings and found her way out. As she made her way over the gravel path, she was relieved to observe that the moving men had heeded her advice and had ceased lifting any more furniture onto the lorry.

"We're checking with our supervisor, ma'am, as you advised," the big, yellow- haired man called out as she walked past him. "Sorry to inconvenience you."

"It's all right. It's certainly not your fault that a misunderstanding has taken place. Thank you for heeding my instructions. And now, good day, gentlemen," she said to all three.

"Good day, miss," they returned in good humor. And with her most valued objects in tow, she found her way to the train station that was only several blocks away.

Although she was sorely tempted to purchase a ticket to Pontypridd wherein she could spend some time with Graham, she knew such action to be ill-advised.

No, she decided, practicing great self-restraint. *I must rectify matters with Percy first, and I don't feel that it is time to do so yet. It must be he who seeks me out. Furthermore, I shall have to firmly establish my position with the Hurleys and earn a good wage in order to provide Graham with all he needs. In the meantime, I will continue to entrust Graham to the care of Mother and Father Hayward and furnish them with enough money to pay for his care. When I have acquired the Hurleys' trust and have achieved a position of responsibility and solid financial remuneration in their household, then I will be ready to have Graham join me in Newport. I will then be in a position to provide him with everything necessary to ensure his well-being.*

CHAPTER 36

Love in Bloom

IT WAS LATE AFTERNOON WHEN she finally returned to the Hurleys' home

"Are you all right, dear?" Doris asked anxiously, upon seeing Katherine. "We were awfully worried about you."

"Didn't you receive my note?" asked Katherine.

"Oh, yes. But both Trevor and I could not help but feel that something troublesome had occurred."

"No," Katherine lied as gracefully as she could, "I'm . . . everything is perfectly all right. My . . . uh . . . business was successfully concluded and on my way back here I managed to stop at my former home in Aberdare to collect and bring a few of my favorite belongs."

"Good," smiled Doris. "Trev and I had hoped all would be well." Katherine was touched by Doris' genuine concern. Within the brief period of time she had been with the Hurleys, she, Trevor, and Doris had grown quite fond of one another, and Katherine had been quite consistently overwhelmed by their kindness and thoughtfulness.

Trevor, too, had taken Katherine aside following dinner. They were the only ones to remain in the dining room as the others made their way to the library to relax. "Are you quite certain that everything is all right?" he had asked solicitously. "Is there nothing we can do to assist you in your . . . er . . . endeavors?"

"You are most kind," she replied, blushing under his gaze. "But I assure you all is well."

"Truly?" he inquired, looking into her eyes. She was surprised by the fluttering of her heart as he drew near, and most particularly, when he took her arm and asked in a quiet, steady voice, "May I speak with you frankly?"

She nodded dumbly, too overcome by sudden shyness to speak.

"First of all I should like to say that we—my father, sister, and I—should be most grateful if you would remain here as a permanent member of our staff. We are most pleased with your contribution thus far and regard you as an asset. Secondly, our housekeeper has assured us that she will not be returning as we had expected, and we would be most appreciative if you could take over some of her responsibilities—such as complete supervision of our domestic staff. We would, of course, reward you financially for your expanded services. Please say that you'll stay on with us," he added finally.

Katherine could not help but feel that there was an undercurrent of strong emotion behind his words; that he had, drawn her aside for another purpose in addition to the business proposition.

"I'm afraid that it's not quite so simple, Mr. Hurley."

"Trevor," he stated.

"What?" she looked up into his eyes.

"Do call me Trevor," he said warmly.

"Oh, oh, I see," she stammered, as the color rose into her cheeks, "Well, you see, Mr. Hurley . . . er . . . uh . . . Trevor, things are far more complicated than they appear. You know . . . the recent loss of my . . . er . . . husband and the separation from my child has caused me great pain and suffering. And, as one might expect, great anxiety as well. My husband left me with few possessions and many debts, and frankly, it is simply too early—it would be premature—to make a commitment. If my son or family should need me in any way, for example, I must be free to come to their aid at once."

"You need say nothing more, Katherine," his silken voice caressed each syllable of her name, and he moved even closer to her than before. Taking her hands in his, he said, "You will enjoy complete freedom here, to come and go as you wish. And you will stay for as long as you please. You will be under no obligation whatsoever to us. I stand personal guarantor of your liberty. Is that fair enough?"

"Oh, yes, indeed, more than fair," she stammered, in embarrassment. "It is most generous of you—and unexpected." By now, she was feeling self-conscious and ill at ease under his direct gaze, and wished only to escape from the room. There was a brief silence, during which Katherine wondered how to graciously conclude the conversation. But, as though sensing her desire to leave, Trevor held her hands more tightly in his and spoke in a soft voice, deep with feeling.

"I feel that I must tell you the truth, Katherine. I can no longer repress my feelings. You are unlike anyone I have ever known before, and . . . and I love you . . . dear."

Katherine's astonishment was inexpressible. She had in no way been prepared for such an admission. Now, more than ever, she longed to escape. She would have given anything to avoid responding. But although her mind was racing and her heart pounding, she somehow managed to smile feebly and utter, "I am flattered by your words, and hardly know what to say. During the short time I have been here, I have grown very . . . er . . . fond . . . of you and Doris. I like you both very much—and am most appreciative of your kind words. And now, I am feeling very tired, so if you will excuse me . . ."

"Oh, please don't go yet," pleaded Trevor, looking more handsome than ever. "We have so much to discuss—our future together, for example."

"Oh, Mr. Hurley . . . I mean, Trevor, there is no future for us. Don't you see? I have a husband and a son . . ."

"A husband? But aren't you a widow?"

"Oh, yes, yes, of course I am a widow, but. . ." Her mind was racing madly. *I can't let him know about Percy. It will ruin everything. And I cannot afford to get romantically involved with Trevor—it is absolutely essential that our relationship remain strictly professional. I do not wish to jeopardize my professional future in the Hurley household. Perhaps if I tell him I am engaged to another, he will leave me alone. Yes, that's it!"* A triumphant gleam had come into her eyes which Trevor could not help but notice.

"I am a widow, Trevor," she said demurely. "But I have recently promised my hand in marriage to another—a gentleman of rare refinement and breeding who was a close friend of the family for years. So you see, I do not feel it advisable for us to continue this discussion any further." Trevor had listened intently to her words. His astonishment was evident. He had become pale with anger, and was now struggling for the appearance of composure.

"Am I to believe that you are engaged to another?" he asked unsteadily, releasing her hands from his.

"Yes," she replied, unable to look him in the eye.

"And what is the name of this most fortunate gentleman?"

"His name?" Katherine repeated, thinking furiously. "Oh, well his name is . . . uh . . . uh . . . Mr. Fletcher." For some reason, the name of the healer had passed through her mind at this juncture.

"Indeed," Trevor murmured cooly. "Do you know something, Katherine?" he said suddenly. "I cannot help but feel that you are not very deeply involved with this uh . . . Mr. Fletcher?"

"Is that so?" she replied haughtily. "I do not see that my . . . er . . . involvement with him is any concern of yours. Look, I will gladly adhere to your request and assume total responsibility for the supervision of your domestic staff. I will be glad to assist you professionally whenever there is a need. But I do not think it wise to complicate our professional relationship for many reasons. And so, if it is all right with you, I would like to terminate this conversation now and in the future. As I have already explained, I am very fond of both you and your sister, and I should be happy to assist you both in whatever areas I can. But I am afraid that my personal life must remain precisely that: personal. And now, I really *must* say good night." She turned and started toward the door but Trevor caught her by the arm.

"Must you?" he murmured in an odd voice. Confused for a moment, her mouth fell open, and before she was able to utter another word, Trevor had swept her up into his arms. He held her so close that she could feel the texture and folds of his coat and hear his heart beating rapidly. His strong hands gently slid up her arms, and then found their way around her shoulders. She was too startled by the abruptness of the action to move or speak. Furthermore, there had been something vital, vibrant, electrifying about his touch, and in a way she did not want him to relinquish his hold of her at all. Now, his lips were gently brushing against hers. Then his mouth became insistent, and he kissed her with greater intensity. She began to feel dizzy, helpless, intoxicated as she instinctively succumbed to his charm.

"I love you, Katherine," he murmured tenderly. For a single instant more, she allowed herself to respond. But, then, recovering her senses, she pulled away from him. Still trembling at the nearness of him, she could not meet his eyes as she spoke.

"I am sorry, but I really must go now. I will see you in the morning." She turned away and hastily slipped out of the room, aware that his eyes were following her every movement. It was not until she had tumbled into bed that she was able to think about what had taken place. And for the very first time it occurred to her that she might just be falling in love with the heir of the Hurley estate after all.

She certainly had not planned it, but she had been helpless to prevent it. In fact, she would not have believed it possible to fall in love with anyone ever again. She, who desired freedom above all else—she who had no time or use for any romantic involvement—had found it impossible to avoid falling deeply in love with Trevor Hurley.

He possessed all of the qualities and was everything she admired and could have wished for in a man. Tall, lean and athletic, with his even virile features, expressive eyes, and high cheek bones, he was extraordinarily handsome. Furthermore, he was graceful, articulate, and surprisingly gentle for so wealthy and powerful a man. He also was thoughtful, witty, and charming, and Katherine had learned from Doris and other members of the household staff that Trevor had been loved and admired by many women and had even been engaged several times. Apparently he was a great favorite in Newport society—despite his deeply rooted sadness and modesty—due to his kindness, wit, and generosity; everyone liked Trevor! And Katherine simply could not be insensible to the compliment of such a man's attentions.

Following that fateful evening after her return from Aberdare during which Trevor had first revealed his love, Katherine had done everything in her power to resist the strong attraction she felt toward him. She painstakingly sought to avoid him. She ignored him whenever she could. And when circumstances required their physical proximity, she maintained an attitude of icy civility. But Trevor had been relatively unaffected by her deliberate coldness; if anything, he seemed amused by her behavior.

"Can you not see that our togetherness is inevitable?" he whispered one evening over dinner, his eyes laughing as he saw her cringe in embarrassment. "Don't worry. No one can hear me. No matter what you say or do, I'll love you always." Fortunately, his father and sister were engaged in deep conversation and oblivious to the communications taking place between Trevor and Katherine. But Katherine had reddened and remained self-conscious for the remainder of the meal.

In time, as Doris grew to rely upon her to a greater extent, Katherine was required to work more closely with Trevor than ever before. She began to take a greater interest in both their domestic and business responsibilities, helping them to manage the staff and daily operation of The George 'N Dragon as well. Within a matter of months, all three had become close personal friends as well as collaborators in the truest sense of that word. Because of her cleverness, diligence, and efficiency, Katherine had become a highly valued and respected employee—and one in whom both Doris and Trevor shared implicit faith and confidence.

Yet, however rapid her advancement in the Hurley household, Katherine was far from happy. Although she was by now regularly communicating with her little boy by telephone, she missed terribly Gray's physical presence. Furthermore, she was in a state of constant turmoil regarding the outcome of the inevitable confrontation she would have with Percy that would determine her future life. And, she lived in a constant state of anxiety lest Trevor or Doris discover the truth about her background or the subterfuge concerning her "widowhood" and her new fiancé, Mr. Fletcher, to which she had impulsively resorted in order to avoid their involvement in her personal affairs.

I'll be ruined—lose my job—if they ever find out about Percy, about my past, she thought in an agony of fear. She was fairly certain that few so-called respectable middle-class women had backgrounds as "colorful" as her own, and she knew that she would never have been so desirable to the Hurleys had it not been for her air of solid, middle-class respectability and dependability. "Oh, well," she would sigh when all alone in her room. *I will have to tell them the truth sooner or later. Trev is becoming impossible, I know he senses something peculiar about my past, and I know that he's suspicious of Mr. Fletcher. Oh, dear, whatever prompted me to tell such an absurd lie?*

But she knew that she had been unable to do otherwise and that she would resort to the same subterfuge again, if circumstances required it. The intensity of her feelings about Trevor both disturbed and confused her. Deeply fond of and attracted to him, she wondered what their relationship might have been had she not lied about her widowhood and her fiancée. Would they have become engaged—then married? Would she have become accepted by his upper class friends? She loved him more deeply than any other man—and was tortured by her own circumstances and duplicity. However, she adored Trevor, she cherished her freedom above all else.

CHAPTER 37

A New "Mr. Fletcher" Pays a Visit

LATE ONE AFTERNOON, APPROXIMATELY THREE months after she had begun working for the Hurleys, she, Trevor, and Doris were industriously poring over the hotel's business records in order to determine how they might reduce expenditures that had been steadily multiplying during previous months.

"I say, haven't we all had enough for this afternoon?" said Trevor suddenly rising from his position at the large desk in the library. "Let's forget budgets and figures, debits and credits for the remainder of the afternoon and take a rest."

"All right, dear," agreed Doris good-naturedly, also rising from her chair. Yawning and stretching his long body, Trevor walked toward the large leaded glass window where he intended to reduce some of the sharp sunlight that flooded the room by partly drawing the draperies.

He stood transfixed at the window for several moments before he blurted out, "I say, there's rather a strange chap out in the garden who appears to be 'lost.' Perhaps he is looking for someone. Perhaps he is looking for you, Mrs. Hayward. One never knows—it just might be your mysterious fiancé. What's his name? Ah, yes, Mr. Fletcher, isn't it?" teased Trevor in fun.

Katherine never knew what it was that caused her to leap from her chair and rush toward the window at which Trevor was standing. But somehow an internal alarm had gone off, and she had responded, "Oh, God." She groaned inwardly as she identified at once the stranger who was lurking about the garden of the Hurley mansion. It was none other than Percy

Hayward. *What on Earth shall I do?* she wondered in desperation. In the meantime, Trevor had not failed to note the surprised expression on her face, and was most curious as to whether or not she knew the gentleman.

"You are quite correct in your determination of the identity of the man outside," she found herself saying coolly. "He is my fiancé . . . my . . . er . . . Mr. Fletcher." Trevor's jaw dropped in amazement. "If you will excuse me, I shall go to him at once."

"Keep on walking until I tell you to stop," she ordered Percy once she had embraced him in greeting in the manner expected of a couple sufficiently in love to wish soon to enter the blissful state of matrimony. She knew that Trevor was watching her every move from the library window, and she could not wait to get Percy as far away from the Hurley residence as possible.

"But, Katherine, my love," Percy had protested, his joy at seeing her apparent.

"Don't speak," she muttered under her breath. "Just walk. Here—take my hand, as though you were delighted to take it."

"But I am delighted to take it—to see you again, to be with you," stated Percy happily.

"Shut up," advised Katherine, "and walk with me to the rose garden."

"All right love, anything you say," agreed the nonplussed Percy.

When they finally managed to get out of view of the house, Katherine explained to Percy the nature of the events that had taken place during the past three months and described in detail the story she had invented regarding her recent "widowhood" and her "fiancé," Mr. Fletcher.

"You simply must not jeopardize my position, Percy. I have enjoyed great success here. The Hurleys are paying me a handsome wage, and I will not have you interfering with my life any further. Do you understand?" Percy nodded miserably.

"The Hurleys know nothing whatever of your existence, and I want to keep it that way. I would like to bring you back to the house and to introduce you to Trevor and Doris as my fiancé. If you play your role in this little charade successfully, I will go out to dinner with you this evening and discuss our future together. If you are unwilling to participate in this way, I assure you that I will have nothing further to do or discuss with you ever again. Have I made myself understood?"

"All right, love. I'll do whatever you wish. And if it's Mr. Fletcher you want, why, then, it's Mr. Fletcher you shall have."

"Good," smiled Katherine. "I was hoping you would see it my way. Ready, then, Mr. Fletcher?"

"Ready," sighed Percy. And leaving the rose garden, the two strolled arm-in-arm toward the Hurley residence.

They arrived at the precise moment the butler was announcing tea. And although Katherine would have given almost anything to avoid the meeting between Trevor and Percy, she thought gratefully to herself that the ritual of tea might afford enough distraction to lessen the impact of the meeting. "Now behave yourself, Percy, or I will never forgive you as long as I live," she whispered to her husband as they made their way into the dining room.

Would she ever forget the look of disappointment on Trevor's face as she formally introduced Percy to him as her fiancé. She would not wish to relive those painful moments for anything. For Trevor had obviously been deeply disturbed by the incident. The two men had shared a suspicious dislike of one another immediately, and had this situation not been so grave and her future not in jeopardy, Katherine would have derived considerable amusement from the childish manner in which these two grown up men were behaving. *Why they're stalking each other like two jungle animals*, she observed.

When Percy toasted Trevor's health, Katherine nearly fell off her chair so obviously insincere was his manner and his meaning. *I must conclude this parody at once*, she thought desperately. *I've got to get Percy out of here.* She knew that Trevor was terribly hurt and disappointed by the entire episode; she knew beyond a shadow of a doubt that he was deeply in love with her, and that it had been agony for him to watch Percy and her together. For his eyes had betrayed him. Not since she had first met Trevor had his eyes looked so sad.

Oh, whatever have I done? she asked herself miserably. *What a fool I've been to get involved in such a silly charade.* And as she studied Trevor's forlorn figure, she realized how very deeply she loved him. After an appropriate amount of time had elapsed, Katherine excused herself from the table.

"We have several errands to complete, and must be on our way," she lied as gracefully as possible. And finally, thankfully, she and Percy made their way out of the dining room. "Thank goodness that's over," she murmured to herself as she escorted Percy out of the house and off the premises.

"Come on," she muttered, once out of the hearing range of Trevor and Doris, "let's go for a walk. We'll dine in the city."

"Whatever you wish, love," replied an unusually docile and cooperative Percy. Katherine could see that he wished to make amends and to resume their relationship.

"Won't you return home with me tonight?" he implored several hours later as they enjoyed a lovely dinner at Iris' Restaurant.

"No, Percy," she had responded, simply gazing directly in his eyes. "I will not return tonight or any other night. I will never again live with you as your wife unless and until you have managed to acquire a good job; a real home; have managed to put aside, at least, one thousand pounds in a savings account; and until you have decided to have nothing to do with pubs or liquor of any variety ever again. Only under those conditions can I possibly even think of serving as your wife."

"Don't you love me anymore Katherine? How can you be so cold-hearted?" asked Percy, truly taken aback by his wife's detached manner. "What shall I do in the meantime?" he pleaded, thinking that it would take many months, most likely years, before he would have the opportunity of living up to Katherine's demands.

"I could divorce you, Percy. I certainly have grounds," stated Katherine simply. "But I won't—more for Graham's sake than for either of ours. For he dearly loves and needs both of us. We will continue to see each other—spend time together—you, Graham, and myself—but we shall remain separated until you have achieved the demands, the criteria set forth in my ultimatum. It is as simple as that. We will live apart, but we will always share friendship. And although I no longer love you as I did in the early years of our marriage, I will always be very fond of you Percy. Very fond."

"I see," murmured Percy, in deep disappointment.

"I do wish that it hadn't turned out this way," said Katherine gently, "but it has. And so, here we are. Don't be sad, love. It will all work out. Truly it will."

"I'll love you, Katherine, until the day I die. I'll never love another woman."

"No, I don't think you ever will love another woman," said Katherine slowly. "But if ever you should, Percy, I should, upon your request, grant you a divorce with no contest."

"I will never desire a divorce from you, Katherine. Let's remain husband and wife—if only for Graham's sake. Even if we must live apart from here on," his voice choked at the words.

"All right, love," agreed Katherine. "That's fine. For truly I know that I shall never marry again."

"No?" asked Percy, obviously relieved.

"No, love," smiled Katherine.

It was not long after their reunion that both Percy and Katherine agreed that at least for the present time—while both were so unsettled and insecure—that little Graham would from hereon be cared for by Katherine's mother and father in Abercumboy. Graham had always adored Gwilym and Elizabeth and they, he. Furthermore, Katherine was aware that Graham would receive the care, attention, freedom, and understanding that the precocious, high-spirited little boy required above all else. And because of their sophisticated grasp of life's meaning and purpose, she knew that all of little Graham's questions would be answered to his satisfaction and her own.

As Katherine's duties and responsibilities expanded to incorporate the daily management of The George 'N Dragon Hotel, she had recognized the impracticality and ill-advisability of raising her son in such an atmosphere. In this instance, she heartily agreed with her mother that a hotel was in no way the proper atmosphere in which to rear a child. *It's just no place to raise a child as sensitive as my little Graham*, she thought ruefully, remembering all-too-vividly the strange mixture of humanity who had taken temporary respite at the inn. And although she had been devastated by the separation from her son, she realized that she had no alternative at the present time. *Perhaps I'll soon able to afford a home for us,* she thought hopefully.

It had not been easy to explain to Graham the nature or rationale behind the changes that had taken place. Although the little boy dearly loved both sets of grandparents, he felt sharply the absence of his own Mum and Dad. He missed his old home and friends, and he simply could not comprehend why his parents were no longer living together, if they still loved him and each other as Mum had said.

"It's better this way," Katherine had informed him on numerous occasions, but Graham never quite believed her. With Percy now living with his parents, the little boy saw both his Mum and Dad frequently—often two or three times a week. Percy and Katherine would, on these occasions, take him to the park, shopping, to the cinema, out to dinner, or some other diversion. He noticed that his Mum and Dad seemed to be getting along and enjoying each other's company far more now than when they had lived together. And, in time, Graham grew to suspect that perhaps his mother had been correct when she had said, "It's better this way." Still, for a time the little boy felt abandoned and terribly sad and lonely. Only with the slow, steady passage of time and increasing maturity were his wounds healed.

CHAPTER 38

The Interim

⁓

KATHERINE DISCOVERED LIFE AT THE George 'N Dragon to be more demanding than ever. And she soon found her efforts to resist Trevor's charms futile. Actually, the two fell in love within as brief and painless a period of time as possible. Trevor had been persistent—relentless in his pursuit of her. Not boldly or obviously, but cleverly and subtly—for the most part—had been his overtures. Always exceedingly kind and good-humored, he had waited patiently for her to change—to "come round"—and acknowledge that she loved him as deeply as he loved her. And one day, all barriers simply dissolved, the two were in love. It was as simple as that.

Eventually, when Katherine's future in the Hurley household seemed secure, she told Trevor and Doris the truth about her background and confessed that her engagement—indeed the very existence of Mr. Fletcher—had been invented.

"I knew it!" Trevor declared gleefully. "I knew there was something decidedly peculiar about you and old Mr. Fletcher!"

"Now there's nothing to interfere with our happiness, darling. You and I shall be free to marry," Trevor had stated earnestly, late one December evening. "I love you, Katherine. Will you marry me?" He held her tenderly, his whole heart in his eyes. There was a long silence during which she appeared to be lost in thought.

"No, Trevor, I'm terribly sorry, but I can't," she replied at last in a low voice.

"But why not, my love? You can divorce Percy. Graham won't mind now. He's grown quite fond of me, you know." He was referring to the number of times that Katherine had brought her boy to visit with the Hurleys. They had gotten along very well together and had shared many games together and funny stories. "And you know that I adore him."

"It's not that simple," Katherine answered slowly. "And it really isn't because of Graham—or Percy—that I won't marry you, Trev. It's because of me. I shall never marry again. I wish to be free—I must be free—to carry on my real work in the manner in which I was intended to do so. I cannot give myself wholly to any human being, Trevor, and no matter how much I love you, I could never make you truly happy—not in the way a wife ought. You see, my work would always come first—before anyone or anything else."

"That doesn't matter, Katherine. I shouldn't mind taking second place to your work."

"Oh, yes, you should. A man wants to be loved and cherished and regarded with the esteem and attention of a loving, doting wife. I could never provide all that a good wife should. You would always crave more than I could give you, Trev. You would be unhappy with me—truly, you would."

"No, I wouldn't, Katherine, You're being absurd. We would get along beautifully—you know we would."

"I am sorry, Trev, I can't. I don't think I'll ever be able to make you understand the way I feel. And although I love you as I've loved no one before, the rest of my life is to be dedicated to my work. That is the way it must be. And that's the way it is," she said with an air of finality.

"You won't change your mind, love?" said Trevor softly.

"Never, my darling."

"I shall never love anyone else, Katherine," said Trevor after holding her tightly to him and kissing her passionately.

"I know, Trev," she said faintly. "And I shall never love anyone as I do you. We will share our lives for as long as it is God's will; and then, if need be, we will go our separate ways," she said softly, as tears suddenly stung the lids of her eyes.

Although Trevor and Doris were members of the Church of England and had never before been in contact with anyone who believed as Katherine did, they were both receptive to and influenced by her teachings. Furthermore, both believed that their own mother had indeed survived "death" and had been instrumental in bringing them all together.

"Mother has been close by. I can feel her presence," Trevor had marveled on many occasions. And Katherine would agree, going so far as to describe in detail the nature of the work in which Mrs. Hurley was engaged on the Other Side and delivering specific messages from her to her children.

"It's uncanny," Trevor had stated when first Katherine had demonstrated her mediumistic abilities. But he had never been frightened or disturbed by them. Rather, he had declared once in an unusually serious tone, "Someday, when the time is right, I too, shall become involved in this work. But not now. There are things in the material world I must accomplish first. You aren't disappointed?" he asked as a little boy might of his mum.

"No, love," smiled Katherine warmly. "I agree with you wholeheartedly. And I could never be disappointed in you, Trev—never!"

As soon as her own personal affairs had been resolved satisfactorily, Katherine once again turned her attention and energy toward "the work." Having devoted any free time to further research, she had visited numerous Spiritualist Churches, New Thought societies (as these metaphysical groups were often called), and psychic research centers in the Newport area. Only one such church had impressed her to any degree, and she began to spend much of her time working with its director, septuagenarian, Mrs. Carolyn Hillman, who had been one of the most respected, brilliant, and gifted Spiritualist mediums and thinkers in the Newport area. Mrs. Hillman had immediately recognized Katherine's abilities and introduced her to many prominent Spiritualist and "New Thought" thinkers and spokespersons in the area, helping Katherine to establish a reputation.

It was Mrs. Hillman who reintroduced Katherine to the importance of physical phenomena as a powerful means of persuading even the most skeptical of life's continuity.

"It is time for you, my dear, to lend your energies toward the cultivation of positive proof of survival. You must lend yourself to the Invisible ones so that you and they together may develop physical phenomena of such a caliber that it may prove beyond a shadow of a doubt that there is no death. The strictly material concerns of the vast majority of men must be altered into those of a spiritual nature. For times are changing; the world is changing, my dear, and we are among those who are helping people to draw closer to an understanding of our true nature. But we must provide evidence—material evidence—in order for them to believe what you and I know to be true. No one can doubt or negate what they themselves have experienced with their physical senses. And so, let us work toward achieving publicly a perfect demonstration of life's continuity by means of a perfect full-body Spirit materialization. Think of the response of even the greatest cynic or skeptic upon witnessing the process whereby a Spirit Being takes on a material substance, becomes solid and seems to our physical senses as tangible and real as any ordinary human being. My friends in the Spirit Worlds have described the procedure in this manner. Firstly, the spirit body of the one to be materialized is reduced in pitch of vibration to that approaching the material world and becomes etherealized to the solidity of smoke or vapor. Then, ectoplasmic substance, made up by combining matter drawn from the physical medium and sitters with a substance brought from the Spirit World, is imposed upon and blended with the coarsened body of the materialized spirit, and is vitalized by forces of that spirit and by forces added by the materialization group. The result of course is the creation of a solid, three-dimensional Spirit Being who looks like any member of the human race. What greater proof could one require than to see, touch, and hear a full spirit, materialization?"

And, adhering to Mrs. Hillman's advice, Katherine began to conduct her own investigation into physical phenomena in the hope of finding a physical medium who would be willing to demonstrate his or her gift of full body spirit materialization to the public. During this period of research, Katherine came into contact with a great number of those who were commonly regarded as the greatest physical mediums of the twentieth century.

Through Helen Duncan, Katherine witnessed phenomena, the magnitude of which she had never seen before. By means of Mrs. Duncan's gift, Katherine was afforded the opportunity of witnessing perfect full body materializations of her Spirit Guides including White Eagle, Bright Eyes, and Marie-Therese.

White Eagle was a tall, stately, bronze figure with exquisite, pale blue eyes, an imperious nose, high cheek bones, and a beautiful, sensitive mouth. His expression bespoke indescribable peace, compassion, and love. He was graceful, majestic, and resplendent in his white chieftain's attire and glorious headdress composed of translucent, shimmering white feathers trimmed with blue and. gold. Bright Eyes was a slim, merry black child of eight with large luminous brown eyes and numberless small braids. Marie-Therese had dark hair, ivory skin, and beautiful indigo eyes and wore the black and white habit of a nun. Each one of these materialized spirits looked every bit as real and solid as any other human being. The caliber of the materialization was commensurate upon the gifts of the medium, and in Katherine's opinion, Mrs. Duncan was one of the greatest.

On one occasion, Katherine brought Graham to one of Mrs. Duncan's séances. And firsthand, the boy saw his great grandfather, James Coleman, of whom he had seen many detailed photographs, materialize right before his very eyes—every line, every feature, the texture, and color of James' skin—exactly as it had been while the old gentleman had been "alive."

"Come on, Gray," the Spirit had coaxed. "Shake my hand." It was a gesture that Graham would never forget as long as he lived.

"Wow, Mum, Grandpa's hand is warm! He looks and feels just like he's alive."

"I am alive," James smilingly reminded his great grandson.

Time in Newport passed quickly indeed, and to Katherine it seemed that months, rather than years had elapsed by the time she had begun to form her own development circles designed to produce the finest examples of physical phenomena. Having witnessed numberless demonstrations of every imaginable variety of physical phenomena, Katherine was now interested in developing and refining those physical mediums with the greatest potential in order that they might exhibit, on a consistent basis, before the public, their remarkable gifts.

By the time Katherine was thirty-eight, she had worked with virtually the greatest and most highly acclaimed mediums in England and Wales. Furthermore, she had conducted as well as participated in numberless séances, lectures, classes, and workshops in and around Newport, agreeing with Mrs. Hillman that the demonstrations of physical phenomena nearly always had a transformational effect upon those who witnessed it. No one could ever be the same—maintain the same attitude regarding religion, life, and death—after seeing, meeting and talking with a Spirit Being. Such a demonstration virtually always served as a powerful catalyst—prompting man's investigation into the meaning of life and death.

After all, had not such prominent public figures as Sir Arthur Conan Doyle, Sir Oliver Lodge, W. T. Stead, and Stainton Moses conducted great research after having been exposed to physical phenomena? Once they had experienced such "proof," they had been unable to refrain from sharing their experiences with others. It had been at a great personal cost that Sir Arthur Conan Doyle, author of the widely read Sherlock Holmes mystery novels, jeopardized his reputation, risked public derision, and devoted time, energy, and expense to advance the cause of spiritualism, writing and publishing many of his own books in its behalf. And, the eminent physicist and scientist, Sir Oliver Lodge had publicly expressed his views in his autobiography, *Past Years*,[1] in which he stated:

"My testimony, and that of others, to the reality of a spiritual world is based upon direct experience of fact, and not upon theory. Test the facts whatever way you choose, they can only be accounted for by the interaction of intelligences other than our own. A spiritual world is the greatest of realities, but we cannot fully comprehend it yet. Everything tends to show that this short material existence is intensely important, and constitutes a unique opportunity. Infinite possibilities for progress lie ahead, yet it behooves us strenuously to make the most of the present possibilities of earth-life."

---

1 New York: Charles Scribner Sons; 1932.

Throughout her years of research, Katherine had willingly traveled anywhere in search of potential talent. Through advertisements in the psychic journals and newspapers, by word of mouth, often by what appeared nothing more than chance or good luck, Katherine would manage to locate the finest physical mediums available. On one occasion—an icy, bitterly cold January evening—it was Mrs. Hillman herself who persuaded Katherine to visit the mountain home of an eight-year-old girl and her seventeen-year-old brother, both of whom were said to be excellent physical mediums. Katherine quickly discovered that the abilities of these children had not been exaggerated.

Upon arriving at their home, she had been startled to witness an oil painting—portrait of a pair of young male twins—dancing of its own accord in the hallway. The painting led Katherine into the séance room, and once she was seated, glided into its rightful position among other paintings hanging on the wall. The teenage boy, through whom much of the phenomena was taking place, sat bound and gagged in the center of the circle of sitters who had come to witness the demonstration. As soon as Katherine had settled comfortably in her seat, the lights began to flicker and dim. Light bulbs popped out of the lamps and chandeliers. And the moment that Katherine had begun to feel irritated by the loud ticking of the old clock on the mantle, the clock floated past her and into the next room. Soon, every object, every piece of furniture in the room was in motion—including the chairs in which the sitters were seated.

Within a short period of time, the boy, who had been bound into his chair with heavy rope, was free; and, with no outside intervention, was transported across the room and had been placed on top of the eight-foot high oak armoire. Shortly after this occurred, the boy's sister literally flew across the room and landed in Katherine's lap. Such demonstrations reminded Katherine of the physical power of the Spirit Beings and of the extraordinary "proof" available to those who were willing to examine life objectively.

Weary of the public's concept of the séance room as "spooky" or unpleasant, she was determined to display phenomena under "normal" circumstances—in bright light or daylight. Furthermore, she was determined to rid the séances of unnecessary and meaningless ritual. "Make it appear as 'normal' as possible," Katherine would advise her mediums and sitters. "We don't want to scare the nonbeliever away. Remember, we want to convert the nonbeliever into a believer."

During this time, Katherine never abandoned her own work or unique gifts. She continued to teach, lecture, and heal throughout southern Wales. Literally hundreds of healers and mediums were trained personally by her at this juncture.

In late March of 1937, Katherine slipped and fell on the highly polished and freshly waxed hardwood floor of the Hurleys' library and found that she had broken several ribs and suffered internal hemorrhaging as a result. Although she made light of the fall, she knew that she was far more ill than anyone suspected. But she had refrained from undergoing the surgery her physician recommended for a very good reason. For, on the day after her fall, she had received word from her mother that her father was dying. And Katherine was determined to spend time with Gwilym before his death.

In spite of her own excruciating pain, then, Katherine made the journey by train to Abercumboy. And, in spite of her sadness and fear, she was profoundly moved by the courage and confidence demonstrated by her father. For, at this time of transition, he experienced no fear, no apprehension, only the unwavering certainty that he would soon enter the glorious realms so often described by the Spirit Beings. Katherine could see that he had serenely surrendered to the Power which had first provided him with breath and which was now retracting it. With tranquility, grace, and patience did he wean himself from the earthly life and attempt to prepare himself for the new life to follow. So, although Katherine loved him dearly and knew she would miss him sorely, she could not grieve.

"You understand, love, don't you?" he asked hoarsely. She had nodded through her tears. "I've earned the right to leave. The body has served me well. But now, it's time to move onward."

"Yes, Dad," she had whispered, "I know."

His passing was simple. He had refused to remain in the hospital and had adamantly refused all medication. "Remember Mr. Fletcher's advice? No medication." Soon, most of his time was spent in sleep. And, finally, in the same manner in which he had drawn his very first breath, he quietly drew his last. And, although they missed him deeply, neither Katherine nor her mother mourned him.

Shortly after her father's death, Katherine underwent surgery for the internal injuries she had suffered in conjunction with her fall. At the same time, Elizabeth sold her property in Abercumboy and relocated to the lovely seaside town of Bournemouth where she and her sister Mariah, who had also recently lost her husband, purchased a small but charming house together.

In the interim years following Gwilym's death and before England's declaration of war upon Germany on September 3, 1939, Katherine remained with Trevor and Doris at The George 'N Dragon. But she had become, by now, a full partner in the business and was, by most standards quite well-off financially. Her relationship with Trevor had remained essentially the same, for in spite of his frequent proposals of marriage and her own deep love for him, she had adhered to the words she had spoken so many years before: "I shall never marry again." Still, the two were deeply in love and shared a joyous relationship.

In the meantime, she and Percy remained separated but the very best of friends; spending a good deal of time together and with their son. He had been unable to achieve the terms of his wife's ultimatum, but they had never divorced officially for Graham's sake. Little Graham—now a handsome young man preparing to enter Cardiff's Technical College as an engineering student—had grown up in the home of Gwilym and Elizabeth. And Katherine was convinced that he was the better for it for she still felt very strongly that a hotel was no place in which to raise a young, impressionable boy.

By 1938, the world situation had steadily deteriorated and, much to his mother's dismay, Graham had voluntarily joined the Territorial Army. Katherine and Doris matriculated in several nursing courses, and it seemed that the United Kingdom was preparing for war. With each day that elapsed, the atmosphere grew more unsettled, more uncertain. In spite of the changes that were taking place throughout the country—or perhaps because of them—Katherine continued to work at a feverish pitch, traveling to all parts of England and Wales in order to "prove survival" to those whose sons, husbands, and lovers would soon be going off to battle, and in order to convince as many as possible that peace was still a possibility, that England need not involve herself in the war.

"We must all work for peace," she told her audiences. "True and lasting peace. It's not too late. We can prevent any further warfare by thinking peace, by praying for peace." But it was too late for thinking and praying. The war machine had already been activated. And Katherine's days at The George 'N Dragon were rapidly coming to an end.

CHAPTER 39

Moving to London

DESPITE MUCH HEATED DISCUSSION OF war, few had been truly prepared for it. Memories of the horrors of the First World War were still far too vivid in the minds of the majority. England was a peace-loving nation, and pacification through the settlement of issues by negotiation and compromise (referred to as "appeasement") had been employed by the British government in the hope that the impending holocaust might be averted. "Let us remember," Neville Chamberlain had stated, "the desire of all peoples of the world still remains concentrated on the hopes of peace."

Who had not been relieved upon hearing Chamberlain's words following his private conference with Hitler in Munich in 1938? "I believe it is peace for our time." Who, among the British, had not wanted with all their hearts to believe their prime minister's words?

Yet, how vastly had the situation altered only one year later after Germany invaded Poland and a heartbroken Chamberlain announced to the House of Commons: "Everything that I have worked for, everything that I have believed during my public life has crashed in ruins." And, within an amazingly brief period, Britain had made what Churchill called, "the immense, delicate and hazardous transition from peace to war." A wartime regimen including conscription, rationing, blackouts, air raids, and the evacuation of women and children from major cities was introduced. And still, Katherine and her coworkers continued to work and pray for peace. Alas, it was too late. Neither they nor numberless similar groups and organizations were powerful enough to prevent what seemed inevitable.

"Mum, is that you?" It was with a great sigh of relief that Katherine heard Graham's excited voice at the other end of the line.

"Yes, love. I've been trying to reach you for hours."

"I suspected as much." She could hear the grin in his voice. "The lines have been tied up ever since the announcement came over the wires. I take it you've heard."

"Yes, love," Katherine replied gravely. "We were preparing for lunch when word came over the BBC. Dreadful news, isn't it?" Katherine sighed again, this time in despair.

"Not so bad, Mum. You know England has no choice. Mr. Chamberlain did everything in his power to prevent it from taking place. But that bastard Hitler just went ahead and did what he wanted anyhow. Why, . . ."

"Now, no more of that Gray."

"Aw, now don't worry, Mum. I'll be all right. No harm will come to either one of us."

"I know, love," she replied wearily, unable to control the tide of emotions that had gripped her from the moment she had heard Mr. Chamberlain solemnly announced that England was already at war with Germany. Poland had been attacked by Germany at dawn on September 1, 1939. The mobilization of British forces had been ordered during the morning. A British ultimatum had been given to Germany at 9:30 p.m. on September 1, and this had been followed by a second and final ultimatum at 9:00 a.m. on September 3. And then, at 11:15 a.m., Mr. Chamberlain made the fateful broadcast, after which neither England nor the world would ever be the same.

"Are you there, Mum?" Graham asked following a particularly lengthy silence.

"Yes, yes, of course, dear. Just know that I'll be with you every step of the way, and that no harm can come to my brave boy. You shall have some remarkable experiences and some close calls, but no real harm will come to you." There was another pause. "When do you leave?"

"Don't know yet, Mum. We expect to hear sometime this afternoon. Rumor has it we're to be sent to Dover first for field training, and from there wherever we're needed."

"I see," said Katherine, the slightest hint of a quiver in her voice. "Ring me up, love, as soon as you hear anything."

"I will, Mum."

"I expect we had better get off now and let someone else use the line, eh?"

"Right, Mum. You'll hear from me soon. Promise."

"All right, my precious. I . . . I love you, Graham," she choked.

"I love you too, Mum." Graham was suddenly aware of the lump in his throat, and he had difficulty swallowing. "Bye, Mum," he finally managed to get out.

"Goodbye, my love." She remained on the line until she heard the click of his receiver. "Bless him, God, and protect him from all harm and danger," she prayed aloud.

And although she was deeply saddened by the turn of events, she did not shed a tear. She saw Graham only once before he was called to active service. On this occasion, she and the lovely young nursing student whom he had been courting for the past two years, Beryl Jones, had met him in Cardiff shortly before he was scheduled to depart for southern England. It was not an easy parting for any of them, but with admirable courage and deliberate lightheartedness the three managed to enjoy the time together without voicing their doubts or fears.

Katherine noticed with maternal pride that her boy was all grown up and looking ever so dashing in his uniform. Graham, in turn, took particular delight from the sight of his two favorite women in the world who seemed at this time to complement one another beautifully. Despite an age difference of twenty years, Katherine looked as though she could be Beryl's sister. In her beautiful, classically tailored costume that showed her slender figure to advantage, with her thick glossy hair styled in the new bob that was all the rage, and her regal carriage, Katherine was the epitome of elegance and sophistication.

"She's a real looker," noted Graham with satisfaction as he observed his mother—her svelte figure, creamy complexion, pretty features, and the shrewd, good-humored eyes that tilted upward at the ends. Without a doubt, Katherine was the more striking of the two women. But Beryl was lovely in her own way—dainty, delicate, with an ivory complexion, and honey blonde hair. Furthermore, she possessed a gentle loveliness and a refreshing girlish charm.

All three would remember with special fondness that lovely golden September afternoon wherein a deep bond of affection and understanding had been forged between them—a bond that would endure the remainder of their lives. And the pleasant memory of that golden afternoon would sustain them through countless hours of darkness and despair throughout the War years. Only for an instant—shocking in its clarity and abruptness— were all three aware that this might be their final togetherness.

"If I don't see you back here, Mum, I'll see you at the place we know so well," Graham had whispered in his mother's ear as they prepared to separate.

"You'll see me back here, Graham. Don't think for a moment you won't," she warned fiercely.

"All right, Mum, as you say," he said, with a crooked grin. And that was that. Graham was gone and many months were to elapse before Katherine was to see him again.

Now, England began to get down to the serious business of being at war, although for some months after she had declared war on Germany, there was only a prolonged and oppressive pause which Mr. Chamberlain described in a private letter as "twilight war." Soon, nearly all the men that Katherine knew had enlisted in the armed forces. Percy, who was now forty-one years old, volunteered his time to the War effort. While even poor Trevor who, as a result of severe childhood illness, had failed to pass the physical examination, served as a street warden by day and as a member of the fire brigade at night.

In the meantime, Katherine and Doris, desperately desiring to be of service, matriculated in the Red Cross nursing program. For Katherine, who had not attended school since the age of seven, the rigorous training program was traumatic. But she was determined to succeed, and succeed she did. She was both proud and relieved to receive her certificate of completion. So pleased was she, in fact, that she vowed at this juncture that she would one day return to school and obtain a college degree.

As a result of their service requirements, Katherine, Trevor, and Doris had far less time and energy to devote to the maintenance of The George 'N Dragon which, even during wartime, was doing quite a flourishing business. During the early stages of the war, it had been, to a great extent, business as usual. Toward the end of 1940, the effects of the war were being keenly felt everywhere. Shortages of staff and supplies soon made it impossible for The George 'N Dragon to function as it had. And with the decrease in responsibility, Katherine became increasingly bored and restless. Fortunately her boredom was soon alleviated by a huge surprise that arrived by telephone as Graham announced his sudden plans to marry Beryl Jones as quickly and unceremoniously as possible while he was on a short leave.

On September 29, 1940, almost exactly one year after England had declared war on Germany, Graham had married Beryl Jones in a simple ceremony at St. Ann's Church in Ynyssia where Della still resided part of the year and near the Abercumboy home wherein Graham had been raised since the age of eight by Gwilym and Elizabeth. Due to the austerity of the times, neither family had wished to make an elaborate display, but the wedding, in its simplicity, was beautiful. And Katherine had been forced to whisk out her handkerchief and dab the tears that had appeared at the corners of her eyes as her son looked straight into Beryl's eyes and said, "I do." How proud she had been of her son—so dignified and handsome in his full army regalia—and her daughter-in-law—so fresh and pretty and happy-hearted. She and Percy had sat together and watched in amazement as their little boy became the husband of Beryl Jones.

"They're too young to be married," Katherine observed in a whisper to Percy.

"You forget, my dear, they are older than we were when we got married," Percy reminded her.

Although they had initially intended to wait to get married until after the war, the grim days and weeks had passed endlessly, the end was nowhere in sight, Graham's future was uncertain, and so the two had hastened to the altar desiring to spend what time remained to them as man and wife. Countless other young couples had been determined to grasp at happiness while they could and did the same. So many decisions were, of necessity, made rapidly, and so many changes were taking place at an accelerated pace.

In spite of the fleeting joy and beauty of her son's wedding which offered a brief escape from the wartime regimen, life rapidly resumed its dismal pace as reality set in.

Reminders of the horrors of war were everywhere to be seen. Observing the trainloads of little children who were being evacuated from the large cities and relocated to the country, Katherine felt terribly depressed and helpless. But, far worse, were the trains which, one after another, passed through Newport transporting the wounded soldiers who were to receive treatment at the local hospitals. There were so many of them—so many young lads whose youthful minds and bodies had already been irrevocably scarred and ravaged by war and Katherine could hardly bear the sight of them. Nothing—not the wail of the air-raid sirens, not the black-outs or Anderson shelters, or the droning of enemy airplanes or the screaming ambulances or fire brigades—had upset her so deeply as the young men on crutches or swathed in bandages being huddled together on the gloomy grimy platforms of the train station or milling about outside the depot as they waited for ambulances and lorries to transport them to the hospital. It was this simple symbol of the human suffering and wanton carnage that made Katherine feel violently ill and terribly sad. The nursing that she had been doing no longer seemed enough. She began to feel as though somehow she might be doing more, something greater to assist in the war effort. *I know that I can be of greater service*, she thought to herself as time elapsed and Hitler's campaign grew more intense. *I think it's time to make changes.*

She was not terribly surprised, then, when her sister, Della, telephoned with a business proposition. "Katherine," Della had squealed in excitement. "The most marvelous thing has happened. Frederick, my brother-in-law, owns a lovely beauty salon in Woolwich outside of London. He's been too ill to manage it, and he wants me to buy it from him. For a song. He says the shop is very lucrative—and has done well even during the war. Well, what do you say? That you and I go into a partnership, I mean? We could each pay half. Oh, doesn't it sound too marvelous? We could have ever so much fun! Don't you think?"

"Um," Katherine was thinking swiftly, as a plan began to solidify in her mind. *I've done all I can do in Newport. I'm ready to move on. And I've always relished the idea of living in London. And I'd have my own business and my own income. Della and I get along beautifully.* "It does sound like a wonderful opportunity, Della. Tell me more about it."

"Well, dear, I've seen it. It's located at 16 Vincent Road. It's a three-story brick structure and across the road from a great office building and catty-corner from the Woolwich Arsenal—right in the heart of the city. Nice middle-class clientele. Ooh la! Just think of the fun we should have together, darling! Our own business to run just as we choose!"

Katherine was silent, carefully calculating the possibilities and consequences of such a move. *I'd have to leave Trev and Doris. But they really don't need me any longer. After all, business has been slow. I could sell my percentage of the business back to them and come away with quite a tidy sum. I could reinvest some money in the beauty salon, make a good profit, and then do the real work for free. I would be free to work in and around London. There must be literally hundreds of Spiritualist churches and New Thought societies that would have me as a lecturer. And I could counsel privately as well.*

"Oh, by the way, dear," Della was saying. "You could live above the shop if you wish. There are large, pleasant apartments on the second and third floors. And you wouldn't have to `pay a farthing for rent. And you know how much flats go for in London—a small fortune, no less. Well, what do you say?"

"I say I would like to see the shop," replied Katherine, most interested in the proposition by now.

"Good. Can you meet me in Woolwich tomorrow afternoon at, say, one?"

"How about half past one?"

"Perfect. We'll meet at the train station at half past one."

"Good. See you then."

"All right then, love. Goodbye."

"Goodbye, dear." A broad smile had crossed Katherine's face as she clasped the receiver of the phone to her breast. *It may be just the opportunity I've been hoping for,* she thought happily.

The next day, upon seeing the salon, Katherine knew at once that Della had in no way exaggerated its virtues. *Why, with a little bit of sprucing up, it could be quite a showcase,* she thought to herself. After discussing the shop's financial history with Frederick, Katherine was convinced that it was an opportunity she simply could not afford to refuse.

"Congratulations, madam partner," Della had declared, warmly embracing her sister after the transaction had been finalized.

"Ditto, sister," teased Katherine, and the two were on their way as business partners.

Because there was a severe shortage of hair and beauty products as a result of the war, Katherine and Della emphasized and advertised only the simplest of styling services, which included primarily haircuts and sets. Even such limited salon services were in great demand, however, and such a shop afforded a luxury-starved people a much appreciated luxury. *Yes,* thought Katherine, *with a minimum of time and money, I can make this place quite profitable. The London location is ideal, and such a venture will provide me with sufficient time and income to enable me to devote the majority of my days to the work.*

It was not easy saying goodbye to Trevor and Doris. The three had become extremely close. *Why, we're family,* thought Katherine ruefully, as she gazed lovingly at her two dearest friends in the world. *However, I simply must get on with my life.* Katherine made a brief announcement before both of them. But she later took Trevor aside.

"I love you, Trev. And always will. I'll come visit often—really, I will. It's not so very far from Newport to London, you know. And I shall be delighted to assist you and Doris whenever you are in need. Holidays, vacations when the hotel is busy, let me know. And I shall be happy to come. Don't think it's the end—we will see each other often, I promise."

"I love you, Katherine. Don't you see? I want you to stay here with me—marry me, my darling. Please," he had implored, his eyes searching hers for some sign that she might acquiesce. But he knew by her expression that she had made her decision long ago and that it would never alter. She started to speak, but he placed his finger gently on her lips. "It's hopeless, isn't it? You've made up your mind?"

"Yes," she admitted, her face white and strained and her eyes suddenly brimming with tears. "You must believe me, Trev, when I say that this moment was inevitable. I must go my way and you yours. I shall love you always. But you have your life and I have mine. I know you don't believe me when I tell you that I could never make you happy, but it's true. The work will always come first with me, Trev. Do try to understand. You have the properties and businesses to look after—not to mention Doris who adores you. I would only be a liability to you. You need a lovely, caring partner who could serve you and your interests to advantage. I am afraid that I am just not the stuff of which good wives are made. But that does not mean that I shall ever stop loving you or caring for you one iota less than I already do. I . . . I am truly sorry, Trev. I've only ever wanted to bring you and your family happiness. I never intended to hurt you or anyone."

"You have brought me the greatest happiness I've ever known," said Trevor softly. "I shall never love anyone again as I have you." Yet, while Katherine knew Trevor to be deeply hurt and disappointed, she knew also that on an intuitive level he thoroughly grasped her reasons for leaving. He had always understood and accepted her without attempting to change her in any way. He had understood her as no one had before—or would again, for that matter. Fourteen years had elapsed since Katherine had first set foot on the Hurley property.

And so, in September 1941, Katherine left Wales for London. The transition was nowhere nearly as difficult as she had feared, and she was comfortably settled in Woolwich in no time. She had always loved city life, and she was intoxicated by London.

CHAPTER 40

World War II

INITIALLY, THERE WAS A GREAT amount to be learned about the new business. But, as happily as girls, Della and Katherine plunged in. As diligent and persistent as ever, Katherine actually managed to persuade the manager of one of the finest hairdressing salons in London (located at Oxford Circus and boasting to be "Hairdressers to the Queen") to instruct her in all phases of the business. And Katherine derived considerable delight not only from the challenging financial aspects of running a business but also the aesthetics of cutting, curling, coloring and permanent-waving. Within ten months' time, she had become an expert in the salon business.

A testimony to the talents, ambition, and hard work of the sisters was the almost instantaneous success of the Vincent Street Salon. Having tastefully remodeled the shop and modernizing it to the extent they were able during wartime, they also hired—or, at least, attempted to hire—those who were most compatible with the shop's pleasant, middle-class clientele. But, in spite of their early success, they experienced their share of difficulties, frustration, and even hilarity.

For the persistent shortage of supplies posed many problems as well as many amusing adventures. Could Katherine ever forget the man whose face had been literally dripping with the new vegetable dye with which Della had been experimenting, so that his face was the same purplish-brown color as his hair? Or the recipient of one of Katherine's first haircuts whose thick, becoming hairdo had been cropped and thinned to look exactly like a man's as Katherine had tried to make the sides "even"? Or the lady who had brought in her own black-market dye and whose hair had been altered into a soft pink color? Or the woman who had entered the shop with a fine head of hair and left with a great bald spot as a result of exposure to a defective hairdryer? Or the hearing impaired couple who had been hired as hairdressers and who made more fuss and commotion than the entire staff put together? And exposure to the diverse types of people who entered the shop afforded Katherine the opportunity to assist them in ways she had never thought possible. For virtually all of her clients had been adversely affected by the war; and Katherine took advantage of the time they spent in her salon to heal, comfort, and counsel. Although she did it so subtly, few were consciously aware of that dimension of her work. They only knew that they nearly always left the shop feeling stronger, happier, and healthier than when they had entered it.

As Katherine had hoped, it was not long before she began to see a sizeable return on her investment. And, only a short time followed before she was afforded the financial freedom and flexibility of schedule that would enable her to devote the majority of her time to "the work." Furthermore, the shop's proximity to London was a godsend. For Katherine could now travel easily from one end of the city to another and lecture and demonstrate her gifts before thousands she could never have hoped to reach otherwise.

It had not been difficult at all to establish herself in London for she had already achieved a name for herself in many other parts of England. Her reputation having preceded her, she received numerous invitations to appear on Spiritualist platforms and as a guest lecturer for many New Age societies. Through word-of-mouth, her reputation continued to spread throughout London, and Katherine soon became well-known and respected in such circles. During this period, her abilities to "prove survival" were more in demand than ever before, as literally thousands of desperate human beings learned that death is not the end of life, but the beginning of another, more beautiful and joyous experience.

Often two, three, or even four nights of the week were devoted toward public demonstrations of her mediumistic abilities. Other evenings and any free hours of the day were devoted to nursing—as a volunteer nurse with the

Red Cross, she had easily been able to transfer to a local chapter and hospital near the business. Any other available time was spent conducting healing circles or counseling those who had attended one of her public meetings and desired further counseling or training in metaphysical areas. And at least once a month, at their request for help, Katherine returned to Trevor and Doris to assist them at The George "N Dragon.

Twelve to sixteen hours a day, seven days a week, she worked in one capacity or another to help those in need and to promote peace on earth. She, Della, and so many other women as well, worked in many different capacities during the war to help those in need and to boast public morale. At last, Katherine felt satisfied that she was contributing to the welfare of her country and the world as a whole. And although such a rigorous schedule might have resulted in fatigue or weariness in another, Katherine thrived on the constant activity and stimulation and was virtually inexhaustible. She had always appreciated a good challenge, and now, nearly every hour of every day posed some new problem to be resolved or obstacle to be surmounted.

As Katherine traveled from one end of England to the other, she could not help but marvel at the changes that had taken place in her country since war had been declared. Men and women in uniform were visible wherever one went—on every city or village street, at the bus and railway stations, in the theatres and restaurants, galleries and museums. Air raid shelters; the drone of military planes soaring overhead; fire brigades and ambulances scrambling to the scene of some disaster; newly established arsenals replacing what had formerly been laboratories or factories; shattered glass, decay, and rubble where great buildings had once stood; trainloads of children or wounded soldiers all were a part of the "new" England.

My God, it's as though the entire world has been transformed!, She thought, astounded at the magnitude of the changes that had occurred. *I don't think England—or the world as a whole, for that matter—will ever be the same*, she reflected. And she was correct. Not only would the physical landscape alter, but war was considerably accelerating basic social changes that had been taking place very gradually during the years of peace. The Britain that was to eventually emerge from the war would be vastly different from pre-war Britain.

Even while her country had been held in the grip of desperation as Hitler's blitzkrieg continued unabated in extensive night-bombing raids, and following the Battle of Dunkirk, as well as other major battles, Katherine was deeply impressed by the indomitability of spirit, stoicism, grace, and courage of her countrymen. For, in a time of immense sadness and fear, and of enormous personal loss, fearlessness and honor and a cheerful jocularity characterized their behavior. It was with pride that she observed their heroism.

While many well-intentioned friends and relatives had cautioned her against extensive travel during such precarious circumstances, Katherine calmly ignored the warnings, sincerely believing that no harm would come to her. Nonetheless, there were many close calls as she traversed all parts of London, England, and Wales. Often her train and automobile rides were accompanied by the sounds of antiaircraft guns, bombs exploding, screaming sirens, falling rubble, buildings clattering down in dust. Yet never did she experience fear. It simply did not occur to her to do so. Like her mother who had said, "No harm will come to my chicks," Katherine possessed devout faith that no harm would come either to her or to any of her loved ones and that both her death and theirs would occur at the appointed time—neither sooner nor later. She felt certain that despite grave difficulties and great odds that the people of Britain, and that Britain herself would emerge victorious and that good would triumph over evil.

Yet, as the intensity of Hitler's campaign to destroy the Royal Air Force and break England's morale increased, Katherine and countless others became even more determined that this should never take place. With equal fervor as though to offset the intensity of Hitler's efforts, Katherine threw herself into work with a vengeance—determined to share her understanding and her remarkable healing abilities with as many as possible. It was through nursing as well that she was able to reach an untold number of young men and women, their families, and loved ones who had returned home from the battleground.

Katherine had been overwhelmed by the vast numbers of sick, half-dead, and dying members of the Armed Forces—mostly young men in the prime of their lives—who literally poured out of the trains and into the hospitals. Never had she witnessed such suffering. Never had she experienced such simultaneous revulsion and compassion.

Under the guise and protection of conventional medicine, she was able to employ her own unorthodox methods of healing. And to so many—at the crossroads of their young lives—she was able to deliver a message of hope and inspiration and to administer a healing touch. Not infrequently, so-called "miracles" occurred, as those patients under her supervision and care for whom doctors had "no hope" survived and became full of hope and faith that despite all present pain and havoc, peace would be restored and a more meaningful and joyous life established for all people everywhere.

"You certainly have a way with the patients," Katherine had been informed by ever so many physicians. But she never revealed the manner or method by which she accomplished her results. She wondered how the medical community would react to the true response to their inevitable question, "What is your secret, Mrs. Hayward? How do you achieve such extraordinary results?" Ruefully, she recalled her own suspicion and dubious response to Mr. Fletcher—and the unusual methods he had employed to heal her father so many years ago.

No, I don't think that the medical community is quite ready for my explanation, she reflected, sadly, feeling that far greater results could have been achieved if they had been ready to listen to the truth about her healing work.

It had not been easy for Katherine to nurse. Frail and delicate, she had always been sheltered from life's uglier aspects. Her parents, then Percy, and, most recently, Trevor and Doris had protected her from the cruder, harsher aspects of life. Now, she was forced to watch helplessly the young men and women—often mere boys and girls of eighteen or nineteen—as they experienced agonizing physical pain; as they struggled to make sense of the horrors they had witnessed; as they attempted to justify the pain and/or murder they had inflected upon other human beings; as they sought to interpret the significance of the battles in which they had fought that had seemed terribly meaningful before but which now seemed not only purposeless but senseless. Many of these lovely young men—full of youthful optimism, vigor, and courage—had been hopelessly shattered, disfigured, scarred, or maimed—their morale severely damaged, their desire to go on living virtually nonexistent. So many of the soldiers had been mere boys studying at the university or apprenticing at a trade, in love, and looking forward to raising a family, preparing for a happy married life—completely unprepared either for the battlefield or worse, perhaps, what lay beyond. To so many, war had been little more than a game, a great adventure, a means of testing one's mental acuity and physical agility, or a contest that one could overcome through cunning and courage. Now, as they lay writhing in physical and mental anguish, the contest was over and it seemed that no one had won. All aspects of the experience were a puzzlement.

Although she had tried not to pity them—those who were physically and psychologically damaged—she could not help herself, observing the overcrowded infirmaries filled beyond capacity with bleeding, bandaged, moaning, tortured bodies, she wondered that any man could think that hell awaited following death. *If this isn't hell, I don't know what is*, she would think to herself, simultaneously wondering how anyone could ever have been so foolhardy to actually want the war.

With amazement, she observed these who were recent arrivals at the hospital and their gradual realization of where they were and what had transpired. Some, as they lay in the hospital beds attached to all kinds of tubes and machines, believed that they were still in the trenches, amidst the raging battle fire. Others shook and shivered, quivering uncontrollably in response to any sudden or unexpected noise. There were those who screamed and bellowed; those who sobbed aloud; those who cried quietly within; still others who were far, far away from everything and everyone. Not one who had actively been engaged in warfare would ever forget the abrupt, violent explosions of grenades and gunfire; the inexpressible shock and horror of witnessing the brutal death and carnage of another human being; the constant terror of enemy fire, of the minefields, and the presence of nameless, personality-less human beings whom they were told were THE

ENEMY. Few could hope to eradicate the violent spectacle of the battlefield from memory. And Katherine knew that the road to recovery would not be an easy one for any of them. For, along with their youth and health, these young men had forfeited their dreams and ambitions and, in spite of the fact that they continued to breathe, regarded their lives as over.

Yet although many had wished to die, and in truth, would have died during the previous World War, the advancement of medical technology made these deaths virtually impossible. The lives of many whose injuries were extensive and would have resulted in death before were now spared. And often, these cases were the most difficult for Katherine to treat—for example, those who sustained traumatic brain injuries, those who had multiple amputations, those who had been severely burned, those who were profoundly disfigured, and so on. For these men the likelihood of leading a "normal" life was nonexistent, and the hopelessness and despair that resulted from their awareness of this fact prolonged or postponed the recuperation process. Yet as a result of Katherine's healing abilities, many who had sincerely longed for death had changed and made remarkable progress.

One such patient had been near death when he had been brought into the ward in which Katherine was working. Having been severely burned over most of his body, he was literally swathed in bandages from head to toe. No one had believed that he would survive. So extensive was the damage that many secretly hoped that the boy would not make it. But Katherine had known through her psychic abilities that the boy would survive, and she knew that it was up to her to strengthen and prepare him for the changes that had taken place and for the new life that would follow as a result.

Upon reviewing his medical charts, she had been aghast to learn that he had been an actor prior to the war. One young lad, who had fought alongside of him, had informed her that he had been quite staggeringly handsome before—before a grenade had exploded in his face and a swiftly moving ground fire had erupted in the area in which he had been standing. *How dreadful*, thought Katherine, but she braced herself for the task at hand. Utilizing her own healing abilities along with the techniques demonstrated by Mr. Fletcher, Katherine began to work with her patient. Her hands lightly traveled over the bandages that covered his entire body, and massaged where she could. And although the boy was, for the most part, unconscious, she spoke to him in a low voice so that no one else could hear. "You are going to survive. You will recover from your wounds. You will achieve remarkable results, and your mind and body will serve you very well. You'll see. Through plastic surgery and other medical procedures, your appearance will return to normal. Your life will be healthy and normal. Don't give up, lad. You are meant to continue on this plane. Don't grieve. Don't despair. You will make a miraculous recovery."

Katherine devoted a portion of every day for a month to the boy, and she observed his progress with astonishment. There could be no doubt that he was responding to her treatment. She had felt the healing energies pouring forth from her hands, and had seen the boy respond. Intuitively, she knew that on some level he knew exactly what was taking place. Initially, his hand had reached out for hers; later he had nodded or shaken his head in response to her queries or comments. In time, he was addressing her in his feeble voice. It was she who had encouraged, then persuaded him first to consume water and later to eat and drink the food that was brought to him. Within six weeks of his arrival at the hospital, he was deemed well enough to be transferred to a hospital renowned for its superb plastic surgery staff and facilities. Tears of gratitude welled up in her eyes as she wished the boy—who had been like a son—goodbye.

"God bless you, my dear boy. You'll see that your life is a great blessing after all," she had whispered.

"Thank you, Mrs. Hayward. I could never have made it without you."

"Nonsense," she scoffed. But she would never forget the expression in his eyes—as though she had given him the greatest gift of all—the will to continue. Nor had she been prepared for the gratitude of the boy's widowed mother.

"I shall never forget you as long as I live, Mrs. Hayward. My boy is alive, thanks to you. I can never thank you enough," the woman was positively radiant, and her eyes shone with joy.

"Please don't thank me," Katherine said quietly in earnest. For she had been reminded of the humble healer who had taken no personal credit for saving her father's life. "It is God to Whom you must give thanks. It is Our Creator Who works through me."

No one—not even Katherine herself—could recall how many lives had been improved or saved as a result of her intervention, Not only were her healing abilities invaluable, but also her clairvoyance proved to be of great benefit. As a result of her abilities, she was able to diagnose and formulate prognoses and prescribe treatments for patients. In addition, she was able to know in advance when danger was imminent. Countless lives had been saved after Katherine gently insisted that staff members or patients relocate from one room or wing of the hospital in a sufficient amount of time to prevent them from being victims of an explosion or some other disaster. In conjunction with several such demonstrations, Katherine had begun to acquire quite a reputation with her coworkers, and few of them took any action without first consulting her. Doctors, nurses, the relatives and friends of patients—all had learned to seek and trust Nurse Hayward's advice. Never had her psychic powers been employed to such advantage, and Katherine felt a deep sense of gratitude for the privilege of sharing her gifts with those in need.

Expending an incalculable amount of time and energy with her patients, she could not help but hope that her Graham was being equally well cared for, and that if ever he were in need, he would meet similar kindness. For, despite her frantic schedule, Graham was rarely far from her thoughts, and she could not help but wonder where and how he was. His sporadic letters were far from comforting, for they were subject to Army censorship, and Graham had not been permitted to divulge his true whereabouts or circumstances. And Katherine had been able to glean little of real significance from them. All she could determine was the fact that Graham was still alive and that he did not seem to be minding the experience too much. The letter in which he had written, "Boy, were you right, Mother, when you said I'd have some remarkable adventures and some close calls," hardly put her at ease.

By the early 1940s Britain had fully accepted the idea of the state's ultimate responsibility toward its less fortunate members—as government policy on pensions, housing, and unemployment benefits clearly indicated. Furthermore, divisiveness in the form of class distinctions and labels was disappearing as aristocrats and members of the lower class alike shared the cramped quarters of air-raid shelters, stood together in ration lines and ubiquitous queues, and as individuals in the Royal Armed Forces advanced on the basis of individual merit rather than social status.

During the Second World War, economic pressures influenced the wage structure sharply in favor of the working class as a whole, while state intervention became an accepted part of life of every member of the community, and not merely of the underprivileged. By 1945, the principle of the "welfare state" was acknowledged by both major British political parties. Furthermore, as a result of the war, the focus of the nation had become external rather than internal, international rather than national. British insularity had been superseded of necessity by active world involvement. In short, her position as a world power had changed fundamentally, as the nation that had formerly "stood alone" against the might of Hitler's Germany, after 1945 now recognized her interdependence with the United States and with the non-Communist nations on the continent.

At long last, in spring of 1945, it had become increasingly apparent that the war was finally drawing to its conclusion. Graham had hinted in a recent letter that he would soon be returning home permanently. *Uncle Glyn has already promised me a position with the Ministry of Defense, and Beryl can't wait to settle in London. Our work in Italy is almost finished. I shall be home to stay, Mother; everyone around me seems to feel that this bloody mess will be over within the next few months.* Katherine's hands had trembled so that she could hardly hold on to the letter. "Home," she murmured. "My boy will soon be coming home." She would not have long to wait.

By the end of April, Mussolini had been shot and the Russians had reached Berlin. By May 2, Berlin surrendered to the Allied Forces, and armistice in Italy had become effective. On May 5, German forces in northwestern Europe had surrendered, and by May 7, the Germans had unconditionally surrendered at Reims in France. All hostilities ceased at midnight on May 8.

May 8 was V-E Day in Britain. And as Winston Churchill acknowledged, "The unconditional surrender of our enemies was the signal for the greatest outburst of joy in the history of mankind." As official word came over the BBC that England was no longer at war, Katherine wept. She could not recall when she had experienced such profound joy, gratitude, and relief. "Thank the Blessed Lord," was all she had been able to say upon hearing the news, as she and Della embraced.

Never before had she witnessed, or would witness again, such a joyous celebration or demonstration of brotherly affection as that which overtook the city of London on V-E Day. It seemed to her that everyone in the whole of England had traveled to London as citizens paraded down the streets en masse singing, dancing, laughing, and shouting to one another. Many were openly weeping or praying, and St. Paul's and other churches were filled to capacity. The rich and the poor, city and country folk, the illiterate and well-educated—all were united in unequivocal joy, triumph, and relief. Restaurants, theatres, and pubs were filled with merrymakers, as the city itself acquired an air of ebullience, exhilaration, and optimism.

To Katherine, this day represented the closing of an era, the conclusion of one of the darkest chapters in the Earth's history. And she and her coworkers prayed in earnest that there would be no further war; no further suffering of such enormous magnitude. Silent tears streamed down her face as she realized with profound gratitude that there had been no casualties, no losses in her family. As she had envisioned, no harm had come to her loved ones. Overcome by emotion, she had knelt in prayer.

"Thank you, Dear God. Thank you for this great and blessed day in the history of humankind."

But although the war was now officially over, Katherine realized that she—that no one who had ever experienced such sadness and destruction—would ever be the same. Memory might dim or soften some of the harsher images, but she knew that for the rest of her life, she would be haunted by the ghastly headlines of the daily newspapers that had chronicled Hitler's rapid advancement throughout Europe; the terror that the grim announcements of traitor and Nazi radio broadcaster Lord Haw-Haw had evoked in her heart; the hospitals as infernos of pain, suffering, and despair; the crowded railway stations filled with soldiers and their families and loves ones; the postal offices teeming with those anxious to hear from their loved ones who were far away; the cramped and miserable quarters of the air-raid shelters; the wail of the air-raid sirens; blackouts; the horrible sound of bombs exploding; the shortage of nearly everything; and the sight of rubble where a landmark or a favorite haunt of hers had stood. No, she would never, as long as she lived, forget the horror of these years.

Now, she knew that it was time to recover, repair, and rebuild. To employ the past to create a future. A future free of conflict and suffering and destruction. A future in which all might flourish together in peace. She was not the only one to dream of peace. There were many who longed, hoped and prayed for it—among them those who were laboring to create a world organization: the United Nations. Everyone wished to usher in a golden age of peace, prosperity, and progress—an age of kindness and beauty.

Progress, Katherine thought to herself. *A new world. No more violence or bloodshed. Man had learned from his mistakes. He will be transformed and manifest the Great Creature and Divine Being he truly is. And now, we shall progress. I know it. No more war, no more violation of human rights. We shall construct a magnificent new world. That is what I shall be working for from hereon.*

CHAPTER 41

Graham Hayward

&

"HELLO, MUM? IS THAT YOU? It's me, Gray. Can you hear me? The connection's bloody awful. Are you all right?" Her heart missed a beat as she recognized the voice. It seemed so dim and far away.

"Graham, Graham, is that you? You sound so different. Are you all right, love?" she asked anxiously.

"I'm all right, Mum, only very tired, that's all."

"Is everything in order?"

"Yes, Mum. Everything is fine. In fact," he stated confidently, "that is precisely why I've rung you up to inform you personally that not only is everything all right but to let you know that everything is more than all right. " His speech was garbled, and Katherine could hardly make out his words.

"What's that, Graham? I can't hear you properly. I can't make any sense out of what you're saying," she was genuinely mystified by now as to the purpose for his telephone call. In the meantime, Graham smiled to himself, biting his lower lip to keep from laughing aloud.

"Actually, it's quite simple, Mum."

"Simple. What's simple, Graham? Please do get on with it, will you? And kindly advise me as to exactly what this is all about." Graham smiled once again, visualizing the impatient scowl upon his mother's face that he knew all too well.

"If you'll just be patient, Mum, I'll explain everything."

"I should certainly hope so dear," she said icily.

"Well, all that I am trying to tell you is that I am to be released from the Royal Engineers tomorrow, and that I shall be returning home permanently. In fact, I am scheduled to arrive in London next Tuesday sometime after mid-day."

There was a silence, and Katherine was utterly still as the meaning of his words sank in. "Mother, are you there? Did you hear me? I said that I am coming home." Still, she could not trust her voice enough to speak.

Sensing his mother's reaction, Graham continued teasingly, "Well, Mum, if you don't want to see me on Tuesday, just tell me. I am certain that I can arrange to extend my stay in the military. And France really is so lovely this time of year . . . "

"I have never wanted anything so much in my life as to see you next Tuesday," Katherine finally replied fiercely. "And don't you dare think of staying in France a single moment longer than is absolutely necessary. Do you understand?" she warned. Her voice was unusually husky.

"I can't believe it's true," she whispered, hardly daring to breathe. "Have you told Beryl the good news?"

"Yes, Mum. And she's positively thrilled. I've never heard her quite so happy. Why, I believe she's even more excited than you."

That's possible, but not likely, she thought to herself, feeling that a mother's love was deeper than any other.

"Well, then, Mother, I will look forward to seeing you sometime next Tuesday afternoon. I had better go now. See you soon!"

"Yes, my darling. I will see you soon," she said happily. Even after he had hung up, she cradled the telephone receiver to her bosom, rejoicing in the news. Quickly she calculated the number of days and hours that would elapse before her boy would return safely to her arms. It was Friday. "Tuesday," she murmured aloud. "Graham and I will be reunited on Tuesday." She was able to think of little else for the remainder of the day.

It was the second week of October in 1945, and few could deny that winter was already in the air. The weather was uncharacteristically wet and cold, and thunderstorms one after another erupted throughout southern England. "The past two weeks have been perfectly miserable," Katherine sighed, as she stood at the bedroom window and stared at the dreary street below. Glancing at the watch on her wrist, she was astonished to note that it was only half past one in the afternoon. Graham had telephoned less than an hour ago to inform her that he would be coming home for sure on Tuesday afternoon. She did not know how she would survive the next few days. Every time the telephone rang or someone knocked at the door, her heart leaped to her throat. *It's Gray*, she would think instantly. And she would wait for him to appear. But, of course, he did not.

It had been decided that Beryl would join her and that Graham would meet them both at the Woolwich apartment Katherine had prepared for them. Unbeknownst to Graham, the women had prepared a small party in honor of his homecoming. Della and George along with some of Katherine's oldest and dearest friends would collect in Katherine's apartment in antici-pation of Graham's arrival.

But on Tuesday morning, Katherine awoke to the sound of rain spat-tering on the street, and the fierce whistling of the wind. She had awakened feeling unrefreshed and with a feeling of inexplicable foreboding. "Gray!" she cried out, suddenly remembering that this was the day upon which he was to return. Literally tumbling out of bed, she temporarily forgot the feeling of foreboding and hastened to get the flat ready for his arrival. Throughout the morning, she plunged into her work; first cleaning the flat and preparing refreshment for the evening's celebration and then attending to business at the salon. She felt tired and strained, but was not certain why.

Two o'clock came and passed, then three, four, and five, and without any word from Graham. The feelings of dread and foreboding that Katherine had attempted to suppress throughout the day became even more powerful. *Something awful has happened!* she thought suddenly in desperation as the clock on the fireplace mantle chimed six. *Oh, God*, she prayed rapidly, *please let my boy be alive. I'm not ready to give him up. Please spare him.*

But Tuesday evening had come and gone without a trace of him. Desperately appearing to be at ease, Katherine had decided not to cancel the homecoming party. But she had fooled no one least of all Della whose own two sons had only recently returned from the front.

"Don't worry, love," she had patted her sister's arm comfortingly. "We'll telephone Gray's division office in the morning. I'm certain there's a good explanation for the delay."

"I'm sure you're right," said Katherine, feeling somewhat better.

Finally, managing to fall into a fitful sleep long past midnight, Katherine awoke early the next morning to the sound of thunder and torrential rain. *Something has happened to Graham's plane,* she thought helplessly, as she raced to the telephone to contact anyone who might have knowledge regarding her son's present whereabouts. But although she spoke to one officer after another, no one was able to give her the information she required.

"I'm very sorry, Mrs. Hayward," the last officer to whom she had spoken said kindly. "But we haven't heard a word. The weather has really loused up all communications. I assure you we shall notify you as soon as we hear anything."

And so, Katherine was forced to spend another day in a state of anxiety and desperation the likes of which she hadn't previously experienced.. Poor Beryl had been remarkably patient, calm, and optimistic knowing full well the possible scenarios Graham faced. She maintained her faith that all was well and that she and her husband would soon be together again.

Early Thursday morning, she was startled out of her sleep by the ringing of the telephone. The male voice that politely announced itself as Captain Harrison at the other end of the line was tense, and it was evident that he was finding the message difficult to deliver.

"I regret, Mrs. Hayward, that your son is missing. He was traveling with a group of bomber planes—one of which—I am so sorry about this, Mrs. Hayward—ran out of fuel and crashed in the Channel. Because of the foul weather, our communications have been poor, and we simply do not know at this time if your son was on board the plane that fell. I sincerely wish that I could tell you more, but that is all we know at the present time. We will notify you the moment we acquire any further information. I am sorry, Mrs. Hayward," he said gently.

"Thank you, Captain," were the only words she could manage to get out. In a daze, she placed the receiver down and sat at the edge of her bed, staring into space. For some moments, she sat in stunned silence. Then gradually, life flowed back into her body. Her wit restored, she began to contemplate the Captain's words.

"No," she shouted suddenly. "I don't believe it! I don't believe that Graham was on the plane that crashed. I feel that he is alive. Lost, perhaps, but alive. I know he shall return home to me. I know it!" The remainder of the morning was spent on the telephone, as Katherine contacted every officer and department that might have further information regarding Graham's circumstances and whereabouts. Unfortunately, her efforts were futile, and by noon, she had, more or less, become reconciled to the fact that she would have to wait until someone contacted her. In the meantime, she and Beryl comforted one another as best they could, and went about their daily affairs to the extent to which they were able. Always finding strength and solace in her work, Katherine plunged in with renewed fervor determined not to dwell upon her son's well-being. "He's going to be all right," she told herself. "I'm certain he'll be all right."

It was not until Friday morning that she and Beryl received word that Graham had not been a passenger in the plane that had crashed in the Channel. "Oh, Beloved Lord, thank you," she had cried in gratitude upon hearing the news. Still, her son was missing, and no one seemed to know his whereabouts.

But, knowing that he had not been killed in the fatal crash, she was no longer worried. "He'll be home soon, Darling," she told Beryl who was still all atremble.

"I do hope you're right," Beryl had spoken hopefully in her soft voice, looking more like a little girl than ever. In spite of her own grief during the past three days, Katherine's heart had gone out to her young daughter-in-law. *Poor darling, as if the years of separation from Graham haven't been enough for her to bear,* thought Katherine, ruefully studying Beryl's white face and sad expression. Frankly, Katherine had been surprised by Beryl's demonstration of courage throughout the ordeal, for her daughter-in-law had hardly broken down at all, and had made every effort to hide her true feelings. *God, I hope that she and Gray will be together soon. They deserve every happiness in the world,* thought Katherine.

She was seated at the small table in the kitchen drinking a cup of tea and poring over the newspaper when she heard footsteps in the hallway outside her front door. She knew at once that they were neither Beryl's nor Della's. *Who could it be?* she wondered, rising from the chair. Then, suddenly, her heart began to hammer wildly in her chest, and the color rose to her cheeks. For the past three and a half days, she had expected Graham's telephone call or his appearance at her front door. Now, as the doorbell rang, she felt instantaneous elation. She knew, positively knew, that her son had finally arrived.

"Graham!" she cried, reaching out for him as though afraid he were a mirage that would vanish into thin air. "Oh, Graham!" she could hardly stifle the tears that had risen instantly to her eyes, nor could she control the shaking of her knees so unsteady beneath her, and she could not control the quivering of her voice. "Is it you, my love? Is it really you?" she asked pulling him to her, then hugging him as though she would never let him go.

"Oh, Mum. Mum. It's so good to see you again. You are a sight for sore eyes. God, it feels good to hold you in my arms!" he had said, with deep feeling. For several minutes, they were locked in an embrace, appreciating the comfort and warmth of one another as they never had before in their lives.

Thank God for this moment. Thank God. Now the war is really and truly over for me. My son is home again, thought Katherine, as she held him in her arms. And then, all of a sudden, as though she were releasing the combined tension, fear, pain, and suffering that she had experienced over the past six years, she began to sob uncontrollably.

"It's all right, Mother," Graham whispered reassuringly. "Everything is all right."

"I know" wailed Katherine. "But I can't help it. All the waiting . . . and the worry . . . and wondering if you were gone forever . . . if I would ever see you again . . ." And a fresh wave of grief overcame her, and she sobbed even more loudly and intensely. Soon, Graham's chest was heaving and tears were streaming down his cheeks and the two were crying in each other's arms.

"This is positively absurd," Graham finally announced, pulling away and drying her tears first, then his own.

"It is, isn't it?" she sniffled, smiling through her tears. "Do you know that this is the first good cry I've had since the war began? All those emotions have been bottled up in me for years," she said, blowing her nose.

"I know what you mean. I guess it's been a great release for me too," he admitted. "You can't imagine what I've been through during the past few days. I'm not at all certain which was worse—the war itself or the experiences of the last week." His voice cracked, and tears reappeared in his eyes. Katherine escorted him to the sofa as he collected himself.

"Now calm down, dear. We have plenty of time to discuss all that has happened. Let's not try to cram the experiences of an entire war into a few minutes." But he proceeded to describe the events of the past few days in some detail.

"Although our pilot was instructed to return to Calais almost immediately due to the severity of the weather, he refused. Felt we could make it safely home, I guess. Anyway, the weather grew worse steadily, and we were tossing and turning like you can't believe. And there was virtually no visibility. Our pilot got terribly lost, our men very ill, and we were forced to land at the nearest field we could find—which happened to be near St. Mawgan in Cornwall—and where, of course, not a living soul was expecting us. You can imagine the mess. All communications systems were down due to the dreadful storms and we were forced to make an unexpected landing at an airfield that was already overcrowded and could not accommodate another plane.

"I won't go into the frightful details. But almost immediately upon landing, we were advised to get back in the plane, resume our flight, and land at another airfield—this time in Peterborough in eastern England, seventy-five miles from London. Suffice it to say, that through an endless series of bureaucratic errors and red tape, we were sent from one base to another—in the wretched weather—and throughout the process absolutely forbidden to communicate with anyone outside the service until we were officially cleared by military security. Hence, I was unable to contact either Beryl or you; knowing very well that both of you would be mad with worry. After being transported by train from one end of England to another, we were all finally cleared and officially released from service. And, well, to make a long story very short, here am I in your midst."

There was a slight twinkle in his eye as he smiled at the absurdity of the situation. And, as he sat in the late afternoon stillness, Katherine had the opportunity to observe him closely for the first time. Although she could not pinpoint it, she was aware that there was something different about him. Although he looked somewhat paler (beneath the sunburn), a little thinner, perhaps, and very tired, he was as handsome as ever. There were fine lines around his eyes and he was unshaven and he had aged somewhat. But there was something else about him that had changed. And then, as she gazed into his eyes, she realized immediately what the difference was. *Why, he is no longer a boy—he is a man. My boy is all grown up*, she marveled.

There was an air of maturity and efficiency about him; and his eyes looked as though they had seen much suffering—and that there was little in life that could ever again surprise him. For a single instant, she wished that she could have protected him from all he had obviously witnessed and experienced. But she knew that he had learned and grown tremendously over the past years. Tears stung the back of her eyelids as she thought of the horrors he must have experienced. Well, thank God the war was over. She would do everything in her power to make her boy happy. Now that her Graham was home for good at last, she would make sure that he was well looked after.

CHAPTER 42

A New Thought Center

⟶

FOR NEARLY A YEAR, GRAHAM and Beryl lived in the flat below Katherine's in Woolwich. And, more so than during any other phase of their lives, this was a period of readjustment in England. Married life was entirely different now than it had been during the war, for rarely had Graham and Beryl spent longer than a few consecutive weeks' time together, and never had they lived together as "normal," happily married couples had before the war. Now, they were forced to get to know one another in a vastly different way. Furthermore, Graham had left Cardiff a boy, a happy, carefree, and idealistic student, and had returned to London a serious man of responsibility who had risen in the ranks of the Royal Engineers from "sapper" to captain. Both his mental prowess and physical agility had been constantly tested throughout the years with the Royal Engineers; and he had rather grown accustomed to the frantic pace and constant challenge of life in the service. Having borne witness to untold suffering and misery and having been exposed to considerable constant danger, he had been forced to develop and mature in ways that would never have been possible in times of peace. Like his country, Graham had changed dramatically and irrevocably in certain fundamental ways.

Neither Graham nor Beryl was happy living in post-war London. Having grown up in rural Wales, Beryl missed the simplicity and beauty of life in the country. And even Graham, who had always loved London, found the city ugly, dreary, and depressing with its crowds of soldiers from all over the world; the tortured and the maimed who were ubiquitous on

London's streets; the burnt-out buildings, rubble, shattered glass, and gaping holes where buildings once had stood. It seemed a burned-out shell of its former vibrant self; and it was a grim and constant reminder of the worldwide devastation that had taken place since 1939. And so, when Graham received the lucrative offer to assist his Uncle Glyn in the post-war construction and renovation business he had established in association with the Ministry of Defense (which required him to relocate to the picturesque town of Whitstable in Kent), he was only too happy to accept.

"There's an enormous amount of money to be made in the construction business, my boy," Glyn had intimated. "And I plan to take you in as a full partner one day soon—that is, if you're as good as I think you are," he winked. "Mark my words, boy, we'll be the biggest and the best construction firm in all of England and Wales. I'm happy to have you with me, son." And so, Graham and Beryl left Woolwich and settled in Whitstable. By early 1947, Graham had been promoted to director of the firm which had, indeed, become one of the most powerful and prestigious construction outfits in southern England, and he and Beryl had bought their very first house. On March 28, 1947, Beryl gave birth to a little boy named David Grant.

"Peace at last," Katherine thought, upon receiving the letter in which Graham had proudly described his beautiful new home in full detail. But even though he and Beryl had often mentioned their desire to have a family, no one had been more surprised than she by Beryl's announcement that she was pregnant. And no one could have been more thrilled than Katherine upon learning of the birth of her first grandchild—a beautiful little boy with black hair and deep blue eyes. At age forty-eight, she had become a grandmother.

Relieved and grateful that her children were finally well settled, Katherine was devoting her time to her public work, was still very actively involved in the Vincent Street Salon, and had also begun to assist Trevor and Doris at the lovely country inn they recently acquired in Christchurch, north of Newport, which was called The Greyhound. For years, Trevor had talked of getting a country place—he had grown tired of Newport and had yearned for the beauty and serenity of country life. And toward the end of the war, this wonderful business opportunity had been presented to him. It was an offer he dared not refuse and Katherine had never seen him so content.

From the moment that she had first seen the charming Tudor structure, with acres of surrounding gardens and land, Katherine had been enamored of it. "I shall spend my summers here with you," she had informed the delighted Trevor. "Perhaps I'll be able to come for other holidays as well."

"You know you're always welcome here," was Trevor's heartfelt response. And because she was insistent upon helping them each time she visited The Greyhound, Trevor and Doris were equally insistent upon paying her for her services. And so, although her "holidays" in the country turned out to be "working" holidays, they were always delightful and invigorating. And the additional income came in handy, for Katherine had only recently decided to invest virtually all of her savings into a psychic research center of her very own. Not quite yet, but very soon, she planned to open her center.

Having appeared by now on numberless public platforms and having worked in conjunction with an incalculable number and variety of psychic and New Thought societies, organizations, and churches throughout England and Wales, Katherine had seen and experienced enough to feel that she was ready to establish a base from which she could propagate her own unique viewpoints and abilities. She was tired of traveling from one end of England to the other. Furthermore, she was equally tired of being misunderstood and misrepresented by those factions that chose to label her and her work as part of their own. "My teachings are different," she longed to cry out to those who misunderstood her. "They are broader, more universal in scope than yours." A natural born leader, Katherine was ready and willing to stand on her own, and, in an atmosphere devoid of any outside interference, she felt her work would flourish.

After Graham and Beryl moved to Whitstable, Della's husband George was taken seriously ill and advised to leave London and recuperate in the country. Unable to look after her share of the business, Della had little alternative but to relinquish her hold on the Vincent Street Salon.

"Why don't you just buy me out, Love?" she had inquired of her sister. But, although the business had been more lucrative than either of them had ever imagined when first they had begun, Katherine refused the offer.

"No, dear, I think it's time to sell the shop, and keep whatever profit we can get. I think we are both ready to move on." And so, the happy partnership between the sisters was dissolved. And Katherine was on her way. *Toward what?* she wondered. But she did not have to wait long to find out.

Only one month elapsed after the Vincent Street Salon had been sold when Katherine received a telephone call from her younger sister, Olwen, who was presently residing in Bournemouth. "Katherine," she had said excitedly, "I have decided to sell my properties here and am looking for a business opportunity in London."

"Oh, no," replied Katherine, the purpose for her sister's call all too evident.

"Pardon?" said Olwen.

"Nothing," murmured Katherine. "Go on."

"Well, dear, you know how you've always talked about establishing your own psychic research center. Well, you also know that I am a registered nurse. And, well, I was thinking, that perhaps we—you and I—with our combined savings could open a New Thought Center of Learning—you know the sort of place where you could lecture, conduct classes, hold meetings, and so on, while I could treat patients with their physical problems. You know, I've been researching metaphysics in my own way ever since you and Mum and Dad told me about your amazing experiences."

"In your own way," Katherine repeated, seriously questioning the nature of Olwen's investigation. For she knew that although well-intentioned and hard-working, her sister was not the most dependable person in the world. Not too many years ago, Olwen had been severely burned in a fire that had broken out at home, and ever since she had been very nervous, self-conscious, and terribly high-strung; only recently she had been through a painful divorce. Throughout these challenging experiences, Olwen had derived considerable comfort and pleasure from her nursing. After the wonderful care and attention she had received in the hospital by members of the medical profession, she had yearned to provide similar care to those in need.

"We could get a charming place—you know, one of those grand old Victorian homes in a suburb of London—and set up a center where people could recuperate, rest, and conduct research simultaneously. My properties are worth quite a bit of money, and I know that you've been saving for a center of your own. Why not pool our resources? I think we could make a real success of it. What do you think?"

While Olwen had been rattling on, Katherine's mind had been racing. *Perhaps it would be wise to open a center with Olwen—and share the investment. After all, she is intelligent and hard-working—perhaps she would attend to the business aspects and other areas with which I would really prefer not to involve myself. And, then, I could devote my time and energies to teaching and lecturing.*

"Well, dear, what do you think?" Olwen was saying at the other end of the line.

"Well, love, it is an interesting proposition. But I shall have to think it over very carefully before making any decision."

"Oh," said Olwen, the disappointment evident in her voice.

"I'm sorry, Olwen, but I couldn't possibly decide on so important a decision and investment without careful deliberation." And deliberate was precisely what she did. For several weeks following her telephone conversation with Olwen, Katherine debated the advisability of entering into a business partnership with her younger sister. But, finally, keeping in mind her previous success and happiness with Della, she decided to accept Olwen's proposal. Even as she had agreed to the collaboration, uneasiness had gnawed at her, and she was reminded of the inner voice that had assured her since the early days of the work, *You will work—you must work—alone.* Yet, in the excitement of searching for an appropriate residence and location, the voice was temporarily ignored.

It was not until approximately one year later—after Katherine had invested a substantial portion of her savings in a beautiful, spacious residence in the hospitable middle-class suburb of Cricklewood—that Katherine was once again reminded of the warning. For, despite the enormous amount of time and money she had expended toward the establishment of a successful center, her efforts had seemingly been for naught. Having entrusted a realtor with the responsibility of locating for them a suitable residence, neither Katherine nor Olwen had realized until it was far too late that their psychic research center was situated in the very heart of a predominantly Jewish suburb in which Spiritualism and New Thought were largely nonexistent.

Although Katherine had widely advertised and distributed brochures announcing forthcoming activities at the center, she received no response worth mentioning. Her first public meeting in the area had taken place on an evening during which one of the hardest, most persistent rains she could remember had fallen, and only ten people appeared in the large hall which could accommodate several hundred. As one might well imagine, Katherine was terribly disappointed by the unexpected turn of events. But, far more disturbing than any other factor regarding the acquisition of the Cricklewood residence, were the financial difficulties that had plagued Olwen following the purchase of the property and involving several other pieces of property and which forced Katherine to employ virtually her entire savings to cover the steep monthly mortgage payments as well as the numerous additional debts that had been incurred in conjunction with the daily operation of the center.

Katherine—who had always been so prudent and frugal, who had diligently and conscientiously saved her money for years in order to one day establish a research center—now found herself forced to employ nearly her entire reserve of money in order to keep and maintain a center from which she was not only deriving no profit but from which she was actually operating at a loss. After spending nearly a year in this manner, the heartbroken Katherine was ready to admit that she had made a grave mistake, and that she was most anxious to forget this segment of her life. She would get rid of the property once and for all. She and Olwen finally managed to sell the house at a substantial financial loss. But, in spite of the loss of a large portion of her savings, Katherine felt enormously relieved to be free of the great burden that had fallen upon her shoulders. Furthermore, she had learned several invaluable lessons. Firstly, she would, from hereon, work alone. Secondly, she would never again buy property of her own. She might rent or lease, but would never assume the financial burdens and responsibilities associated with owning a center. Furthermore, she would assume complete control of all facets of her work and activities—business or otherwise.

CHAPTER 43

The Aftermath

~~~~

FOLLOWING THE CRICKLEWOOD DEBACLE, KATHERINE, whose finances were now the most limited that they had been since she had left Aberdare for Newport over twenty years ago, accepted brother Glyn's generous offer enabling her to reside in an attractive, pre-war apartment building he owned on lovely Pendennis Road in a suburb southwest of London called Streatham. Best of all, in addition to affording her a pleasant environment in which to live, there were suitable accommodations on the ground floor beneath her own apartment which she felt would serve as a small but effective center or, at least, a place where she could teach and heal and hold public meetings.

For the present time, she felt it would serve her well. *All it takes is a little fixing up for it to be ideal*, she had observed, and then set about the task of remodeling and redecorating so that in several months' time, it had become a charming and hospitable base from which to do the work in her own unique manner on a small scale. Unfortunately, several days before it was scheduled to open officially, the rooms comprising the center—the new furnishings, draperies, and rugs, etc.—were flooded and irreparably damaged after several water pipes had been incorrectly installed by a workman. Thousands of pounds had been poured into the renovation of the center-to-be; and now, as the combined result of this with the Cricklewood disaster, Katherine was virtually penniless and disillusioned.

It had finally begun to occur to her that perhaps she was not meant to serve as head of her own center after all. She had worked throughout her entire adult life in order to achieve sufficient financial freedom to enable her to do the work in her own way. But, now, perhaps, she was no longer meant to do the work. *And what would my life be were I not to do what I love most deeply?* she wondered sadly. It was the first time since the age of twenty, when she had first entered into communications with the Spirit Beings, that she was at a real crossroads and knew not which way to go. "Show me the way," she begged of God.

Suddenly, He seemed very far away and unapproachable. Although she did not speak of her hurt and disappointment, her weariness and despair, her brother, Glyn, had sensed her deep distress and genuinely wished to help her. "I can lend you the money—I should regard it as a privilege to *give* you the money to open a center. I've seen your work. And there's no one to compare with you, Katherine. Don't give up—whatever you do. You have far too much to give the world." Tears had risen to her eyes at his words, but she was adamant. She no longer believed it advisable to carry on.

"All I have ever lived for has been to serve Thee, God," she said fiercely. "Why then have you rewarded me in this way? What is it you wish me to do? Where do you wish me to go? Please make Thy presence, my purpose known to me. For I am lost, and know not what to do." And in the midst of her despair, she had slipped on the wet pavement and had sprained her ankle. She was forced to accept Glyn's hospitality and remain under his family's care and supervision. And so, the angst-ridden Katherine was house-bound and bed-ridden for nearly six weeks.

A dark and difficult period ensued during which Katherine sincerely wondered why she had been forced to meet with such sadness and how she would spend the remainder of her days. But always, always, throughout this time of doubt and self-pity, she was reminded of Dr. Evans' words, "Surrender to the Great Eternal Spirit and say, 'Thy will, oh God, be done on earth, in my life . . . Thy will, not mine.'" She adhered to this advice, and waited for the answer to her prayers. Never did she doubt that they would be answered. And so, regardless of her own searing disappointment, it did not occur to her that there was no meaning or lack of purposefulness to everything that had taken place.

An answer did arrive to her prayers, but not in the form she had anticipated. Some weeks after the bandages had been removed from her foot, she received by mail an engraved invitation requesting that she audition for a position at The Society for Psychical Research—the foremost Spiritualist society in London, perhaps in all of England.

However did they hear of me? she wondered, for during the past few years, she had gone out of her way to remain autonomous and free of the influence or control of any church or organization. And generally, resisting all labels and stereotypes normally associated with "mediumship," she had gone about her work quietly and independently. She could not imagine, therefore, why she had received such an invitation. With some misapprehension, she dialed the telephone number of the Society and scheduled an appointment to audition within the week.

"Perhaps such an experience would be good for me. It might not be so bad—working for such a prestigious organization," she told Glyn halfheartedly, trying to convince herself.

"I'm sorry, love," he had said in reply. "I just can't see you working for anybody else—and especially that stuffy, snobbish group. Nonetheless, I wish you good luck at your audition."

"Thanks a lot," Katherine murmured wryly.

In the meantime, Katherine could not help but wonder why she had received the invitation or what was in store for her. She had always been so certain that she was meant to serve as a leader, stand at the helm of an avantgarde organization of her own creation and under her management and jurisdiction. Frankly, she could not imagine herself working for someone else at this phase of her career.

Now, fifty-one years old, Katherine weighed the alternatives. She knew that Trevor and Doris would gladly take her back as a partner in the business, but although the money was tempting, she knew that she could never return to business. Her heart and soul were dedicated to the work, and she no longer wished to do anything else. Furthermore, she began to realize now that she was more curious than ever to discover the truths of life—to find out more about herself and her true purpose and identity.

Although the Spirit Beings had provided satisfactory answers to her questions so many years ago, she now yearned for an even greater, richer, deeper knowledge and understanding. "Who am I? From whence came I? Whither will I go after death?" were the questions to which she longed for answers. Although she had experienced intimately every type and phase of mediumship, and although she had received constant proof of life's continuity following death, she had recently recognized that these experiences had not brought her any closer to a genuine understanding of either herself or her Creator. Powerfully, sincerely, she yearned, hungered to know God. Although she had learned an enormous amount about life and human nature and herself as a result of her mediumship, she had begun to realize that mediumship was but one small, relatively insignificant step toward realizing one's true potential. Now, she longed to come into real contact/communion with her Creator, her Father, and Mother God. "Seek and ye shall find; ask and ye shall receive; knock and the door shall open," she repeated, longing above all else to know, to directly experience God.

In fact, most of these ideas remained unformed, unexpressed, inchoate; she was not yet able to translate such deep, complex, and compelling feelings into words. At present, she was consciously aware only that she was maturing, and that major changes—both internal and external—were taking place. Now, upon careful scrutiny of the invitation she had received from The Society for Psychical Research, she was once again forced to marvel at the careful guidance and direction she had received throughout her entire life.

How could I be so silly as to doubt the future? she wondered, feeling genuinely ashamed of her lack of faith. *Why, it's obvious that I have been guided every step of the way right up until the present moment. And I know that I shall be carefully guided the rest of the way. And although I've certainly had my share of sorrows and difficulties, I have never truly been disappointed in the past. I have learned from everything I've done—failures as well as so-called successes.*

And, as she looked out from the living room window of her Pendennis apartment onto the pretty residential street below, she smiled with pleasure. With renewed confidence and vigor, she said aloud—almost as an oath—" I know that no matter how bleak things may appear, I shall never be disappointed in the future. I shall never fail life, nor shall it ever fail me."

CHAPTER 44

Wood Court

In the summer of 1949 Katherine and Cora had visited Wood Court on their way from Newport to London. They had stopped at the fashionable resort and New Thought Center for a few days, but the beauty and peacefulness of the spot had deeply impressed them and had not easily been forgotten. The New Thought movement originated in the 1830s with roots in United States and England. It was characterized by creative visualization, the law of attraction, affirmative prayer, and higher consciousness. It was labeled by psychologist and philosopher William James as "the religion of healthy mindedness."

Situated on thirty-three acres of lovely wooded land in Cobham, Surrey (only half an hour's drive from the heart of London), Wood Court was said to have belonged to former Prime Minister Neville Chamberlain. The residence—a great stone structure of imposing beauty—was elegant and immense, and yet seemed completely attuned to the surrounding landscape, which included gentle slopes, velvet green lawns, a charming rose garden, quiet woods, and a small stream that picturesquely wove its way in and out of the rolling hills. In addition, the property contained numerous pretty cottages that had, in the past, obviously been used as servants' quarters but were now employed as guest houses for visiting members of the staff. As Katherine walked across the neatly trimmed lawn toward the stream, she was delighted by the natural beauty and serenity of her surroundings.

"One could not imagine a more ideal spot for a New Thought Center," she had whispered to Cora, her gaze taking in the distant hills, pleasant meadows, and the clusters of shade trees. "In fact, it's exactly the sort of place I would choose for my work. "

It was during this visit that Katherine had received from Dr. and Mrs. Roberts, (Wood Court's present owners and proprietors), a standing invitation to join their staff. "You would be a marvelous addition, Mrs. Hayward," stated Dr. Roberts warmly. "I've seen quite a lot of your work, and you would fit in beautifully. Why, we should make use of all of your wonderful gifts here, Mrs. Hayward, and recompense you well."

"I'm afraid that I can't accept your kind offer at the present time. You see, I am currently running my own organization as well as lecturing all over England. But, perhaps someday in the future, I will be able to come here to work. Frankly, I can't think of a more delightful atmosphere in which to share our gifts. You are very blessed."

"We are indeed," admitted Mrs. Roberts.

"Do you know," Katherine had exclaimed suddenly, "that I should be most surprised if you both remain here at Wood Court. In fact, I should say that by the time of my next visit here, both of you will have sold this property and will be in another part of England altogether."

"Is that so?" Dr. Roberts queried in a polite voice.

"Yes," replied Katherine. "See if I'm right, won't you? I believe that you will decide to sell Wood Court within the year."

"Indeed," Mrs. Roberts had responded condescendingly. "Well then, Mrs. Hayward, you are a welcome guest here at Wood Court or at any other center we may establish. We should be pleased to have you on our team wherever we find ourselves."

Although she had been flattered by their generous offer, she refused. Graciously, she demurred, volunteering to serve as a guest speaker whenever the opportunity arose. "We should be pleased to have you under any circumstances," Dr. Roberts had smiled warmly, enthusiastically shaking her hand.

In the meantime, during her brief stay at the New Thought Center, Katherine devoted a good portion of her time examining its structure—internal and external—interviewing its patrons and staff members. It seemed that one came to Wood Court for many reasons but predominantly for healing, recuperation, a holiday, or for further study in such diverse New Thought areas as mind-science, hypnotism, mediumship, psychic development, healing, spiritual unfoldment, astrology, numerology, radionics, and yoga. Seemingly, Wood Court had something for everyone interested in New Thought.

Katherine left Wood Court feeling wonderfully refreshed and revitalized and with the strong desire to model any future center of her own along its lines. Furthermore, she felt that it would not be long before she herself would return to Wood Court. *Perhaps for further personal study,* she speculated. For she personally had, for some time, desired to study formally those areas of metaphysics and parapsychology that the Spirit Beings had advised her not to study so many years ago. In the past, they had quite justifiably requested that she and her family avoid reading or studying in order to receive their instruction undiluted or distorted by the opinions of others.

"You must receive our teachings first," she recalled Dr. Evans' words so many years ago. "Then in later years, you may read and study whatever and however much you wish." Now, in addition to the formal study of metaphysics, Katherine began to seriously consider the possibility of obtaining a university degree and becoming a psychologist. *As a means of enhancing my credibility with the public,* she had thought.

At any rate, Katherine had, at frequent intervals following her visit to Wood Court, remembered the New Thought Center with fondness. And recently, in light of her failure to establish a successful center of her own, she had begun to seriously consider the possibility of accepting Dr. Roberts' frequent invitations to join Wood Court's staff. *Perhaps I should telephone Dr. Roberts and advise him as to my availability and interest in a position. After all, what have I got to lose?*

And, finally, one crisp, clear September afternoon, only several days after receiving the invitation to audition for The Society for Psychical Research, Katherine managed to locate Dr. Roberts' telephone number that she had scribbled in an old diary and decided to ring him up.

"My God!" she exclaimed suddenly as she began to dial his number. "I predicted that he and his wife would leave Wood Court within the year. I wonder if they are still there? Oh, dear, it would be too embarrassing if he was still there after all and I had been wrong. That certainly would raise grave doubts regarding my gifts. On the other hand, if I can't rely upon my own abilities, by now, I don't deserve to have them! I will be courageous and contact Wood Court regardless of Dr. Roberts' whereabouts or any faulty mediumship on my part."

She nearly laughed aloud. When, after dialing his number, she heard the voice of an elderly gentleman announce that Dr. Roberts and his wife were no longer at Wood Court, that they had sold the property, and that the center was now under new management. "It is my own sister, Mrs. Liebie Pugh, who purchased the estate from Dr. Roberts," the gentleman was saying. "Would you like to speak with her?"

"Oh, no, I don't believe so," was Katherine's response, but the older man did not appear to have heard her. He did not reply, and there was a long silence at the other end of the line. Just as she was debating whether to hang up and forget the whole incident, she heard the rustling noises of someone picking up the receiver at the other end, and she decided to remain on the line after all. *I'll briefly explain what has happened and then get off*, she planned. She had not been at all prepared for the soft, gentile, unmistakably aristocratic voice of a woman whom Katherine guessed immediately to be her own age or perhaps a little older.

"Good day. My name is Liebie Pugh. May I be of assistance to you?" the lovely voice was saying. Katherine noticed that it was a cultured voice, and that it was slightly tremulous.

"Why, no. I don't believe so," Katherine stammered politely. "You see, I am an acquaintance—well, really a coworker, you might say—of Dr. Roberts, the former owner of Wood Court. And, well, you see, Dr. Roberts offered me a position on his staff, which, frankly, I had been seriously considering. I have only just this moment learned from your brother that Dr. Roberts is no longer at Wood Court."

"Oh, I see," murmured Mrs. Pugh regretfully. "Yes, I have only recently purchased Wood Court, and have been here only for a few months. Are you still interested in a position on Wood Court's staff?" she inquired.

"Well, I don't really know," murmured Katherine. "Is it still functioning as it was under Dr. Roberts' direction?"

"I'm afraid I don't know exactly," replied Liebie uncertainly. "I'm afraid I don't know very much about the manner in which he managed the Center."

"Oh, I see," returned Katherine. "But it is still a New Thought Center?"

"Oh, yes, indeed it is. You are interested, then, in Dr. Roberts' work, are you?" Liebie was saying slowly, as though thinking aloud. "Are you by any chance interested as well in the work of Yogananda?" Now, the telephone connection was not as clear as either one would have wished, and Katherine mistakenly thought Liebie was referring to the great man, Mahatma Gandhi, who had led India's struggle for independence through nonviolence, and, accordingly, she replied.

"Oh, yes, I am deeply interested in his work. Why he is one of the most remarkable men of our times."

"Oh, I'm so glad. For he is one of my own personal heroes, and has set such a great example for all of us," Liebie was saying, obviously pleased to find someone who shared her opinion. "Well, my dear, I do feel that you and I should get together. Are you by any chance free on Monday afternoon—say at 4 o'clock? I should be most happy to have you visit me here at Wood Court. We could share our views at that time."

Not at all certain that she ever wanted to meet with Liebie Pugh, Katherine hesitated, and Mrs. Pugh chose to regard her silence as an acceptance to her invitation. "Well, my dear, it has been lovely speaking with you. Thank you for ringing us up. And I shall look forward to our meeting on Monday. Good day."

And, to her amazement, before she had an opportunity to speak again, Mrs. Pugh had hung up. Katherine listened to the click of the receiver, too dazed to utter a sound. Several minutes later, after recovering her senses, she began to hunt for her appointment book. With amusement, she noticed that her audition at The Society for Psychical Research was on the same day she had just inadvertently scheduled her appointment with Mrs. Pugh. *It's too funny*, she thought to herself, and began to laugh aloud. *No promise of a job for months, and then two prospective positions on the same day. I wonder what it's all about.*

She did not have to wait long to find out. Monday arrived cool and clear with the delightful scent and feel of autumn in the air. She wore a navy blue light woolen dress that framed her lovely figure becomingly and matching high-heeled slippers, a long strand of pearls with matching pearl studs at her ears, and she looked rich and elegant. "Anything but what I am," she murmured in wry good humor, as she stared at her reflection in the mirror. Grabbing her matching leather handbag and camel hair coat, she was soon out the door and on her way from Pendennis to the headquarters of The Society for Psychical Research. She was glad that she had decided to take a bus into town from Streatham, for the journey enabled her to relax somewhat and to ruminate as to the manner in which she had come to receive an invitation from the prestigious society that boasted the finest minds and mediums involved in the New Thought work.. It suddenly occurred to her that it was on the occasion that she had been required to substitute at the last minute for the great physical medium, Joseph Benjamin, that one of the heads of The Society for Psychical Research had approached her.

"Your work is exceptional, Mrs. Hayward. Why have I not seen you before?" the old gentleman had asked. "I should like to see more of your work and I should very much like my associates to see you. You have a lot to give to the world, Mrs. Hayward. You should be giving it."

"I am giving it," she felt like saying, "in my own way, that is." But she merely bit her lip and smiled. She was accustomed to such flattery, and only rarely did it affect her. She had never sought a national or international reputation. She had been content to serve in her own way—free from outside domination or influence. And to the extent to which she had been able, she had resisted affiliations with the numerous prestigious organizations that had expressed interest in her abilities. As a guest speaker, she had seen far too many demonstrations of pettiness, divisiveness, snobbery, and cliquishness among the members of such societies and she had, therefore, for as long as she could remember, desired to remain independent "free of all the rubbish," as she viewed it. Now, as the bus drew close to the street upon which the society's headquarters were situated, Katherine had serious misgivings about the interview, finally deciding that *as I've come this far, I may as well see the bloomin' thing through all the way.*

She entered a great white stone structure and approached the receptionist.

"Please have a seat. The committee will be with you in just a few minutes," advised a disagreeable-looking young man with thin lips and a pasty white complexion, and a Cambridge accent of which he was obviously aware and proud.

"Thank you," murmured Katherine politely, taking the opportunity to study her surroundings. Her appointment had been scheduled for 11:00 a.m., and she had arrived at 10:45 a.m. The small antechamber was terribly warm and uncomfortable, and Katherine fidgeted in her seat. She waited and waited, growing more irritated and impatient by the moment. *Who do they think they are to keep me waiting in this manner? After all, my time is valuable. I really cannot afford to waste any further time waiting,* she had been thinking.

Finally, she rose, walked over to the desk at which the young man was seated, and addressed him as pleasantly as she could under the circumstances. "My appointment was for 11:00 a.m. It is now half past eleven. And I am afraid that I cannot afford to wait any longer. I have another commitment following this one requiring me to travel to the opposite end of London."

"What is your name?" inquired the young man with obvious disinterest.

"Mrs. Katherine Hayward," she replied somewhat haughtily.

"And did you request an interview with us, Mrs. Hayward?"

"Indeed, I did not. As a matter of fact, I received a written invitation from your Society requesting an interview with me. You may examine it if you wish. I have it right here with me." She had already begun to grope through her handbag.

"Oh, that really isn't necessary, Mrs. Hayworth."

"Hayward," she corrected him.

"Right," he said. "I shall notify the committee of your difficulty."

"It is not my difficulty, it is yours," she had begun but it was too late. The young man had already risen from his desk and was on his way into the meeting room. He emerged several minutes later with an air of triumph.

"You may go in now," Mrs. Hapworth," he smirked.

"Hayward," she reminded him once more. But he did not seem to hear.

"Follow me," he said with an insincere smile. And taking a deep breath, she silently followed him into the conference room. Frankly, no matter how grave had been her reservations regarding the procedure, she had not been prepared for what she found—either the harsh, austere setting or the grim, lifeless faces of the thirty-odd committee members who sat in rows of five in front of a small platform. As she strode purposefully through the room and in front of the committee members, she wondered dazedly how many gifted mediums in desperate need of a job had passed this way before her and had been expected to demonstrate their abilities in such a somber atmosphere.

It's no good. I can't do it, she thought suddenly, as she stood before the group. *It's simply no use. I could never sacrifice my own freedom to work in such a place—I'd rather starve. No, I know now that this is not for me.* All these thoughts raced through her mind as an elderly white-haired gentleman reviewed her background and introduced her to the rest of the committee. After he had finished his introduction, he smiled condescendingly. "And now, Mrs. Hayward, if you would be so kind, please give the committee a demonstration of your abilities."

"With pleasure," smiled Katherine. But just as she was about to begin, she felt compelled to speak. With customary forthrightness, she addressed the group. "Ladies and gentlemen, I wish to express my gratitude to you for inviting me to appear before you this morning. But I must confess that I have already made my decision regarding our future association. You see, I could not possibly work in so sterile and solemn and uncomfortable atmosphere as that which I find here."

She heard someone gasp aloud at her words, but she continued undaunted. "You must believe me that I did not know—until I set foot into this room—that this was so. For surely, I would not have wished to waste either your precious time or my own. But now that I am here amongst you, I feel that each one of you would benefit from hearing from the perspective of an auditioning medium. For you see, as the head of countless development circles and several centers, I have learned a great deal about mediums in addition to being one myself. And I must assure you that the atmosphere you have established here is in no way conducive to the successful demonstration of any facet of mediumship. I assure you that even the greatest mediums whose abilities you may have witnessed here in this room have not been fairly represented, and I would speculate that you have seen only a fraction of their true potential. Virtually every medium I have ever known is acutely sensitive and receives thoughts, feelings, and impressions not normally perceived by the 'average' human being. He is, therefore, far more sensitive, as well, to his environment. And, in such a cold, formal atmosphere, he cannot function nearly so successfully as he can in a friendlier more casual environment.

"From my own personal experience, I have found it most beneficial to audition mediums in their own environment where they are most relaxed and receptive. I truly hope that I have not offended any of you or your organization—of which I have heard only that which is highly favorable. But I truly feel that the medium must be viewed as an artist and respected as a highly unique individual. You must become more attuned to the needs of such people, and you must establish different criteria in terms of assessing the talents of such men and women who are able to foretell the future and produce physical phenomena of such a nature that it proves life's continuity, man's immortality, to numberless human beings. In short, learn to value the medium for the vast resource he or she really is, and cultivate the best rather than the worst of their abilities.

"And now, if you will permit me, I would like to demonstrate my own abilities for this group just so you know that I am speaking from personal experience." And from hereon, Katherine described the past and predicted the future with astounding accuracy for several members of the committee, continuing until she felt thoroughly satisfied that her gifts had been fairly represented. When she had finished, she smiled graciously, thanked the committee for their forbearance, and bade them farewell. "You've been most kind and generous," she told the stunned group. And, with no further fanfare, she calmly stepped down from the platform and strode out of the room. She never looked back.

And, suppressing a strong desire to laugh aloud, she made her way past the reception desk, through the narrow hallway, and down several steps to the foyer. Once on the street, Katherine breathed an enormous sigh of relief. "Well, that's that," she sighed, grateful that the ordeal was finally over. It was a glorious autumn day, the sun shining through a clear cerulean sky, and Katherine decided to walk through Knightsbridge to Victoria Station. She had always loved London—felt at home here—and she took particular delight from her surroundings this afternoon.

As she strolled through the busy streets, she reviewed the events of the morning. Certainly, no one had been more surprised than she by the manner in which she had behaved at the Society. In the back of her mind, she had rather hoped that the outcome of her audition would have resulted in a job offer at the prestigious institution. Now, obviously such an offer was out of the question. Now, she seriously questioned the wisdom of traveling all the way to Cobham, Surrey, to meet with Liebie Pugh at the Wood Court Hotel. *It seems a great waste of time*, she thought to herself in anticipation of the journey by bus. But, after stopping for a small luncheon, she found herself walking briskly in the direction of the station and mentally preparing for her interview with Mrs. Pugh, and although she had been disinterested and disinclined to make the journey, she now felt compelled to do so.

CHAPTER 45

Liebie Pugh

＿ℴ

SHE ARRIVED AT WOOD COURT at ten minutes before four o'clock—ten minutes before the time she had been scheduled to meet with Mrs. Pugh. A young male secretary advised her to "please wait just a moment." Now, as she relaxed in the small room outside Mrs. Pugh's office, Katherine studied her surroundings with a contented air. *I like this place. There's something so peaceful, so calming about it.* Her gaze took in the view from the window which consisted of beautiful rolling hills and the trees that were now changing into brilliant color. She sniffed the fresh country air with delight and once again she was as deeply impressed with the spot as she had been during her first visit here over a year ago. Lost in thought, she did not hear the sounds of Mrs. Pugh's footsteps in the corridor or the door open softly.

"Lovely, isn't it?" said Liebie Pugh in her soft, aristocratic voice, her gaze following Katherine's. Katherine started at the sound of the strange voice, then turned to face the owner and proprietor of Wood Court. She was astonished by what she saw. For it was immediately apparent that Liebie Pugh was unlike anyone she had ever met.

Liebie was tall and slender, with straight mahogany-colored hair closely cropped to the head like a man's, a high forehead and cheekbones, a creamy complexion, handsome nose, sensitive mouth, and beautiful, expressive dark eyes that bore a kindly expression. Liebie's appearance was not only unconventional but arresting and unforgettable. It was obvious that Liebie had no interest whatsoever in dressing for any purpose other than comfort. She wore a baggy taupe woolen skirt, a deep blue woolen turtleneck sweater, and a light blue cardigan with white silken gloves on her hands and funny fur-lined boots, so odd that Katherine was forced to smile in spite of herself. *She is definitely an original*, thought Katherine, not suspecting that Liebie had drawn the same conclusion about her.

After only a brief exchange, Liebie had been aware that Katherine Hayward was no ordinary woman. *Why she's both charming and uncommonly intelligent. And her candor is most refreshing*, thought Liebie. *And I cannot help but, feel that she belongs here with me at Wood Court.* Nor could Liebie dismiss the odd feeling that Katherine's presence there was very much needed.

"Let us continue our conversation in my private apartment where we can be more comfortable," suggested Liebie, not long after the two had introduced themselves.

"As you wish," agreed Katherine, happy to oblige. She followed Liebie through the maze of corridors and stairways that led to her quarters, her admiration for both Wood Court and its present owner increasing by the moment. The residence was every bit as beautiful and luxurious as she had remembered it.

Throughout their conversation, Katherine observed Liebie closely, aware that she was in the presence of an extraordinary human being. Liebie's carriage and bearing were regal; her manner gentle and refined, yet for one of such obvious wealth and breeding, Liebie displayed a surprising lack of snobbishness and was unexpectedly open and unaffected. But it was Liebie's poise—her quiet strength and dignity, the lovely peacefulness that she radiated—that affected Katherine most deeply. Her features shone with spiritual light, purity, and kindness of heart; her eyes were full of trust, wisdom, and compassion. With a sudden gasp, Katherine realized that she and Liebie had been destined to come together and that Liebie Pugh was the most enlightened and highly spiritually evolved people she had ever met.

Almost as astonishing as Liebie's physical appearance were her living quarters. For on the second floor, in the midst of the luxurious elegance of the rest of the rooms of the palatial residence, Liebie's apartment was small, austere, and sparsely furnished. Furthermore, the stark, sterile atmosphere of a hospital pervaded the suite, for there were no richly woven rugs or tapestries, no tantalizing bibelots or objets d'art to relieve the monotony of the hardwood floors, oak dados and trim, and pale draperies. The walls were white, the rooms immaculate, and the furnishings clean and simple in design and purely functional. Frankly, Katherine found the atmosphere both disconcerting and repugnant. *Why would anyone choose to live in such a manner?* she wondered, wrinkling her nose in distaste. Liebie had impressed her as an artist, and Katherine could not imagine why one of such rare refinement, breeding, and artistic ability would willingly live in such a starkly simple off-putting manner.

Katherine was further surprised when Liebie, seated on the long, pale beige sofa, failed to remove the spotless white gloves she had been wearing and had continued to speak completely oblivious to the impact that she and her quarters were having upon her guest.

"Now, my dear, please do make yourself comfortable," Liebie was saying. And, at her words, Katherine settled back in one of the white, modern armchairs. "May I get you a cup of tea?" asked Liebie politely.

"That would be lovely," smiled Katherine. And Liebie, still wearing the white gloves, picked up the house telephone and dialed one of the servants and requested tea for two.

"Thank you," she had murmured to whoever had responded to her call, with sincerity, then hung up the phone.

"Now then," Liebie began, looking Katherine directly in the eyes. "You must be wondering how it is that I have come to own and manage Wood Court."

"Why, yes, as a matter of fact I have been rather curious. You see, I am familiar—at least by name—with most of the New Thought societies and their leaders in England. And although you are running this great center, I had never heard your name before last week."

"Quite so," murmured Liebie, observing Katherine with genuine friendliness and admiration. "I have always been deeply interested in philosophy—particularly religious philosophy. During my adolescence, I investigated nearly all the major world religions and then some. I became deeply interested in the writing of Mary Baker Eddy and in the religion she established known as Christian Science, but also continued to explore many other religions as well. I must say, however, that it was through Christian Science that I became acutely aware of the enormous power of the human mind. All through these years of intense research, I became enamored of many ideas and began to synthesize what I viewed as the best concepts and principles and to formulate them into my own religious system, or way of life. I have never been able to accept or adhere to any one formalized religious system, but, rather, have embraced the best of all of them.

"At any rate—" she was interrupted by gentle knocking at the door. "Please come in," she called out. A pretty young serving girl—whom Katherine guessed to be about nineteen or twenty—with light blonde hair and a rosy complexion, appeared at the door with a tray brimming with tea, biscuits and jams, cream, and scones.

"Here you are, Mrs. Pugh," she said, setting the tray down on the large square oak coffee table.

"Thank you, my dear. We will serve ourselves."

"As you wish," the girl murmured politely, and turned and left the room. And Katherine watched as Liebie, still wearing the white gloves, systematically arranged the cups, saucers, and silver and poured the tea.

"Now then, where were we?" she asked, after the two were comfortably fixed with refreshment. "Ah, yes. I was telling you a bit of my background. I married at an early age, and as both my husband and I came from wealthy families, I was able to devote my time both to my research and my art. You see, I am a sculptress by profession. I have spent most of my adult life searching for and investigating the Truth. I have been told by so-called masters on this plane as well as the Other Side that I am highly intuitive and spiritually evolved and would become a great spiritual teacher."

I thought so, Katherine mused—now also realizing that being a sculptress must be the reason she continually wears those absurd white gloves.

"During the latter years of my husband's life," Liebie continued, "he became severely arthritic, consumed with pain and confined to a wheelchair. But, shortly before he died, he came into contact with a remarkable healer who eased his pain to a great degree and assisted him in making the transition to the next world peaceful, nearly painless. Do you know that for a while, under the healer's careful guidance, my husband's health actually improved to such an extent that we thought he might fully recover? But obviously this was not meant to be. Even my husband was aware that he was not meant to live longer. Yet he was so profoundly grateful to the healer for his wonderful assistance that he volunteered to stand as guarantor for the New Thought Center the healer had informed us he was going to purchase. This center was known as the Wood Court Hotel.

"To make a long story very short, our 'healer' turned out to be a bit of a crook. After we signed as guarantors, he went bankrupt, disappeared for a while, then left the country and left my husband and myself as the inadvertent owners of this enormous estate. Legally, we were now required to assume full financial responsibility and ownership of the property, for we never heard from the healer again. And although we could have sold Wood Court, my husband and I decided to hold onto it for a while and to maintain the healing center that our healing "acquaintance" had intended to develop.

"Shortly after we moved here, my husband became terribly ill and required extensive medical treatment and twenty-four-hour supervision. My husband lingered between life and death for several months in this manner, and, as a result of some disastrous business transactions, the acquisition of Wood Court, and the costly medical attention, our financial resources were almost virtually depleted. Although I still own various properties throughout the country, I am afraid that my present financial circumstances make it impossible to manage Wood Court in the manner I would have wished. Nonetheless, it is a lovely spot, and I am certain that it can serve as a center of inspiration, healing, and illumination for those who are drawn to us. It has been only two and a half months since my husband's passing away and, currently, I am in the process of reorganizing and restaffing Wood Court. But it is a difficult process for, unfortunately, I know very little about business, and I am afraid I know even less about running an organization. I only know that I wish to gather together the finest available talent in our field and develop a research center that might serve as a prototype for all others in New Thought."

"I see," said Katherine, after Liebie had finished. "In other words, you wish to make Wood Court the very finest of New Thought Centers."

"Exactly," said Liebie, eyeing Katherine appreciatively.

Why is it that I'm so drawn to her? wondered Katherine, . *After all, we're not at all alike. And yet, I really do feel somehow that we belong together, that our work is linked together.*

"Now, *you* must tell me all about yourself," said Liebie with a smile. And beginning with a description of the out-of-the-body experience she had at the age of seven, Katherine spoke of her clairvoyance and mediumistic abilities, the communications with the Spirit Beings at age twenty, and the public work that she had been doing right up until the present time. It was nearly seven when Katherine finished. Glancing at her watch, she apologized for taking so much of Liebie's time.

"I am so sorry for rattling on that way. It's terribly late and I'm afraid I must be going."

"But won't you do me the honor of joining me for dinner?" Liebie asked gently.

"Oh, I'm afraid I couldn't . . .," Katherine protested, thinking of the journey back to London which she dreaded to make late at night.

As though reading her thoughts, Liebie smiled warmly and said, "I would be honored if you would spend the night here at Wood Court as my guest."

"Oh!" Katherine exclaimed, startled by the generous offer. *Say yes!* something inside her said, and she found herself accepting Liebie's invitation.

Dinner was a pleasant affair, and Katherine was introduced to several members of the staff who were presently residing on the premises. She was particularly impressed by a handsome healer and radionics expert, Paul Flemming, who spoke with enthusiasm of holistic medicine. "One must not isolate a diseased organ from the rest of the body and attempt to treat it as a separate unit. Rather, we must begin to see the body, mind, and emotions as one great organism—one unit working together—and attempt to diagnose and treat the entire being rather than one small segment," he had informed Katherine. And, later on in the evening, he had demonstrated the use of an instrument with calibrated dials that enabled him to measure disease reactions and intensities in his patients.

"Accepting that all life is energy operating at different rates of vibration, radionics sees organs, diseases, and remedies as having their own particular frequency or vibration," Paul told her. "These factors can be expressed in numerical value and are known in radionics as 'rates'; hence the calibrated dials of the radionics instruments upon which the frequencies or rates can be placed for diagnostic or treatment purposes. Each life form has its own electromagnetic field which, if distorted to a certain degree, will result in disease of the organism."

"Is it not true that ESP, or extrasensory perception, also plays a critical role in your radionics?" asked Katherine.

"Indeed, that's quite true—much as a dowser detects the location of water or gold or whatever he might be searching for by means of his ESP so does the radionics practitioner."

"Fascinating," murmured Katherine. And soon she, Paul, and Liebie were chattering away as comfortably as old friends. Upon hearing of Katherine's plan to return to London the following day, Paul was troubled.

"But surely you can stay with us another day?" he pleaded, his black eyes caressing her figure so that she turned crimson under his scrutiny.

"Yes," agreed Liebie, "please do stay on with us. Somehow I can't help but feel that the three of us belong here together."

"Very well," Katherine acquiesced, feeling the truthfulness of Liebie's words. *Somehow we do belong together,* she felt in her heart.

Katherine spent three days at the New Thought Center before returning to London. Before departing, she had agreed to consider Liebie's proposal that she assist her as the co-director of Wood Court.

"Do say yes, my dear," urged Liebie.

But Katherine only smiled and said, "I shall have to carefully think it over Liebie. I will let you know my decision as soon as possible."

"See you soon," whispered Paul, his eyes laughing, as he helped her into the waiting taxi that would drive her back to London. She did not reply.

Although Liebie could not afford to pay her very much, Katherine decided to accept her offer. Shortly after their initial meeting, then, Katherine joined Liebie Pugh as co-director of Wood Court. Katherine made it perfectly clear from the onset that her personal freedom was of critical importance to her, and the she must be free to come and go as she pleased.

"You see, I must have leave to visit my friends and family whenever it is necessary. Weekends and holidays are reserved for my dear friends, Trevor and Doris in Newport." But Liebie seemed to understand Katherine, her nature, and her strong yearning for freedom and autonomy and agreed to all of her demands upon hiring her.

"As you wish, my dear," was all that Liebie said in conjunction with the numerous requests Katherine had outlined.

Although Katherine insisted upon retaining her Pendennis apartment, she quickly discovered that the vast majority of her time was being spent at Wood Court. Within several months of her arrival at the New Thought Center, she had become indispensable to Liebie Pugh. It was she who organized and restructured the budget and all financial aspects of the center, thereby enabling Liebie to concentrate upon the administrative and creative aspects of running a large center. With Katherine's assistance, Wood Court soon became a viable money-making business enterprise in addition to serving as a center for healing and research and for both spiritual and psychic research and development.

In the meantime, Katherine and Liebie became close friends as well as coworkers, and a deep bond was established between them. Prior to Katherine's appearance in her life, Liebie had been lonely, isolated, and insulated from the rest of the world. No one but Katherine had been able to penetrate the veneer of reserved politeness, for Liebie had deliberately chosen to remain removed and remote. It was Katherine who taught Liebie to mix with all types of people.

"You have so much to give to the world," Katherine had informed her surprised friend. "You will touch thousands, perhaps millions of people through your work. You must learn to be among the people—as one of them—not isolated and withdrawn in your own private studio or quarters. Get rid of your white gloves, they are odd and off-putting. Take some interest in your appearance. You must meet and greet the public on their own terms," Katherine persuaded her coworker. And soon, to the astonishment of the entire staff of Wood Court, Liebie—distant and forbidding to so many—learned to socialize, entertain, and belong.

"No one would have dared to say the things you have—to be so blunt with me," Liebie confessed one day.

"I know," agreed Katherine. "That's why we're together—to learn from one another."

"I am so glad you've come—so grateful to you," admitted Liebie. "I feel that we will do great work together."

"So do I," said Katherine, smiling warmly at her new friend.

Once Wood Court was running smoothly, Katherine began to tire of the responsibilities that had fallen on her shoulders. After all, she was anxious to continue her own work and research. And one evening, while she and Liebie were sitting quietly together in the peace of the night, Katherine went into a trance-like state and spoke under the influence of her spirit guide Hassan and addressed Liebie:

The invisible is to become visible. Picture for a split second all who have gone beyond your sight. Picture the marvel of that world, with special thought of the great ones of your Earth—the saints, sages, scientists, artists, masters— all becoming able to manifest themselves to you—to show themselves so that you may seem them, hear them, touch them, spend time with them learning of the world the inhabit. You would be able to understand and appreciate the glory of their life, the great power of the power of thought, the brilliance and beauty of the actuality of spiritual existence—all beyond your present conception—far beyond. But all to be revealed to you in the near future.

From hereon Katherine is to be trained by you in order to be a vehicle for the highest possible form of mediumship, so that the highest, purest teachings

may be delivered through her to humankind. Eventually your training and work together will enable the most highly evolved beings to manifest visibly, to ordinary humanity, apart from the normal visitations and communications of the typical séance room. You two and the radionics practitioner whom you call Paul will sit together as often as possible for further psychic development and unfoldment. You will establish a special room—a sanctuary—specifically designed for the purpose of the aforementioned. Here, you will build a formation of gradually solidifying spiritual substance in which the great ones can manifest themselves and communicate through each of you in accordance with your own unique gifts, and the needs of the moment.

Shortly after this experience, Katherine, Paul, and Liebie referring to themselves as the "inner trio," began to sit regularly for development as mediums capable of manifesting the highest and the finest spiritual teachers. Frequently, they sat twice daily, and after some months, in accordance with the specific instructions of Katherine's Spirit Guides, several more members were added to the group until there were six all together.

In March 1953, the "Gold Room" was established in one of the charming cottages on the property, wherein the group persistently worked for the development of what Katherine called "the perfect materialization." As this work expanded, Katherine's interest in the project intensified and she persuaded Liebie to write to the finest physical mediums in the country and recruit their cooperation in this endeavor. As Liebie had become equally absorbed in the remarkable undertaking, she complied. And soon, many of the greatest physical mediums as well as sitters (participants who were spiritual advanced and whose physical and emotional support was beneficial to the medium) had been brought together to create the perfect materialization of a highly spiritually evolved being.

Not since the early six-month period of communications with the Spirit Beings nearly thirty-four years ago had Katherine been so excited or enthusiastic about a project. Although she continued to assist Liebie in the daily operation of the hotel, her heart was in the work of establishing a materialization that could be witnessed by anyone, at any time in any place and regardless of the skepticism or religious views of these witnesses. In time she began to relegate her own administrative and financial responsibilities to others on the staff upon whom she and Liebie had grown to trust and rely, and she devoted the vast majority of her time and energy toward the remarkable work that took place in the "Gold Room."

What appeared to be an amazing series of coincidences had been responsible for the appearance at Wood Court of a number of gifted mediums, among them a young man named Jim Hutchins, who possessed the gift of direct voice, whereby ectoplasm would be drawn from the mucous membranes of the medium's throat and nasal organs and used to create a materialized larynx and apparatus of speech and that could speak from anywhere in the room or through a trumpet that floated through the air. After many months of diligent work, Jim was producing materializations of a fine caliber, and Katherine, justifiably proud and pleased with the results of her experimentation, was certain that her goal was within reach.

Unfortunately, when it seemed that Jim's work was ready for the public's scrutiny, internal difficulties arose in the group in the form of bitter divisiveness and dissension. Neither Liebie nor Katherine had been prepared for the pettiness, jealousy, and suspicion that arose among the mediums who were envious of Jim's success and desirous of receiving recognition for their own work. First shocked, then appalled, Katherine next experienced one of the deepest disappointments she could remember in a lifetime that had been full of sadness, hurts, losses, and sorrows. She could not believe that such pettiness would impede the progress of so important a discovery. Sadly she became aware, little by little, that humankind was not yet ready to receive such a revelation. *They really are like naughty children*, she thought ruefully of her coworkers and humanity as a whole. *I know of no choice but to abandon the project for the present time.*

By 1954, Katherine was ready to leave Wood Court and to move on. Weary and disillusioned, she was determined to devote the remainder of her life toward teaching those who were ready and receptive toward her own personal research into the various "-isms," as she called the other religions. Beyond a shadow of a doubt, she had learned an enormous amount at Wood Court and through

Liebie. In truth, Katherine had never before known a human being so kind, compassionate, patient, generous, and wise as Liebie Pugh.

She is a great teacher, thought Katherine, genuinely grateful for having been privileged enough to share the past years with her. In times of trial and tribulation, financial, physical, and emotional pressures, Liebie had remained calm, gentle, loving, and in possession of great strength and deep faith. Everyone adored her, the staff as well as visitors, for Liebie never judged or criticized. *She's only ever offered loved everyone*, marveled Katherine, at the equilibrium and poise in which Liebie dealt with life. *She has been a great teacher for me.*

"It's time for me to move on," Katherine explained gently one rainy spring afternoon, as the two gathered for tea in the sitting room.

"What do you mean, dear?" asked Liebie in her tremulous voice, hardly daring to look into Katherine's eyes. Katherine had become her dearest friend, her closest companion in the world, and she simply could not bear for her to leave.

"I mean, I cannot spend any further time here at Wood Court," said Katherine simply in a quiet voice. "I want to travel, see the world, study on my own. I believe that I've done all I can here." The hurt and disappointment over the Gold Room failure were evident in her voice. Tears rose to Liebie's eyes, as she recalled the years of diligent work and enormous effort and sacrifice that had been dedicated toward the Gold Room work, but she held them back.

"Do you know something? I have been doing some thinking, and I believe that I will sell Wood Court. I think that the purpose for which I came here has been fulfilled. As you say, I believe it is time to move on; for me as well as you," said Liebie slowly, feeling the impact of her words as she spoke. Katherine looked up, startled.

"Sell Wood Court? But where would you go, Liebie?"

"I don't know," answered Liebie honestly. "I just don't know. A smaller place, perhaps? Where we could conduct our own manner of research without the constant stress and strain of such a large financial burden. What do you think?" she asked timidly.

"I think quite honestly, that you must count me out of all your subsequent work. I am tired of centers and wish to go off by myself. Somewhere . . . somewhere peaceful and lovely." Liebie said nothing, but there was just a hint of a smile about her lips, the meaning of which Katherine could not interpret.

Not for a moment do I believe that our work together is over, thought Liebie, as she studied the unusually subdued countenance of her best friend in the world. *The world is in great need of our work, and I'll see it through to fruition if it's the last thing I do. Man must receive the physical evidence he requires in order to fully understand and believe in life's continuity, man's immortality.*

And taking Katherine's hands in her own, Liebie smiled comfortingly, looked directly into her eyes and spoke. "I do believe that you will be surprised where we end up, my dear. Very surprised, indeed." And, squeezing her friend's hand encouragingly, Liebie softly chuckled.

CHAPTER 46

The White House Chapel

"KATHERINE, MY DEAR, ARE YOU certain that you're awake?" the pleasant, unmistakable voice of Liebie Pugh inquired at the other end of the telephone. Several months had elapsed since Katherine had informed her friend that she wanted to move on from the Wood Court Center, to travel and see the world. During this period, Katherine had been true to her word. Putting the sadness and disappointment of the final days of Wood Court behind her, she had first traveled to The Greyhound to assist Trevor and Doris during the busy summer months. Then, one day in late October not long after she had arrived in Newport, she had taken particular satisfaction from announcing before both of her friends, as though deliberately showing off her ability to exercise the power of the mind, "I am going to go on a tour of Europe. I won't have to spend much money, and I will be accompanied by several delightful and well-to-do companions."

Never knowing quite what to make of Katherine's unorthodox behavior, Trevor merely started. Doris smirked, sincerely doubting that Katherine would truly live up to her words. After all, the summer holiday season was nearly over, most business people were back on the job. Whoever would Katherine find to accompany her all over Europe this time of year? But Katherine was sincere, and determined. And sure enough, only several weeks after she had issued the bold statement, she received the invitation from her sister Cora requesting that she join her and her wealthy friends, the Darcy's, who were visiting from New Zealand, on a leisurely motor trip through Europe. "Europe should be lovely this time of year without the usual throngs of tourists!" exclaimed Cora. "The Darcy's would be thrilled to have you along."

"I told you! I told you!" Katherine cried gleefully, embracing Trevor and Doris. "I'm going to Europe just as I said I would!"

Now, both Trevor and Doris stared at her wonderingly. Although she had repeatedly demonstrated her ability to place mind over matter, to translate dreams into material reality, and although they frequently doubted her, they never ceased to marvel over the way things seemed "to go her way." Jubilant, Katherine hastily packed her belongings and prepared for the journey. It had been decided that Cora and the Darcy's would pick her up at The Greyhound and, starting out in France, they would then travel north through the Netherlands, and then south through Belgium and Luxembourg and onward through Germany, Austria, Switzerland, and Italy.

"Wherever the car takes us, we'll go," all four gaily agreed, as they embarked on the first real holiday Katherine had enjoyed in years.

It will do me a world of good to get away for a while, she mused. And when she met the Darcy's—a handsome, well-mannered, and altogether delightful couple—she was convinced that it would be appropriate to join them. And so, in the Darcy's brand new light blue Bentley, the four traveled in luxury and comfort, for the Darcy's made certain that the car was always filled with an enormous luncheon hamper stocked with all sorts of delicious local fare, several fur lap robes, assorted road maps, and numerous books and magazines. For nearly five months, the four traveled, reveling in the charm, beauty, and history of the Old World. For the first time in many years, Katherine was free of the responsibilities and pressures of family and business, and she thrived in this freedom. By the time she had returned to her Pendennis apartment in early March, she was thoroughly refreshed and ready to return to work.

She had, in fact, been back in London only a few days when Liebie had telephoned her early in the morning.

"What time is it?" Katherine had demanded sleepily.

"Nearly half past eight," replied Liebie cheerfully.

"Oh," groaned Katherine, suddenly recollecting the fact that she had not fallen asleep until nearly three o'clock in the morning.

"You must listen, dear," Liebie was saying. "It's quite important."

"What is?" asked Katherine, rolling over onto her back, stifling a yawn.

"What I am about to tell you," replied Liebie calmly.

"Oh," said Katherine once again.

"You know that ever since I sold Wood Court, I have been searching for another smaller, more suitable piece of property upon which to establish a New Thought Center. And well, my dear, I do believe that I have found the ideal spot at last. It's a large white stone house located at 8 Oakhill Road, Surbiton, Surrey—a great old building that has been subdivided into eight individual apartments for which I could receive a nice rent, and has a grand downstairs that contains several more apartments, a beautiful entrance hall, and numerous large rooms perfect for the kind of work in which we were involved in the Gold Room. Furthermore, The White House, as it's called, is much closer to central London than Wood Court. Katherine, I do think it's precisely what I've been looking for, and well, I should be most grateful if you would take a look at the property and give me your advice. You know how much I value your opinion. Would you mind taking a look at it, Dear?" Liebie asked in her tremulous voice.

There was a long silence as Katherine carefully digested Liebie's words. As usual, she had intuitively surmised the true purpose for Liebie's call.

"Liebie," Katherine said, awkwardly but firmly, "I have already explained to you that our work together is over—that you are to go your way, and I mine. I really do not think that you should be seeking my advice in areas which no longer concern me." She had not meant to be harsh, but she simply had to give vent to her feelings.

"My dear, I am well aware of your opinion regarding any future professional collaboration," Liebie was saying smoothly, "I am merely asking your advice as a respected, and cherished, friend and former coworker."

"I see," replied Katherine.

"My dear, if you would prefer not to go. . ." Liebie began in a quivering voice, and Katherine realized that she had offended her.

"I'm sorry, Liebie. I don't mean to be difficult or unkind. It's just that, well, I don't see any point . . . " She broke off, suddenly as she was struck by an idea. *Oh, no, God. No. Surely you don't mean it. You really can't expect me to collaborate with Liebie again. At her new place. At this White House of hers. I thought she and I were finished*, were the thoughts that raced through her mind while Liebie said simply, "As you wish, darling."

Oh, no, Katherine groaned inwardly, feeling trapped. She knew that she could not refuse the help Liebie required of her.

"All right, Liebie," Katherine agreed quietly. "I will help you find a suitable location for your new center, and I should be happy to see The White House. But I find it necessary to advise you that that's as far as I go. I want nothing further to do with your center. I want to be free—of any and all centers for a while. Do you understand?"

"Of course, dear," was Liebie's deliberately casual response. "When can we get together?"

"Any time you say," sighed Katherine wearily.

Upon seeing The White House, Katherine knew that Liebie had not underestimated its potential value. After closely inspecting the residence and beautiful grounds, Katherine knew that it was perfectly suited for the work which Liebie hoped to do.

"You're right, love. It's absolutely ideal for a center," Katherine conceded. "It's really a bargain at the price they're asking, the land and setup are all one would wish. I think that you'd be wise to grab it."

"Really?" asked Liebie, her eyes shining in anticipation.

"Really," sighed Katherine, as she braced herself for the next of Liebie's inevitable requests. *Get ready*, she thought. *Here it comes.* And, sure enough, Liebie next asked in a meek voice.

"Would you mind terribly helping me to get the center established? You know just in the very early stages? I would so value your assistance." Recognizing the futility of any further argument or discussion, Katherine acquiesced.

"All right, Liebie," she said defeated.

"Thank you, dear," Liebie had murmured gratefully, her features glowing in happiness. "You won't regret it. We shall have a lovely time together." But although Katherine nodded politely, inwardly she was still groaning. *Oh, God. Here we go again.*

Yet, despite her doubts and reservations, Katherine actually enjoyed helping Liebie to get settled in her new home. The White House—its atmosphere and grounds—greatly appealed to Katherine; and she derived considerable pleasure and fulfillment in preparing the property for its new purpose. Old furnishings, wallpapers, and carpets and draperies were removed and replaced with new ones or those Liebie had taken along with her from Wood Court. And soon the Georgian residence was filled with beautiful works of art and antique furniture—circa 1800 English Regency commodes with Chinese details, early 18th century French Regence armchairs covered in Aubusson tapestry, Chinese Chippendale mirrors, handsome Georgian tables, and cabinets adorned the reception rooms on the main floor—and both Katherine and Liebie had been delighted by the effect of their efforts.

In the meantime, because of Liebie's utter helplessness and lack of acumen in nearly all facets of business, Katherine found herself at the helm of The White House. And, as was the case at Wood Court, she found herself bearing far too much unwanted responsibility.

"Liebie," she had protested vehemently, "you simply must find someone else to help you. I will remain here with you strictly on a temporary basis, until you can find someone else upon whom to rely. But you must become accustomed to the idea of running The White House, or any other organization of your own, by yourself. I wish to be free of all responsibility. Do you understand?"

But although a subdued Liebie had replied, "Of course, my dear," Katherine began to sense the she would remain at The White House, and with Liebie, for quite some time.

It slowly began to dawn on Katherine that in order to leave Liebie permanently, it would be necessary to educate and train her so that she would no longer have to depend upon her or anyone else and would become completely self-sufficient. And so Katherine set about the painstaking task of teaching Liebie the various facets of center management. Furthermore, she taught Liebie to feel comfortable in the public eye. Under Katherine's careful tutelage, then, Liebie began slowly but surely to assume an increasing amount of responsibility for all aspects of The White House's daily operation. To Katherine's relief, then, within a relatively brief period of time, the two were sharing the responsibilities of running a large organization. Needless to say, Katherine was delighted with the results of her efforts.

Once Liebie was able to assume further responsibility, Katherine experienced a greater degree of freedom and was at last able to pursue her own areas of research and to conduct her work as she wished. Now, she continued to lecture, to conduct classes and development circles, to have sittings, and to demonstrate her mediumistic abilities. And although she had not intended or desired it all, she found herself permanently at The White House. Slowly, she had come to recognize the distinct advantages of running, but not owning, a center. And she was, at least for the present time, content with her role as director of The White House.

And although she had truly believed that the work that had been done in the Gold Room at Wood Court was to be abandoned for some time—possibly forever—she had discovered, much to her amazement, that there was a beautiful drawing room on the main floor that was singularly suited to the materialization work. In fact, with virtually no discussion, she and Liebie found themselves intuitively decorating the room with the same furniture and accessories that had graced the Gold Room. Yet, neither she nor Liebie was willing to discuss the possibility of continuing the materialization work until, little by little, Katherine began to realize that her own attitudes and opinions had little impact or influence over what was inevitable.

It quickly became evident that the Gold Room work was not to be abandoned after all. Only several months after Liebie had purchased the new center, a remarkable series of "coincidences" convinced both women that the materialization work must continue. During the final phases of the Gold Room work, the effort to establish a perfect materialization had been marred by the bitter divisiveness and jealousies that had arisen between sitters and mediums. Selflessness, discipline, and diligence had been required of individuals whom Katherine learned subsequently had their own personal welfare and self-aggrandizement at heart. And although Katherine had been sorely disappointed by the outcome of years of hard work, she had understood and believed that her coworkers knew no better, could not help themselves, and were doing the best they could. Even though Liebie had provided these mediums with free room and board in addition to a good salary in order to relieve these hypersensitive souls from the strains and pressures of earning a living while engaged in such demanding work, Katherine realized sadly that even such enticements were not sufficient to alter human nature. And so, coming to terms with the childishness and pettiness of her fellow human beings, she had abandoned hope of ever achieving the desired outcome.

Now, she was amazed to witness the process whereby each one of the mediums and sitters who had participated in the Gold Room work came to The White House under one pretext or another, and ended up renting accommodations from Liebie. Within a few months of Katherine's arrival, all eight apartments that had been rented out under the previous landlord's ownership were vacated and then inhabited by the various mediums who had worked with Katherine and Liebie in the Gold Room. Katherine had watched in astonishment, as one by one, the apartments upstairs were vacated and then occupied by her former coworkers, all of whom were willing and eager to complete the project they had begun together.

Katherine and Liebie had looked at one another in amazement, then burst into laughter on the cold, rainy night upon which Jim Hutchins and his wife Anne had arrived, soaking wet, complaining that they had been visiting the area and had been unable to find a hotel room due to the fact that a business convention was being held nearby.

"Every single hotel in the area is booked. Would it be possible to spend the night here?" Jim had asked, obviously deeply embarrassed but desperate.

"Of course," Liebie had responded with her customary graciousness and generosity. And Jim and his wife never left The White House again. In a similarly unexpected and mysterious way did each member of the original group find his or her way back. Yet, Katherine was adamant. Although she agreed to assist the group in their own development, she would never again strive as she had before to achieve the perfect materialization. In other words, she would work with the group, but not in the same manner or with the same goal in mind as she had in the past.

In light of the peculiar manner in which she had ended up at The White House, Katherine could not be terribly surprised when her dear friend and close coworker Eileen Richards also appeared at the center, expressing her sincere desire to live on the premises and to assist Katherine personally in all facets of her work, "Whatever they may be," Eileen had said, smiling warmly.

From the moment she had first set eyes upon Katherine at the Wood Court Hotel several years ago, Eileen, a guest at the center, had been inextricably drawn to her. And although she initially knew nothing whatever of Mrs. Hayward's background or the nature of her work, she had desired to come to know her better. *There's something extraordinary about that woman. I must meet her*, Eileen had thought, unable to pinpoint what it was about Katherine that so intrigued her.

It was Liebie who had noticed her guest's infatuation with her coworker and had said to Katherine one morning over breakfast, "My dear, see that woman over there?" She pointed to a strikingly attractive dark-haired woman elegantly attired and with a beautiful figure. "She is a guest. I've noticed that she simply cannot take her eyes off of you. I cannot help but feel that she has come to Wood Court to be with you to receive what you have to teach," Liebie said in her quiet, tactful way, her eyes rich in wisdom and compassion. "Go to her, my dear." And Katherine, looking directly into Liebie's eyes and then at the woman, knew that Liebie was right.

"All right, Liebie. I will do as you wish. I will introduce myself to her." And, taking one last bite of her hot buttered biscuit, she excused herself and walked over to Eileen's table.

"I am Katherine Hayward," she began. "Co-Director of Wood Court. May I join you?"

"Oh, yes, please do," replied the woman, who Katherine noticed at close range was her own age. She had appeared far younger from a distance. Katherine knew at once that Liebie had been right. The woman was obviously delighted that she had joined her.

"My name is Eileen Richards," she said graciously. Looking into Katherine's eyes, Eileen could not help but feel that she was talking to an old beloved friend, one whom she had known forever. "To tell the truth, I know almost nothing about metaphysics," Eileen admitted. "I happened to discover a brochure for Wood Court and was, for some reason, drawn to the place. Prior to coming here, I had been rather troubled and was seriously contemplating divorcing my husband. I guess you could say that I have been searching . . . for something. But I'm afraid I do not know what. Do you know something, Mrs. Hayward? From the first moment I saw you I could not help but feel that there was something very familiar about you, and you had the answers to the questions I've been asking for a very long time. Oh, dear, I do hope I'm making sense."

"My dear, you are making a lot of sense. More than you can possibly know at the present time. And I must say that I do feel that you have come to the right place to receive the answers you desire. If you would like, you and I can meet privately, and I shall be happy to introduce you to the work we do here at Wood Court."

"Oh, Mrs. Hayward. I would be thrilled to work with you. To tell the truth, if you hadn't approached me now, I don't know what I would have done. For frankly, I was seriously contemplating leaving Wood Court. When can we start?" she inquired, her eyes glistening with joy.

From that moment forth, Katherine had taken Eileen into her own personal care and begun teaching her privately. In Eileen she had discovered an earnest and diligent pupil. *Why, she reminds me of myself,* thought Katherine, marveling at Eileen's enthusiasm and dedication. For nearly a year, at Wood Court, Katherine worked with Eileen, training her as she herself had been trained so many years ago by the Spirit Beings. And once Eileen had begun, there was no stopping her. As anxious and determined as Katherine to discover the truths of life, Eileen read and researched with a zealousness and fervor that could compare only with Katherine's. And soon Eileen and she were inseparable, for Eileen took it upon herself to assist Katherine in any way she could.

"My life has been transformed," she told Katherine gratefully. "I will never be the same. Thank you."

"Don't be silly. Don't thank me. Thank God. It is your greater self who has guided and directed you all through your life. Which is guiding and directing you at this moment. We are all manifestations of God—God manifesting through various forms and formats," Katherine replied, unwilling to accept credit for the transformation that had taken place in Eileen's life.

Within a relatively brief period of time, the two had become inordinately fond of one another, and Eileen had become virtually indispensable to Katherine. Maternal and solicitous, it was Eileen who made certain that Katherine was afforded sufficient rest and respite from the seemingly endless round of daily activity; it was she who scheduled Katherine's public lectures and demonstrations; who handled her heavy correspondence and who screened her private interviews. Furthermore, it was Eileen who introduced Katherine to the book that transformed Katherine's life.

It was at the age of fifty-six, now at the White House, that Katherine, upon Eileen's recommendation, read *The Autobiography of a Yogi* by Paramahansa Yogananda. A factual and moving account of one man's search for the truth, it was *The Autobiography of a Yogi* that further inspired Katherine to regard mediumship as a useful and purposeful gift and, far more importantly, as a means of introducing human beings to their own vast potential, however, it was not the end point of one's spiritual unfoldment or development.

Upon reading Yogananda's uplifting account of his own search, Katherine began to realize consciously what she had always sensed intuitively but had been unable to express: that man was destined to one day recognize his own divinity; that he would one day understand that he and the Father are One; that the Kingdom of Heaven is within him; and that all life is one life manifesting through myriad forms. And although some of the concepts presented by Yogananda were couched in different terms other than those with which Katherine had been familiar previously, she knew at once that they were, in essence, exactly the same as those that had been imparted by the Spirit Beings over thirty years ago. Reincarnation, karma, the immortality of man's soul—all were familiar concepts to her. And now, somehow she found it extremely comforting and reassuring to know that millions of people believed as she did, even if the customs, culture, and lifestyle of those who believed as she did were vastly different than her own.

From Eileen and her husband Frank, Katherine learned much about India and its people. Frank had served in India as a member of the Foreign Service for many years and knew the customs, rituals, and culture of India very well. From the Richards Katherine learned about the yogis (those who were earnestly aspiring to achieve conscious union with God and were following a scientific technique for this divine realization), their gurus (spiritual teachers who have achieved true union with the divine spiritual essence within and are truly able to dispel the darkness that separates his devotees from a similar awareness), and the ashrams (spiritual communities wherein various gurus and their disciples live and study and practice yoga). Now, in conjunction with the Richards' descriptions of life in India and *The Autobiography of a Yogi*, which so beautifully revealed the depths of the Hindu mind and heart, Katherine became increasingly desirous to visit the land in which spiritual unfoldment rather than technological advancement or material acquisitions were revered. She yearned to study firsthand the country whose politics and policies were predicated upon spiritual attainment rather than economic achievement.

Although Liebie had spoken of Yogananda in the very early days of Katherine's arrival at Wood Court, it had not been until Frank and Eileen had insisted that she read Yogananda's autobiography that she had felt compelled to delve deeply into a study of Indian culture and philosophy. Now, she was very excited about kriya yoga—a technique for God-realization advocated by Yogananda: "the union with the Infinite through a certain action or rite (kriya) - an ancient science and a simple, psychophysiological method by which human blood is decarbonated and recharged with oxygen. An instrument through which human evolution can be quickened."[2]

Katherine sought further information regarding this scientific system whereby one could achieve the goal of self-awareness. Furthermore, she had been profoundly affected by Yogananda's description of the reappearance, or resurrection, of his guru Sri Yukteswar, following his so-called death. *So he too desired evidence of life's continuity, and received it,* she mused, feeling a powerful bond with Yogananda.

"Grieve not for me," Yukteswar had entreated his disciple. "Rather broadcast everywhere the story of my resurrection. New hope will be infused into the hearts of misery-mad, death-fearing dreamers of the world."[3] Had not Katherine since the age of twenty infused hope into the hearts of millions as a result of her mediumistic abilities? Finally, she had read of an Indian philosopher who willingly acknowledged the importance of such work as she had been doing throughout her adult life. *He, too, is aware that the proof of survival is the first in a long series of steps that leads one to discover the truth,* she marveled. *Someday, some day, I shall visit one of Yogananda's ashrams and see for myself how his kriya yoga works,* she vowed solemnly. The idea of visiting the birthplace of both Yogananda and Mahatma Gandhi greatly appealed to her, and with the passage of time, she grew increasingly determined to see India.

And so, although Katherine remained at the helm of The White House's management, it became clear to Liebie and other coworkers that Katherine's heart was no longer in her mediumship work. While there were some remarkable demonstrations of physical phenomena from her development circle, Katherine was unwilling to devote time and energy toward the achievement of the perfect materialization.

"That part of my life is over," she insisted before the group. It was at this time that Liebie felt inspired to record in writing many of the lectures given by Katherine and her spirit guides at The White House while in a trance state. Although Liebie never intended this to be a lengthy or difficult

---

2 California: Self-Realization Fellowship; 1979

3 Ibid.

project, she found herself devoting more time than anticipated collaborating with Katherine on what she had intended to be a short pamphlet of a series of papers containing excerpts or highlights from Katherine's talks and tracing the development of the work that transpired at The White House. Instead, the short pamphlet became a book published in 1957 by Regency Press in London called *Nothing Else Matters.*

Throughout this period, Katherine had expressed her reluctance to publicize work of such a private nature, but Liebie had been inspired and felt compelled to share with the world some of the extraordinary messages that had been delivered through Katherine's Inspirers. Some of these messages predicted that great day when highly evolved Spiritual Beings would show themselves to those who are ready to perceive them; when the invisible would become visible.

Liebie wrote, "Katherine Hayward wishes for silence and seclusion until the Great Day dawns or, as she would, prefer me to write, until we know from our own firsthand experience that it is going to dawn at all, I, on the other hand, have been so totally convinced that these Great Inspirers of hers know so wholly what They are about that I cannot leave any stone unturned to help towards that fulfillment which I know is to come. All she [Katherine] asks is to say nothing—to advertise nothing—but simply to go on quietly with the work with us while she continues to give herself to spreading light and happiness individually through her great gifts as she has been privileged to do for over thirty-four years—but to say no word to the outer world until some measure of this sublime prophesy has been fulfilled." Despite Katherine's reluctance for public exposure, Liebie's book reached a surprisingly large audience, and the reputation of The White House continued to expand.

Also during this period, Katherine, while in trance, gave Liebie explicit instructions regarding the creation and construction of a chapel or shrine on The White House premises. This little chapel was to be designed as a place wherein the highest forms of communication between the spheres—where the greatest degree of spiritual achievement—could take place and from which the rays of peace could radiate outwardly toward the rest of the world. Although Katherine herself knew nothing of architecture or interior design, she, under the careful inspiration of her Guides, was responsible for the execution of a structure the likes of which neither she nor Liebie had ever seen before.

Designed to accommodate fifty people comfortably, the little chapel consisted of a rookery, a waterfall, walls tinted to suggest the shades of a glowing fiery sunset, a screen on which the deeper more brilliant hues of sunset itself were painted, a simple archway through which could be seen a figure of Jesus with His Hands outstretched in blessing (which Liebie, an award-winning sculptress, sculpted and someone who had been presented at Court had modeled), and an inspirational painting of Katherine's Spirit Guide Bright Eyes as well as other figures and paintings of the great saints and masters who have lived on the earth. No one had been more surprised than Katherine herself as she witnessed the completed project—a little chapel of exquisite design and proportion from which one felt immediately at peace and at home. *It's heaven on Earth*, she thought, marveling at the building's simple beauty. "It is to be dedicated to the purpose of establishing true and lasting peace on Earth," she told Liebie.

Throughout the construction of the chapel, Katherine had felt the influence of Paramahansa Yogananda. It was not until some years later, while she and Eileen were on holiday in the United States, that she discovered the only chapel like hers that she had ever seen, in design and atmosphere: the chapel belonging to Yogananda's Self-Realization organization in Los Angeles, California (which Yogananda himself had founded), which bore an uncanny resemblance to the little chapel Katherine had designed under inspiration for The White House. Once again, she was reminded of and amazed by the extraordinary guidance she had received all her life.

But, as Katherine became increasingly disinterested in psychism and increasingly interested in self-discovery, she grew restless and eager to move onward. Although she adored Trevor and Doris as well as her own family, she was never truly content unless she was doing the work, and so she rarely spent longer than a few days at a time with any of her loved ones. Her teaching, lecturing, demonstrations, and private interviews took up nearly all her time. She had, during her years at The White House, studied formally as she had never done before. From Christian Science to Gurdjieff to Subudh, Katherine read and studied to her heart's content. Furthermore, she did something she had always yearned to do: had managed over a period of years to obtain a Bachelor's Degree in Psychology from Psychology House, Marple County of Cheshire, proving to herself that she could succeed academically. It was quite an achievement, and one of which she was very proud.

Yet, by mid-summer of 1958, Katherine, still at The White House, began to feel "I am nearly sixty years old, and have little to show for it." For years, she had seemingly stagnated. In her mind, she was no closer now toward achieving her true goal of self-discovery than she had ever been. *What next?* she wondered impatiently. *What is next for me?*

She did not have to wait long to find out what was next. No one could have been more surprised than she when, late one afternoon in July 1958, a well-known clairvoyant visiting The White House confronted Katherine in front of Liebie and admonished her loudly, "Whatever are you doing here, Mrs. Hayward? You should be in India. You no longer belong here. It is your destiny to leave and go to India. There is important work to be done there."

Katherine had been too stunned to utter a word. The clairvoyant used the silence as an opportunity to continue. Pointing a finger at Katherine, she said accusingly, "You are working with the energies Divine. You must transmit our Western energy to the East, and bring the East to the West. But you must go at once. You do not belong here," she repeated solemnly. As though this message were not enough of a catalyst, Katherine was, soon after this confrontation, introduced to a couple from India who were equally convinced that Katherine belonged in their native land at the present time.

"Go you must!" they advised.

Although Katherine had longed to leave The White House and to travel around the world, she had postponed her departure until the day when she felt certain that Liebie was fully capable of managing The White House all by herself. In time, that day arrived. And by September 1958, Katherine was ready to leave both Liebie and The White House permanently, and to reclaim her independence. Briefly she recalled the words of the Indian woman who, along with her husband, had recently advised her to visit India.

"It is the mind that makes one wise or ignorant, bound or emancipated. One is holy because of his mind, one is wicked because of his mind; it is the mind that makes me virtuous. So he whose mind is always fixed on God requires no other practices, devotion or spiritual exercises. . ."

"He whose mind is always fixed on God," Katherine repeated, a deep yearning stirring inside her. "I must discover what it's all about. I want to know, to experience, my Creator, the Source of All Life. Perhaps in India I will find someone who can guide me."

She knew that Liebie was deeply hurt and disappointed by her desire to leave The White House.

"I had so hoped you would stay on with me," Liebie had confessed. But Katherine knew that her work with Liebie was over at long last. It was time for both of them to move on, to grow, and develop in new areas. Suddenly, Liebie began to openly declare her desire to sell The White House.

"Perhaps I will retire," she had calmly informed Katherine. Liebie was now nearly seventy years of age. "I've always longed to settle somewhere by the sea, perhaps in Hove." Katherine deliberately avoided reacting to Liebie's plans. She neither encouraged nor discouraged her friend from selling the property.

"What is right will occur," Katherine consoled her.

In the meantime, Eileen had enthusiastically volunteered to accompany Katherine on her trip to India. Eileen could not, would not, leave her beloved friend alone overseas. After all she insisted, "You know that Frank and I have lived there on and off for nearly thirty years with his position in the Foreign Service. I know the language. I know the people, and I understand and appreciate the culture. I could be of great assistance," and Katherine concurred. It was Eileen who made the travel arrangements. The two would set sail on October 20 and stop in Port Said, spend five days in Ceylon, and arrive in Bombay on November 7. They deliberately avoided booking return passage for they did not know how long they would stay.

"It all depends," Katherine had admitted.

"On what?" asked the always curious Eileen.

"On what we find there, of course," teased Katherine. But truthfully, she did not know what to expect, and she was somewhat troubled by the fact that she was permitted by the British government to bring with her only a small amount of currency. She truly hoped that she and Eileen would not be stranded in India with insufficient funds to return home. But Eileen had good-naturedly laughed at Katherine's apprehension.

"You'll see," said Eileen, "it will all work out perfectly."

"Ah, well, I suppose you're right," agreed Katherine. Also, at this time, Eileen planned Katherine's itinerary. "Don't book me for too many lectures," Katherine warned her. "Remember, this is intended to be a holiday."

"A working holiday, you mean," laughed Eileen.

Looking forward with great anticipation to her "working holiday," Katherine shopped for clothing suitable to India's climate and for the accessories and appliances that would make travel throughout India more pleasant and convenient. Thinking, *I am going to enjoy myself, as I've never had the opportunity to do before*, Katherine even brushed up on her dancing by attending a ballroom dancing class prior to the journey. Unfortunately, only two days before their scheduled departure, Katherine tripped and fell while attempting to change the draperies on a high kitchen window at her Pendennis apartment, and broke her right arm. *Silly ass*, she rebuked herself, deciding to take the ocean voyage nonetheless. Now, she was even more grateful that Eileen was coming along.

"She'll have to look after me, after all," murmured Katherine, ruefully surveying the heavy plaster cast on her arm. "But I will not cancel the trip. I've been waiting for years to go." But her enthusiasm was somewhat diminished, for who wanted to travel with a plaster cast on one's arm?

"Ah, well," she sighed. "Such is life."

But, during a time when she had hoped to experience great freedom and was looking forward to the adventure such a journey promised, she had been forced to acknowledge further restriction and limitation.

Katherine and Eileen spent the night before the day they were scheduled to depart completing their packing and finalizing all details that had been saved for the last minute and chattering away as happily as schoolgirls.

"The Taj Mahal; the Ganges River; the burning ghats; the temples; sacred cows; the narrow, windy streets," Katherine breathed, growing more excited by the minute.

"The poverty; disease; misery; despair; the ancient plumbing," teased Eileen.

"Oh shut up," replied Katherine, her eyes shining, refusing to hear anything that might cast a pallor over her notion of the romance and beauty of the ancient land she was about to see for the first time. "Gurus, ashrams, temple ceremonies and great feasts, elephants and monkeys," she continued, lost in reverie. "How very much I hope to learn there," she said dreamily, as she unconsciously attempted to squeeze yet another silk blouse into a suitcase that had already been packed to capacity and whose contents were, in fact, spilling from the sides.

"Don't you think you've packed enough clothing, dear?" Eileen asked tactfully, biting her lip to keep from laughing, She had never seen her mentor like this. Always Katherine was calm, unflappable, and authoritative. Now, Eileen was seeing a very different Katherine—one as happy and excited as a child. But Katherine was not paying attention to Eileen.

"I do have so very much to learn yet," she was saying earnestly, mostly to herself.

Touched by her friend's sincerity and childlike naiveté, Eileen smiled and said softly in a maternal manner, "I know. We all have so much to learn. I must say that I cannot help but feel that you will learn an enormous amount in India. Perhaps even more than you've bargained for."

"Yes," agreed Katherine quietly, slowly coming out of her reverie. "Perhaps even more than I've bargained for." But she did not—could not—say aloud what she felt so deeply in her heart. *All I really want is to know God. It is for that reason, and for that reason only, that I am going to India.*

Turning to face Eileen, she smiled radiantly. "I'm ready if you are," finally managing to close and lock her suitcase.

"I am indeed!" laughed Eileen.

"Well, then," said Katherine, with an impish grin, "India, here we come!"

CHAPTER 47

The Journey Begins

NEVER FOR A MOMENT DID Katherine regret her decision to go to India despite the inconvenience of a broken arm. As soon as she was comfortably settled on board the luxurious ocean liner, she knew that it had been right to leave England. For too long she had yearned for a rest and a change. And she was certain that the ocean voyage would fulfill both of these ends.

As the great ship edged away from the pier, accompanied by the thunderous boat whistles and the vibration of the vessel's motor, Katherine became exhilarated, and a glorious sense of peacefulness overcame her. An ebullience—borne of the knowledge that she was no longer responsible to or for anyone or anything—settled over her, and she felt happier, more light-hearted than she had felt in years.

She and Liebie had bid one another a bittersweet farewell in the pretty seaside town of Hove where Liebie owned a luxurious apartment in one of the great buildings along the ocean. Now, as the ship rolled majestically out to sea, Katherine recalled the wistful features, the forlorn figure of Liebie, as they embraced one last time before Katherine's departure. Her heart had gone out to her dear friend and coworker, for she knew that Liebie would miss her terribly. Liebie was closer to her than to anyone else and, in a way, she hated to leave Liebie behind. Yet, at the same time, she knew their separation to be inevitable.

We've learned so very much from one another, marveled Katherine as she thought of the many years the two had spent together in such close physical proximity. Now, she could not help but wonder what would become of Liebie. *Will she retire? Sell the White House? Remain in Hove?* Shrugging, she realized that only time would tell, and that Liebie's life was no longer of concern to her.

Suddenly, all thoughts of Liebie, the White House, and the past in its entirety vanished from her consciousness, as Katherine felt the unsteadiness of the deck beneath her feet, saw the gray-violet water below, and swallowed, in enormous gulps, the deliciously cold fresh ocean air. At least for the present time, she was leaving everything behind her. As the breezes grew fresher and cooler, Katherine began to feel lighter and cleaner. Mesmerized by the rolling of the ship and the heaving water that enfolded it, she watched the last vestiges of the English coastline disappear into a tiny pinpoint of muted green and brown. Then there was nothing to be seen but the waves lapping and nipping below; she turned and walked toward her stateroom.

She was genuinely moved by what she saw upon entering her room. For it was filled, almost to overflowing, with lovely flowers, fruit baskets, plants, candies, and gifts from her friends and former coworkers. Everyone had sought to wish her well on this, her first trip to India.

"How thoughtful—and dear—they all are," murmured Katherine, tears rising to her eyes. Unfortunately, her room was quite small and could not comfortably accommodate the elaborate displays of affection. And so, Katherine was forced to have the steward—a funny, white-haired man with a Cockney accent—remove the majority of them.

"But what shall I do with them, mum?" he had asked in despair.

"Whatever you wish," replied Katherine firmly.

"As you say, mum."

Following the steward's departure, Katherine had surveyed her now nearly empty room with satisfaction. Sighing in relief, she solemnly vowed, *No one will disturb me or in any way interfere with my holiday. I am not going to inform a single individual anything about my background. God! If word gets out that there's a psychic on board, my serenity, not to mention my privacy, will be violated. I must warn Eileen not to say a word to anyone about my psychic abilities.*

And, although Eileen assented verbally to Katherine's demands, she knew that there was little hope of Katherine's remarkable personality or unique abilities going unnoticed or undetected. Ever since she had met Katherine, she had been aware of the attention that her friend inadvertently attracted for no obvious reason. "You are a lovely woman," or "There is something very special about you," or "Don't I know you?" Strangers would approach Katherine on streets, in railway stations, at bus stops, in theatres, or at the market and blurt out such statements.

"Whatever prompts these people to behave in such a fashion?" Eileen had asked Katherine in the early stages of their relationship.

Smiling mysteriously, Katherine had whispered, "The energies. The energies that I receive and transmit cause them to react in that manner."

"Oh, I see," said Eileen. Not seeing at all, but too embarrassed to proceed any further. And so, ocean or no ocean, holiday or no holiday, Eileen was prepared for the worst.

In the meantime, the two were as carefree and gay as they could be. They took leisurely strolls on the decks, shopped, sun-bathed, read voraciously, danced to their hearts' content, attended concerts in the ship's salon, and dined on the superb Continental cuisine offered in the restaurants.

"Do you know," Katherine had said to Eileen during their first day on board, "I shouldn't be at all surprised if we were invited to dine at the captain's table?"

Now why on earth should we be invited to the captain's table? wondered Eileen, in light of the fact that they had taken great pains to obscure their positions and identities. But she said nothing, having learned to trust Katherine's predictions by this time.

Several hours later, the two were comfortably ensconced in the colorful chaise lounges, each absorbed in reading. The intense heat of the afternoon sun beating down upon them was only somewhat tempered by the fresh ocean breezes.

"I sure could go for an ice cream!" Katherine blurted out suddenly, placing her book in her lap and gazing at the people around her. Peering at Katherine from behind her book, Eileen sighed, yawned, and stretched, and then put the book aside, marking her place with the flap of the jacket. Rising and then stretching her slim, elegant figure, she looked Katherine squarely in the eyes.

"What flavor?"

"Oh, dear, I didn't mean to interrupt, and I certainly don't expect you to get ice cream for me," Katherine protested feebly.

"What flavor?" persisted Eileen in an authoritative voice.

"Vanilla," admitted Katherine.

"See you in a moment," Eileen called out before Katherine had a chance to protest any further. At almost the same instant, Eileen vanished from view, an elderly fastidious, gray-haired steward approached Katherine.

"Are you Mrs. Katherine Hayward?" he asked politely.

"Why, yes. Yes, I am," admitted Katherine, rather taken aback.

"Well, Mrs. Hayward, it is my privilege on behalf of Captain Morrow to ask you and your companion, Mrs. Richards, to please join the captain for dinner at his table this evening and for the remainder of the journey. He would be most honored if you would accept his invitation."

"I see," replied Katherine. "Well, please do tell the captain that my friend and I should be delighted to accept his kind invitation."

"Thank you, madam," he replied in his elegant accent. "I shall be pleased to relay your acceptance to the captain." Katherine half expected him to bow in farewell, but he did not. "Good day, madam."

"Good day to you," smiled Katherine, then went back to her book. She was engrossed in reading by the time that Eileen returned.

"Here you are," murmured Eileen, handing Katherine a dish of creamy vanilla ice cream.

"Thank you so much, love." And as the two enjoyed the afternoon treat, Katherine described what had taken place in Eileen's absence.

"We're to dine with the captain at his table at half past eight this evening," Katherine said nonchalantly.

"I don't believe it!" laughed Eileen, wondering if her friend was teasing.

"Nonetheless, it's true," sighed Katherine.

And Eileen was forced to accept her friend's account. *Who would have thought it possible?* Eileen mused, but then she recalled all the mysterious and delightful things that had happened to her and Katherine throughout the years and questioned no further.

"What are we going to wear?" she asked instead.

"I really haven't thought about it," returned Katherine. And looking down at her arm in its plaster cast and sling, she said unhappily, "I'm afraid none of the new frocks I bought are going to look very becoming with my arm in this bloody mess. And to think we're going to meet most important people on board while I'm wearing this awful thing. Oh well!" she sighed. "What can one do?" But as she surveyed her arm, an idea suddenly occurred to her.

"I know precisely what one can do. I'm not going to wear this thing one moment longer than absolutely necessary!" she exclaimed. Her face had changed, and now there was an expression of grim determination about her. Jumping gracefully up from her chair, she quickly combed her hair and added a dash of lipstick. "See you later!" she called out to the stunned Eileen.

"But where are you going?" Eileen began, rising from her seat.

"Now you stay where you are," ordered Katherine. "I've got a little business to take care of. Meet me in my room at five o'clock."

"All right," agreed Eileen, reluctantly, having no alternative but to resume her seat. *I wonder what she's up to?* she wondered, as Katherine disappeared from view. But she wasted no further time in speculation. For Katherine was capable of doing anything at any time. Picking up the novel she had been enjoying throughout the day, she soon became absorbed in her reading and was, several hours later, astonished to see, upon glancing at her wrist-watch, that it was ten minutes after five. *Oh, dear. Where has the afternoon gone? I'd better go. I promised Katherine I'd meet her at five o'clock.*

Putting on her dark glasses and collecting her belongings, she found her way to Katherine's room. When she arrived there, Katherine was standing in front of the mirror looking rather pale and with a strange expression of satisfaction upon her face. Upon seeing Eileen's reflection in the mirror, Katherine smiled mysteriously.

"Now, Mrs. Hayward. What is all the mystery about? Wherever have you been all afternoon. You look like the proverbial cat who swallowed the canary. What is going on around here?" Eileen demanded, settling in one of the arm chairs.

"Well," said Katherine, with an odd smile, "if you would really like to know. Take a look." And to Eileen's horror, Katherine held out her right hand—which was now free of the cast in which it had been encased for the past several days.

"Katherine Hayward, you're crazy. You only just broke your arm three days ago. You may injure it permanently if you aren't careful. Do yourself a favor, and have the ship's physician make you another cast." Eileen was genuinely worried.

"Not on your life. Not after all I went through to have the other one removed. Aren't you going to ask me how I managed?" she asked gleefully, refusing to be disturbed by Eileen's warning.

"I wouldn't put anything past you," said Eileen darkly. "All right. Tell me what happened."

"Well, you know how disappointed I was at having to wear that awful thing. Do you know how many sad, pitying glances I've endured during the brief time we've been aboard? Well, I decided, that I couldn't stand wearing that clumsy thing a single minute longer, and so, I managed to persuade one of the engineers to remove it. You should have seen them hammering and sawing that thing—plaster all over the place," she giggled at the memory. "You see," she whispered confidingly, I told them that the cast was due off yesterday, and that I simply was unable to arrange to see my physician at home. They really were lovely—the engineer and his assistants."

"Oh, Katherine, how could you? Approach perfect strangers with such an outrageous lie? And implicate innocent by-standers in your subterfuge?" Eileen was clearly horrified.

"Now, don't be so serious," Katherine pleaded with her friend. "After all, it's all over now. And I made three perfectly lovely gentlemen friends."

"Three?" asked Eileen, raising her eyebrows.

"Uh-huh, and handsome ones at that. In fact, I told them all about you, and they can't wait to meet us this evening at the dance after dinner."

"Oh, Katherine, you are impossible," chided the staid Eileen. She was appalled by her improper behavior.

"And you are too respectable," returned Katherine. "I thought we were going to be carefree and have some fun, some excitement . . ."

"Yes, but we didn't agree to behave like spoiled children or to throw caution to the wind," insisted Eileen. "Now do be sensible and have that arm of yours looked after properly."

"I won't. I've already made up my mind. So you had best drop the subject, dear," said Katherine, beginning to lose patience. Fortunately, the discussion was interrupted by loud, persistent knocking of the steward.

"Tea, ladies?" he asked.

"Yes," answered Katherine, grateful for the interruption. "Please come in."

Thankfully, the argument had ended. Following tea, as Eileen prepared to leave, "Don't worry, love," Katherine had squeezed Eileen's hand and whispered, "Don't worry—I'll be very careful I promise." And from thereon neither introduced the subject again. For the remainder of the journey, Katherine wore her arm in a dainty silken sling.

Dinner at the captain's table was a pleasant affair. The captain himself was an altogether charming and charismatic fellow who delighted in sharing tales of his adventures at sea in addition to bawdy anecdotes which his guests found irresistible. Jovial and hearty, he had red cheeks and twinkling eyes that were accompanied by a keen intelligence, wry wit, and a definite eye for the ladies.

"However did you find out who I was?" Katherine had inquired of the captain after they had become quite friendly.

"I didn't," he admitted with a merry gleam in his eye. "In fact, I knew nothing whatever about you other than that I thought you and your companion to be the most attractive—and interesting—ladies on board. And I personally was dead-bent on getting to know you."

"No," Katherine exclaimed, turning red. "Is that true?"

"On my honor as a gentleman," laughing at Katherine's discomfiture. Under his gaze, she was now blushing from ear to ear.

Then, recovering her composure, as well as her sense of humor, she smiled and said, "I must say, I do think that your opinion of me was quite justified."

At this the captain laughed heartily. "Mrs. Hayward, I must say you are one of a kind."

"And I must say that I quite agree," returned Katherine immodestly but with characteristic candor.

"Do you mean to say that we were invited to the captain's table simply because he found us attractive?" Eileen queried later on that evening.

"Oh, no," replied Katherine mischievously. "Not because we were attractive. But because we were attractive—and interesting—and because the captain wished to become acquainted with us."

"Well, I never! I can't believe it!"

"Nonetheless," Katherine said wryly, "it appears to be true."

They dined with the captain every evening for the remainder of the voyage and felt both privileged and grateful to be included among the captain's guests, which included not only members of the British aristocracy but also political figures from several different countries around the world. It was only after Katherine had become acquainted with several of her dinner companions that she became aware of the real reason she had been invited to dine with the captain. For she soon discovered that three of the gentlemen at the table were of great political influence in their own countries, that their countries were undergoing massive political and social upheaval, and that each was in dire need of guidance—the type of guidance at which she was expert. Two of the men were from the Middle East and the third was from Ceylon. All wielded enormous power at home and abroad and all were at personal and political crossroads. Although she intuitively knew the nature of the difficulties and challenges they faced, she was helpless to assist until they, of their own conscious volition, sought her advice. *Unsolicited advice is seldom, if ever, appreciated*, she thought to herself. *They must truly desire my help for it to be of use to them.*

Although she had fully intended to keep her psychic abilities a secret from anyone on board, it had not taken her fellow passengers long to deduce that she was a woman of rare insight and intuitive ability. Few had failed to notice her powers of perception, and too many had been taken aback when Katherine, unwittingly, rattled off facts and figures pertaining to their lives that no one outside of their immediate families could possibly have known. Furthermore, as Eileen had feared, nearly everyone was drawn to her friend, and Katherine was nearly always surrounded by a group of admirers.

And she calls this a holiday, Eileen thought to herself, observing her friend's animated features and expressive delivery, as she attempted to answer the questions of her fellow passengers.

"I don't know what it is about you, Mrs. Hayward," a plump, red-faced woman had said. "But I just feel that you know me so well. That we're like old friends."

"I know what you mean," Katherine had replied, hiding a smile. And she proceeded to counsel the woman as no one ever had before.

"Thank you, thank you, Mrs. Hayward. Your advice has been astonishingly sound. I don't know how you know what you know—but it really is quite extraordinary. I must tell my friends about you."

"Oh, please don't do that," replied Katherine, not so much out of modesty as a genuine desire to spend the rest of the trip in peace. But the woman did send her friends and Katherine's reputation on board continued to expand until nearly everyone was seeking out her advice.

It was while she was sitting on deck one afternoon, absorbed in re-reading *Autobiography of a Yogi*, that the brother of one of the top Ceylonese government officials introduced himself and asked if he might take a look at her book.

"Of course," she had replied graciously. For some minutes, she watched him as he examined its contents.

Finally, handing it back to her, he said, "Would you mind lending it to me for a while?"

She nodded, feeling that there was something else he wanted to say.

He then continued, looking directly into her eyes and speaking in a low, intense voice. "Mrs. Hayward, God has sent you to me in answer to my prayers. My country is in grave danger—my brother's life and career are in jeopardy. I would be most grateful for any assistance, any guidance, you can provide. I have felt compelled to meet with you ever since we met."

I see," she said slowly, scrutinizing his face for several minutes. She then proceeded to describe in detail the difficulties that had plagued his country since it had become independent from Britain. "I see that there has been great brutality and conflict between the Sinhalese and the Tamilis and that countless Tamilis have been displaced." At the present time she addressed the manner in which his brother was confronting these challenges. "Your brother must not do anything hasty or impulsive. Nor must he adhere to the instructions of the militants. He must detach himself from those who wish to overthrow the existing government and remain true and steadfast to his own beliefs. They will carry him forth and sustain him through the tumultuous period to follow."

"I knew it! I felt it to be precisely as you have said. My brother must not be associated with those who seek to destroy the existing government. You see, my brother is a great believer in peace."

"And he will emerge victorious," stated Katherine in a serious tone.

"Thank you, Mrs. Hayward!" the man exclaimed excitedly. "I shall never forget what you have done for my family and my country. You knew nothing at all about me, and yet you described my circumstances, the circumstances of my country with profound accuracy. I will never forget you. You would do my family and myself a great honor if you would spend time with us at our residence in Ceylon when the ship arrives there. We live in the capital city of Colombo, and you would be welcome to stay with us as our guest for as long as you wish. I am so very grateful to you, Mrs. Hayward. Please accept my cordial invitation."

"Thank you so very much for your kind invitation. But let me refrain from deciding now. I prefer to see how I feel at the time of our arrival in Ceylon, if that is all right with you," she said honestly.

"Certainly. Whatever is your wish," he said, lifting her hand to his lips and kissing it.

In subsequent days, Katherine and the gentleman from Ceylon, along with his family, kept steady company and became close friends.

"If you would spend time with us in Colombo," he had implored, "I would arrange for my brother and his coworkers to meet with you at my home. Your words would mean so much to them. Please do say you'll stay with us."

"Well, all right then," Katherine finally agreed, feeling the inevitability of such a visit and recognizing the value of the service she might conceivably render to so many members of the Ceylonese government. "I humbly accept your kind offer."

"Wonderful," the man said, grinning. "We greatly look forward to the time you will spend with us."

The days on board the ship passed joyously and all too swiftly. So pleasant and peaceful was the atmosphere on board that she felt that she could remain there forever! All sense of time and space had been temporarily suspended, and she felt liberated, exhilarated by the rolling, sunlit reality of her new surroundings. Furthermore, the numerous cities and ports at which the boat docked—Lisbon, Portugal; Tangier, Morocco; Algiers, Algeria; Port Said, Egypt; Tunis, Tunisia; Tripoli, Lebanon; and Alexandria, Egypt—were terribly exotic and assumed a fairy tale quality. Katherine could not remember when she had felt so healthy and exuberant. Little by little, the weariness and exhaustion that had characterized her mentally and physically during her final days at the White House disappeared, and she felt ready to move forward.

CHAPTER 48

Ceylon

—⤸—

BEFORE DOCKING IN CEYLON, KATHERINE was approached by each of the three world leaders, and as she had for so many years, for persons of diverse social and political backgrounds, she advised them as best she could in the areas where they required her unique brand of guidance. All three were deeply impressed and satisfied with the information she provided. She learned, some months hence, that virtually everything she had predicted for each one had come about precisely as she had prophesied.

"And you wished peace and rest above all else," Eileen reminded her friend.

"I know," Katherine acknowledged. "But I cannot shirk my responsibilities. And those men needed me."

"I know, love. But it does seem a shame sometimes, doesn't it, that one's holiday must be spent working?"

"You know that my work is a joy to me," stated Katherine simply. "And that, frankly, I'd rather be doing it than anything else in the world. You know that, don't you?"

"Yes, dear, I suppose I do, at that," smiled Eileen.

Despite the inconvenience of her broken arm and the counseling she found herself doing for her fellow passengers as well as the crew, she had ample opportunity to relax and enjoy the pleasures of being on board a large luxury liner which boasted all manner of comforts and diversions. She shopped, swam, walked the decks, danced, read, mingled with her fellow passengers, dined on the exquisite faire, and enjoyed the films and concerts that were offered as entertainment.

"I wish it would never come to an end," she sighed wistfully to Eileen, the night before they were scheduled to arrive in Ceylon, as the two stood at the rails watching the last golden and amethyst vestiges of the sunset. "I wonder what Ceylon is like," she mused.

"Well, we shall soon find out," noted Eileen wryly. "We are supposed to dock there at about ten o'clock."

It was on November 2 that they arrived in Ceylon, and both Katherine and Eileen fell in love at once with the beautiful tropical island.

"It's heaven on earth, isn't it?" breathed, Katherine, gulping hungrily the fragrant air filled with the rich perfume of flowers she had never seen before. She and Eileen had decided to spend the first few nights of the five-day visit in Ceylon in a hotel. The remaining three days would be spent at the residence in Colombo of the gentleman whom she had counseled.

"At least we'll have a few days to ourselves." Eileen had observed happily.

"Yes," agreed Katherine. "We're under no obligation to anyone. We can come and go as we please."

The coconut palm trees; the busy docks where tea, rubber, cocoa, cinnamon, and tobacco were loaded onto the great mercantile ships for export; the dagobas (hemispherical structures built of brick that were said to contain relics of the Lord Buddha, or of Buddhist saints); the busy streets on which ox-driven carts, rickshaws, and motor cars traveled side-by-side; the colorful roadside stands at which all manner of local crafts were sold; and the elaborate mosques and ornate churches and forts were all a part of the exciting landscape of Ceylon from which Katherine and Eileen derived considerable delight.

Having hired a car and driver, they were able to indulge in the beauty of the countryside surrounding the city. Unfortunately, their freedom was short-lived, for upon returning to their hotel following a day of unceasing activity, they learned from the hotel concierge that a gentleman had called upon them in their absence to welcome them to Ceylon.

"But no one knows we're here!" protested Eileen. "We've told no one our itinerary. Who could have discovered our presence here?"

"I've no idea." replied Katherine. "Let's just pretend it never happened, shall we? Let's rest for a short while, change, and go out for dinner. Then, perhaps, we could take in a movie. I'm really too tired to do much more than that."

"Sounds like a great idea to me," agreed Eileen, stifling a yawn. "I'm exhausted. Let's go up to our rooms now and rest for a while." Several hours later, the women emerged from their rooms somewhat refreshed and starved but still too tired and weary to roam too far away.

"Shall we dine at the hotel tonight?" Katherine suggested.

"Fine with me, love. And I really do think that both of us should go to bed early and get a good night's rest." Katherine nodded. Immediately following the meal, as they prepared to leave the hotel, Katherine noticed that it had started to drizzle.

"Oh, dear, I've just set my hair, and I don't want it to get ruined," wailed Eileen. "I'd better run upstairs and fetch an umbrella."

"All right," sighed Katherine. "I'll wait for you in the lobby." Katherine did not know why she felt so queer and uneasy. *Something peculiar is about to happen,* she thought to herself. *Someone is looking for me. I can't help but feel it.* A sudden chill swept over her, and the sky outside seemed grayer and drearier than ever. *Oh, dear. Perhaps I had better get out of here at once. I'll wait for Eileen outside.* But just as she caught sight of her friend emerging from the elevator, her name was paged over the loud-speaker.

"Katherine Hayward. Mrs. Katherine Hayward. Please come to the concierge desk. Mrs. Hayward. Mrs. Katherine Hayward, if you are in the lobby, please come to the concierge desk. Thank you."

Oh, dear, she thought. *Perhaps I should just ignore it?*

But somehow she could not. And so slowly, reluctantly, she turned and crossed the hotel lobby. As she approached the desk, a short, stocky, round-faced Ceylonese man with inscrutable features and of middle age, cordially extended both his arms in greeting.

"Welcome, Mrs. Hayward. I am Amil. On behalf of the Subud, we welcome you to our country. It is indeed a pleasure to meet you."

"Why, thank you," Katherine replied graciously, raising a questioning eyebrow to Eileen who had by now joined her.

I know nothing at all about any of this, Eileen's expression revealed.

"How, may I ask, did you learn of our arrival here?" inquired Katherine politely.

"Ah, it was Mrs. Alice Fitzgerald of the London branch of our organization who notified us as to the date and time of your intended arrival. She has notified us of your interest in our master, Bapak Subud, and the work that you have done on his behalf in the United Kingdom. Mrs. Fitzgerald has informed us that you have been made an honorary 'helper'—an 'opener'—an individual whom our master has designated to 'open others'—to pass on his energy to others."

"Yes, that is correct," replied Katherine. In conjunction with her constant research and investigation into the various New Thought societies and movements, she had come into contact with a group near the White House headed by Mrs. Fitzgerald that had been called "Subud" and, having completed a course of study in Subud, she had been honored with the title "helper," or "opener"—a teacher and catalyst—a conduit for the divine energies that could be directly experienced by those participants of the "latihan"—an Indonesian word that can be translated as training or exercise and that could connect one with the "higher emotional center"— what Katherine called the "higher or greater self." Vaguely she remembered discussing her intended itinerary with Mrs. Fitzgerald.

"And, now, if you will permit me," the little man was saying, "I would like to transport you and your companion to the celebration that has been arranged in your honor. Our master himself, Pak Subuh, will be there to greet you."

She stared at Eileen helplessly. *What choice have we got?* her eyes were saying. *None whatsoever*, Eileen's eyes signaled back.

"You are most kind." Katherine acquiesced. "My friend and I accept your invitation. Only I am afraid we're not properly dressed for such an event. Would you mind terribly if we return to our rooms to change our clothing? It will take only a few minutes."

"Certainly not," replied the man. "I shall wait for you here."

"Thank you," she said, and she and Eileen hastily made their way to the elevator and up to their rooms.

"How do we manage to get ourselves into such scrapes?" asked Katherine remorsefully.

"Don't look at me," warned Eileen darkly. "I'm not the one who is a helper or opener or whatever he called you for Subud. I hope this experience will teach you to be of a less inquisitive nature."

"Perhaps it will at that," replied Katherine wearily.

For nearly two hours, they rode in the limousine driven by the little man, growing more tired and impatient by the moment.

"Where on earth is he taking us?" whispered Eileen angrily.

"Shhhh!" Katherine admonished. "He'll hear us. I have no idea where we're going."

Through the mist and rain, the countryside appeared grim and foreboding, and Katherine was genuinely regretting her decision to accept Amil's invitation, when finally the car appeared to be slowing down.

"Here we are!" Amil announced gaily. "Now I will introduce you to our master and his devotees in Ceylon. All look forward to meeting you."

"Lovely," replied Katherine insincerely. By now, she wanted nothing but to return to the hotel. "I shall sleep all day tomorrow," she whispered to Eileen, as the little man led the way to the front door of the residence which obviously doubled as a headquarters for the Subud.

"Where on Earth are we?" Eileen wondered once inside this home in the middle of the countryside.

"God only knows," said Katherine, eyeing her surroundings wearily. Bracing herself, she prepared to meet those who had gathered to welcome her.

She was genuinely moved and gratified by the kindness and generosity that they demonstrated. After several hours of greeting and chatting with these people, she was ready to return home. It was well past midnight, and still there had been no appearance by Bapak Subuh. When she was so exhausted that she could stand it no longer, she sought out Amil and told him, "I am afraid I can wait no longer for the arrival of your master. I am thoroughly exhausted. And my friend and I really must return to our hotel. Please offer our apologies to him . . ."

Her voice trailed off as she caught sight of the man whom she knew immediately to be Bapak Subuh. She froze in her place, as he approached her. *He is indeed a master*, she thought to herself, as he came nearer, for she could feel the enormous energy, the effulgence, and radiance that he emanated. Although he was far more Western and modern in appearance than she had imagined, Katherine recognized him instantly as one who had achieved mastery over and understood the truths of life.

"You, my dear, have come to the world to do the work, just as I and many others like us have come to prepare the way for what is often called the 'New Age,'" Pak Subuh said in his heavily accented but musical voice. "You did not receive formal education in the way you would have wished because you did not need it. You see, you already possess great wisdom and insight and have attempted to share it with others. You go to India to share with the Indian people the energies that will facilitate their growth and development. Soon, you will go to the United States to do the same thing. Then you will no longer be British but American citizen. You have much work to do yet, Mrs. Hayward. Much work. God bless you. It is an honor to have met you," he said beaming. He then turned and walked away, and Katherine saw nothing more of him. After he had vanished from view, Katherine decided to depart.

"The Master is wonderful," she had said to Eileen on the trip home. "What a privilege it has been to meet him; however, I would rather not participate in any further Subud activities. I am worn out."

"You'll be clever to avoid that," Eileen warned. And she was proven correct. For the next day, shortly after breakfast another member of Subud arrived at the hotel prepared to escort them to yet another get-together. And Katherine did not feel it wise to refuse these offers. These meetings continued, until thankfully, she and Eileen became the guest of the gentleman from Ceylon they had met onboard the ship. Finally, they were afforded an excuse that prevented them from participating in the constant round of Subud activities.

As her friend from Ceylon had promised, Katherine was introduced to nearly everyone of importance in the Ceylonese government, and she was able to counsel them in accordance with their needs and the needs of the country as a whole. Both she and Eileen thoroughly enjoyed their stay at the palatial residence with its glorious tropical gardens and luxuriously exotic furnishings.

On the night before they were scheduled to set sail for Bombay, their host and his family threw a lavish garden party for Katherine and Eileen. It was at this time that Katherine realized how fortunate she had been to spend time with these lovely people in their magnificent home. Every moment of that final evening in Ceylon was perfect—from the superb cuisine to the balmy moonlight to the air fresh and filled with the scent of exotic blossoms to the companionship of those generous and warm-hearted Ceylonese who had become her dear friends. As she stood basking in the moonlight and staring at the stars which seemed to fill the sky with their radiance, Katherine felt filled with a peacefulness she had not experienced since the childhood days she had spent in "her meadow" at the Somerset home of her Aunt Mariah and Uncle Charles.

"Oh, I wish it could go on forever" she whispered to Eileen, tears filling her eyes in response to the exquisite beauty and peace that enfolded her.

"I know what you mean," Eileen whispered back. Neither wished to disturb the atmosphere in any way. They stood gazing at the heavens for some time. When Katherine finally recovered her senses enough to realize the time, she saw that it was nearly dawn.

"My God," she cried aloud to Eileen, "do you realize we're scheduled to set sail for Bombay in three hours? We'll never make it!"

"Shhhh, love, calm down." advised Eileen. "I had a feeling something like this would happen, so I took it upon myself to cancel our passage on the ship and make airline reservations instead. Most of our luggage has been sent on ahead, and we're to be at the airport at half past nine. I figured we could save time by flying to India. Don't forget you are scheduled to deliver a speech on Sunday morning."

"And what's today?" inquired Katherine.

"Friday," answered Eileen.

"Oh God," Katherine groaned. "And when do you expect to sleep so that I will be sufficiently awake to give a speech?"

"On the airplane," replied Eileen without hesitation. "On the airplane," mimicked Katherine.

"On the airplane! You know that I've never been able to sleep for one minute on a train or airplane. Oh, well, what's the point of worrying? We will manage somehow."

"In the meantime, let's enjoy the sunrise, shall we? I don't think I've ever seen anything so sublime."

"No," agreed Katherine, feeling as though she should be speaking in hushed tones. She noticed that a hush had fallen over the rest of the crowd, as they observed in awe the grandeur of the scene unfolding before them. Although the sky had been the color of a dove's wings when they first began to watch, it had seemed only a matter of an instant before the dove's wings were dotted with sparkling topaz and then with ribbons of pale, shimmering rose. The rose then somehow expanded into crimson and the crimson into a flame color that seemed to light up the heavens and disperse the gray into streamers of brilliant color, tinged with deep green, amethyst, and turquoise. Katherine gasped as she saw the heavens come to life with the dawning of this new day and the appearance of the sun in its full golden glory.

Not until she had seen the sun assume its rightful position in the heavens did she make any motion to leave. Thanking their host profusely for his hospitality and promising to return in the future, she and Eileen took their leave and were soon on their way to the hotel. Hastily packing the few belongings that remained, Katherine also bathed and washed her hair so that she would not have to be burdened with this task upon her arrival in Bombay.

"All I plan on doing upon our arrival in India is sleeping. I shan't meander anywhere outside my hotel room for at least two days," she vowed.

"We shall see," said Eileen wisely, politely suppressing the desire to laugh aloud at Katherine's appearance. For her friend had taken none of the usual measures to make herself attractive. Pale and utterly exhausted, she had not stopped yawning since they left the home of their Ceylonese friends.

Katherine suspected but was never quite certain as to whether or not she had fallen asleep on the airplane after all. She only knew that there had been an inordinately brief interval between the time she had boarded the plane and the announcement by the pilot that they were ready to land in Bombay. Almost as soon as she had become comfortably settled in her seat, she decided to set her hair in the metal curlers she had brought along so that she would not have to be bothered with this task later on and could go directly to bed once she arrived at the hotel. When this task was completed, she wrapped her head in a silken scarf and then dozed off. The next thing of which she was cognizant was the captain's voice announcing that they were preparing to land, a brief view of the city from the air, and then the dizzy taxiing of the plane down the runway.

"Wake up!" Katherine nudged Eileen impatiently with her elbow. "We're landing in Bombay! Get up!"

"What is it, for God's sake?" Eileen asked irritably, abruptly awakening from a deep sleep.

"Look!" cried Katherine excitedly pointing to the colorful buildings below signifying Bombay.

"Uh-huh," yawned Eileen.

"Is that all you have to say? Where is your sense of adventure?" teased Katherine.

"Not on this airplane, I assure you. Perhaps I'll rediscover it after I've slept for about two weeks without, waking up."

"I know what you mean," agreed Katherine dryly. "I simply cannot wait to sleep in a soft comfortable bed."

As Eileen hastily scrambled to retrieve her small travel case, they heard the captain's words over the public address system, "It has been a pleasure having you on board. We wish you all a pleasant time in Bombay. All passengers may disembark now. We thank you all for flying with us."

"Well, kid, that's us. Let's go," said Katherine, rising from her seat.

"Hey, Katherine, look! " Eileen pulled her back into her seat.

"What is it?" she tried to follow Eileen's gaze. Eileen was staring at a group of people gathered at the gate. "What of it?" Katherine asked.

"Don't you see?" Eileen said impatiently. "The cameras and microphones? They're obviously here to meet someone. There must be a celebrity on board."

"Oh, is that all?" replied Katherine indifferently. "I hadn't noticed any celebrities. Come on Eileen, let's go. I'm exhausted."

"Oh all right."

And the two struggled down the narrow aisle toward the exit.

"There could be a million celebrities on board, and I don't think I would pay them any mind," observed Katherine wearily. "Perhaps if one was dressed as a pillow or a coverlet or a bed. Then, perhaps I would be interested . . . " Katherine was rambling on in this manner when Eileen suddenly blurted out.

"Oh my God!"

"Oh my God, what?" asked Katherine.

"You're not going to believe this!" continued Eileen breathlessly.

"Believe what?"

"Well, we seem to be the last ones off of the plane."

"That's what you're 'Oh my God-ing' about?"

"No, of course not. Don't you see?"

"Don't I see what? Come on Eileen. I'm really too tired for such games. Just come out with it."

"All right," sighed Eileen. "But brace yourself, Mrs. Hayward, because I have a feeling that the crowd outside is a group of photographers and journalists and that they are waiting for you,"

"For me?" muttered Katherine. "Eileen, don't be absurd. Why would reporters be waiting for me?"

"God only knows. But I swear it's true. I feel it!" At that juncture, one of the flight attendants, an attractive Indian girl, approached them.

"Is either one of you Mrs. Katherine Hayward?" she asked.

"Why, yes, I am she," replied Katherine. "What can I do for you?"

"Well I was just asked by several of the reporters outside to check the plane to see if you were still on board. They have been waiting for you, and thought, perhaps, that somehow they had missed you."

"Oh, thank you," said Katherine weakly. "Oh my God!" she groaned after the girl had left. "That crowd down there really is waiting for me! I'll have to put some make-up on and remove these ridiculous curlers. Excuse me, I won't be a minute." And within a matter of moments, Katherine emerged from the lavatory looking rosy and blooming and as chic as ever.

"Let's go!" she directed, and the two made their way briskly toward the crowd. For nearly forty-five minutes, she was barraged by questions: "Why have you come to India?" "Do you regard yourself as a guru?" "What is the nature of your work in the United Kingdom?" "How long will you be staying in our country?" "How do you feel about India's current political status?" "What is the real Katherine Hayward like?"

To this last question she replied in earnest, "That is what I have come to India to discover. Let me make your task simple, ladies and gentlemen. And just let me say that I do not regard myself as a guru, but rather as an explorer, a researcher, an investigator into the truth. And as to the nature of my research, well it has taken many forms including that which has been read and that which has been personally experienced and that which has been taught to me by others. When you ask why I have come to India, I would reply that it is for several reasons. One, to find true peace of mind. Two, to teach and to learn. Three, to discover and then to develop fully my own divine potential as a human being. I hope this information is of assistance. I'm afraid it will have to suffice, for I have no further time to give you. My friend and I have been several days with virtually no sleep at all and are most anxious to get to our hotel. So do please excuse us and thank you for your patience."

"I wonder who is responsible for all of this?" Katherine asked in a low voice to Eileen, as they found their way through the crowd.

"It is I, Mrs. Hayward, who am responsible for all of this. I do hope you haven't minded," she heard a man's voice saying. Katherine turned in surprise and found herself standing next to a slim, handsome, distinguished looking Indian gentleman who spoke perfect English and was impeccably attired in a classic, tailored Western suit.

"Who are you?" she asked, quickly, searching the man's eyes to discover the motive behind his words.

"Please let me introduce myself. I am Bhaskar Singh, friend and benefactor of Mr. Wilfred Hastings, the president of the Spiritualist Church for whom you will be lecturing this Sunday morning. Having seen your photograph, resume, and biographical data, I was intrigued, and could not help but feel that you had something very special to offer our people. You see, they know so little of Western mysticism, psychism, and so forth. Therefore, I felt compelled to introduce you to as many influential Indians as possible, and with your permission, I would like to arrange numerous public engagements for you, Mrs. Hayward."

"Why, that is most generous of you," said Katherine, blinking. "But I hardly know what to say. I shall have to think about your offer."

"As you say. But do not forget that our need is great. And now, if you would permit me, I should be happy to escort you to the limousine I have obtained for your use throughout your visit in India. I wish to make you as happy and comfortable as possible. We hope that your stay will be a long, fulfilling, and joyous one. Furthermore, my associates and I would like to arrange financial matters so that you will feel free to remain in our country for as long as you wish! But let us not speak of all this now you are tired. Come, follow me." And Mr. Singh led them to the waiting limousine. "Now, then. Welcome once again to our country. We will discuss all future plans and activities in the near future. I will telephone you tomorrow morning to arrange another meeting between us, if that is all right with you."

"Oh, yes, certainly," Katherine agreed, hardly knowing how to react to such excessive generosity. "Thank you so very much. I shall look forward to hearing from you," she called through the window, as the limousine sped off.

CHAPTER 49

Katherine the "Guru"

⟿

"FINALLY, WE MADE IT!" KATHERINE cried, as she prepared for bed. The two had no difficulty at all checking into the Ambassador Hotel which, they were relieved to observe, was comfortable in accordance with the English standard of the day. Eyeing her bed longingly, Katherine hastened to complete what little unpacking was necessary and changed into her bedclothes.

"Blessed sleep," she sighed, while washing her face in anticipation of the relief soon to follow. It was while absorbed in the task of brushing her hair that Katherine heard a faint knocking at the door of her room, *It couldn't be anyone for me*, she thought, startled. *It must be next door. I gave explicit instructions to the concierge that I was not to be disturbed under any circumstances.* Still, the knocking persisted, and Katherine finally realized that there was most assuredly someone at her door.

"Who is it?" she called out.

"Very important, Mrs. Hayward. Very important," was the only response she received to her query. The voice was male; the accent Indian.

"Just a moment," she called out impatiently, wrapping a pale blue chenille robe around her body.

"Yes?" she asked politely upon opening her door only several inches— enough to see who was there. She beheld a tiny, disheveled-looking Indian man who wore a rumpled brown cotton suit that looked as though it had been slept in. "What is it?" she demanded, as the man stood silently gawking at her.

"May I come in and speak with you, Mrs. Hayward.? Very important I see you. Urgent I talk now. I am reporter for *Times of India*. It's essential I speak with you. Please let me in."

Sensing the desperation in the little man's voice, she opened the door a bit farther. "I'm afraid I am too exhausted to give you more than a few minutes of my time. Can't you return tomorrow? I should be happy to see you then." she added graciously.

"Oh no!" the man exclaimed, turning ashen. "No can return tomorrow. Have deadline. Article I write about you must be turned in tonight!"

"I'm sorry, but it just isn't possible," she began. But the reporter was cleverly edging his way into her room while speaking.

"Please help me, Mrs. Hayward. My position with the *Times* will be in jeopardy if you do not grant interview today. And," he said dramatically, "I have wife and three children; cannot afford to lose job!" Was it her imagination or were his eyes filling with tears? And she had most definitely heard a quiver in his voice.

"Oh, all right," she finally conceded. "Come on in. I will give you a brief interview, but then you must leave. Do you understand?"

"Oh, yes. Yes, I understand perfectly," he returned, his eyes shining with happiness. "Thank you, Mrs. Hayward. Will never forget you for such a kindness." And for the next hour and fifteen minutes, Katherine answered the man's persistent and probing questions. She ended the interview with a demonstration of her clairvoyance so accurate that the man left the room positively mesmerized.

"How you know? How you do that?" he asked over and over again. "How you know about my wife and family? Mother and new job? You are great lady, Mrs. Hayward. Never before seen one like you. No one ever spoke before like this to me. Thank you. So grateful. I take my leave now. You give me great story—no lose job now. Thank you," he said again, bowing at the waist. He was so deferential that Katherine felt inclined to laugh aloud.

But practicing restraint and civility, she only smiled and said, "You are most welcome."

"And now I go," he said, bowing once again. And soon, thankfully, he was gone. Hastily, she discarded the chenille robe and climbed into bed, solemnly vowing to let nothing further interrupt her sleep. She fell asleep at once.

She did not awaken until nearly noon the following day. And preferring to have a cup of tea before proceeding a single step farther, she ordered a pot along with a copy of the *London Times* and several local newspapers. She spent several minutes thoroughly enjoying the luxury of absolute privacy and relaxation as the sunlight streamed through the open windows and a gentle breeze stirred the languid atmosphere. It was one of those mornings when she genuinely felt glad and grateful to be alive. "Who could ask for anything more?" she sighed happily, taking one last sip of her tea and munching on a delicious pastry.

As she leafed through one of the local newspapers, she was suddenly aware that it was the paper for which the funny little man who had interviewed her yesterday was employed. Staring at the front page, her gaze was suddenly drawn to an article at the bottom of the page. It was entitled, "Spiritual Leader Arrives In Bombay." Her heart began to race as she read on.

Katherine Hayward knows all about you. A godly woman, she perceives the truths of life and shares them with the public. She seems to know everything about everyone. She can tell you all about you—your past, present, and future. We welcome this illumined soul to our country. It is clear most of us have much to learn from her. This guru from the West not only possesses great wisdom and insight but can perform the miracle of proving that life continues after death. Do not miss the opportunity to meeting her while she is in India. Her first public meeting in our country will be this Sunday at eleven a.m. at the Royal Hall. I would not miss it for the world. See you there!

Blushing from ear to ear, Katherine reread the article. "What rubbish!" she exclaimed finally, putting the paper down. The telephone rang, and she temporarily forgot her embarrassment. *I wonder how many people will have read the article?* she mused. But soon after this, doing her best to recover from her journey, and to refresh and revitalize her mind and body, she dismissed the entire episode from her mind. Now all she wished for were peace and quiet.

It was not until Sunday morning shortly before she was scheduled to deliver her first address in India that she had an inkling as to how many people had read the article. The wide streets outside the hall in which she was to speak were filled with people. Throngs of them—Indians, Westerners, Indonesian—white, black, and yellow—literally lined the streets. Many of them sat in the lotus position at the side of the roads or on stoops. All had come to pay homage to the guru from the West and to hear her speak. The open limousine managed to crawl through the waiting throngs and, at several junctures, Katherine herself was forced to stand and beg the crowds to disperse so that the car could get through. She was reminded of the excitement preceding her very first public meeting in Mt. Ash nearly forty years ago. "Little did I imagine then that I would be in such a place as this today!" she marveled.

"Here we are, Madam," the driver announced, stopping before a large, ornate building. Katherine, who had expected to speak before perhaps several hundred people, was astounded to see that the hall itself could easily accommodate one thousand. As she entered the building, she heard the cries of those waiting in the street, "There she goes! It is the Great One from the West. That is Mrs. Hayward!"

She began her talk at eleven a.m. When, finally, she was finished it was nearly three, and she was almost faint from the heat and exhaustion. Still the crowds stamped and cheered, whistled and applauded.

"I've never seen anything like it!" Eileen gasped, as the two tried to make their way out of the hall and into the waiting limousine following the meeting.

"Neither have I!" replied Katherine, feeling totally drained as a result of the ordeal. "I'm glad that's over!"

"Shall we stop at a restaurant for lunch?" Eileen asked later on, when, at last they were comfortably sprawled out in the back of the car.

"You mean dinner, don't you?" quipped Katherine, glancing at her watch and noting that it was near four p.m. "Actually," she said, "I think I'd rather return to the hotel, bathe, change, and then eat a meal, if that's all right with you."

"Fine, it would do both of us good to rest after all the excitement," agreed, Eileen. "We can order some tea and biscuits to tide us over, can't we?"

"Lovely," Katherine agreed, closing her eyes.

Both were thoroughly exhausted by the time they returned to the hotel and glad they had made the decision to postpone going out. As the two alighted from the limousine and prepared to enter the lobby, they were taken aback by the number of people milling about.

"What is this all about?" Katherine wondered aloud.

"I've no idea," murmured Eileen. "Perhaps they're here for a conference or convention of some sort."

"You're probably right. Let's slip through as quickly and unobtrusively as possible. I've had enough of crowds today to last my entire life!"

"Ditto, I'm sure!" Eileen concurred.

And noticing the crowd standing by the elevator, Katherine whispered, "Let's take the stairs." But both were astounded to see the crowds extend into the stairwell along the corridor and in front of the door to her room. Many smiled beatifically at Katherine—some bowed. Others knelt. Still others saluted her. She did not know how to interpret these gestures. As they had outside the hall that morning, many were sitting in the lotus posture. As she struggled to find her key in her handbag, she was forced to literally step over several bodies.

"Now this is positively absurd!" she said with annoyance. "I'm going downstairs to register a complaint and to find out what this is all about! Will you join me?"

"With pleasure!" returned Eileen.

"What is going on here?" Katherine demanded of the concierge, a middle-aged English man with thinning hair and a wide, flat face, and florid complexion.

"You should know better than anyone, Mrs. Hayward," he replied curtly.

"I'm sure I haven't any idea as to what you mean," she said icily.

"Well, Mrs. Hayward. These people are your devotees. You are their guru," he explained simply.

"Devotees? Guru," sputtered Katherine fiercely. "You can't be serious! I have no devotees, and I am most certainly no guru."

"Well, then, why have all these people come to pay you homage?"

"I'm telling you that I have no idea," replied Katherine. "Nothing like this has ever happened before—truly." The man looked dubious, but said nothing further. "Isn't it possible to somehow, someway to make them leave?" she pleaded, staring at the enormous group which filled the lobby. "Isn't there a translator in the hotel that can explain that I wish to—that I need to—be left alone?"

"Mrs. Hayward, each one here has come for darshan."

"Darshan?" asked Katherine, puzzled.

"Yes, for the holy sight of the guru."

"Look, must I keep on telling you that I am not a guru?"

"It matters not what you tell me, Mrs. Hayward. What matters is what all these devotees believe, and they believe you to be a guru. Furthermore, each one wishes to meet with you privately—so that you can help, heal, and predict the future for them."

"I see," Katherine acknowledged. "Well please do find a translator to inform them that I will be happy to schedule private appointments for a fee if they contact me by telephone, and that they must leave this hotel at once. I must have peace and privacy!"

"All right, Mrs. Hayward, as you wish," replied the concierge with obvious distaste for the entire situation.

"Thank you very much indeed," replied Katherine politely. By the time she and Eileen arrived at their rooms upstairs, the crowds had already begun to disperse.

"Thank goodness," Katherine sighed gratefully. But once she had managed to get safely past the crowd and into her own quarters, she realized that there was to be no respite after all. For now the telephone rang incessantly with those anxious to meet with her privately.

"It's the secretary of the Maharani of Cooch Behar," Eileen whispered, putting her hand over the receiver, after the telephone had rung once again. "He wishes to know when you can meet with the Maharani who is one of the wealthiest and most powerful women in India. This is the third time he has called this afternoon."

"I don't care," was Katherine's defiant response. "I don't have time to meet with her. There are many others who have requested an interview, and I am booked every day from morning until night for the next two weeks. But I shall certainly be glad to see her if I have an opening. I will notify the Maharani as soon as I receive word that someone has canceled his or her appointment."

"Hold on just a moment, please," Eileen said politely into the telephone, then placed her hands once again over the receiver and said urgently, "Katherine, don't be pig-headed. You are insulting the Maharani by refusing to see her. Just agree to meet with her."

"Why?" asked Katherine, her eyes smoldering. "Just because she is wealthy and influential and accustomed to pushing her weight around? Absolutely not. I will not indulge her whims at the expense of someone in need simply because she is a member of the Indian aristocracy. She will have to wait her turn just like everyone else."

"Oh, all right. I see it's no use arguing with you on that matter . . . I am very sorry, Sir, but Mrs. Hayward insists that she has not a moment to spare right now for the Maharani, but that she will contact her the moment time becomes available. Thank you for your patience in this matter," Eileen said, then hung up the phone.

"Who does she think she is?" Katherine was fuming. "Obviously expects the world to be handed to her on a silver platter just because she happens to have been born into the aristocracy. Expects to take the place of some poor bloke who really needs what I have to give just because she wields a certain amount of power. Well, she won't get away with it with me!"

"Calm down, Katherine. Really, you're overreacting. Furthermore, you don't even know why the Maharani wanted to see you."

"Oh, don't I!" snapped Katherine, her eyes blazing. "What color shall I paint the servant quarters? Will I acquire another million rupees? Where shall I go for my summer holiday?" Katherine said sarcastically, mimicking the Maharani.

"Now, I really don't think that's fair. She may be a lovely person and have a motive altogether different from that which you imagine."

"Perhaps," said Katherine slowly. "Nonetheless, I am very glad that it did not work lout that I was able to see her. You know me well enough to realize that I will not grant favors to anyone simply on the basis of their wealth, power, or social position. Everyone is equally important in my eyes regardless of their outer circumstances."

"All right, all right. I understand." Eileen admitted grudgingly. "But I still feel that it's important for you to meet her," she persisted. "I have a hunch you two belong together."

Later that day, finding herself with some vacant moments and remaining true to her words, Katherine advised Eileen to schedule an appointment with the Maharani. "I find that I am free tomorrow afternoon, Monday, from half past one to three. If that is convenient for the Maharani, I shall be happy to meet with her then."

"Bravo!" Eileen applauded, racing to the telephone.

"Don't 'bravo' me," murmured Katherine, "it just so happens that I have received a cancellation, that's all. Now we shall see how accurate your hunch is."

"Good," declared Eileen, unperturbed by Katherine's sarcasm.

In fact, Eileen's hunch did prove correct. Furthermore, the next afternoon as they were ushered in to see the Maharani at her palatial residence in Bombay, Katherine realized that the meeting had, in a way, come about as a direct response to her own prayers. Having been permitted to take out of England only a fraction of the money she would have wished to bring to India and, as a result, frankly worried as to how it might be possible to remain in this country indefinitely, Katherine had boldly declared before leaving England, "All right Maharajahs and Maharanis of India. Come forth. Support my work in your country, so that I need not think of money at all and will be able to do and travel as I wish throughout my stay in India." Although she had uttered these words in half-jest, she was suddenly reminded of them as an Indian manservant escorted them into the great chamber in which they were to meet the Maharani.

The Maharani of Cooch Behar was nothing like Katherine had imagined her. Far from being snobbish or arrogant, she was unaffected and down-to-earth with a warmth and charm that were delightful to behold. Katherine liked her at once. Furthermore, the Maharani, having been educated in England, spoke perfect English and had a wonderful sense of humor. She came to the point of their meeting almost immediately.

"I attended your meeting yesterday, Mrs. Hayward, and enjoyed myself very much indeed. You see, I have spent many years in the West and have studied many branches of philosophy and mysticism. What you said yesterday corroborated my own viewpoints. But this is not the reason for which I desired to see you. Rather, I could not help but feel that you had a great deal to offer my countrymen. I felt that if you could stay on in India indefinitely, you could reach many here who are in great need of what you have to offer. I would simply like to offer my assistance to you in your work, and to provide you with accommodations here at the palace and at my residences in all parts of India so that you may stay in our country for as long as you wish and travel freely without any financial responsibilities. I would feel grateful and privileged if you would be my guest," she said simply.

"And . . . and that is the purpose for which you sought an interview with me?" Katherine stammered, a blush creeping over her cheeks. She was by now sorely regretting the sharp words she had spoken to Eileen regarding the Maharani.

"Precisely," replied the Maharani warmly.

"Thank you so very much for your most generous invitation," said Katherine, feeling more ashamed than ever of her previous false assumptions and misconceptions regarding the Maharani's motive for inviting her to the palace. "We should be delighted to accept your kind offer," said Katherine suddenly, after a moment's deliberation.

"Good," smiled the Maharani. "You shall have your own private quarters—a bungalow with your own staff. You may move in as soon as you wish."

"Thank you so very much," replied Katherine gratefully. "We shall notify you when we're ready to move in, if that's all right with you. It will be sometime within the next few days."

"Very good," said the Maharani. "We look forward to your stay."

It did not take them long, nor was it at all inconvenient to settle into the charming bungalow adjacent to the Maharani's residence. Beautifully furnished, it was equipped with every known luxury and a full-time domestic staff.

"What more could one ask?" Katherine exclaimed, studying with pleasure her new surroundings. "And don't say I told you so!" she warned Eileen whom she had always been able to read like a book.

"All right," laughed Eileen, "but I'll think it just the same."

Through the Maharani (whom both she and Eileen grew to love dearly), Katherine and Eileen were introduced to nearly everyone of influence in Bombay, and Katherine's reputation as a great teacher from the West expanded within a very brief period of time. Katherine's days were filled with appointments with friends and relatives of the Maharani, and she was required to give frequent talks and demonstrations by night. Not a single day had elapsed wherein she was free to conduct her own personal research or to do as she chose.

"I came here both to teach and to learn," she had wailed one day to Eileen. "And so far all I've done is teach. I really must get on with the work for which I've come to India."

Explaining to the Maharani the true purpose for which she had come to India and that she had been inspired by Paramahansa Yogananda by means of his *Autobiography of a Yogi*, the Maharani was most sympathetic and desirous that Katherine should be free to do and study as she wished.

"I myself should like to learn more about this guru, Yogananda," the Maharani declared. "In fact, why do we not visit one of Yogananda's spiritual communities—what we in India refer to as ashrams."

"An excellent idea, Eileen and I have intended to visit several of them in fact, to meet members of the Self-Realization Fellowship and study kriya yoga." And so, as a result of the Maharani's influence and intervention on their behalf, it came to pass that all three were introduced to the heads of the Self-Realization Fellowship—one of which was a particularly gifted and inspired devotee known as Sri Daya Mata—who would later become President of the Self-Realization Fellowship. All three—Katherine, Eileen, and the Maharani (whom Katherine affectionately called "Mah")—studied diligently the teachings of Yogananda in the peaceful atmosphere of one of his own ashrams.

Meditation, yoga, yoga postures, chanting, philosophy, and practical spiritual living were integral parts of the daily program the three experienced here under the meticulous guidance and training of those who were experts in the ancient science of kriya yoga. Yet, although deeply interested in the philosophy and lifestyle advocated by Yogananda and his disciples, Katherine, after several months of study along these lines, realized that despite the beauty, purposefulness, and appropriateness of his philosophy for countless people that this was not the spiritual path for her. In the meantime, she was also introduced to a number of other highly respected yogis and gurus who also claimed to know the pathway toward God-realization. Open-minded, Katherine studied, with equal fervor and diligence, their methods of attaining God. She spent the greater part of nearly four months in Bombay and the southwestern portion of India visiting ashrams, conducting research, and visiting many other cities including Karachi, Bangalore, Madras, Calcutta, Benares, and Darjeeling. She insisted upon meeting the various well-known yogis and gurus of the areas, meditating and conversing with those who were deemed knowledgeable in the areas in which she so desperately sought knowledge.

Yet, although she, herself, had come to India in search of greater wisdom, to her astonishment, virtually everywhere she traveled she herself was hailed as a guru. Welcomed throughout the country, she continued to lecture and to demonstrate the proof of survival, and to conduct countless private interviews with individuals of every conceivable type of religious training and background. Hindus, Moslems, Sikhs, Buddhists, Jains, and Christians—mostly the affluent and well-educated representatives of these religious groups sought contact with her. There was little doubt that both she and they were learning and sharing their wisdom and experience in remarkable ways.

CHAPTER 50

Maharani of Cooch Behar

YET IN SPITE OF ALL she learned about Hinduism, the predominant religious system in India, from a variety of sources, she had difficulty reconciling the acute poverty, disease, and starvation she witnessed with a philosophy that maintained each human being is divine; each is Brahman; each is Shiva; that God dwells within each one as Him.

"How is it possible for you to sit in the lap of luxury—experience enormous wealth and power—while witnessing the suffering and despair of your brothers and sisters?" Katherine inquired of the Maharani, at the risk of offending her benefactor. "How do you justify such disparity between the social classes or castes?"

"I do not attempt to justify anything, Katherine. You see, the Hindu merely accept one's circumstances and those of others as God's will and as the result of the universal law of karma which suggests, as does your own Christian Bible, 'As you sow, so shall you reap.' So many Westerners have difficulty understanding the Hindu belief. But you see, those whom you pity, those who appear to be suffering so greatly, regard it as their karma to live in this way. They believe that they are reaping what they have sown during previous lifetimes. They have 'earned' their present lifestyle, as I, perhaps have earned mine. My people do not believe in such a thing as injustice. Nor do they judge one another. For they recognize that we, as human beings, do not possess sufficient knowledge or understanding to comprehend the whys and wherefores of life, but rather that all of us are evolving at different levels and rates into a state of perfection wherein we

458

will ultimately live in the eternal ecstasy of union with the Absolute. Only the infinite Spirit that pervades all living things is responsible for the creation, sustenance, and dissolution of all living things knows the complete and true picture. We, as mere human beings, see with limited vision and operate with limited consciousness.

"Therefore, what appears to you to be profound suffering, may indeed be God's grace, for only through this suffering is the soul becoming stronger and drawing closer than ever to its Creator. Furthermore, do not overlook the fact that you are viewing 'success' by Western standards and that the Hindu concept of so-called success and failure are vastly different from your own. For the Hindu does not think in material terms, but rather in spiritual terms. The degree to which man knows himself, his true nature, and potential, that is the means by which he determines success. That is why in our country it is the holy man, the saint, teacher, the Enlightened One, guru who is revered. He who knows himself, the True Higher or Greater Self, is the true king among men and beyond all suffering. Therefore, if you were to interrogate many of those poor, starving, diseased human beings on the streets, you would discover an attitude of acceptance, submission to God's will, and the realization that their prospects for a joyous prosperous life the next time around are being considerably increased.

"From the yogis and gurus you have met, you are aware that the ordinary creature comforts so important to most human beings in the West are of little value or significance to them. Some require very little food or water for their sustenance; most of these Great Beings are so exalted in the presence of the Holy Spirit that resides within and without that they have learned to perform what ordinary men call miracles. These Great Souls are in such a state of ecstasy and eternal beauty that they transcend material wants or needs. These Souls bless and benefit the whole of humankind and the Earth itself by means of their presence on the planet. It is this state of perfect peace, of everlasting joy that results from the knowledge that one is the Self—on the truest and deepest level—universal, indestructible, omniscient, and omnipotent. "

"It seems impossible to reconcile such lofty aims and ideals with the pitiful sight one sees on the streets," Katherine remarked.

"I imagine that it is difficult indeed for Westerners to comprehend. For most are so caught up in the material concerns of life and judge success in terms of material success. The Hindu, on the other hand, attaches little significance to material achievement and places value upon success in accordance with spiritual attainment. He regards any so-called 'social injustice' as a very temporary status, as a means toward an end. Only spiritual achievement is enduring."

"I see," Katherine remained unconvinced but attentive. "Does not karma, as you view it, bear a striking resemblance to the Christian concepts of hellfire and damnation? Are not then poverty, disease, misery in the outer world punishments for what one has previously sown?"

"Superficially, it may appear this way," returned the Maharani. "But the Hindu does not view karma as a system of punishment but as a means of teaching certain cosmic truths and as a universal law—scientific and precise—that states that every cause has an effect. And, like Newton's Law of Gravity, which indicates that what comes up will surely come down, one does not view the 'coming down' as a 'system of punishment.' It is an observable phenomenon—a scientific fact—one that remains in effect in the same manner regardless of mans' attempts to interpret or extrapolate any hidden purposes or meanings to it. Do not the mountains, flowers, and trees exist regardless of whether we view them as beautiful or ugly or whether or not we are indifferent to them? In the same way, it matters not how one interprets 'karma'; the Hindu only knows that it exists as surely as the skies above or the Earth beneath his feet. He knows that a man cannot escape the effects of his own actions—that every action has a reaction."

Still, although much of what the Maharani and others told her rang true, it remained difficult for her to observe the seeming misery rampant throughout India—the invalids; the beggars; the homeless; the thousands who slept and lived on the city streets—and believe that these poor souls were but reaping what they had sown.

Yet I have no better explanation, she thought ruefully. *Who am I to dis-agree with this belief system? No one seems to have any tangible proof of any-thing. I guess there are certain things that one must learn to accept on faith. Yet, had I not myself seen, touched and spoken with Spirit Beings would I have believed in life's continuity? Even though countless individuals had told me of their own experiences? I just don't know. I want to know and experience—not merely to think or believe—but I want to know, with every nerve and fiber of my being, that Power that sustains me and every other living creature with breath. I must know the truth!* she declared passionately.

But she instantly recalled the words of one of the yogis whom she had recently met in Calcutta: "The truth resides beyond the mind—beyond the physical senses and any physical reality—although the Mighty Power penetrates and permeates the physical existence. It is only truly discernible by one who has truly come to know, through meditation and pure living, the Self within—the Knower, the Supreme Witness. The mind is the great obstacle that keeps us from knowing the Self. The sages of the Upanishads taught that the mind is the body of the self, and that the true Self is the witness of all our thoughts, actions, and words. Only through yoga and meditation—when the mind, which is normally focused upon external ob-jects and circumstances, is focused deeper and deeper within—can it touch its own source. The Katha Upanishad says that the one that perceives both dream and waking states is the all-pervasive self. The self is the supreme Truth. Is it not this supreme Truth which you are seeking, Mrs. Hayward?" he had asked gently, his eyes smiling with compassion.

Katherine knew he had been aware of the inner torment, the yearning that had led her to come to India, which had, indeed, propelled her from one point to another throughout her entire life.

"You will never find that which you seek from any book or school. Only by stilling the mind and dwelling inwardly can you hope to discover It. Self-Realization is nothing but the merging of the mind in the Self. As un-happiness is the result of our own thoughts, when we go beyond the mind, beyond thought, we experience the true and lasting bliss of the Self."

It was only when the yogi began to discuss the necessity of finding a guru that Katherine became disillusioned. "Realization of God is possible only through a guru. Only through the grace of a guru can you unfold and grow. Only the guru—one who already knows the truth and who possesses spiritual power—can awaken you to the supreme bliss of the Self, only he can liberate you from the bondage of earthly life."

"I see," Katherine had said slowly, feeling inexplicably saddened and disappointed by his words. "But I thought you said one can achieve Realization by going inward, by meditating."

"Yes, but it is through the guru that we are initiated into the path of meditation. The guru has the power to transform his disciple completely."

"This system is not for me," Katherine realized suddenly, tears of disappointment stinging her eyes. "I cannot accept the concept of a guru or believe that it is necessary for any other person to guide me along the path toward God-Realization." Finally, she had put into words what had disturbed her ever since she had come to India—the fact that virtually everyone she had met who was yearning for spiritual unfoldment had depended upon her or a "guru" to do the work, to assume the responsibility for them.

Why the spiritual path is nothing more than an acceptable means of escaping life's responsibilities, she thought to herself. *What finer way to escape the hardship and frustration of the outer world than by living in an ashram—under the care and tutelage of a guru?* She began to realize, for the first time, that many sought to escape the harshness of everyday life in the outer world by retreating into these spiritual communities.

I don't want to escape from my responsibilities, from my obligations, she thought suddenly. *I want to know God and bring Him to those in the outer world—to show them that all can live a godly existence—not simply those who have chosen to retreat from the outer world. And I simply do not believe that I must have a guru in order to achieve Self-Realization. Somehow, I have always felt that the true teacher resides within me—that I need no outer guide or teacher. But who knows? Perhaps I will discover differently at a later time. Nonetheless, for the present, the ways taught in India are not for me.*

It was a realization that deeply saddened and disappointed her. She had come to this country full of hope. Now, the reality of her circumstances hit her hard. And she wondered if ever she would discover the Truths for which she had so earnestly searched throughout her life. Once again, she was reminded of the words of Dr. Evans, which had been uttered so many years ago: "There are no mistakes. Everyone is in precisely the right place at the right time in order to acquire those experiences which are necessary for their own soul's growth." And, as she had so often throughout her life, she said simply with utter sincerity, "Not my way, oh God, but Thy way. Thy will be done on earth as it is in heaven."

And although she used the remainder of her time in India to conduct further research, her heart was no longer in this effort. She had begun to realize that the knowledge she had so desperately sought for so long was still a ways off. And so, she continued to bring what wisdom she had acquired to those who would benefit. As the guest of the Maharani, she was treated as royalty wherever she went, and her lectures and demonstrations were highly praised. Many she met in India seemed so familiar—"as though we've always known each other"—that she was once again struck with the utter sensibility and practicality of the belief in reincarnation.

She truly felt "at home" in all parts of the world, and had never felt fearful or suspicious of anyone or any place she had visited. From the mysterious little man who had volunteered to serve as their chauffeur in Calcutta, to the marvelous swami whom they met at the Serampore hermitage of Sri Ukteswar (Yogananda's guru), to the saintly gurus who radiated blessedness and peace, to the queer wiry Indian man with dark, penetrating eyes who showed up at the door of her Bombay residence several days before her scheduled departure home who had volunteered to escort her to the Himalayas wherein she would be afforded the privilege of seeing the Akashic Records,[4] Katherine experienced the feeling that all life was indeed one life and that, accordingly, all men and women were her brothers and

---

4 A celestial ether that fills all space and upon which are recorded every thought, action, and word in existence since the beginning of the world.

sisters. Reincarnation, an acceptable theory before, had assumed new meaning and significance, and had become a reality to her.

By the end of her fifth month in India, Katherine had had enough. She was restless and homesick and anxious to make some kind of order out of all she had seen, studied, and experienced on the trip. As Eileen was equally ready and willing to return home, Katherine wasted no time in notifying Graham and Liebie that they could expect her in England sometime in February 1959. She was surprised to receive a letter from Liebie in response.

"Katherine, let me meet you in Gibraltar," she had written back. "From there we can travel in Spain for a month or so, and then return to England. I feel we have an enormous amount to discuss and plan."

In spite of her reluctance to extend her absence from home, Katherine found herself accepting Liebie's proposal. *Perhaps she'll be able to assist me in sorting out and interpreting my experiences. Perhaps we'll plan the next phase of our work.*

"I'll meet you in Gibraltar on the 27th of February," Katherine wrote back. "I'm looking forward to seeing you." In the meantime, it was decided that Eileen would forgo the trip to Gibraltar and return home to England. She would stop at Gibraltar to see Katherine and Liebie safely together.

There could be little doubt that the time in India had been invaluable. She had studied and learned and experienced firsthand so much which had been only theory before. She did not doubt that she had grown and matured in many ways. In addition, she had met an extraordinary number of people and had made a wide circle of friends which would never be forgotten.

"Goodbye, and thank you," the Maharani had tearfully embraced her, as she prepared to leave the palatial residence that had served as her home for so many months. "You have taught me the importance of acknowledging what I know and what I don't know," the Maharani smiled through her tears. "I will never forget you, Katherine."

"Nor will I you," Katherine replied. "I am eternally grateful. Together, I believe, we have done much to help your people. Now, life's continuity is no far-fetched theory or dream, but a practical reality."

"Yes, and for this, we are more thankful than you can ever know," the Maharani had said, hugging Katherine close to her in one final embrace. "I love you," she said softly.

"And I love you," returned Katherine.

Now, as she and Eileen boarded the plane that would fly them to Gibraltar, Katherine wished with all her heart that she could have returned to the West in possession of the peace and wisdom she had come to India to find. But, bravely swallowing her disappointment and her tears, she decided to let go her hopes and dreams for the time being and to dwell in the present. As she had on so many occasions in the past, she faced the future with quiet courage, dignity, and optimism.

Ask and ye shall receive; knock and the door shall open; seek and ye shall find, she thought paraphrasing Jesus' words. *I won't give up*, she vowed solemnly. *I'll never give up my search for God. And one day soon, I know that I'll find exactly what I've been looking for. He can't hide from me forever.* Heartened by this realization, she smiled at Eileen, and then settled back into her seat.

No, she promised herself. *I will never give up.* A gentle smile played about her lips, as the plane made its way through the heavens toward Gibraltar.

CHAPTER 51

Reunion

SHE RECOGNIZED LIEBIE AT ONCE. Despite the many months they had been apart, in spite of the noisy crowd that had assembled at the gate, Katherine had no difficulty distinguishing the closely cropped dark hair, pale oval face, serious deep-set eyes, slender figure, and boyish attire. Even from a distance, she saw that Liebie's eyes were dancing with excitement, and she knew that this excitement was due, at least in part, to their imminent reunion.

"Katherine!" Liebie cried happily, as she caught sight of her. Normally cool and reserved, the aristocratic Mrs. Pugh almost flew into Katherine's arms. "How lovely to see you. How I've missed you!" exclaimed Liebie, as the two friends embraced enthusiastically. "I've so much to tell you!"

"Ditto, I'm sure," replied Katherine, her eyes sparkling.

"I've sold the White House," Liebie began, "for a good price, too."

"No!" squealed Katherine. "So you did sell it after all?"

"Yes, and for the present time, I am settled in Hove. For the first time in years, I am free of a center and all the responsibilities that go with it. But, I may buy another in the near future. One never knows, does one?" asked Liebie with deliberate naiveté.

"Now, Liebie Pugh, none of that. I don't feel that I will ever again want anything to do with a Center—or the type of work in which you and I were involved before. I want to move forward—work in new directions. But we can discuss all that some other time. I have so much to tell you about my journey—Port Said and Tripoli, the three world leaders I met and advised, Ceylon and the Subud and India and the Maharani . . ."

"Maharani?" inquired Liebie.

"Yes, you cannot imagine how much we experienced; India was not at all the way I imagined it to be."

"No?"

"No," replied Katherine shaking her head. "But you really must go, Liebie. The atmosphere is like nothing I ever experienced before."

"And . . . and did you discover all that you set out to discover?" asked Liebie awkwardly, reluctant to intrude upon Katherine's privacy. There was a brief silence, as Katherine digested the full meaning of Liebie's words.

"No," she said quietly, "I did not." Disappointment was evident in her voice.

"I see, love," said Liebie with compassion. "Perhaps you will tell me all about it . . ."

"Yes, I will, Liebie, but not just yet. There is so much that I've simply not been able to absorb or interpret for that matter. I . . . I . . . we'll discuss it after I've had the time and opportunity to draw a few conclusions—that is, if you don't mind . . ." she whispered earnestly. "I hope you understand," she added, looking directly into Liebie's eyes. Liebie's heart went out to her for she understood the disappointment that lay behind her friend's simple words.

Taking Katherine's hand in her own, she smiled in her gentle way. "I understand, my dear. You will tell me all about it at some later date—when you are ready to talk about such things."

"Thank you, Liebie for . . . for . . . for," Katherine choked. She was surprised by the depth of her feelings—apparently, the disappointment she had recently experienced was far greater than she had been aware.

"For what, my dear?" inquired Liebie gently, her sharp eyes observing Katherine's features.

"For . . . for . . . all that you are."

The days on Gibraltar passed quickly and happily, as the two shopped, swam, took pictures with the famed monkeys, and hiked and delighted in the unique beauty of the spot. It was during this time that Liebie informed Katherine of her future plans.

"I shall open a small center by the sea in Hove. There, I will continue the work that we began so many years ago at Wood Court. You know I have continued to believe, through all these years, that we would achieve all we sought to achieve during those early days. Won't you join me, Katherine, in the continuation of the work we began so long ago? The world is in great need of the proof we could offer them."

Katherine had searched Liebie's face, in order to determine to what extent Liebie was relying upon her acceptance of the proposal. But Liebie's face was inscrutable.

"I hope that you are in no way depending upon me in regard to your future plans," said Katherine quietly. "You know that there is no future for us together, Liebie. I will always be there for you as a friend. But nothing further. My work no longer includes you, Liebie. Nor does yours concern me. Although we will always remain friends and although I will most certainly lend you a helping hand, whenever you require it, we must go our separate ways. Now, more than ever I must be free!" she said with an intensity that took Liebie quite by surprise.

Several moments elapsed before Liebie said tremulously, "I cannot say that I am not deeply disappointed. But, I understand your need for independence. Let's leave it this way, shall we? When we return to Hove, you will remain with me for as long as you find it convenient to do so. At your request, we have already scheduled a series of lectures based upon your experiences in India. After you have delivered that series, you are free to do and go as you wish. From thereon, we will work together—be together—only to the extent you wish. Is this agreeable to you?" asked Liebie, as tactfully as possible.

"Perfectly," nodded Katherine. "And now that our professional relationship has been resolved, I have no wish to discuss it any further. From here on, let's enjoy the time we spend together. Let's have some fun!"

"Agreed," smiled Liebie.

From thereon, they got on beautifully and enjoyed their holiday together immensely. Yet before leaving Gibraltar and traveling north to Spain, Katherine was to have an experience unlike any she had ever had before.

Seldom had she dreamt by night. In fact, the number of dreams she could recall having had in her entire life could be numbered on the fingers of one hand. Yet, one night shortly after her arrival on the Rock, she had a dream so terrifyingly vivid that the events that took place in the dream-state seemed very real to her, as though she actually had lived through those events. She awoke trembling with fear and cold, beads of perspiration dotting her forehead! The horror of the dream remained with her for some time. She had difficulty falling back asleep, and had sat up in bed for half the night reading, in a futile attempt to forget the dreadful episode.

The following morning, looking pale and ill, and tired, she met Liebie in the hotel dining room for breakfast. "Whatever is wrong?" Liebie blurted aloud, at once, gasping at the sight of her friend.

"Well, Liebie," Katherine began in a weak voice. "It seems that I've had a dream—at least I think it was a dream—but now, I'm really not sure what it was." So startlingly vivid had been the dream that Katherine was able to recall it in perfect detail. "All I know is," she continued, "that I was traveling—perhaps gliding is a better word—over the Rock. I could see everything—its full geography from my viewpoint, as though I were flying above it all."

"Yes?" said Liebie intently, as Katherine paused to collect her thoughts.

"I have no idea how it came about, but, all of a sudden, I seemed to find myself in this . . . cave . . . it was really a gaping hole at the side of a jagged, barren hill. The interior was dank and dark and draughty. There was a pathway in the cave, but I was too frightened to follow it very far. There was, along the pathway not too distant from the opening, a large pool of muddy, murky water into which water, tepid water, continued to drip from the ceiling. For some reason, the atmosphere in this place was very unpleasant. It seemed that something—something terrible—had taken place there or at least nearby. I stopped for several moments, wondering why I felt so uneasy. But then, suddenly, from a distance, I heard what sounded like a groan. I paused to listen intently now, listening for further sounds. I remained frozen to the spot. I couldn't move at all. Suddenly, a blood-curdling scream pierced the atmosphere. But I could do nothing. I was still somehow riveted to my spot. Soon, it sounded as though an entire chorus of voices—sobbing, moaning, wailing. I'd never heard anything like it. After some moments, I finally gathered enough courage to move and proceed in the direction from which the voices were coming. Deeper and deeper along the treacherous pathway I ascended. The voices kept growing louder and louder, more and more pitiful. It was agony to listen to them. Just when I was about to turn back in the direction from which I had come, I saw!" Her voice quivered now, and her eyes were as large as saucers.

"What is it you saw, Katherine?" prompted Liebie. "What happened?"

"Oh, Liebie, it was awful. I've never seen anything like it in my life!" She flinched, as though in actual physical pain.

"It's all right, Katherine. Remember, it was only a dream. No do go on with it."

"Well, well, there was a horrible stench in the air, and the sobs and screams grew louder and more frequent and more intense. And then, suddenly, I began to realize that some of these cries were those of human beings calling for help. 'Please help me! God help us! Get us out of here!' the voices seemed to be saying. I continued along the pathway until the noise was unbearable, and then, then I saw them! Oh Liebie, it was horrible!" she grimaced at the recollection.

"Go on," Liebie prodded gently.

"Well the maimed and mutilated, the dying . . . There was blood everywhere. Limbs scattered hither and thither . . . Bodies and parts of bodies strewn all over the pathway . . . corpses—and heart-wrenching sobs. Oh, God, Liebie I've never seen anything so gruesome." She shuddered at the memory. "The cries of agony. Oh, Liebie, it was so vivid! What can it possibly mean?"

"My dear, I have no idea at all. I think it best that you attempt to forget it all as quickly as possible," said Liebie in a queer voice. "Everyone has nightmares every once in a while," she added.

"I haven't," admitted Katherine. "This is the first one I can remember having. And I hope I never have one again!" she smiled feebly for the first time that day.

"Come on, Katherine. Let's go exploring, and forget all about the entire episode. How would you like to take one of those guided tours of the Rock?"

"I'd love to," murmured Katherine. "Good, I'll make the arrangements. I believe the next tour bus leaves in half an hour!"

"Perfect!" breathed Katherine, relieved to have at least shared her terrifying experience with another. *Thank God, that's all over!* she thought to herself, as she and Liebie boarded the bus that was to visit the points of interest on the Rock.

Unhappily, as they drove through the country, Katherine began to feel increasingly queer and uneasy. *What is the matter with me?* she wondered, feeling ill and out of sorts. The landscape, the atmosphere—the flora and fauna—everything seemed vaguely, disturbingly familiar to her. A strange, foreboding feeling overcame her. *Don't be such a ninny!* she chided herself, having no idea why she felt so peculiar.

Yet, as they traveled over the rocky terrain, Katherine could not help but feel that she had seen all this before. *But where? How?* she wondered. *I've been here—I know that road, and that pathway,* she marveled. It was not until the bus stopped at the foot of a great hill at which she and the passengers alighted that she began to realize where she had seen all this before. *Oh my God!* she thought suddenly to herself. She pulled Liebie aside so that no one would overhear her.

"Liebie, this is the place I saw last night in my dream—we're here. Everything is familiar. Look, I'll bet you anything that the cave I saw last night is over there!" she pointed to a tall lone pine tree standing as a sentry to a great limestone hill.

"Do you want to explore it?" asked Liebie.

"You bet!" replied Katherine with far more bravado than she actually felt. "Let's go!" The bus would be stopping here for a half hour, and so the two had a sufficient amount of time to go off and explore by themselves.

"Be careful, ladies," advised the driver. "Those rocks can be treacherous. Also, there are caves in those hills."

"Caves!" exclaimed Katherine under her breath, more convinced than ever that this was indeed the spot she had visited last night in her dream.

"I'm beginning to wonder if it was a dream after all," she mentioned to Liebie as the two gingerly climbed the hill in which "her" cave could be found.

"This is giving me the creeps," said Katherine, with a shudder, as she recognized the landscape as that which she had "visited" the previous night. They made their way through the cave, and sure enough, the pathway, which Katherine had seen, the pool of murky water, the dripping ceiling—every detail—the flora and fauna, the formation of the rocks, etc. were exactly as they had appeared in her dream. Thankfully, however, as they approached the spot wherein Katherine had expected to see the maimed bodies and corpses, there was nothing. Yet, even so, the atmosphere was unusually bleak and grim. *There is death and suffering here,* thought Katherine to herself. Yet, although they searched the area for several minutes, they found no sign of any living human being. They continued to scour the area until Katherine felt certain that the bodies she had seen last night were not present.

Upon returning to the bus, the driver, who had spotted them coming from the direction of the cave, remarked, "Pretty scary up there, isn't it? You know during the last World War that cave was used as a temporary shelter for wounded soldiers—that is, until they could be transported to the hospital. Hundreds of men remained up there—many died while waiting to be rescued."

"I see," said Katherine slowly, as an idea suddenly dawned upon her. They re-entered the bus, and sat in silence. Katherine was hardly conscious of the chattering around her. She remained lost in thought for the remainder of the tour.

"Whatever is on your mind?" Liebie asked after they had returned to the hotel and were lounging in Katherine's room. "Do tell me what you were thinking about all the way home from the cave."

"Well," said Katherine slowly, "let me explain what I believe has taken place. Firstly, I believe that what I thought to be a 'dream' was no dream at all, but, rather, an example of astral projection."

"What does that mean?" asked Liebie.

"Well, you are already aware that each human being possesses, in addition to the physical body, many subtler bodies including an astral body, which might be defined as the ethereal counterpart of the physical body, which it resembles and with which it normally coincides. Although the astral body normally coincides with the physical body during the hours of full, waking consciousness, in sleep it withdraws from the physical body, to a greater or lesser degree depending on the soul's level of spiritual awareness. In the case of the so-called, 'average' human being, who is as yet unaware of occult truths, the astral body usually hovers several feet above the physical body, neither conscious nor controlled. In the case of some highly spiritually evolved human beings, the astral body may be consciously, voluntarily projected to travel to places and view scenes that he has never seen before. He can, at will return to his physical body and recall vividly all that he has seen or experienced.

"Furthermore, he can verify the truth of these experiences by visiting the site of his experiences, as I did this afternoon here in Gibraltar. As one travels astrally, one is connected to the physical body by means of the silver cord. Years ago, the Spirit Being, Dr. Evans, explained that only if the silver cord is severed, can death result. This cord is enormously elastic and capable of great extension. At any rate, I feel that I traveled astrally last night and actually witnessed what was taking place on the astral plane. And on this plane were many—whom I would call 'lost souls'—who, as a result of a harsh, abrupt or unexpected death or through long, extended suffering, are unaware that they have discarded the physical body and are presently existing in a state of limbo in the astral world which bears a striking resemblance to the Earth plane. Believing that they are still 'alive,' these poor souls cling to the Earth life, hover in the area in which their 'deaths' have taken place, and resist making progress on the Other Side.

"For these souls, the awakening process is very slow, for they are too wretched and caught up in the physical world to be receptive to the gentle, loving influence of the illumined souls in the realms of light who wish to guide them onward in their new environment. Refusing to believe they are dead, these souls continue to suffer in the same manner as that which preceded their deaths. Last night I saw numberless men and women who 'died' in the cave, but who still believed they were alive. I believe that I was afforded that experience in order to assist those miserable souls."

"But how could you possibly assist them?" asked Liebie, genuinely mystified.

"By means of a rescue circle," replied Katherine calmly.

"A what?"

"A rescue circle wherein we, with the assistance and cooperation of our Spirit Guides, communicate with those lost souls and explain to them what has transpired. You see, Liebie, my so-called 'dream' was the means whereby my Spirit Guides chose to inform me of the problem and enlist our aid. We must help those souls to progress."

"We?" asked Liebie weakly.

"We," confirmed Katherine.

"But what can I do? I know nothing about any of this."

"Don't worry," smiled Katherine. "My Guides will speak through me and instruct us as to the procedure. We need only follow their explicit directions. We will meet here in my room tonight at midnight, when the world is quiet and at peace and when there is a greater likelihood of achieving clear communication. In the meantime, let us both rest. This work won't be easy, I assure you."

"All right, my dear," said Liebie, "I will meet you here at midnight."

When the sky was inky black and the world still, Liebie crept stealthily into Katherine's room, and the two prepared for the arduous task at hand. They sat together in silent prayer. As they attuned to their Helpers, the Enlightened Forces, Katherine was strongly reminded of the excitement and adventure of the early years of communication. As she had predicted, however, this task was neither pleasant nor easy in spite of the wonderful advice and cooperation they received from Katherine's Guides. Her guides inspired her words and actions; they requested that she and Liebie sit in quiet communion and to attune to the vibration of those in need of release from the bondage of the earth. Those who had been left to die in the cave responded to the energies and messages Katherine and Liebie transmitted to them. Soon, Katherine and Liebie were able to communicate with and be understood by them.

"You are no longer alive," Katherine informed the dazed, restless, and bewildered souls who hovered near the Earth. "You no longer inhabit the physical body, but are, instead, in a body of a finer, lighter substance called the astral body. You no longer reside on the Earth, but in the astral world which closely resembles the physical world. You are being guided by Teachers and Helpers nearby who wish to introduce you to your new home. Let go of the Earth—let go of the physical body. You are spirit. You are spiritual beings. The new world in which you inhabit is beautiful, and filled with light and love. Your companions are guiding you toward the Light. Go, move, travel toward the Light. You will acquire peace and well-being as you move toward the Light. Go on. Go on. Go on!"

Gradually, Katherine and Liebie felt that their words were being understood. The communications between the spheres took place for many hours. Finally, Katherine knew that the lost souls had comprehended and were ready to relinquish their hold upon their physical bodies and the Earth.

"Your friends and loved ones are welcoming you," Katherine told them softly, tears filling her eyes, as she sensed the joyousness, the serenity finally settling over these tortured souls, these men and women who had suffered in agony for so very long. "You are on your way. You are ready now to inhabit the glorious world of peace into which you have entered. The Earth no longer has any hold over you; it has no further meaning. You have entered the land of light. You will remain there. God bless you—all of you—always!" Katherine prayed.

She felt like sobbing aloud, but there was only an odd, strangled feeling in her throat, which made it ache. When finally the Guides announced that the group could disband, that the work had been successful, she and Liebie had burst into tears, and had remained pale and motionless in their seats, too exhausted and drained to budge. With heavy hearts, the two stared at one another neither one yet strong enough to rise or to speak. Finally, perhaps half an hour after Bright Eyes had announced that the so-called "lost souls" were now under the guidance of their Spirit Helpers, Katherine spoke. "Thank God that's over."

"Yes," breathed Liebie, still overcome by the experience. When finally the two recovered, they were still far too wound up to sleep. After a cup of tea, they spent the remainder of the night discussing all that had taken place. Gradually all fear and depression dissipated, and the two finally fell asleep at dawn.

Not long after this episode, Katherine and Liebie decided to leave Gibraltar and travel on to Spain. "No one could be more deserving of a carefree holiday in Spain!" Katherine teased, thoroughly prepared for the next few weeks to immerse herself in nothing more demanding than sightseeing and merry-making.

"I couldn't agree with you more, my dear," admitted Liebie. And so, the two set about to enjoy themselves. Barcelona, Madrid, Valencia, Segonia, Avila, Seville—all with their diversity of climate and altitude appealed greatly to the two women—as did the Gothic and Romanesque cathedrals, the grand Moorish palaces; the ancient citadels and fortresses; the aqueducts and ruins; theatres and museums. Mostly, however, they delighted in the beauty of the countryside in southwestern Spain. They traveled throughout Spain for nearly a month.

Then, suddenly, early one morning in late April 1959, Katherine awakened, feeling very strongly that it was time to return home to England. It was with surprise that she realized the she had been away for so long.

"Why, it simply doesn't seem possible! How the time has flown," she had remarked to Liebie.

Always ready to placate Katherine, Liebie was, nonetheless, also ready to return to England. They made plane reservations to leave Spain the following day.

"I've had a wonderful time, Liebie. Thank you for inviting me," Katherine had said as they boarded the plane which would soon land at Heathrow.

"I'm so glad," murmured Liebie, gazing fondly at her friend's animated features.

Now, as Katherine settled comfortably in her seat on the plane, she began to feel more homesick than ever. *Why, I really can't wait to go home!* she mused. She began to think. *My traveling days are over. It's time I settled down.* During the past ten years, she had traveled extensively. *The only place I haven't seen is the Orient. Hmmmmmm, now that would be fun, wouldn't it? Perhaps . . .* she suddenly caught herself. *No,* she vowed, *no more traveling for a while. I'm nearly sixty. It's time to settle down.*

Suddenly, the faces of Graham, Beryl and David, Trevor and Doris—all those whom she loved—flashed before her. *It will be marvelous to see everyone again.* Next Wood Court, the Greyhound Inn, Pendennis, and Cheltenham (wherein Graham and Beryl had just purchased their lovely new home), and London loomed before her.

"I can't believe we're almost home!" she had squealed to Liebie excitedly, as the pilot announced that they were flying above the United Kingdom. She could not wait to see her loved ones, her beloved country once again. Never had the mere thought of "home" seemed so attractive and enticing.

CHAPTER 52

A Sad Farewell

~&~

MAY 5, 1959

FINALLY RETURNED TO LONDON FROM Spain after seven and a half months of life overseas. London is even lovelier than I remembered. I never thought it possible to miss a city so. How wonderful it feels to be home again!

Katherine had written in the small travel diary that she had maintained throughout the journey. Seldom in her life had she taken time from her busy schedule to record her feelings or experiences in writing, but, on this occasion, her heart full of joy and genuine appreciation for her loved ones and country, she paused briefly to express herself in writing. To the above words, she added, *I am thoroughly rested and refreshed and more than ready for what is to come. For perhaps the first time in my life, I am content to remain here in England. In fact, it feels to me now that I shall never wish to leave home again . . .*

This attitude prevailed for some weeks following her arrival back in England. During this time, she was content to divide her time and energy between Pendennis and the delightful furnished apartment near Liebie's in Hove which she decided to rent for an indefinite amount of time. She also learned from Graham that Percy had retired and was now living in the beautiful county of Cornwall. She seldom spoke or wrote to him but Graham maintained contact with his dad until his death from a heart attack in 1961.

Yet, although she enjoyed the excitement, frenetic activity, and publicity that accompanied her return, and although she had quickly become as absorbed in her work as ever, there was an odd, unfamiliar, and unsettled quality to her life—an undercurrent—that she could neither describe nor comprehend. She only knew that despite her effort, her life lacked its previous gusto, charm, and fulfillment—something was lacking.

What is wrong with me? she wondered impatiently from time to time, when afforded the opportunity for reflection. When she was no longer able to approach her work with her old vitality and enthusiasm, she decided to postpone a series of public lectures she was scheduled to deliver for one of the local societies and to temporarily withdraw from public life in order to take stock of her present circumstances. No longer certain of the nature and scope of her work, after the initial excitement of her return, a restless spirit possessed her, along with a feeling of discontent and a yearning for she knew not what. Having failed to discover what she had traveled to India to find, she felt it imperative to review, reassess and perhaps redefine her dreams and objectives.

Where from here? she wondered patiently. It hadn't occurred to her that she was almost sixty years old, that she had worked very hard throughout her entire adult life, that she was well-to-do financially, and that she could now easily afford to retire. On the contrary, she was now more determined than ever to execute the vow she had made long ago, "I will carry on with the work until I draw my final breath . . ."

It was a golden, sunlit morning in early June. The day was unusually warm for that time of year. And one could already feel summer in the air. The sky was a deep, brilliant turquoise dotted every now and then with tiny wisps of billowing white; the sun's rays cast a shower of white and gold upon the glistening waves as they rose and fell; a soft breeze stirred the branches of the oak and maple trees nearby. For some time there was no sound but the sweet murmur of the wind and the gentle lapping of the tide.

Katherine and Liebie were virtually alone on the ocean front, for it was still too early in the season for the majority of tourists. But for the two women, it was the most pleasant time of year. There was a lightness, purity, and freshness in the atmosphere and inexpressible peace. Today, they were remarkably still—absorbing the glorious peace of their surroundings and the beauty of this near-perfect day. For a long time, Katherine observed the tiny buoy, gray birds that darted back and forth along the coast. But then her attention was drawn to the white-winged seagulls as they swooped then soared high into the sky and finally vanished from view. Suddenly the old restless spirit overcame her, and she felt inexplicably sad and lonely. She wished that she, too, might soar high into the heavens. Sighing wistfully, she turned her attention to the ocean and to the laughing waves breaking along the shore. Then suddenly, as she watched the waves heave and ripple, she was struck by an idea—one so ordinary and fundamental that she found it impossible to believe that it had not occurred to her before.

"Liebie!" she cried, her voice full of excitement. Her eyes were suddenly blazing with an emotion Liebie had seldom seen before. "Liebie! Do you realize that I've never been to America?"

"What!" exclaimed Liebie, uncomprehendingly.

"America—the United States. I've never been there," Katherine continued breathlessly, her eyes shining. "The one country I have truly wanted to visit all my life—the country in which I was conceived. Why ever since I was a child and heard Mother talking about it, I've longed to go. Now, all of a sudden, I feel that somehow I must go there—that I must see America before I can settle permanently here in England. You know, it's odd but I can't help but feel that I belong there."

"Well! I hardly know what to say!" murmured Liebie in an odd voice. Having only just recently regained the companionship of her dearest friend, she hardly relished the idea of another separation. But, upon observing the instantaneous change that had taken place in Katherine's demeanor, Liebie cleverly concealed her own disappointment and smiled softly. "When shall you go?"

"As soon as possible," declared Katherine vehemently. "Of course, I must tie up some loose ends first—you know, visit with the children, spend time with Trevor and Doris, fulfill my business obligations. It's now June. Probably, I will leave early in the fall—yes, that's it! I shall go in the fall!"

A curious sense of lightness, of freedom, had come over her now that she had a plan, a definite course of action. She did not know that her face had changed, that the bored, listless expression had vanished completely and that she was literally aglow with excitement. Despite her own doubts and reservations, Liebie could not help but smile at Katherine's girlish enthusiasm.

"My dear, it sounds like a wonderful idea. How long will you be gone?"

"Oh, I don't know. Perhaps only a month or two," replied Katherine whose mind was busy working out the details.

"Oh!" Liebie's face fell. But Katherine was too absorbed to notice.

"How is it that I never thought of going before?" she wondered aloud, genuinely amazed by the fact. Now, she struggled to recall each word her mother had used to describe life in America. *How lucky that I postponed that lecture series,* she mused. *Now, I have no major commitments and am really free to do as I wish.*

"America," she murmured aloud, caressing each syllable of the word. "America," she repeated, growing more excited by the moment. A string of visual images unfolded before her—largely a composite of the things her mother had told her about this country and also what she had seen in American films. The Capitol, the White House, the skyline of New York City, Broadway—all held an irresistible charm and fascination for her. "I am going to America," she announced once more happily and fully satisfied with the decision she had made.

For the remainder of the morning, she busily patterned her visit. *It will be sort of a working holiday,* she decided. *I shall contact the Americans I met at Yogananda's ashram in India, that spiritualist minister from Seattle, and several others. I'm certain that they will be happy to have me as a guest speaker. Yes, I would like to do some public work in America in addition to seeing the country itself. It should be a marvelous trip and a marvelous opportunity to make many new friends!* she thought, little suspecting the extent to which her words would materialize.

Only one disturbing thought occurred to her in conjunction with the proposed trip to the United States. *How shall I break the news to the kids?* she wondered in despair. *They already think I'm mad as a hatter coming and going wherever and whenever I choose.* It was not difficult to imagine the incredulity in Graham's voice. "But, Mother," he would say disapprovingly, "you've only just returned from India, Ceylon, and God-knows where else. Shouldn't you rest and wait a decent interval before dashing off again?" She giggled ruefully at the thought. Kind and well-intentioned, her son was rather condescending and overly solicitous where his mother was concerned. *Oh, never mind*, she thought, *I'll soon set him straight*. In spite of her concern over Graham's reaction, her face lit up at the prospect of seeing him. Instantly, she planned to visit her entire family before embarking on her trip to America. *It will do me a world of good to see them again. I'll go to their new home in Cheltenham for a couple of weeks, then travel on to Christchurch to see Trevor and Doris. They'll all think me mad, no doubt, but what the dickens! I shan't stay long in America—I've always longed to go—and I may never have the opportunity again!*

Feeling much better about life as a whole, now that she had a new goal and renewed purpose, she devoted the next few months toward the completion of all prior commitments and to the preparation for the new adventure.

"I am certain that I shall settle down once and for all following the trip," she informed a dubious Eileen. "After all there's nowhere else I'd like to go."

Although Eileen felt like saying, "I don't think you will ever settle down," she only smiled and nodded wisely. She knew her friend far too well to rely upon any of her plans or proposals, for seldom, if ever, did they turn out as anticipated.

"By the way," Eileen asked casually one warm June afternoon, "how would you like a traveling companion?" There was a silence, as Katherine attempted to determine the true nature of her words.

"What do you mean?" she asked finally, earnestly searching Eileen's face.

"Well, I mean that I would very much like to accompany you to the United States in the fall of this year of Our Lord, 1959."

"I see," said Katherine slowly, deeply moved by her friend's proposal. "I should be delighted to have you as my companion on my first trip to America," she said heartily.

"Good," smiled Eileen, "then it's settled. We will have a wonderful time together. I'm sure of it."

"I have no doubt of it," said Katherine, fondly squeezing her friend's hand. She knew that Eileen loved a good adventure as much as she herself did. Eileen subsequently made arrangements for them to sail across the ocean on the *S.S. United States*. They would set sail from England during the last week of October almost exactly one year from the time they had left for India.

In the meantime, Katherine's days were devoted to meeting those obligations she had incurred upon her return from India. Lectures, both formal and informal, classes, workshops, demonstrations, private interviews, counseling—she simply could not neglect her work, although she managed to convince herself that her load was lighter than it had ever been. In truth, she was as busy as ever. Only her attitude and focus were different as she prepared to face the inevitable challenges and experiences to be met abroad.

For the first time in years, she spent more than a day or two at a time with her family—her mother (as wise, down-to-earth, and wonderful as ever) and her brothers and sisters. *What a distance we've traveled.* Katherine had marveled upon realizing for the first time that even the babies, Leonard, Megan, and Mauve, were all grown up with lives and families of their own. Furthermore, during this period, she was able to spend more time with Graham and Beryl than ever before. Now residing in the fashionable city of Cheltenham, Graham was now well-established and comfortably situated in his own large and attractive home here. As owner and director of his own expansive construction firm, he was well-to-do and influential; and both his home life and social status reflected his success. Accordingly, although Katherine had hoped to share a great deal of time with her son, he was far too busy and preoccupied to devote more than a few scattered hours here and there with his mother. With a mixture of pride and regret, she began to realize that he was all grown-up and independent.

Where have the years gone? she mused, feeling no different, certainly no older, than when she'd been forced to leave Graham with her parents while working at The George 'n Dragon. Now, witty, charming, and amusing, her "Gray" was calm, confident, and obviously capable of handling the heavy responsibilities that had fallen upon his shoulders. *He's everything I could have wished for in a son,* she thought, tears of pride filling her eyes. Observing his every word and gesture with pleasure, she felt profound gratitude for his presence in her life. *I, who, in the early years, never wanted either marriage or a family, now could not imagine life without them,* her gaze lovingly enfolded her son, his wife, and her handsome, dark-haired grandson, David, whose high spirits, wit, and precocity set her heart soaring. Of course, he was the most remarkable child ever born, and he could do no wrong in the eyes of his doting grandmother. *He's beautiful,* she would think to herself. "Mark my words, that boy is going to go far," she was fond of telling David's mother, gazing rapturously at the boy's large blue eyes, high forehead, gentle mouth, and sensitive features.

"I can't help but agree with you," replied Beryl beaming, and without a trace of apology. "He really is exceptional, isn't he?"

"Absolutely," Katherine would respond, without a moment's hesitation.

"Aren't you, my love?" she would ask the embarrassed boy, while tenderly embracing him. She was convinced beyond a shadow of a doubt of his utter charm, brilliance, and innate superiority in all areas of life.

Katherine had almost laughed aloud at Graham's response to the news of her intended visit to the United States. It was almost verbatim as she had predicted. "But Mother," he entreated in his most paternal voice, "America? All the way across the ocean—at this time in your life? Whatever for? Why, you've only just returned from India, Ceylon, and God-knows where else. I don't advise it," he said flatly. He looked worried, and his forehead was wrinkled in concern.

"Nonetheless, my love," she replied lightly, "all the arrangements have been made, and Eileen and I are to set sail for New York City on October 20."

"Can't you stay put for a while? Really, Mother, must you go gallivanting all over the world at your age?" asked pouted Graham disapprovingly.

"I'm afraid I must, dear," said Katherine simply, concealing a smile. "You know I've never been exactly what one might call a homebody, don't you, darling? And now, I really feel the strong desire to go to America. I wouldn't be content to remain here at home—I'd be restless, bored, frustrated . . . And you wouldn't want me to be unhappy, would you dear?"

"Oh, of course not, Mother. But it seems that we never really have a chance to spend time together—to talk about the things in life that matter the most. You know, 'the work'—your work—I mean. I've always been keenly interested in it. Someday, I thought I'd assist you in it. . . Well, anyway," Graham sighed, "I suppose you're right. If you really wish to go, I suppose you must. Right?"

"Right, my love," said Katherine, gently patting her son's arm. "Don't worry, I'll be fine. After all, I've got Eileen to look after me. And, furthermore, I won't be gone long. When I return to England, we shall be able to spend plenty of time together."

"Sure, that's right. We'll have lots of time together," agreed Graham, with a forced smile, wondering why the words rang hollowly. Somehow in the back of his mind, he could not help but feel that a long separation was at hand. Yet, he was helpless to prevent what seemed inevitable. He knew that once his mother's mind was made up, one had little hope of changing it.

"I shall write to you as soon as I arrive in New York," Katherine promised, amidst tearful goodbyes, shortly before leaving for America.

"Don't go!" Graham had implored once more, as the two were locked in an embrace.

"I must, love," returned Katherine, not knowing why she felt so queer and heavy-hearted. She could not recall seeing Graham, Beryl, and David look so forlorn, "Cheer up, will you all?" she demanded. "I'll be back soon. Promise!"

"All right, Mother," sighed Graham uneasily.

"Have a wonderful time!"

"I shall, dear. Of that you may be certain."

"This isn't as easy as I hoped it would be," Katherine sighed regretfully, a short time after she had left her children to visit with Trevor and Doris in Christchurch to inform them of her intended journey. "I love this place," she sighed wistfully, as she took in the sights and sounds of The Greyhound and the beautiful countryside surrounding it. "It's perfect for Trevor and Doris. I wish it were right for me, too . . ."

Trevor was standing in the doorway as she arrived, and they embraced warmly. "God, you're a sight for sore eyes!" he had remarked enthusiastically, putting his arms around her and guiding her into the hotel. "You look better than ever!" he exclaimed, hardly taking his eyes off of her.

"You look pretty wonderful yourself, sir," she teased lightly, feeling unusually self- conscious. *What on earth is the matter with me?* she wondered, her heart hammering madly. *I feel sixteen and as shy as though I were with my first beau,* she mused, before Trevor drew her close and kissed her passionately in the foyer. His touch was electrifying. His mouth was hard and unrelenting on hers, and Katherine returned his kisses' unable to resist.

"Trev!" she finally whispered, pulling away. "We mustn't!"

"Why not?" his lips grazed her shoulder, then her neck.

"Trev!" she cried in a feeble voice. "Stop! What if Doris should see us?"

"What of it? She knows we're in love. Everyone knows we're in love."

"Oh, Trev," she started to say miserably. .

"Come on, Katherine," begged Trever, his blue eyes pleading. "There's no reason for us to be separated any longer. We love each other. We have a right to be together. Marry me, my darling. You'll see, everything will work out magnificently. We'll be so happy together. I promise."

"Oh, Trev. I wish it were that easy . . ."

"But it is that easy, my darling," he said eagerly. "We could spend the rest of our days together here in the country—amidst indescribable beauty and luxury, enjoying one another as we have never been able to before."

"Trev, you are missing the point. Don't you see? Things are as they've always been with us. I must have my freedom, to do as I want, to come and go as I choose. My work still comes first. And no matter how dearly I love you or how enticing your proposal, I cannot accept. So, please do let us drop the subject once and for all and remain grateful for the time we do have together. We have been greatly blessed—you and I—to have loved each other all these years. And I shall cherish every moment we've spent together for as long as I live. Each moment with you has been more precious to me than you will ever know," she said quietly, the words catching in her throat.

Touching her cheek lightly, he only said, "I understand." But she felt the hurt and disappointment underlying his words, and she felt terribly saddened by the episode. Their days together passed all too swiftly and without any further opportunity to share their deepest thoughts and feelings.

"I . . . I came back to say goodbye," Katherine admitted awkwardly, shortly before she was scheduled to return to London.

He had hesitated only a moment before saying quietly, "How long this time?"

"I . . . I don't really know."

"Where?"

She could not meet his eyes, "The United States," she said slowly.

"Oh, I see," his voice was expressionless, his features impassive.

"Don't be upset, Trev," she said finally, clasping his hand in hers. "I'm sure it won't be for long. And I shall, more than likely, settle down when I return."

"Settle down? You?" Trevor laughed uneasily. "I don't believe that you will settle down here or anywhere ever."

"We shall see," she said wisely. "I'll miss you, Trev," she added, after yet another pause.

"And I you, my love," he replied, holding her close.

"I'll write—promise!" she whispered, tears brimming to her eyes. For a single instant she held him tightly wishing that they could remain locked in the embrace forever. Next to the time she had been compelled to leave Graham at age eight with Mother and Father Hayward in Pontypridd so many years ago, it was the most difficult goodbye she had ever spoken.

CHAPTER 53

America

WHILE IN INDIA, KATHERINE HAD been introduced to several Americans including Sri Daya Mata, soon-to-be president of the Self-Realization Fellowship, and a lovely Spiritualist minister, Mr. Wendell Phillips, from Seattle, who had eagerly invited her to spend time in the United States as a visiting lecturer at his congregation. Not having the foggiest notion as to what or where Seattle was, Katherine graciously accepted the invitation. Once again, she, as a British citizen, was not permitted to take much money out of England, and so she welcomed any opportunity to earn an income while in the United States.

Unfortunately, as the date drew near for her scheduled departure from the United Kingdom, she received notification from Mr. Phillips that certain unforeseen circumstances had arisen that would temporarily preclude her visit with him.

I do hope you will forgive me, but knowing of your eagerness to work in our country, I have taken the liberty of scheduling your lecture series in Long Beach, California, instead. A dear friend and respected coworker of mine, Mrs. Hilda Wilcox, who is currently the president of the Long Beach spiritualist society, is most anxious, upon my recommendation, to engage your services. With your gracious permission, I shall make all further arrangements including hotel accom-modations. I am mindful of your request for accommodations adjacent to any center for which you are scheduled to speak. So don't worry about a thing. Hope your journey to the New World will be pleasant and fulfilling in every way. Once again, please accept my apologies for any inconvenience this change has caused you.

Yours Sincerely, W. Phillips.

Accustomed to British geography and thinking that Long Beach must be near Seattle, Katherine gratefully accepted Mr. Phillips' kind offer and began to look forward to spending time in this pleasant-sounding city.

It was Katherine's intention to travel all over the United States. And, as she had in England and Wales, Ceylon, India, and in many parts of Europe, she would both demonstrate the proof of survival to American audiences and share with them the information she had acquired from the Spirit Beings. Furthermore, as had been the case in the past, she would both teach and learn. As had been her pattern since the time of her first public appearance, she would first schedule a large public meeting. From the publicity resulting from this initial meeting, she would receive numerous offers and invitations for further public engagements—*enough to keep me busy for as long as I like*, she thought to herself. *Perhaps I will do some television and radio as well*, she mused, planning how best to reach the greatest number of people within the short amount of time she intended to stay in the country. *Oh well, no use to plan any further*, she sighed. *It's best to leave it to God. No doubt, I shall be surprised by what takes place anyhow. I always am*, she murmured wryly.

She and Eileen arrived in New York City on October 24, 1959, following one of the most difficult and unpleasant trips they had known. For the *S.S. United States*, upon which they had booked passage, seemed intent upon making the voyage from England in record time, and had raced through the choppy waters of the Atlantic at such a pace that the two women (as well as the majority of other passengers) had been seasick, dizzy, and nauseous throughout the journey.

"I can't remember when I've ever been so out of sorts in all my life," moaned Katherine, hardly noticing the Statue of Liberty or the New York City skyline, which she had for so long wanted to see. Nor was there much relief on land, for the docks were terribly crowded, and the weather was chilly and uncomfortable.

"Oh, why ever did we come to this Godforsaken place? What was I thinking?" Katherine wailed to Eileen, as the two sat in the back of a cab that sped over the busy, dilapidated streets of New York. "It's a good thing we didn't have any lunch," observed Katherine as the taxi weaved in and out of the heavy traffic, bumping and grinding its way to their hotel. The two were tense, wet with perspiration, ill, and exhausted by the time they arrived at the elegant St. Moritz located on Central Park South. When finally they managed to get to their rooms the two were ready to sleep for the next few days.

"Don't forget," Eileen whispered suddenly as they unpacked their wardrobes, "you are scheduled to speak at eight o'clock this evening at my Uncle Robert's church. It's in Queens, and I must get directions from him. Remind me to ring him up later—after a nap."

"Oh, God," moaned Katherine. "I'd forgotten all about your promise to your Uncle Robert. Why an Episcopalian congregation would want to hear from me is beyond my comprehension."

"Uncle Robert says it's a liberal congregation."

"It can't be that liberal!" said Katherine wryly.

"Well, all I know is that he definitely wants you there tonight at eight," said Eileen, rather peeved.

"Oh, don't worry, I'll be there I promise. I don't know how—but I'll be there! I wouldn't miss my first public engagement in America for anything!"

"Good," sighed Eileen.

"How do I manage to get myself into these situations?" Eileen overheard Katherine say to herself and had to bite her lip to keep from laughing aloud.

Following a brief nap, the intrusion of a maid who insisted that Katherine change rooms "because the plumbing in yours doesn't work, ma'am," a meal at a coffee shop adjacent to the hotel, Katherine and Eileen were ready to leave for Katherine's first public meeting in the United States.

"Would you please order a taxi for us?" Katherine had graciously requested of the bell captain several hours before she was scheduled to depart.

"Oh, don't worry, Ma'am, you'll have no difficulty getting a taxi here in New York. All you have to do is stand outside the hotel and hail one. You'll see the street will be teeming with them!" the man smiled jovially.

"You're certain of this?"

"Oh, of course, Ma'am, I've lived in New York all my life. You'll have no problem getting a cab, I assure you."

"Oh, all right then," said Katherine dubiously.

She wished she had never seen the bell captain several hours later, after he had so nonchalantly advised her she would not need to make a reservation to get a taxi. She and Eileen, dressed in their long, formal gowns and furs, were standing and waiting in front of the hotel—no vacant taxi in sight.

"Oh, what are we going to do?" wailed Katherine. "We're due at the church in less than an hour, and every cab that comes near is already full!" It was cold and dreary and it had begun to drizzle slightly, and the traffic was extremely heavy.

"Come on," Katherine finally snarled impatiently. "Let's walk!"

"I am not walking all the way to Queens," protested Eileen angrily. "That sounds far away."

"I am not planning on walking all the way to Queens, love, only to another street where we'll perhaps have better luck."

"Oh, all right," muttered Eileen, growing more anxious and nervous by the moment. But they had no better luck several blocks away.

"This is incredible!" Katherine remarked. But suddenly spotting a group of passengers enter a bus, Katherine shouted, "Come on, Eileen. We've got no choice. We'll take a bus!"

"You've got to be kidding!" Eileen protested. But she had no further opportunity to give vent to her true feelings, for Katherine took her by the hand and dragged her all the way to the bus stop. After making numerous inquiries from those boarding the bus and then the driver himself, the two managed to locate a bus that would take them to their destination. To their dismay, this bus was packed to capacity, and the two elegantly coifed and attired women were forced to stand and bear the curious scrutiny of the other passengers for the remainder of the journey.

"I don't know about you," teased Katherine, "but I've had enough of America. I'm returning home to England tomorrow."

"Can't say I blame you, lady," a large, balding man with fat, red cheeks who had overheard her, said cheerfully. Katherine and Eileen looked at each other, and burst out laughing. They were in good spirits by the time they arrived at the church.

"Thank goodness we made it," sighed Katherine in relief, glancing at her watch she saw it was ten minutes before eight.

"I can't believe we're on time."

"I wouldn't have thought it possible," observed Eileen in amazement.

Thankfully, the evening proceeded smoothly from thereon. And, in spite of feeling tired, flushed, and disheveled following the journey by bus, Katherine managed to deliver a polished entertaining talk—one for which Eileen's Uncle Robert and his congregation were most appreciative. Katherine was frankly surprised by the warmth of her reception, and she was delighted with her audience.

"Why, you've all been wonderful," she told them, following her talk.

"And so our work has begun auspiciously in America," she commented happily to Eileen later on that night.

Five hectic days later, she and Eileen were seated on a Greyhound bus en route to the nation's capital. *I'll do no more work until I get to Long Beach,* Katherine decided. *I want to travel—see the country first.*

"What's the best way to see the United States?" Katherine had asked the travel agent in the hotel.

"Try a bus," he had advised. "You'll really get a feel for the country."

"All right, then, please book us. We'll travel by bus all the way to California."

"Alrighty then," the travel agent replied and purchased the tickets on their behalf.

What fun, thought Katherine looking forward to the trip. Tiring quickly of New York's (its filth, crowds, noise, and traffic had been too much for them in the aftermath of the rugged ocean journey on the *S.S. United States*), they embarked on the bus trip, ready to see the rest of the country.

"Isn't this wonderful!" breathed Katherine, as the large bus lumbered along the highway leaving the glorious skyline of Manhattan behind.

"What a lovely idea to travel by bus," smiled Eileen.

"Now, we're really seeing America," said Katherine.

"Um," agreed Eileen, engrossed in the flashing landscape before her. It took them approximately two hours to tire of the novelty of bus travel and wish that they were flying instead of riding in a bus to Washington and the other parts of the country. They rode through New Jersey, Maryland, and finally arrived in Washington, DC, in the midst of a raging thunderstorm. By the time they arrived at their hotel in the heart of the city during rush hour and in the pouring rain, the women were ready to call it quits.

"Nothing like a touch of home, is there?" said Eileen only partly in jest, as she surveyed the typically English landscape—gray, dreary skies and sloshy wet streets from her hotel room.

"To think I left England for this," agreed Katherine in mock despair. The two remained in Washington for several more days, hoping that the weather would improve and that they would be afforded the opportunity for extensive sight-seeing. But the rain only intensified.

"It feels like forty days and forty nights, doesn't it?" Katherine had laughed. Finally, growing increasingly bored and impatient, they decided to catch the next available bus to Chicago.

Although there were distinct moments during the bus ride wherein they genuinely enjoyed themselves, these were few and far between. The two, for the most part, were too bored, restless, and tired to continue their bus journey. After spending several days in the Windy City, they decided to fly to

Los Angeles, even though the plane fare would sadly deplete their financial resources.

"I don't care," said Katherine defiantly, "if it takes every last penny we've got. I can't endure any more of the bus! And, after all, I'll be earning once we get to California." She was brightened by the prospect. And, so, the two ended up flying from Chicago's O'Hare International Airport to Los Angeles. "Never have I made a wiser decision," Katherine smiled broadly once she was safely on land in California. "I never want to see another bus as long as I live!"

CHAPTER 54

California

—⌒—

THEY ARRIVED IN LOS ANGELES on November 10, 1959. And, in spite of the unexpected hard rain and fierce winds that nearly swept them off their feet, Katherine liked the city at once. *So this is sunny Los Angeles, with its tropical climate and sprawling beauty.* She had not been informed that November marked the beginning of the city's rainy season. As in Washington, DC, they bundled up in their mackintoshes and galoshes and hired a taxi to take them to the residence of one of the members of the Long Beach Spiritualist Society for whom Katherine was scheduled to speak.

"Here we are, ladies," the driver said, pulling up in front of a small, rather dilapidated clapboard house in a rather dingy middle-class neighborhood. Katherine and Eileen looked at one another in dismay.

"Are you sure that this is the address we gave you?"

"Yes, ma'am," replied the driver. "Here it is all right, 3918 Pacific Avenue, Long Beach."

"Oh dear!" began Eileen.

"I see," said Katherine slowly, secretly hoping that there had been some mix-up, but in her heart knowing this to be the right place after all. "Well, I guess this is it!" said Katherine, with false cheerfulness. "Let's go."

A slight, diminutive woman with a pale complexion, knowing smile, and gray hair neatly pulled back and tied in a knot at the nape of her neck (who Katherine guessed to be somewhere in her seventies) came to the door.

"You must be Mrs. Katherine Hayward from England. I am Lucille Watson from the Long Beach Spiritualist Society. How lovely to meet you. Welcome to our country!"

"Thank you, thank you very much," said Katherine graciously.

"Please do come in," chirped the tiny lady who was obviously lonely and thoroughly delighted with the prospect of having house guests for the next several days. Upon entering the little woman's modest home, Katherine knew at once that she could not spend more than a single night here.

"We'll find a hotel first thing in the morning," Katherine advised Eileen, as the two struggled to make themselves comfortable in the tiny second bedroom Lucille Watson had set aside for them. Poor Eileen was forced to sleep on an army cot while Katherine made a futile effort to fall asleep on a small, hard sofa.

"I told you we should have left this country," grumbled Eileen.

"Yes, I do wish I had listened to you," Katherine conceded as the two prepared to fall asleep later on that night. "Don't worry," Katherine added warmly, "it will all work out, it always does. You'll see. Everything will fall into place."

"Well, I certainly hope it falls into place soon. I can't stand too much more of this," continued Eileen, feeling quite sorry for herself. A wealthy woman, she was accustomed to the luxury of first-rate hotels, restaurants, and service.

"Just be patient," advised Katherine. "We both must be patient."

"I don't suppose we can do much more, can we?" agreed Eileen, displaying a spark of her usual good humor.

"I can't imagine how we ended up here with Miss Watson," said Katherine, thinking aloud. "You know I always request hotel accommodations adjacent to the hall in which I'm scheduled to appear. And I remember specifically requesting such accommodations in my correspondence with Mr. Phillips. Apparently, Mr Phillips had not conveyed this information to the director of the Long Beach Spiritualist Society. Oh well! Not much point in thinking about all that now," she sighed. At that juncture, their conversation was interrupted by the intrusion of Miss Watson.

"May I come in?" she inquired politely, once she had already knocked and entered. For the next two and a half hours, the lonely, garrulous old woman shared her life's history with the two women who were thoroughly exhausted and longed only to fall asleep. Finally, the woman excused herself, at last noticing the profuse yawning and sleepy responses of the guests.

"Well, then," she had said, reluctantly, finally glancing at her wrist watch, "I guess you two must be pretty tired after your plane flight and everything. You had best get some sleep," Katherine was too tired to utter a word, and could only nod dumbly. "Good night, then," said Miss Watson. "Sleep well."

"Thank goodness," declared Katherine when, finally, she had closed the door behind her and the two were alone. Neither had any difficulty falling asleep at all.

The following morning, they managed to tactfully extricate themselves from Miss Watson's home, and to check into a hotel nearby. That evening Katherine delivered her first formal public address in the California.. Although friendly and receptive, the audience was far smaller and seemed less sophisticated than those to which she had been accustomed in England. And she could not help but feel rather disappointed. As she had hoped, however, in conjunction with her talk, she received numerous invitations to speak elsewhere as well as requests for private interviews.

At least I'll be able to pay our hotel bills, she thought with relief, following the talk.

One pleasant young man with boyish good looks who came to Katherine for personal counseling politely advised her, "If you don't mind my saying so, you don't belong here in Long Beach, Mrs. Hayward—or at a Spiritualist society. I know of a wonderful psychic research center that would suit your style and message perfectly. Why not visit the place with me? I should be happy to escort you to one of their evening meetings. If you like the center, why, then, I should be pleased to introduce you to its owner and director Mr. William Armstrong. I've got a feeling that you and he would work well together. It seems to me that you two share similar philosophies."

"Thank you for mentioning this," said Katherine warmly. "I should be most happy to attend a meeting with you." She made arrangements to visit the center on Sunday.

Mr. Armstrong was a tall, handsome, and impeccably groomed black man whom Katherine liked immediately. Articulate and refined, humble, and in possession of a delightful sense of humor, she knew at once that, as the young man had suggested, she and Mr. Armstrong would work well together. Both the manner in which he spoke as well as the content of his speech appealed to her, and she was not at all surprised when, at the end of the meeting, while giving a demonstration of clairvoyance, he addressed both her and Eileen.

"My dear," he said in a kind, full voice to Eileen, "you must return to England—to your home and family. Both your husband and your son need you." At this, Eileen gasped audibly. "Do not worry about the future of your only son. He will enjoy a successful acting career—he will be called a 'star.' But, in the not-too-distant future, you son will make a career out of what is presently his hobby—photography. He will be highly successful in this field as well. Worry not, madam. All will be well. Your husband will be delighted at your return, and you two will enjoy the golden years of your lives in marital harmony. I hope that you are able to follow what I've said," he smiled.

"Oh, yes, indeed," whispered Eileen. "Thank you very much."

"Thank you," replied Mr. Armstrong. "And now, dear lady, to you," he said, pointing to Katherine. "Would you like me to speak with you this evening?"

"Yes, please," replied Katherine eagerly.

"Good," returned Mr. Armstrong grinning at her enthusiasm. "Well," he said with rather a curious tone, "it seems I am about to tell you the opposite of what I have just told your friend. You must not return to England. You are to remain in the United States to teach and to serve as you always have." Now, Mr. Armstrong's face clearly showed his bewilderment at his own words. "It seems," he said slowly, "that it is I who will assist you in establishing a working base here in the United States. It is I who am to arrange a large public meeting for you here so that your reputation will expand. The ways and means will be indicated by our Spirit Guides as we work together. Please come see me following this meeting, and we will discuss these matters further. Thank you."

"Thank you," replied Katherine, quite taken aback by his words. *He simply cannot be correct. Stay in America? He must be mad. Why, my life, my family, my work—all are in England. Why would I settle in the United States this late in my life? After all, I am over sixty. No, he must have made some kind of mistake,* thought Katherine, her mind trying to make sense of Mr. Armstrong's words. Yet in spite of her initial skepticism, something stirred deep within her. *Who's to say if he's right or wrong? Only time will tell. After all, anything is possible.* And after the meeting, she could not help but feel impressed by the strength of Mr. Armstrong's conviction. He was positively convinced that it was her destiny to remain in the United States for the rest of her life.

It was at this juncture that she was suddenly reminded of the words of the Subud Master, Pak Subuh, "You have come to the world to do the work. You go to India to share with the Indian people the energies that will facilitate their spiritual growth and development. Soon you will go to the United States to do the same thing. Then you will no longer be British but American citizen. You have much work to do yet."

I wonder if he's right? mused Katherine. *After all, he is a great teacher and I know that stranger things have happened.*

In the meantime, she was overwhelmed with Mr. Armstrong's generosity. At his request, his entire staff was at Katherine's disposal. "We'll start you out properly, Katherine," he had said, with a pleasant twinkle in his eye. "Brochures, publicity, the use of the hall, my staff—anything you wish is yours."

"I . . . I don't know how to begin thanking you," she began, genuinely moved by his persistent magnanimity.

"No thanks are necessary," he said softly, with sincerity. "You and I happen to be working for the same Boss, that's all, and the Boss wants me to help you get a good solid start in business out here in these United States. You see, we have different standards and practices than in your country. But we are all working toward the same goal, aren't we, Katherine?"

"Yes, I suppose you're right," she conceded.

"Good, then please stop thanking me. As I see it, we're here to change things—transform our fellow humans—and our world—together."

Although the first public meeting arranged by Mr. Armstrong and his staff did not turn out precisely as Katherine would have wished due to the fact that the brochures were inadvertently forgotten and not sent out until the last moment, it was a modest success. Although the audience numbered approximately sixty, Katherine was pleased, for, by now, she was acquiring familiarity with American audiences and learning to feel comfortable with them. And once again, she was quite surprised by the apparent differences between British and American audiences. And so, the meeting was successful insofar as she received numerous other invitations to guest lecture and to counsel privately. In addition, she was deluged for requests for private "readings." As a result of her public work, then, she was indeed establishing a foundation for all future work in the United States, and she was also earning enough to support her visit to this country. Still, she had no intention of remaining in the United States permanently.

One public meeting quickly followed another. And for the first few months of her visit to the United States, she continued to appear in Los Angeles and throughout southern California at local New Thought centers and churches. Her reputation slowly but surely expanded in these circles. She and Eileen moved from the Long Beach hotel in which they had been staying to one more conveniently priced and located in Hollywood. Even at this juncture, however, Katherine was still intent upon returning to England.

"We'll stay just another week," she would tell Eileen time and again. But, after a week's time had elapsed, she would say once again, "Oh, let's just stay one more week."

By the end of three months, however, both agreed that it was time to return home even though Katherine had the uneasy feeling that she had not yet accomplished all she set out to achieve. Nonetheless, they had a wonderful holiday, and had met some altogether charming and fascinating people, and were now, more or less, ready to pick up where they had left off. Katherine had been in frequent contact with Liebie who not only sorely missed her but spoke of various research projects that she felt certain would interest Katherine upon her return. Intuitively, Katherine knew that Liebie had also postponed making several important decisions until her return.

In the meantime, Katherine, throughout her visit to Los Angeles, had repeatedly made an effort to contact Sri Daya Mata and several other members of the Self-Realization Fellowship she had met during her trip to India. They had deeply enjoyed one another's companionship in India, and Daya Mata had cordially invited Katherine and Eileen to be her guests if ever they were in the United States. Self-Realization Fellowship's international headquarters was based in Los Angeles, and it was likely that Sri Daya Mata would spend a good portion of her time here. Katherine found Daya Mata to be warm, intelligent, unaffected, and not in the least bit sanctimonious as so many so-called "religious leaders" often are. The two had enjoyed exchanging ideas and information, and Katherine had truly hoped that they would one day meet again. Unfortunately, Katherine learned that Daya Mata was out of the country throughout the duration of her visit to Los Angeles. "Please leave her a message that we've called. If by chance, she returns, she can reach me at my hotel," Katherine informed Sri Daya Mata's secretary.

Only several days before their intended departure back to England, Sri Daya Mata returned Katherine's call. "Oh, but you can't think of returning to England without seeing us. In fact, my coworkers have arranged a welcome home party in my honor this evening. Won't you and Eileen please come—if only for a short while? There is so much I would like to share with you."

"Oh, dear. It's such short notice. And we have so many details to look after before our trip back."

"Please," urged Daya Mata softly. Something in her voice made Katherine stop and pause.

"All right," she sighed. "We would love to come to the party tonight."

"Wonderful. I look forward to seeing you then." Katherine could hear the gentle smile in her voice.

The invitation from Sri Daya Mata marked a turning point in Katherine's career. It was as a result of her happy reunion with Daya Mata and Daya

Mata's invitation to remain as her guest at the Self-Realization headquarters in Mt. Washington that Katherine and Eileen decided to postpone the trip home and stay in the United States indefinitely. In fact, the day after the party given in honor of Sri Daya Mata's return to America from extensive travel abroad, Katherine and Eileen gratefully accepted her invitation to visit the beautiful self-realization retreat and hermitage at Encinitas, north of San Diego. Spending nearly a month in the peaceful surroundings, they were afforded the rare opportunity to rest, relax, and reflect while adhering to the daily steps and principles of living recommended by Yogananda.

So deeply impressed was Eileen with the quality of lifestyle and sense of community here, that she seriously began to consider joining the self-realization movement as a devotee of Yogananda and becoming a "sister" in the monastic order. She made preliminary plans to notify her husband, Frank, of her intention to serve in this manner and to remain permanently in the United States. Only after a frantic telegram from Frank and a long, intense conversation with Katherine regarding the full, long-term ramifications of such action at this juncture of her life, was it that Eileen agreed to postpone such a plan and to return to her family in England. It was decided that she would travel by train to New York, and then fly from there to London. Although the two struggled to hold back their tears, Katherine and Eileen were optimistic that their separation would not be permanent. Although the separation might be painful, and the future uncertain, both had learned that there was little value in challenging the inevitable.

"We shall meet again, dear friend," Katherine had murmured as the two embraced one last time in farewell. And soon Eileen was on her way, while Katherine remained behind in America.

Still, Katherine had no intention of remaining in America permanently. Intuitively, she understood that she had not yet achieved the true purpose for which she had come and that it might be necessary to spend several more months here. But she still never seriously considered the possibility of establishing her permanent residence in the United States. Now, alone and really rather lonely (in spite of the many kind and generous individuals she had met here), she was determined to devote all her time and energy to the work.

As she had virtually her entire adult life, she would teach and demonstrate the "proof of survival" to those open-minded enough to receive it.

It was during one of her early public appearances in Los Angeles that she attracted the attention of a successful talent agent named Renè Taylor, who was deeply impressed by Katherine's mediumistic abilities as well as her charismatic manner of "teaching." It had been as a result of a devastatingly accurate personal message that Katherine had imparted to Renè during a public meeting, that the agent began to feel that the public should know more about the remarkable English psychic, Katherine Hayward. So impressed had Renè been, in fact, that she shared her views with a business associate, Lee Atkinson, arranging for her to meet Katherine.

Lee, a noted publicist, who was active and influential in metaphysical circles, was so excited about Katherine's abilities that she agreed to represent her at once. Employing and popularizing the term ESP to convey to the press and media her client's gifts, Lee quickly managed to arrange numerous radio and television appearances for Katherine. This early media exposure, along with a carefully planned and publicized appearance at the large Wilshire-Ebell Theatre in Los Angeles, helped launch Katherine's career in the United States. From here on, she was inundated with work—radio and television appearances, lectures, workshops, demonstrations of ESP, and constant requests for private interviews or counseling. It was following her first appearance at the Wilshire-Ebell (the extensive publicity for which evoked the crowds, chaos, and pleasant excitement associated with her first public meeting in Bombay), that Katherine began to realize that she was in the United States to stay.

In truth, Katherine had grown to love California. Its climate, natural beauty, with its mountains, orchards, and foliage, as well as its kind-hearted people greatly appealed to her, and she enjoyed better health and greater vitality here than anywhere. Furthermore, so long as she was teaching—sharing that which was of greatest importance with those who would benefit as she herself had—she did not really concern herself with geography. As long as she was doing the work, virtually nothing else mattered.

CHAPTER 55

Marie-Therese

⟶

THROUGHOUT THE EARLY MONTHS, KATHERINE maintained close contact with Liebie Pugh primarily through written correspondence. Not long after Katherine left England, Liebie's work began to assume a new dimension and direction. This work was of such an unusual nature that Katherine knew for certain that she would never again be a part of Liebie's work. For Liebie had, through a series of remarkable coincidences, met a physical medium and great healer named Mr. Richard Grave, who claimed that Christ appeared to him daily and would make a great universal revelation of His presence by Christmas morning of 1967.

Skeptical at best, Katherine refused to assist Liebie in her effort to "spread the news," and tried to dissuade her former coworker from any further personal involvement. "As you have asked my advice, I shall be perfectly frank," wrote Katherine to Liebie in 1961. "I do not feel that there is any evidence at all to support Mr. Grave's incredible claim that Christ will reappear on earth in 1967. I, personally, find it absolutely impossible to believe as you do. Therefore, I do not feel able to assist you or support this new endeavor. In fact, I would appreciate it if you do not associate me or my name with this facet of your work at all. I regret to inform you that I firmly believe that there will be no appearance of Christ on Earth in 1967 or on any date in the foreseeable future. Let me make a prediction. Although some sort of scandal or a controversy will surely erupt over this man's bold assertion, you, my dear Liebie, will no longer be in the physical body when this takes place. Do try to be sensible, Liebie, and know once and for all, our work together is over. You can be of good cheer, for your good name and reputation will be spared in spite of the adverse publicity that will surround Mr. Grave's 'mission.'"

Yet, even following her blatant refusal to cooperate in Liebie's new project, Katherine continued to receive numerous entreaties from Liebie to reconsider her position along with articles, essays, and editorials concerning Mr. Grave, his unique gifts, and his prediction. Only with the passage of time did Liebie's letters and frantic telephone calls become less frequent and intense. Soon, the vast physical distance and diverging interests played their role in separating the two women once and for all. In the meantime, Katherine could not imagine why someone so intelligent, discerning, and utterly guileless should become so deeply involved in such a bizarre project. But knowing that "God works in mysterious ways," she had to be content to understand that she was at last truly free of Liebie Pugh and that she was hereby absolved of any further responsibility toward her former coworker. The independence she had craved so many years was finally hers! The phase of her work that involved Liebie was now officially over.

Amazingly, each time she planned a trip home to England, someone or something would, at the last minute, interfere with her plan. Either a job, someone in need, or someone willing to assist in the propagation of her work would appear at precisely the moment necessary to prevent Katherine's departure. *It's obviously meant that I stay*, she would surmise until the next time she grew homesick or anxious for a rest. Furthermore, she was astounded by the care, solicitude, kind attention, and generosity she received from the Americans with whom she came into contact. One gentleman, discovering that she was staying in a second-rate hotel, graciously found and insisted upon paying full rent for a luxurious apartment.

This gentleman stated further, "If there is anything you need, please let me know. I shall be glad to subsidize your work. The need in our country for what you have to offer is great."

Clients and coworkers, friends and strangers, everyone treated Katherine with extraordinary kindness. And somehow, whenever Katherine began to fret or fear financial difficulties, someone would come to her aid in the nick of time. She was deeply impressed by the obvious guidance which she was constantly receiving.

It was with amazing rapidity that time moved on and Katherine became increasingly well adapted to serving those in need. She embraced Americans and quickly assimilated to the American people and their way of life.

Early in 1962, Katherine agreed to fly to Carmel in northern California and to perform an experiment for several members of Duke University's medical staff who were studying the effects of the drug LSD upon the human mind. Although she had never accepted such an offer before, she felt it advisable to participate at this particular juncture of her life. She had seen, heard, and read so much about the "mind-expanding" capabilities of the drug, that she was most anxious to ascertain for herself its effects. Only in a scientific context under careful supervision would she ever have agreed to submit to such an experiment.

Although she spoke into five different tape recorders simultaneously for nearly five hours under the influence of the drug, and although all five devices designed to record her words were in perfect working order, not one of the machines registered or recorded a single word she had spoken. Those administering the experiment were flabbergasted.

"How is it possible?" asked one doctor, several days after the test, obviously deeply disappointed.

"May I venture an opinion?" asked Katherine politely, wondering if it was out of place to make such a request.

"Certainly, Mrs. Hayward," replied the doctor.

"Well, I feel that my Spirit Guides are unhappy with my decision to participate in your experiment. Furthermore, what has been spoken through me was intended only for those who were present—no outside person was to know what took place," she said simply.

Although the doctors looked dubious, they had no better explanation for what transpired. The experiment was regarded as inconclusive and unsuccessful. Yet, although further experimentation was requested of her, she refused. Feeling weak and ill in conjunction with the ordeal, she vowed that she would never again submit to anything like it. For many months following the experiment, Katherine continued to feel the ill effects of the drug.

Shortly after her visit to Carmel in 1962, she traveled all over the country as part of a national lecture tour. Embracing the opportunity to see the various parts of the country as well as to meet its diverse population, she was pleased that she was at last fulfilling the purpose for which she had come to the United States. *I am acquainting hundreds of thousands of people with themselves—their True Selves*, she thought happily. *I am tilling the soil, sowing the seeds which will surely blossom forth in these human beings—if not in this lifetime than in some other. But the seeds of spiritual awakening have been planted.*

Colleges and universities, churches, social clubs and civic organizations, radio and television programs—Katherine thrived in the constant challenge each audience posed. Wherever she lectured, in addition to demonstrating ESP and the proof of survival, she spoke urgently of the need to expand individual or national dreams and goals to incorporate global brotherhood and peace. "All life is one life. Each one of us is an integral part of the whole. Any weak link weakens the whole. As it has been stated, a chain is only as strong as our weakest link. If we and the world are to persist, you must begin now—each one of you—to think peace, pray peace, see peace. Let nothing deter you from the actualization of your dream, the achievement of your goal. Let nothing cloud the true vision of a world at peace. You—each one of you—is the co-creator of the world. Therefore, use your creative powers constructively to benefit the beloved Earth and the whole of life. The future, indeed the very existence of planet Earth, depends on each one of you."

Following the lecture tour, Katherine returned to Los Angeles to resume the work she had begun. Here, she continued to address a wide variety of audiences, using almost any opportunity to convey her message. By now, her radio and television appearances had become frequent, and she was literally deluged by requests for private interviews as well. *This must stop*, she decided suddenly one rainy December afternoon in 1962. *I cannot continue at such a pace. I want to rest. Furthermore, I would like, once again, to continue the research I began in India.*

By early 1963, Katherine rented a spacious, pleasant building on Holloway Drive in West Hollywood and established her own New Thought center called the Katherine Hayward Psychical Research Society. Quickly attracting a wide membership consisting of over three thousand people, the center was dedicated to those who were interested in discovering and developing their own potential. Here, lectures and demonstrations were given several times a week by Katherine or other authorities in the field of metaphysics. In addition, classes, workshops, meditation and healing groups, and weekly Sunday morning meetings were held.

The center afforded Katherine the opportunity of teaching beginning as well as advanced students, an opportunity for which she was most grateful. Gradually, she became less interested in reaching the many and devoted her time and energy to the "chosen few" who shared with her the earnest desire to know life's meaning and purpose, those who shared with her the burning desire to discover the answers to such questions as, Who am I? From whence came I? And whither will I go after death? And although Katherine had never planned to open such a research center, it had been as a result of the persistent demand for her services on the part of those sincerely desiring to study her brand of metaphysics that she was inspired to establish the society.

Not long after the Katherine Hayward Psychical Research Society was formed, Katherine was introduced to a woman who was to influence her profoundly. In fact, Katherine had learned of this woman's existence and their inevitable meeting during the very early days of communications with the Spirit Beings in Mt. Ash. Then, she had been informed by Dr. Evans that she would one day meet the physical embodiment, the present human incarnation of her Spirit Guide, Marie-Therese. "When the time is right you two will be brought together," he had said. In the meantime, during the past forty-odd years, Katherine had seen many full-body materializations of her Spirit Guide—Marie-Therese, a gentle, lovely, and soft-spoken nun—but she had most certainly not met anyone who was "the physical embodiment" of this Guide.

Now, one Sunday morning, a small group of people arrived late to the weekly public meeting Katherine held at the society. Having already delivered her inspirational address, she was demonstrating ESP and delivering "messages" to various members of the audience when she was drawn to a tall, slender woman with dark hair who stood against the window at the back of the hall. Because the mid-day sun was at such an angle that Katherine's vision was partially impaired, she could not even see the features of the dark-haired woman to whom she was drawn. The bright sunlight obliterated all but her silhouette.

"May I speak with you?" asked Katherine politely.

"Oh, yes, surely," replied the woman in a rich, cultured voice. She possessed a slight, pleasant accent.

"We—you and I—are by no means strangers to one another," began Katherine. "I, Marie-Therese, am now speaking with You, who are also Marie-Therese. From here on, it will no longer be necessary for me to speak through Katherine in this manner. I shall be utilizing your vehicle instead. That is the purpose for which we have come together today—to acquaint both of you with this new dimension of your work."

Needless to say, Katherine was astonished to hear herself impart such a message, but the tall woman did not appear to be at all disturbed or surprised. Following the meeting, she approached Katherine calmly, "I have previously been informed of our inevitable meeting. A master of esoteric science in Italy told me years ago of your existence," laughed the black-haired lady whom Katherine knew at once to be the true physical incarnation of her beloved Spirit Guide, Marie-Therese. The brilliant indigo eyes, the silken complexion, high cheek bones, the tall, slender figure, and radiant personality—all bore an extraordinary resemblance to those of the Spirit Being she had seen on so many different occasions.

"No, our meeting is by no means accidental" said Katherine slowly, carefully studying the woman's features which were animated and seemed to glow from within. "How is it you happened to come here today?"

"Well, my close friend, Moyna, who has attended several of your lectures, urged us to pay you a visit. She says that you are not an ordinary psychic, but rather a spiritual teacher of great depth and awareness. And although neither my husband Gianni nor I am at all interested in psychism per se, we decided to come. Moyna is standing over there with my husband and several of our close friends who are members of an Alice Bailey study group." The woman pointed to a tall, handsome statuesque woman and a distinguished-looking gentleman,

"Ah, yes, of course," Katherine nodded.

"Moyna is a close friend of mine. She has been very kind and helpful to me. At any rate, do you not think it advisable that you and I get together?" the woman was saying.

"Yes, yes, I do," replied Katherine, staring directly into her eyes. She was finding the entire experience unnerving. "I'm afraid that I am booked this afternoon. Would it be possible for you to return next Sunday? We could spend time after the meeting."

"Yes, all right," the woman agreed. "We will discuss matters then."

"Good, I shall look forward to seeing you then," said Katherine, awkwardly holding out her hand. "By the way, I did not catch your name?" she asked. The woman seemed taken aback for a moment. Then her eyes crinkled in amusement, her mouth creased into a wide smile.

A low, throaty-laugh escaped her, as she clasped Katherine's hand warmly and whispered, "Marie-Therese. My name is Marie-Therese Boni." Katherine's mouth fell open in amazement. For several moments she stood, in stunned silence, as she watched Marie-Therese Boni glide gracefully across the room to her friends.

CHAPTER 56

Self Realization

—⸺

As planned, Katherine and Marie-Therese met after the meeting the following Sunday. As had been the case when she had first met Liebie Pugh, Katherine somehow "knew" that she and Marie-Therese "belonged" together and were to collaborate, at least for the present time. Katherine learned subsequently that Marie-Therese's life had paralleled her own to a remarkable degree. Both had decided from a very early age that life wasn't worth living without knowing its true meaning and purpose. Both had traveled around the world in search of the Truth. Both had married at an early age, given birth to one son, and been separated from this son. Both had been intensely involved in metaphysical work for the majority of their lives.

"I was born in Rome, Italy," said Marie-Therese in her rich, vibrant contralto voice. "When I was only a little girl, I was inspired to study the Eastern philosophers. I met then my first teacher, the well-known Italian author, lecturer, linguist, and philosopher, Pietro Rivetta—Toddi as he was known to his close friends and coworkers. Under Toddi's careful guidance, I studied esoteric science. As I studied, I became convinced that people know many things, but they do not know how to live. Following Toddi's death, I continued to study on my own until, in 1958, I came to the United States with my second husband, Gianni Boni, and was introduced to another esoteric master, Dr. Michael Malosek, a Czechoslovakia-born musical child prodigy, who had spent two years in a cave at Arunchala, India, with a guru, Ramana Maharshi. If you like, I should be happy to introduce you to Michael. It is my opinion that he has achieved what every human being comes to Earth to achieve—the final goal, the ultimate realization."

"Do you mean to say that you feel this Michael is self-realized?" asked Katherine, growing increasingly excited at the prospect of working with one who already knew his own true Potential.

"It is impossible to judge another human being," replied Marie-Therese simply. "But personally I do feel that Michael has achieved final and full union with his Creator, that he is self-realized," she said softly, a faraway expression coming into her eyes.

"I would love to meet him," said Katherine breathlessly.

From hereon, Katherine and Marie-Therese worked very closely together. Whereas Katherine had virtually no formal education or training in the field of metaphysics, Marie-Therese had been studying formally, scientifically since the age of fourteen. She had already studied with two European masters of esoteric science; had earned the Baccalaureate at the Cabrini Institute in Rome and then earned an additional degree in the United States. Whereas Katherine acquired virtually all of her training intuitively (most often learning from her own heavily "inspired" talks), and had worked as a medium throughout her entire life, Marie-Therese had little interest in or, for that matter, patience with psychism or mediumship.

"I am a scientist, an objective observer. To me, mediumship is a pleasant diversion, an interesting means of illustrating a tiny segment of man's extraordinary Potential. But it cannot, it will not lead one to the goal, which is mastery over all facets of the physical life and reunion with the Creative Power. I have known far too many psychics or mediums lose sight of the true purpose and goal. They become caught up in the greatness of their psychic powers and become lost in the world of Spirit, Spirit Guides, and so forth. It is very nice to know that such things exist, of course, just as it is comforting to know that there is no death. However, I believe that it is only by turning inward, by meditating upon the Divine Life within each human being, that one can draw increasingly close to his/her Creator and eventually grow so in wisdom and understanding and in love that he and the Creator at last merge into the One, the Whole, the Absolute.

"Forget mediumship, Katherine. Although it has served you well, and you have served countless others in their spiritual growth as a result of your mediumistic abilities, it is time now to move on in your spiritual development. Your Spirit Guides and Teachers will never get you where you want to go. You must leave all that behind and devote the rest of your days to the greater self, toward the greatest self-knowledge of all, the true understanding that we take on a physical body to acquire self-mastery and spiritual enlightenment."

Her association with Marie-Therese, did indeed, mark a turning point in her career as well as her life. Listening intently to her new friend, Katherine could not help but be affected by her words. It was obvious that Marie-Therese possessed a brilliant mind and a great understanding of the Ancient wisdom taught by the great occult masters of all time. The two spent much time together studying, questioning, and exploring.

"You can never hope to know God with the mind," exclaimed Marie-Therese in exasperation when her student asked over and over again.

"Why? On what basis? How is it so?"

"You are still expecting to understand, to uncover the most profound truths, with the limited conscious mind. Don't you see? You shall never achieve union with your Creator by means of the conscious mind, which perceives in a limited fashion, finite reality. You must meditate. God lies hidden in the heart of every human being, not in the mind. You must sit quietly and turn your attention within. Focus upon your inner being. Meditate on the Knower who is always there, who knows everything. You must still the petty, narrow conscious mind, and enter the place of perfect stillness that lies beyond all thought. Then and only then can you expect to come into direct contact with your Creator. Then, and only then, can you expect to experience God.

"The great masters and gurus claim that the experience of God is beyond all thought, beyond all words—and that, it is, therefore, indescribable. They only tell us that it is a state in which one experiences absolute unity with God, perfect peace, infinite love, and supreme bliss. As one patiently, diligently, and sincerely meditates on his own self, his true beauty will gradually be revealed, his True Nature will unfold and he will come to know—not to think or guess, to speculate or hypothesize, or even to believe but will KNOW—that he is God, that everything is God, and that God is everything. The wife, the husband, the child, the trees and the flowers and the mountains, the intellect, and the personality are all God manifesting or expressing through that particular form."

Marie-Therese's viewpoints were corroborated by the guru, Dr. Michael Malosek, a brilliant, radiant man who exuded joy and wisdom.

"Don't question so much," he would tell her with a twinkle in his penetrating eyes. "Don't think or analyze. Trust—just trust."

With the encouragement of these two great teachers, Katherine began to change—imperceptibly at first but noticeably in time. Within several years of meeting Marie-Therese and Michael, she decided to permanently close the society she had established in Los Angeles, withdraw from public work altogether for a while, and to devote herself toward "inner research" as she referred to the search for the Self. During this period, she decided to rent a small, pleasant, and unobtrusive apartment in West Hollywood where her privacy would be ensured.

No one would ever expect to find me here, she thought with satisfaction, studying the modest but attractive white stucco bungalow positioned adjacent to other similarly designed buildings in the neat, well-kept middle-class residential area in West Hollywood. *Surely, it's a far cry from Wood Court or even the White House,* she mused. *Finally, I shall have peace and the opportunity to explore my own potential—to do what I've always longed to do.*

Only her most earnest and diligent students were informed as to her whereabouts, and Katherine continued to work with them privately and in small groups and classes that she could hold in her own home. All other work ceased. With the persistent cooperation and guidance of her two beloved friends and coworkers, Katherine withdrew from the outer world to pursue the wealth of the inner. It was a rewarding and gratifying period as Katherine learned to master the techniques of yoga and meditation taught by Michael and Marie-Therese. And, as Marie-Therese had indicated, the experiences that took place on the subtle, inner levels could neither be shared with nor described to anyone else. They were deeply, profoundly personal and fulfilling as nothing thus far in Katherine's life had been. It was a period as exhilarating and exciting in its own way as those first months of communications with the Spirit Beings that had taken place so many years ago. On several occasions, she experienced that "absolute union with the Absolute, that limitless peace, infinite love, and supreme bliss," spoken of by gurus. On such occasions, she was dumbfounded by the utter simplicity and extraordinary beauty and sweetness of Realization. She studied in this manner for over seven years during which time she had come to regard Michael and Marie-Therese as her family. On the deepest, most important level, the three worked together joyously and harmoniously.

Throughout the years of working together, only the news of her mother Elizabeth's death of heart failure at the age of ninety-five in 1964 saddened Katherine deeply. Katherine had adored her mother and dearly missed her.

It was not long after Michael died at the age of ninety-six did Katherine and Marie-Therese realize that the work they had been destined to do together had come to an end, and that it was now time to go their separate ways. Although the parting was painful, both knew that it was inevitable.

"Thank you for the greatest gift a friend could ever give," Katherine had said, softly, tears of gratitude filling her eyes as she bade farewell to the dear friend who had given selflessly of her time, knowledge, and energy for seven years. "Thank you for your love and support." The vivacious and loquacious Marie-Therese was silent for once. Only her eyes revealed her deep affection and concern for her friend and "pupil."

Not long after their separation, Marie-Therese and her family moved to Sacramento. Some years later, she opened her own New Thought Research Center in Los Angeles. A great teacher and leader, she, like Katherine, taught her own unique brand of philosophy—transforming countless lives in the process.

Several months after Michael's death, Katherine decided to return to England for a visit. Throughout the years of study with Marie-Therese and Michael she had managed to visit several times. Now she felt compelled to see her family, children, and colleagues—including Eileen (who had remained in England with her husband Frank) and dear Liebie who had retired in Hove. Above all, she longed to see her beloved Trevor, with whom she had kept in close contact ever since she had first arrived in the United States. Although the two were still as deeply in love as ever and missed each other terribly, both had learned to stoically accept their circumstances. This time, as she made preparations for the journey, Katherine could not help but feel that something was very wrong. *Something dreadful is about to happen,* she thought grimly, wondering what it could be, but feeling vaguely that it concerned her Trevor.

As usual, her instincts proved correct. Upon arriving in Christchurch, she saw at once that Trevor was ill. *Why, he has aged twenty years,* she thought ruefully, realizing for the first time that he looked like an old man. Chronological age meant little to Katherine, and Trevor was a year younger than she. But now, near seventy, in contrast with Katherine, who looked almost as youthful and radiant as ever, Trevor looked old and frail and feeble.

"How wonderful it is to see you," he said softly, his voice cracking, and his eyes dimming at the sight of the only woman he had ever truly loved. "Don't leave me. Don't go away again, Katherine," he implored. "Stay with me, my darling." She had to turn away to keep the tears from gushing forth.

When she had recovered herself, she only said, simply in a quiet voice, "You know I can't, Trev. I wish to God I could, but I can't."

"I don't know that we shall ever be together again," he whispered weakly. "I don't think I am long for this world."

"Nonsense," replied Katherine, wondering why she felt her throat constrict and her limbs suddenly too weak to support her body.

"You know, I've never loved anyone else, don't you, my darling?" he said, drawing her close and touching her cheek gently. She would never, as long as she lived, forget the love or purity of heart with which he spoke, his eyes tenderly caressing every part of her, as though storing this vision in his mind for all eternity. "I love you, Katherine, I always will."

"I know," she said softly, compassionately. "And I love you, my dearest, darling Trev. I'll return to England for another visit soon," she promised.

"All right my sweet," said Trevor softly. But both of them felt intuitively the imminence of a permanent separation. And because of the strange feeling, they clung to each other, hardly daring to leave one another throughout the visit.

It was only a matter of a few days following her return to the United States that Katherine received the long-dreaded telephone call from Doris Hurley. "Trev's gone," Doris sobbed.

"Oh, my God, no," Katherine had cried out in anguish. "How?"

"A . . . a heart attack, followed by a massive stroke," replied Doris, weeping. "He was in the hospital, attached to all those awful tubes and things. And he seemed all right. And the doctor said he'd get better. But, then, somehow, he took a turn for the worse, and then, suddenly, he was gone. Gone!"

"Now, Doris," said Katherine controlling her emotions so as to comfort the sister of her beloved Trevor in any way she could. "You know that there is no death and that Trev's very much alive, don't you? And he's probably gloriously happy, now that he's in the Land of Light. You know, he'll be with us always, don't you, dear?"

"Yes, Katherine, I guess so. But, I miss him so much now. I would give anything to see him, hold him again." She began to cry again.

"You will, love," murmured Katherine soothingly. "You will, I promise. All will be well, Doris. I know it. You get on with your own life, and don't grieve. You know Trevor would never approve of your mourning him. He'd want you to understand and live as joyously as possible. Do you follow?"

"Yes, Katherine, I do. Thank you. I feel better already," she sniffed.

"Good. Everything will be all right. Get back to work. Manage the Greyhound as Trevor would have wished you to. And remember, love, Trev's still very much alive. I promise. Where there is true love, there can be no separation. If you are in need of anything, don't hesitate to telephone. If you wish me to come, I will."

"Thank you, Katherine. No, everything is under control, and Trev wouldn't have wanted you at his funeral, knowing how you felt about death.

You stay in Los Angeles, and attend to your work. You know, Trev always said he wanted to share your work one day."

"I know," acknowledged Katherine, the tears flowing down her cheeks unheeded. "Take care, my love. I miss you. I'm here if there's any need at all. I'll talk with you soon."

"All right, Katherine. Thank you. Goodbye,"

"Goodbye, my love," Katherine barely got out the words.

For some minutes, she remained perfectly still, cradling the receiver to her bosom as the tears rolled down her cheeks. She wept for many hours following the conversation, feeling bereft and inconsolable. Trevor had always been a part of her life it seemed, and now, suddenly, he was no longer there. It was eerie and most unpleasant, this feeling. She felt empty and sad and lost. Never had she felt so alone and utterly grief-stricken. Just knowing he was alive had been enough to sustain her through many a dark and difficult period. For she had known that always, always he was behind her, loving her, supporting her, caring about her. But now, all of a sudden, he was gone, and she was alone. Dazed and despondent, she could hardly believe it. Furthermore, she was bewildered by the events that had taken place in her life prior to Trevor's death.

What in God's name am I doing in America? Where am I going? What am I doing half a world away from my family? she wondered. But, finally, as the days drifted into weeks and the weeks melted into months, her pain lessened, and the aching numbness that had settled over her for some time gradually disappeared. Knowing only one antidote to her grief, she had resumed her work at a feverish pitch. This and only this afforded her any true solace or pleasure. And, in time, she came to realize, *America is where I belong. I guess I truly belong here after all,* and this feeling of belongingness never left her.

Soon, things began to fall into place, and Trevor's death somehow mercifully receded into the background. Her grief diminished as virtually all of her time and energy once again became dedicated to the work. *I shall never again become romantically involved with anyone,* she vowed. *I know that I shall never love another human being as I have loved my Trevor.*

And, finally, by the middle of the 1970s, Katherine had entered a new phase of her life and career. She had, by now, relinquished her British citizenship to become an American. Never again would she return to England. She was in America to stay. A phase of her life had come to an end. Another chapter was closed.

CHAPTER 57

Twilight

⁓ᐟ

THE YEARS FOLLOWING TREVOR'S DEATH passed swiftly and uneventfully, as Katherine continued to conduct her own brand of "inner research" and taught her philosophy of life to any who happened to find her tiny home tucked away at the foot of the Hollywood Hills. At this juncture, she had no desire or intention of resuming her public work. She had advised her agent Lee and her manager Rene that she no longer wished them to promote her. *Those days are over,* she resolved, her shrewd eyes blazing with determination. *From here on, my life shall be dedicated to the pursuit of self-discovery and to those students who are similarly searching for the truth and who may benefit from having a teacher to guide and direct them along the path.*

Acquiring an unlisted telephone number and firmly resisting all efforts to publicize her work, she was certain that "those meant to find me will." And sure enough, to the amazement of her close friends and coworkers, literally thousands of people hearing of her by word-of-mouth passed through her front door—among those several of the greatest authors, actors, entertainers, politicians, composers, musicians, and playwrights of the time. Anyone genuinely seeking greater understanding and approaching all philosophies with an open mind was a welcome visitor to her home. With those, she willingly shared the knowledge she had painstakingly acquired throughout a lifetime dedicated to research. Over and over again she received fervent gratitude and praise for her work from her students and coworkers: "Thank you, Katherine, you have changed my life. I cannot repay you. I've been transformed by your teachings."

But, with equal fervor, Katherine rejected such praise. "Don't thank me. Thank yourselves. After all, you are God. If you've been paying attention to what I teach, you know that you Are God. That each one of us is God manifesting through that physical form. And that it is your Greater Self that is responsible for the transformation of which you speak. You have finally come into contact with the Divine facet of you, and this is why you are experiencing such profound joy and gratitude," Katherine would snap at an unsuspecting student. "Do not attempt to shirk your responsibilities or ignore your potentialities. I am nothing more than a catalyst who helps to bring to you greater knowledge of the true self—the Guiding Spirit or Force of every human being. Just think of the miracle that you are: infinite love, wisdom, power, and peace these reside within you. All the answers to every question you have ever asked exist deep within you. Remember that you are no different than I in regard to your greatness, your divinity," she would remind any student anxious to relegate responsibility for his life to another. "And no one can discover the real you but you. There may be signposts along the path, guiding you hither or thither. But it must be you alone who does the real work, who travels the steep and often rocky terrain. No one can do it for you."

In the meantime, during these years, Katherine slowly but steadily drew ever closer toward making the discoveries she had sought throughout her entire life. Little by little, she began to experience and to understand in the truest sense of those words her True Purpose and Nature. In conjunction with several startling "revelations," she directly experienced God. And she saw for the first time the truth of the words an Indian Master had once uttered, "The mind is the great obstacle which keeps us from knowing the Self. When we go beyond the mind, beyond thought, we experience the true and lasting bliss of the Self." With greater clarity and deeper insight than ever did she perceive the significance of the words, "I am Divine" or "Be still and know that I am God."

Yet, despite these breakthroughs, she still felt as though something—a piece of the puzzle, as it were—was still missing. She did not feel, even at the age of eighty-four, that she had achieved true and everlasting union with God—that which the Eastern philosophers call "samadhi."

Perhaps, I'm not meant to have this Ultimate Realization in this lifetime, after all, she reflected, trying to accept as courageously as possible the full impact of such a concept.

Oh, well, she sighed wearily. *Even if I don't get at the Truth this time around, I shall never stop questioning. And, if it takes me a hundred or a thousand or a million more lifetimes, I shall find God. I will never give up my search. And one day I know that I shall know Him. I know that I shall know Him,"* she affirmed with the same obstinacy and determination her mother had exhibited throughout her lifetime. Like Elizabeth, once she had made a decision, once she had made up her mind to pursue a particular course of action, there was no one, no external event which could circumvent or cause her to deviate from her chosen path. She was determined.

Not until she was nearly eighty did Katherine seriously consider the possibility of leaving behind her a written record of her life. Although she had been approached on numerous occasions both in the United States and in Britain by well-known authors and journalists eager to write her life's story, she had, firmly rejected all such proposals.

"But, Mrs. Hayward," one young, impatient journalist had protested. "Your life has been exceptional. You have so much to share with the world. So many would be inspired by your story. You must let me write it."

Katherine had only smiled enigmatically and replied, "I'm afraid that now is not the time. Someday perhaps. But not now . . ."

It was shortly after her seventy-ninth birthday that Katherine became convinced that the time was now appropriate to begin such an undertaking. She felt confident that many all over the world would benefit by reading of her experiences.

Humanity must awaken to its true purpose and potential, before it's too late. My book will help them to do so, she now conceded, her sharp eyes gazing into the future. *People will need the wisdom and the information that I have acquired over a long life-time filled with disappointments, difficulties, turmoil, and sadness. They will see that in spite of poverty, an invalided childhood, bankruptcy, a failed marriage, separation from a son loved more than anyone or anything in the whole world, a successful but demanding public career that required me to travel constantly—not to mention living through two World Wars—that the information I have acquired has made it possible not merely to survive on planet earth but to live joyously, harmoniously, gratefully, and fruitfully. Unlike so many human beings, my life has truly been a rich and joyful experience. How many of my fellow humans can make such a statement?* she wondered wistfully.

And so, at the age of seventy-nine, she began the arduous and painstaking task of recalling the series of events, personalities, "seeming" coincidences, relationships, and experiences—both inner and outer—that shaped her life. With the earnest and diligent student (as dedicated and deeply in love with "the work" as she herself had been) to whom she had relegated the responsibility of writing her biography, Katherine shared the remarkable experiences that had comprised her life.

It was with a distinct feeling of awe and reverence for the strength and indomitability of the human spirit and will to survive that she reviewed the incredible array of experiences that had led to the present time. The early excitement of Cardiff; the beauty of Gwaelod-y-garth; the illness and the out-of-the-body experience she had at age seven; the pamphlet that arrived in the mail introducing her to Mr. Mesmer; her first job in Mr. Crouch's jewelry store; learning to read and write from dear, kind, Mrs. Pfyfe; her first meeting with the audacious Percy Hayward at dusk outside the jewelry shop in Pontypridd; the birth of her only son; the full-body materialization in her bedroom of her sister, Catherine Sedonia; the six-month period of communications with the Spirit Beings (would she ever forget the first time Percy was transformed into Dr. Evan Evans?); the excitement and confusion of her family's first public meeting in Mt. Ash; bankruptcy and humiliation and the gradual disintegration of her marriage; her first interview with the Hurley's and the George 'N Dragon; the dreadful War years; the countless séances during which she had witnessed extraordinary demonstrations of physical phenomena of every imaginable variety; the joy and camaraderie of VE Day in London; the anxious moments waiting to learn of Graham's welfare and his triumphant return home from the War; the happy days spent at the Vincent Street Salon; Cricklewood and the Pendennis Center; her interview at The Society for Psychical Research in London; her association with Liebie Pugh at Wood Court; the Gold Room experimentation the White House; India; and finally America. The names and faces of those she had known flashed before her with remarkable clarity as did the physical locations that formed the backdrop of her experiences.

No one can deny that it's been a full life. Katherine thought gratefully, alone in the twilight one cozy autumn afternoon in 1983, as she pored over the recently completed manuscript that was the history of her life. After hungrily reading passage after passage, she finally placed the great number of loose, typewritten pages together in one tidy bundle and carefully laid them aside, as one might physically put aside a lovely romance with which one was still enthralled.

"Eighty-four years," she realized in surprise, feeling no different in many ways than she had as a very young girl. *It's been a long life—a great adventure! There are many, perhaps, who won't believe what has been written here,* she mused, her gaze including the enormous stack of typewritten pages, which now lay in a neat pile upon her small bed.

"But that's all right. Those who are meant to believe it will. Those who are not meant to will regard it as a pleasant form of diversion or fantasy, I expect. Perhaps no one but I myself know to what extent this biography is a factual, completely accurate account of my life. I have done my duty. Now, I can only hope and pray that those who read it will read with an open mind, and receive the inspiration to search in their own way for the Truth. If my life story serves to inspire even one individual to obey the ancient injunction, 'Man, Know thyself,' then it will have succeeded, and so will I. Humanity—poor, dear, long-suffering humanity—must learn its own true potential if our planet is to survive; humanity must grasp its divinity if Earth is to fulfill its glorious destiny. Peace, true love, and brotherhood must prevail in the hearts and minds of all human beings. Then and only then can we hope to achieve universal peace, love, and brotherhood. True peace within and without must be the primary purpose and goal toward which each one must strive. There is no other way for us to continue," she spoke aloud as she awkwardly lifted the manuscript from the bed and moved it into the top drawer of the chest nearby. Before closing the drawer, she affectionately patted the inanimate pile of paper as though it could feel her fondness for it.

"Well," she concluded, "that's that!"

And, now, feeling weak from the exertion of the day, for it had been characteristically busy and fruitful, she reached down to remove the putty-colored sandals—her favorite and most comfortable—and then positioned herself comfortably on top of the bed. She did not remove her gown—one of many long, flowing, multi-colored kaftans she had taken to wearing over the past years "for comfort's sake" rather than appearance.

"One just can't care about appearance at my age as one does when one is younger," she would laugh. A gentle breeze filled with the combined scent of autumn and eucalyptus, stirred the white lace curtains, and she heard the sounds of children laughing and shouting in the distance. She heard the clattering of metal pots and pans next door as her neighbors prepared for dinner. There was something so pleasant, so peaceful about this hour. *It is my favorite time of day*, she thought, watching the ribbons of riotous color fill the sky outside her window. Within moments, street lamps were lit and house lights began to twinkle, as the sun slowly disappeared from view.

As was her custom, Katherine now dispassionately reviewed the events of the day. For once she had made no plans for the evening. And she was relieved. It felt good to relax all alone in the twilight of this pleasant autumn day. *Perhaps I'll take a short nap*, she decided, yawning. She felt unusually sleepy. After recalling the events and conversations that had taken place during the day, her thoughts once again returned to the drawer in which her life's history now rested.

"I pray God to bring my book to those whom it may help," she said aloud. And, turning from her back onto her side, preparing to fall asleep, she uttered the simple heartfelt words that she had uttered throughout her entire adult life every morning upon awakening and each night before falling asleep—the words that formed the foundation, guidance, and inspiration of each moment of every day—"Let thy will, oh God, be done on Earth, and in my life ... Let thy will, oh God, be my will ... Thy will, not mine!" She fell asleep at once. Her face in repose was unutterably peaceful and radiantly content.

About the Author

—᧒

Diane Pomerance is the author of nine books, seven of which are nonfiction about animals. She has a deep love and profound respect for nature and all living creatures, and she writes and speaks of the interconnectedness and interdependence of the whole of life. She is an ardent animal lover and advocate who has rescued, rehabilitated, and adopted more than 46 dogs over the past decades. She is deeply involved with animal welfare and the environment.

Spirituality has been the passion, the calling of her life, and she has dedicated her life to spiritual research and exploration. Diane loves animals and nature. She also loves to travel and has been to most parts of the world from Africa to Australia, South America to Asia, Europe to South Africa. She has an innate love of and respect for indigenous peoples and all nonviolent cultures. Diane holds a PhD in mass media/communications from the University of Michigan, Ann Arbor, an MA in theater from the University of Michigan, and a BA in history and speech from the University of Michigan along with a secondary education teaching certification.

Diane lives near Dallas, Texas, with her 10 rescue dogs (2 of which are Animal-assisted Therapy dogs), and, when not writing, spends time reading, engaging in spiritual studies and activities, rescuing animals in need, volunteering with the SPCA of Texas as creator and director of the Pet Grief Counseling Program, and hiking in the woods near her home.